AN ACCIDENTAL
DIPLOMAT

My Years in the Irish Foreign Service
1987-1995

Eamon Delaney

**NEW
ISLAND**

AN ACCIDENTAL DIPLOMAT
MY YEARS IN THE IRISH FOREIGN SERVICE 1987-1995
First published June 2001 by
New Island
2 Brookside
Dundrum Road
Dublin 14
Ireland

Copyright © 2001 Eamon Delaney

ISBN 1 902602 39 0

British Library Cataloguing in Publication Data
A catalogue record for this book is available
from the British Library

Cover image and design: www.jonberkeley.com
Typesetting: New Island Books
Printed in the Channel Islands by The Guernsey Press Ltd.

3 5 4

Contents

For my mother, Nancy

A diplomat is someone who thinks twice
before saying nothing.

Old French saying

Prologue

Dining Against the Government

I joined the Department of Foreign Affairs (DFA) in 1987, a month before Charles J Haughey returned as Taoiseach, and one of my first tasks was to help the Department in plotting against him.

At the time, I was working in the Department's European Union (EU) Co-ordination Section in Harcourt Street and I had to make contact with an incendiary group gathering in the basement of the Grey Door restaurant, off Dublin's Fitzwilliam Square. Over a long and heavy lunch, embittered senior officials were drawing up 'documents of resistance'. Coming into power, Haughey proposed to abolish the Department's European Affairs Committee and its Northern Ireland Committee and replace them with Committees based in his own Department. These are the two most important aspects of Foreign Affairs business and the mandarins were up in arms. Or at least, at this stage, up in cigars and brandies.

Admittedly, mine was only a peripheral role, crossing St Stephen's Green to collect newer and more militant drafts of this revolutionary Bull, but it offered an early and useful insight into some of the Department's characters and their ability not just to 'dine for Ireland' but to 'dine against the Government'. Haughey was regarded as a *bête noire* for DFA and, after five years out of office, he was back. There was great speculation in the media about what he would do with Foreign Affairs and the apocryphal story was again re-told of how, on leaving a function in Iveagh House, he stopped beneath the

1

Portland portico and shouted back, 'Cut their champagne allowance!'

There is always antipathy between Central Government and its Foreign Service — think of the Foreign Office and Thatcher, or the White House and the State Department. It is to be expected when diplomats go native and 'internationalistic' about issues which they are not elected to lead on. But in Haughey's case the gripe was personal. During the Falklands war he defied most European opinion, and DFA, by wanting a more anti-British stand. In 1981, he tried to shift the Irish Ambassador to the US, Sean Donlon, out of Washington, annoyed by the profile the latter was gaining. Donlon, however, had successfully resisted, helped by senior figures in Irish-American politics, including the so-called 'Four Horsemen'; Governor Hugh Carey; Speaker of the House of Representatives, Tip O'Neill and Senators Ted Kennedy and Daniel Patrick Moynihan. Since then Donlon had become Secretary of the Department. (Ironically, Donlon's re-emergence ten years later, as Northern Ireland adviser to the Fine Gael Taoiseach, John Bruton, would create conflict between the Taoiseach and DFA.)

In general, Haughey felt that DFA should take a more radical stand on Northern Ireland (NI), at least rhetorically. This was ironic given that the Department was probably more sincerely nationalistic than most politicians, including Fianna Fáil, and had actually achieved, under Fine Gael, the Anglo-Irish Agreement in 1985. But this was part of the problem and Haughey, in opposition, threatened not to work the Agreement when he got back to office.

In fairness to Haughey, the intense work on that Agreement had created an extraordinary bond between the upper echelons of DFA and the outgoing Fine Gael (FG) administration. This was particularly the case with Donlon, who worked closely with the previous Minister, Peter Barry. And with Michael Lillis, the head of Anglo-

Irish Division, who used to go on holidays in Cyprus with the FG leader, Garret FitzGerald.

FitzGerald regarded DFA almost as a personal fiefdom having presided over its rapid expansion as a dynamic Foreign Minister in the early Seventies (an expansion that would lead to a terrible promotional bottleneck twenty years later). But it was an uncomfortable relationship. In 1987, when Fine Gael finally and reluctantly went to the polls, they held their opening press conference in the ballroom of Iveagh House. 'We should get the place fumigated,' someone said afterwards, correctly anticipating that we would soon be facing a new regime.

Fine Gael, and their former Labour partners, lost the election and those who were tainted didn't waste much time getting out. Donlon was gone by March and Lillis also departed, but not before a story appeared in the papers saying he had turned down becoming Ambassador to Britain. Stuff like this got right up Fianna Fáil's nose. Lillis and Donlon scarpered off to the private sector and got jobs with Guinness Peat Aviation (GPA), the aircraft leasing group. Others followed and even some Third Secretaries joined GPA. Even old Garret himself got on board. It was like the 'Fall of Saigon', except this time we were leasing the planes.

The promise of Haughey's return to power engendered much gleeful speculation about what he would do with the gin-swilling diplomats. *In Dublin* erroneously reported that the shredders were working 'late into the night' in Iveagh House, as if it really was the Fall of Saigon. In fact such speculation showed little appreciation of the continuity of Government. Or of the fact that the Civil Service is the real and permanent Government and that the politicians are only puppets, time-serving mannequins who, if they are clever, will work to the strengths of their scriptwriting masters.

This Haughey did. It helped, of course, that replacing the departed Sean Donlon as Secretary was Noel Dorr, a monkish and mild-mannered man with a slight stoop. He was the ideal Civil Servant; incredibly bright, attentive but invisible. You'd hardly know he was in the room. For this reason, perhaps, he was known as the Late Mr Dorr. The other reason was his occasional habit of arriving late for meetings, a habit that enraged Haughey. One head of Anglo-Irish who arrived, late and windswept, to a meeting in Government Buildings was told by a typist: 'I wouldn't go in, if I was you.'

'Oh, but I must,' he insisted and when he went in Haughey didn't say anything to him. He just ignored his presence for the whole duration of the meeting. By contrast, Haughey's habit was to arrive ten or fifteen minutes early for events, a tactic that unnerved opponents and put everyone off their guard. Even when his belated humiliation came up at Dublin Castle in 1997, he cheated the waiting crowd and media by arriving into the Castle over three hours early.

In fact, Haughey worked well with Dorr. Unlike other politicians who might resent the intellectual airs of the mandarins, Haughey would use and respect such advice. Dorr had been Ambassador to the UN and, by extension, Chairman of the Security Council when Haughey had tried to change our policy on the Falklands but CJ seemed to have forgiven the difficulties of that time. (Unlike the British, who saw it as a treacherous move, which may have set back Irish-British relations by almost three years).

Although perceived to be close to Fine Gael, having worked closely with Garret and Peter Barry on the Agreement, Dorr was scrupulous in trying to establish an even-handed image for DFA. Or, at least, balanced away from FG. In this, he was helped greatly by Dermot Gallagher, head (or Assistant Secretary) of the Anglo-Irish Division and Ted Barrington, head of Administration.

Nevertheless Haughey would, in 1987, make surgical incisions into DFA, one in taking Northern Ireland 'away' from Foreign Affairs and making it answerable to his own Department (the Department of the Taoiseach retains partial responsibility for Northern Ireland to this day).

The other was in abolishing the European Communities Committee and replacing it with 'the Geoghegan-Quinn Committee', based at his own Department and chaired by Máire Geoghegan-Quinn, his Minister of State. This was the Committee I would work to.

These may seem like significant structural changes. The reality was that the day-to-day work on NI and Europe would still be done at DFA. But they were still too much for the more colourful mandarins and a group was assembled to draw up a document protesting these 'unwarranted changes'. The Grey Door was a fitting venue; around the corner from the Department, it was often used to entertain foreign diplomats. Each time I collected a draft, dragging the pages out of the debris of up-ended glasses and balled napkins, the inevitable vermilion-faced toad would wave away the smoke and shout, 'Send it to Kinsealy!' or 'Wrap it round the wooden stake!' (this last a reference to Conor Cruise O'Brien's famous remark that the only way CJ Haughey could be removed from political life would be if they buried him at the crossroads with a wooden stake through his heart. The Cruiser was ex-DFA, of course).

Mindful of this decadent atmosphere — it was now about four p.m. — my Counsellor came over and apologised for the confusion, but the others mocked his concern, to a chorus of guffawing laughter. 'You guys are going for a hop,' I thought as I fled their laughter and emerged back up into the daylight of the street. They were an eclectic bunch and if the incoming Secretary was around — Dorr was away with the incoming Minister, Brian Lenihan — I doubt he would have approved of such liquid restiveness.

In his absence, the Deputy Secretary, Robin Fogarty was in the chair, an addition which must have given the proceedings an extra charge. Fogarty was a volatile figure. A former Ambassador in Bonn and Tokyo, he had had a tempestuous relationship with Haughey, exacerbated by the fact that both he and Haughey had had a close relationship with the social diarist Terry Keane and reputedly came near to blows over her on the steps of the United Arts Club. (Indeed, Fogarty would later have a splendid reunion with Haughey in 1990 when the Taoiseach flew out for the World Cup celebrations in Rome, but more of that anon.)

The other main figure in the Grey Door was Caligula, who wanted me to sow a little ridge of spring onions. A sulphurous character, he was almost recalled as a European Ambassador when he reportedly insulted a major Irish political figure. Called home to account for himself, Caligula was asked by Noel Dorr, in his rhetorical way, if he 'could see himself to retiring' to which Caligula is supposed to have replied, if Dorr could 'see himself to fucking off'. The story is probably apocryphal but I'm sure the tenor of the meeting is correct. It is almost impossible to fire an Ambassador. Indeed, it is almost impossible to fire a Civil Servant, short of an Act of the Oireachtas, but with Ambassadors this is particularly hazardous, given the possibilities for eccentricity after half a lifetime of walking around in the tropical heat being called 'Your Excellency'. If persuasion to voluntary retirement doesn't work, the only solution is hotter and even more faraway places.

Anyway, going back to 1987, and the Grey Door, there were other characters mixed up in the smoky intrigue but since I'd just joined DFA, I couldn't put names to their mutinous faces. Certainly the big empty desks back in Harcourt Street suggested that most of the Counsellors were there. The document they eventually produced was an extraordinary mixture of high dudgeon protest and special pleading, even if its essential points were valid.

It begins: 'There are negative implications in [Haughey's] decision insofar as the role and standing of this Department are concerned, which are most disturbing.'

'Disturbing' was a word mandarins used about suspected fraud, or a shoot-to-kill allegation in the North, so it was not employed lightly. A more conciliatory opening line had conceded that 'the decision is obviously aimed at streamlining and improving arrangements for the interdepartmental co-ordination of Community policy making.' But this generous observation was vehemently scratched out by the red pen of Robin Fogarty.

The background was then outlined to the 'longstanding and well-established role of this Department which has the primary responsibility for co-ordinating Ireland's overall approach on EU matters'. 'The question must be asked' it continued in a self-pitying whine, 'whether the decision ... reflects dissatisfaction with the working of the previous arrangements and with the role and performance of this Department.' Ouch.

There were descriptions of DFA's Economic Division and of the Permanent Representation in Brussels, and their sensitive and direct roles with regard to the EU. But they were described in that childlike way you use when you want to drum-something-home-with-short-sentences. Do you get me at all? It virtually asked whether the incoming Taoiseach was 'aware that we have an Embassy in Brussels'?

But the real beef was with the new Geoghegan-Quinn Committee, to be based at the Taoiseach's Department. 'Is this Committee to replace the European Communities Committee which has, since Ireland joined the Community, been chaired by the Secretary and more recently the Deputy Secretary of Foreign Affairs?' Ah — the Deputy Secretary Robin Fogarty — the real beef. The marrow in the bone, if you like. Here, perhaps, we began to see the true motivation behind this extraordinary protest.

'If so,' the note went on, developing a 'my good man' tone, 'who is to service the Committee and provide the Secretariat?' (It was a question I personally would answer with my feet carrying documents back and forth across St. Stephen's Green between DFA and the Department of the Taoiseach.) 'The DFA has always serviced the European

Communities Committee and provided the Secretariat,' it concluded on what was either a defiant or defeatist note; it was hard to tell which.

Nor was the composition of the new Committee to their liking; it was be comprised solely of Ministers and the Secretary of the Taoiseach's Department and of the Government. 'It was the practise in the previous Cabinet Committee for senior officials to accompany their Minister. The Deputy Secretary of Foreign Affairs invariably accompanied his Minister.' Ah, Robin again. CJ wouldn't have to look too far to see the real Oxo-cube in this festering stew.

But, lest people think that DFA were just protecting themselves, the note also came to the defence of their old Departmental rivals, Industry and Commerce, whose Minister, strangely, was not automatically on the Committee but would attend 'as required'. Instead, their Minister of State would attend. Roused to protest, the note summoned history to its side and stiffly pointed out that 'since the accession negotiations of 1970, the Department of Industry and Commerce had been one of the "core" members of the co-ordination structure on European Community affairs'.

'The responsibilities of the Minister,' it noted dryly with respect to Community policy, 'are wider than those of the Minister of State at his Department'. No kidding.

This spirited blow for the Department of Industry and Commerce made me wonder afterwards if maybe some of their mandarins had come up from Kildare Street and had been seated around that Grey Door table. It is quite possible given that I didn't recognise all the faces amidst the haze of blue smoke and rebellion. The key may be the curious 'accession' reference for, back in 1970 one of those directly involved in the negotiations around entry to the then EEC was no less than Robin Fogarty himself. And he might well have tipped his cigar towards his old groundbreaking Ind and Comm buddies and said 'Don't you worry, I'll get onto Haughey about this'.

The document should have been the opening salvo in a DFA campaign to protect itself against Haughey but sadly, Haughey was singularly unmoved by the appeals within this unsigned and collaborative protest. And that appeared to be the end of it, especially since the new Minister, Brian Lenihan, was unlikely to take up the cudgels on the Department's behalf. As a living testimony to the failure of this Grey Door intrigue, I was very soon making my way over to the Taoiseach's Department with papers for the new Committee. Presumably, the entreaty just went straight into the mythical shredder. Or perhaps Haughey, realising the venue of its composition, decided to take it with him to his own favourite restaurant, Le Coq Hardi, from where I saw him emerge later that week, very much back in Government. And very much 'unperturbed' by paper jets.

Section I

Ireland

1

Joining Up

In the centre of Dublin, on the south side of St Stephen's Green is Iveagh House, headquarters of the Department of Foreign Affairs, the Irish foreign service. It overlooks the Green and is a fine building, with a white portico frontage and lavender-glassed lanterns which give it an unusually camp quality. At night, beneath the portico, a Garda is on duty, with another inside the house and another outside the Department of Justice next door. On the roof, a large spiky aerial keeps All Missions Abroad (Embassies and Consulates) in constant contact with 'HQ', as they call it. Sometimes, at night, when all the chandelier lights are blazing, the place looks like a Viennese Opera House, which is appropriate given its history and that of its former inhabitants.

Originally, the house belonged to Dr Robert Clayton, the Protestant Bishop of Cork, who fell into public disgrace in the 1740s when he disputed aspects of the Holy Trinity. It then passed to John Philpot Curran, Master of the Rolls in the doomed Irish Parliament of the 18th century, and father of Sarah Curran, fiancée of Robert Emmet, the young rebel and beheaded patriot. In 1856, the Guinness family acquired it and, after an extravagant makeover, the house served as a major venue for Vice-Regal society with its many balls and parties. But Irish independence saw the end of that privileged world. 'Deeply distressed' by 1916 and other 'upheavals', the Earl of Iveagh adjourned to London and, in 1939, his son offered the house to the State. There was a story that when the Taoiseach, Eamon de Valera personally came around to see it, a man, still employed as a butler, and rubbing the sleep from his eyes, came out to open the door. 'Come for the Last Waltz, my lord?'

Inside the house, are some of the most impressive rooms in the city. The stone-flagged entrance hall is adorned with Italian statues of The Sleeping Faun and The Reading Girl. A sweeping, double return staircase, wide enough to accommodate the ball-goers dresses, and surrounded by rococo and neo-classical motifs, leads up to a ballroom at the back of the house, lined with gilt and mirrors and apparently (and, appropriately, given the diplomatic connotations) inspired by the palace at Versailles. Around the room are balconies and alcoves where once dancers retreated to fan themselves and mark their dance cards. It is here that receptions are held, Inter-Governmental meetings and Departmental parties. Materials were sourced from afar; onyx, alabaster, West Indian mahogany. At the core of the house are further ornate rooms, serving as chambers for the Minister, Minister of State and the Department Secretary. In and around these are the secret passageways and back stairs of the servants, now used by lowly officials like myself.

The Minister's offices overlook a back garden with dribbling fountain and somnolent goldfish and, at the gardens' end, there is a stone pavilion done in the Celtic Revival style beloved of the Victorians. Beyond that again, past a high fence and security cameras, are the Iveagh Gardens, which connect to the Department's other offices in Harcourt Street and are used sparingly by the public. For this reason, they are also known as 'The Secret Gardens' and often in the afternoon you can see officers crossing between the trees or engaging in spirit-reviving talks with Northern nationalists, as they stroll past the sunken archery lawn, another diverting offshoot of Victorian neo-medievalism.

The Department has come a long way since the days of its curiously isolationist title, 'Department of External

Affairs' and new sections have been added over the years, including an Anglo-Irish 'hospital' block. But in 1994, the Government generously allowed Iveagh House to be used as a location for a TV version of old *Moll Flanders*. It's not hard to see why. It was to double as a 19th-century brothel, but given all the red damask drapes, crushed velvet and busy rococo, very little additional decoration was needed — apart from some fiery red lamps put along the staircase. 'Sure the place is full of whores already' a Minister is reputed to have told an inquiring press. 'That's right — flat out for our country!' retorted a senior official, to raucous laughter in Hourican's.

It was an interesting variation on the line that a diplomat is 'someone who lies for his, or her, country' and it was into this world that I arrived in 1987, a nervous virgin, at the age of twenty-four. How does one get into 'the game'? I left College in the mid-80s, when there were few jobs to be found. The Department of Foreign Affairs (DFA) was one of them; a permanent, pensionable job, with lots of overseas travel. Not that I planned to be either permanent or pensionable, but I was interested in international affairs. Before going to UCD, I'd travelled in the Middle East and was fascinated by the political turmoil there. I'd also begun writing fiction (a novel was on the boil) and I felt that DFA would give me both the time, and material, to continue such a pursuit. Graham Greene types came to mind; quixotic outsiders dreamily tapping away on sun-soaked verandas. But there was also the specific tradition of the Irish foreign service, where many writers and poets had combined diplomacy with artistic output; poets like Valentine Iremonger and Dennis Devlin and the incendiary pundit, Conor Cruise O'Brien. As I say, quixotic outsiders.

I came from an artistic family. My father, Edward, was a sculptor and a sister and brother were involved in the visual arts, so perhaps, in an act of unconscious rebellion, typical of the reactionary Eighties, I decided to work at a desk, in a suit. For the time being, at least. My mother,

Nancy, however, came from a family with a strong sense of patriotism and public service and, as Mothers do, she stressed the wisdom of a good solid job, especially in an age of recession. So, in many ways, it was a neat compromise all round.

The starting grade in the diplomatic service is Third Secretary (or *Troisième Secretaire* — the French founded much of diplomacy) and selection for it is basically a long whittling-down process. The initial, standard exam is open to honours graduates with 1st class or 2.1 degrees, and is held in curious venues around the country — mine was in a Civil Defence Hall on Leeson Street. The exam seemed to be about testing one's expressive skills, with subjects like 'why is modern art relevant today?' to giving the Unionist perspective on the Anglo-Irish Agreement. Basically, from 'dinner party chatter' to delivering the party line. With a background in college debating, I enjoyed these exercises in devil's advocacy and fired off a spirited Ulster tirade against the 'undemocratic' Anglo-Irish 'diktat'.

The next stage was a sort of aptitude test in the Local Appointments Commission on Lower Grand Canal Street, a grim bunker-like building with all the charm of a 1970s' Civil Service office block. In a linoleum and wood-grain wallpapered room, we were given a *Dr Who*-style aptitude test, with reversed clocks and silhouettes and questions like 'if a 5-sided cube looks like this at 3 p.m., what would it look like at 7 p.m.?' The answer sheets were collected by silent clerks with stopwatches, who handed them on to other clerks. Somehow, I imagined more clerks in white lab coats dissecting them in the vault of this grim building. 'Ah, vat haff we here … ?'

After this, it was the interview process, held in a large room, upstairs in the Department of Justice building, where the Foreign Affairs Administration section was then located. I had to face a table of about four people, all firing questions. Of course, I didn't know who they were at the time, but later I realised they included Ted

Barrington, now Ambassador in London, Mary Barrington (no relation) and Conor Murphy, now Ambassador in Saudi Arabia. It was a sort of 'hard cop, soft cop' routine mixed with St Peter at the Gates of Heaven. 'I notice you spent time in the Middle East' Barrington would say 'Do you agree with Conor Cruise O'Brien's assessment of Israeli nationalism?' But no sooner had had I gone into modern Zionism, than someone else said 'In the mock Leaving Cert, you failed honours Maths. Why was that?'

'Oh, eh …' The mock Leaving? I couldn't believe it. 'Ambition beyond my ability,' I stuttered awkwardly and they nodded firmly; we understand.

They seemed impressed but, a few weeks later, I got a letter querying my Inter Cert results (which I'd done at fourteen!). I furnished them with new results and explained the discrepancies. It appeared to have worked and I was placed on the 'panel', the reserve bench from which new Third Secretaries are recruited. But it was quite a few months before I was called. I got worried. People told me about the rigorous security test which was part of the entrance procedure and I agonised about some of the wilder moments of my youth. This is not as farcical as it sounds. The Department is about to trust you with issues of considerable political and security sensitivity and they don't want moles who are going to lose documents to some 'higher cause'. Consequently, some applicants have been held up for a considerable period while they were being vetted. Most suspicious were candidates with a hard left background, especially Trotskyites, or with Sinn Féin/IRA connections. However, most candidates came through regardless of their history, the Department working on the basis that such characters were 'reformed', and that their erstwhile, ideological fervour was something that went in tandem with ambitious, high achievement, which the Department might benefit from.

In fact, the real reasons for the delay were the Government cutbacks and the onset of the Public Service Recruitment Embargo, which meant that new Third Secs were only being taken on very selectively. Indeed, I was lucky to have got in at all. After me, no one was taken on again for almost two years — an astonishing hiatus. The joke among my colleagues was that they had made such a mistake recruiting me that they had to go away and revise the procedures!

To give some flavour of the Department, I should offer a breakdown of its various Divisions, or an 'organogram' as we called it.

Basically, Foreign Affairs is broken into four major Divisions; the European Union(EU)/Economic Division (where I was first sent), the Political Division, the Anglo-Irish Division and the Administration Division. Of these four I would work in all but Administration during my eight years in the Department.

EU/Economic dealt directly to Brussels and increased European integration. (At the time, of course, it was the European Community.) Thus, it was in a world of its own over in Harcourt Street. With the new business-oriented Government in 1987, it was split into a Trade or Foreign Earnings side and, some years later, this was transferred to the Department of Industry and Commerce in Kildare Street, from which we thought the poor creatures would never return. The turf wars between Foreign Affairs and Kildare Street over foreign trade go back decades, with both Departments spoiling any attempts by successive politicians to marry the two.

EU/Economic also had a Development Aid Division, which dealt with aid programmes to the developing world. As the glossy brochures testify, it is the source of some of the more interesting work abroad, with sun-burnt First Secretaries, their sleeves rolled up at last, directing tractors around the fields of Tanzania and Ministers of State enthralling little children with jokes and stories; a pity they've no votes. Under Labour in the 1990s, this part of the Division grew dramatically.

Political Division is closest to what incoming Third Secretaries imagined themselves doing, deciphering disputes in the Middle East and Southeast Asia and meeting other pressure groups, other diplomats and multilateral organisations. Located at the top of Iveagh House, it inhabits a warren of little offices and sky-lit garrets which, in centuries past, must have served as the bedrooms of the gentry and their overworked servants. No real change there then.

Shielded from the main house by cherry blossoms, is the modern 'hospital block' of Anglo-Irish Division, so called because it resembles a small hospital or nursing home. Anglo-Irish deals with Northern Ireland and British-Irish relations. In 1987, it was only two years from the Anglo-Irish Agreement and a whole mechanism was being put in place to service and develop it. It used to be that a newly recruited Third Sec couldn't begin their career there but this has changed, as has some of the absurdly macho and self-important air of the Division.

The arrival of the Agreement, so hated by the Unionists, meant an overall tightening of security in the Department, with submarine doors at the front and back of the House and a high fence, with cameras, to separate us from Iveagh Gardens. Not only that but there were also secure doors to separate Anglo-Irish Division from the rest of the Department, as if they couldn't trust their own colleagues. Along with mini-shredders attached to Counsellors desks, as if they couldn't trust their own Third Secs and Clerical Assistants. With security like that, was it surprising people became self-important?

Nominally Anglo-Irish had two further functions: the Cultural Section dealt with, and funded, Irish cultural events abroad whilst an Information Section basically produced propaganda, writing leaflets, speeches and 'Facts about Ireland' booklets. This was an area very much cut back in the 1980s. Whereas, in the 1950s, the

Department used to produce films, wallcharts and even hardback books, full of diagrams showing the illegitimacy and 'illogicality' of 'Northern Ireland', with photos showing the Border going across a farmhouse and, in one case, an unhappy dog's back. Also housed in this Division was the all important Press section, a key part of the Department, given that it has to comment on so many issues, from Northern Ireland to Brussels to foreign visits and Irish citizens abroad.

Finally, there was the Administration Division which had all the other interesting bits; the Consular section, which dealt with visas, citizenship and Irish nationals abroad; Protocol, which dealt with State functions and foreign Embassies in Ireland; and the Personnel section, which dealt with all the problems of DFA staff, including children's schools, residences and those awkward burned-out diplomats who had to be brought home early.

Most of Admin was not in Iveagh House but next door, in Justice, the Department with which Foreign Affairs uneasily shared so many issues from Citizenship to the North. In this building was DFA's Legal section, which examined international treaties and other issues. And then, of course, there were the Passport Offices, in Dublin and Cork — an important part of DFA, whose advice and assistance were often badly needed by Irish citizens either going or already abroad.

From time to time, DFA creates new units and sections and then closes them afterwards, but the above is the basic structure. Unlike almost all other Departments, people are moved every few years through the different Divisions, the idea being that no one can stay in any one specialist area The idea, I suppose, is that when you go abroad, you can be a Jack, or Mary, of all trades.

This structure came with its own personnel hierarchy. Divisions were headed by Assistant Secs, sections by Counsellors, and subsections by First Secs, assisted by Third Secs, and assisted again by the Clerical staff. At the very top was Noel Dorr, the Department Secretary, to whom the Assistant Secs reported. Every morning he met them for what was known as 'Morning Prayers'. He was shadowed (and shadowed was the appropriate word) by the Deputy Secretary, Robin Fogarty, who in Noel Dorr's absence, for example, convened the lunch against Haughey. In the normal run of things, however, the Deputy Secretary was a relatively powerless position which was later abolished.

Marginally more important was our beloved figurehead, the Minister. He was the reason for our collective existence, and it was to his large, plush office that most of us were effectively working, especially the Secretary who was located in equally salubrious chambers on the ground floor below. The Minister's office was the nerve centre of DFA and if we weren't always sending our stuff up to him, it was always in his good name, and authority, that we were acting. Through my time in EU Co-ordination, a key 'assembly point', I had a lot of direct contact with his office, which was both interesting and useful for the years ahead.

In my seven years in the Department, I served under five Ministers; Peter Barry of Fine Gael, for about a month, followed by three Fianna Fáil Ministers; Brian Lenihan (1987-1989), Gerry Collins (1989-1991) and David Andrews (1992). These were followed by Labour's Dick Spring from 1992 until 1995, the year I resigned. Collins and Spring were probably the most memorable. The hardworking Spring was particularly impressive and even FF-leaning officials admitted that he was one of the best Foreign Ministers Ireland had had. It helps, of course, if the Minister is also a party leader, and, in Spring's case, Tánaiste, in a high-profile coalition Government. It also helps if the Minister is seen to protect the Department and 'bat' for them at the Cabinet table. Spring and Lenihan were perceived to do this. Unfortunately, Lenihan was absent for much of his tenure through illness. By a grim irony, his duties were taken over by our esteemed Taoiseach. So, technically speaking, Charles J Haughey was Minister for Foreign Affairs. It was enough to have them ordering another round of Remy Martins in The Grey Door!

The Department is defined by its hierarchies and chains of command. The Third Sec works to a First Sec who works to a Counsellor who works to an Assistant Sec who works to the Minister. Of course, in exceptional circumstances, this Gogolian chain of command could be circumvented, especially when you're abroad or 'on the hoof'. Also with the cutbacks, of which there were now many, there was plenty of scope for initiative and the by-passing of empty desks. The embargo on public service recruitment introduced in 1987 had hit quite hard and all around positions were left unfilled. Haughey was now reborn to fiscal rectitude and the Public Sector was feeling it. In keeping with the gleeful expectation of political changes in Foreign Affairs, some of the media also wanted cutbacks for 'the gin-swilling diplomats'. Closing Embassies abroad made good copy, especially for the more populist evening papers. Or for the likes of *Magill* magazine, which, for some reason, particularly disliked the socialising associated with Anglo-Irish relations, even if this wining and dining of Tory backbenchers had lubricated the process of achieving the Anglo-Irish Agreement.

Such cost-cutting proved short-sighted. The cost of running a Embassy is not large, and neither is the cost of running the Department. Also, apart from the insult to the host country, the mechanics of closing a Mission abroad are enormous, with concomitant financial implications. In somewhere like Africa, closing an Embassy can end up costing the Exchequer more than it saves. Then, of course, we have to come along a few years later and open another Embassy. In the meantime, should an Irish citizen be killed or kidnapped, the same media would cry out wondering why Ireland has no Embassy in the region. Today, of course, we appear to be opening Missions everywhere — although, rather selfishly perhaps, the driving force is almost exclusively trade and investment.

In the late eighties, however, morale was low around DFA and people were doing more jobs than they expected. But, in many ways, the cutbacks were an improvement, streamlining work procedures and eliminating a line of bureaucracy. But you couldn't admit these things. Just as you never admitted to not being busy. You were always busy. It was part of the culture, just as it was throughout the Civil Service — just as it was, I suspect, in the private sector. It was the same with the fight for resources. Embassies always 'needed' more people.

The Department is, of necessity, a broad church in terms of Personnel. In recent years, DFA has recruited, and promoted, a more conservative and practical type, less *bon viveur* and more bloodless technocrats. It used to be that the educational background was History or Languages but, increasingly — with one eye on Brussels — it is Economics and Law. Sometimes, one had the feeling that future Caligulas and Robin Fogartys might be thin on the ground. But then, you don't how someone might turn out after the long attrition of a diplomatic career. Robin Fogarty, after all, had probably been the definition of the clean-cut technocrat when he sat down to do that tough entrance exam, all those years ago. The "broad church" analogy could be taken literally — many people are recruited from a Protestant, and Jewish background. This is a deliberate policy and means that when such diplomats are abroad, we can show the non-sectarian nature of both the Department and Ireland. People also joined from a Northern Irish Protestant background, which was even better.

But those who saw the place as a nest of Fine Gael-types, or West Britons or whatever the cliché was, would have been completely wrong. Some of the most nationalist people I've ever met have been in Foreign Affairs, often more Republican than their cynical masters (possibly because they have to deal with the British, and Northern Irish authorities on a day-to day basis). One bearded ex-radical — and there were quite a few — got posted to Paris and found himself bumping into his old comrades from the Irish Republican Socialist Party, hiding out in that capital of refuge. Proof that the Security Test couldn't have been all that draconian.

There was also a strong cultural nationalism, as befits a service which effectively marketed the concept of 'Ireland' abroad. Pinned to the walls of people's offices, you'd see an artful reminder of the old Ireland which, for most of us, was only a generation away. Tasteful black and white photos of decayed currachs and grizzled old men sucking on pipes, were put up next to the children's artwork and the more ironically intended 'man of destiny' portraits of C J Haughey.

As with the rest of the Civil Service, there were many Irish speakers. In our internal phone directory, a G after someone's name denoted, not Gay as someone once told a gullible new officer (more of which anon) but Gaelic-speaking. Sometimes, sitting in the toilet cubicle, reading, and possibly even using, the Delors Plan for European Integration, you'd hear the voices outside, chatting away in Irish as they washed their hands. '*Conor, a chara. Conas atá tú?*' It was good to hear it still being used, especially for those awkward members of the public who insisted on their right to use it.

There was also a large gay contingent. "Foreign travel, fine wines, nice interiors — of course it would attract us," was how one of them put it. The contrary was also true; "Look at the style and service we bring — compared to the smelly socks brigade" This was a reference to the more lumpen Civil Servant, chewing away at his biro. I only realised later how many gays there were when, in the midst of an EU Summit, a journalist teasingly asked me what we were going to "do for a Spouses Association in the future?"

"What do you mean?"

"Oh, come on, your place is like Queer Heaven," he said, with satisfaction, and proceeded to 'out' a whole string of officials. Since the guy was from RTÉ it was a bit like the kettle happily calling the pot pink.

However, there was a gender imbalance, which DFA has recently done much to redress. It wasn't so obvious at home, but abroad you really saw it. The old feminist dilemma persisted as it did in the private sector. Those who wanted to get to the top had to work harder just to overcome the discrimination, and, in the process, might sacrifice marriage and children. This made them hard taskmasters, and according to younger female officers, it often made them less patient of the more easy-going generation who came in later, who had a growing private sector to escape to if DFA didn't work out.

In general, however, the Department has a very strong *esprit de corps* naturally bonded by foreign postings. The atmosphere is bolstered by an active social life. The crowded den of Hourican's on a Friday night, or the other pubs on Harcourt Street, bore witness to a healthy mixture of grades and personalities. And unhealthy; careers were made and broken in the pub and people were under much closer surveillance than they thought. Because of this, some Third Secs in the mid-Nineties broke away to another venue, but this was considered cowardly and not playing the game. The crack was in the democracy of the Irish pub.

Further opportunity for extra-curricular bonding in the form of the Department football team. Languishing somewhere in the lower Civil Service leagues, the team was mostly made up of burly Messengers and clerical staff, with few brave diplomats mixed in. Or 'dipsomats' as the clerical staff called them, especially those in accounts branch who had to deal with our reception expenses. A healthy and understandable tension exists between the 'dipsomats' and their much put-upon support staff, which was given full rein on the football pitch ('Over here, ye gobshite!'). But such differences wilted in the face of our Civil Service opponents, as did some of our strikers. I togged out for a bone-crunching encounter with the Prison Officers, a terrifying experience but one in which, astonishingly, I scored a goal. A deliberately over-powered clearance hit the back of my head and rebounded into the screws net. I was the toast of Hourican's for a week, a dubious honour which probably had as much to do with one of the dipsos getting inadvertently whacked. But our footballers must have learned from these encounters since later, in London, a match between the Irish and South African embassies resulted in a brawl to which the police were called, a fracas which predictably appeared on the front pages of the Irish newspapers.

During the day, there were the Coffee Breaks — a Civil Service institution — when people left their sections and went to visit other areas. At one stage, so many people were coming and going — people in Cultural section on Harcourt Road used to come all the way around the Green to meet their friends — that staff were ordered not to stray from their Divisions. The back of Iveagh House was also host to an amazing institution, known as the Civil Service Club, a Soviet-style cafeteria where retired Civil Servants, of all sorts, hobbled in each day for their Club Milks and catering-issue tea, unable to break the habits of a lifetime. The food was dreadful but, God love them, the Club apparently considered pitching to do a State dinner, an application which drew derisive laughter from Protocol. Tragically, it was ultimately decided that the Club's proximity to Anglo-Irish was a security threat and, within a week, it was demolished. Just like that. Nothing was spared for 'Northern Ireland'; the best computers, extra staff, the demolition of a café.

At Coffee Breaks, you'd see the different types of Third Sec — those who'd been on postings abroad and those who hadn't, those who came in directly from College, bright-eyed and idealistic, and the more cautious ones who'd come in from other Departments. There were also 'The Posties', lucky beneficiaries of the six-month postal strike in 1979 which so damaged Jack Lynch's Government (the other lucky beneficiary being CJH, of course). Unable to correspond with outside applicants, it was decided to hold an internal competition, within the Civil Service only. From this, there was an absurdly large intake (a deliberate ploy to bring in some raw, practical types?) who became known as the Postmen, as in 'the Postmen who never delivered'. By contrast in the late 1980s, talented people were leaving as the public service haemorrhage went on. In Harcourt Street, back then, were people who would go on to prominence elsewhere, like Etain Doyle, the Controller of Telecommunications, and Carmel Foley, the Director of Consumer Affairs.

Social life was particularly active in the summer — work in Brussels and Paris shut down for August — and at Christmas time, when DFA fulfils all the clichés of this bacchanalian season. Beginning with Section lunches, it proceeds to Divisional drinks, Embassy parties and eventually on to the Departmental party in Iveagh House, where the doors are locked and no one is supposed to leave until dawn. The party is an extraordinary affair. You'd see people you'd never seen before, dragged in from forgotten parts of DFA; the translation section or EU Documentation. You'd also meet returned diplomats you'd hadn't seen before. Because of the cyclical nature of postings, you could be years in DFA before you met all its officers. With cross-postings, some people were away for eight or nine years, never coming home.

At the party, there were no spouses and no outsiders, except maybe some people from the Taoiseach's Department. One year Sean Donlon, the former Secretary brought in John Hume, symbolic perhaps of our closeness to the SDLP, but breaking the code. It was like sneaking a non-Muslim into Mecca, to watch us circle the black Kaaba and fire accusatory stones at an effigy of the Taoiseach. The Minister usually stuck around for a while, especially someone like Spring who had become very much part of the culture of DFA. Watching Spring, drinking at a table with Ted Barrington and Seán Ó'hUiginn, you realised just how close he'd become to the mandarins, in many ways like a mandarin himself. Afterwards, he might adjourn, with his Labour Party handlers.

After they retreated, the party seriously got underway, with amorous couples drifting up the wide staircase to the Secretary's Ante Room and darkened Minister's quarters, or down into the labyrinthine basement, with its wine cellar and telex room. The parties were infamous for its liaisons, including one unfortunate who was caught on security camera with his trousers around his knees. In scenes worthy of a French farce (or indeed *Moll Flanders*) the servants had literally 'taken over', often directly under the disapproving gaze of the Second Earl of Iveagh, Benjamin Guinness himself, whose portrait hung upstairs.

Because of its absence of clutter or any signs of work, the Minister's office, with its big walnut desk and warm velvety carpet was also popular with lusty couples. 'Golden shag' — never was a surface more aptly named. And never was the adrenalin of possible discovery quite so palpable, kissing under the appropriately titled De Chirico painting 'Wild Horses', and those gild-edged mirrors which often crop up as TV background whenever the Minister emerges from another 'meaningful' discussion with a visiting opposite.

2

EU Co-ordination

I can't say that I was all that excited about the duties my first appointment — to the EU Co-ordination section in Harcourt Street — entailed. Basically, Co-ordination meant the production of Briefing material and the distribution of papers, especially the voluminous documentation coming in from Brussels.

The section came alive for the Foreign Affairs Councils (FACs) when Minister's Briefs had to be assembled, and for the European Councils, attended by the heads of Government and for which a more elaborate ritual took place. FACs are held every month, and European Councils, or Summits, every six months. Briefing material is among the most important of Departmental activities, summarising for the Minister the information necessary to meet and negotiate, or simply to nod his head like he knows what's going on. To improve focus, the Speaking Points are put on white paper, Steering Notes on yellow and Background Notes on blue. But the bound Briefs often came back to us unread. Why should the Minister bother, when he had officials to brief him orally and steer him through? By contrast, the Briefs of senior mandarins came back, disgorged, underlined and inkily rewritten, presumably after on-the-spot consultations with the Germans and French.

And yet everyone had to have one, especially during the European Councils when people saw what others were getting. But we sometimes filleted the Briefs given to outside Ministers or officials from other Departments.

Post-Grey Door, however, this became complicated, since it was decreed that Foreign Affairs briefs should now be assembled in the Taoiseach's Department, with us ignominiously carrying over our sheaves of papers. We included filler off-the-shelf material, but they had their own ideas anyway and started rewriting material as soon as it arrived.

I also had to assemble a Taoiseach's weekly brief on European Affairs, an informal compendium of material for Haughey's weekend perusal in Kinsealy. But knocking on certain doors, it was hard to get anything. 'I'm working — go away', grouchy officials would say as they focussed intently on some note for a meeting with the European Commission. In the dwindling scheme of things, this seemed to have more importance that an informal package for the Taoiseach.

People were equally unmoved when I chased them for contributions to 'Developments in the European Communities', a six monthly report, which we were obliged to produce by dint of our membership of the Community. The booklet, written in tightly worded officialese, covered all aspects of the EU policies and their relationship to Irish legislation, from fisheries to trade to education. Other Departments had to be ceaselessly badgered to provide material for this and the process brought home the laxity of the Public Service with people constantly 'away from their desks' or not returning calls. Eventually, I had to get our Minister's office to ring their Minister's office saying we needed an urgent response; such calls were like electric shocks into a moribund system.

The report took ages to produce, not helped by its long delay on the desk of the Deputy Secretary, Robin Fogarty, who, once he saw it, wanted it all rewritten, as he did everything else. Fogarty's office was an unfortunate lay-by for stuff going up the line. Formerly The Garden Wing, off the main staircase in Iveagh House, it was known as 'the boudoir', because of its extraordinary wallpaper, a sort of throbbing Barbara Cartland pink, not unlike Fogarty's own face as he sat glowering behind his over-heaped desk. It could also be accessed by a hidden spiral staircase, inside the wall, which led to the floor above and perhaps escape. Fogarty was quite an eccentric. His other stricture was a refusal to use red 'Immediate' tags on Circulation Envelopes, on the grounds that everything was immediate. Sadly it was not a principle he held to himself.

The report was proofed obsessively. All documents were, but particularly official ones — we didn't want to enact a new law by accident — and particularly under Haughey who was passionate about typing errors. Along with punctuality, it was his big phobia. In fact, it was almost a secret weapon; send him a document riddled with spelling errors and when he opened it — ah! eek! — they'd come at him like a plague of locusts. That's what they should have done with the Grey Door caveat, but, unfortunately, it didn't have a single typo, since it had been thoroughly combed through by our perfectionist First Sec.

Once finished, we would take the 'Developments in the EC' report to the printers on the East Wall Road: typically our First Sec would still be manically re-reading it as it went onto the machines. Government Departments are careful about where they get stuff printed. Someone I know laminated maps relating to the Anglo-Irish Agreement. An anonymous man stood by his machine and each time there was a dud copy, he took it and put it in a box. Afterwards, people in suits could be seen in the yard going through the skips and the bins.

The report was then laid before the Dáil and there was a lengthy debate, with a long statement from the Minister and supporting contributions from well-meaning politicians; very few people were against 'Europe'. In the chamber, the officials sit near the Minister inside a rail near the wall. On the TV, it appears as the section just beyond the Taoiseach — a sort of non-elected cage.

Whereas most people look at the TV to see what politician is speaking, Civil Servants look to see which officials are pulling the strings. Visits to the Dáil were always a bit of crack. You'd swan around the circular corridors in the company of older officers, and watch them receive welcomes from politicians who remembered them from visits abroad, usually in a previous incarnation for both.

The highlight of my time in Harcourt Street was the rejection of the Single European Act by the Supreme Court in 1986, a rejection that many people felt was not unconnected to the belligerent attitude of our own Mr Fogarty down in the Courts — 'this is the Government speaking' — which only roused the beaks. The rejection meant that a referendum had to be held and a Guide produced which was supposed to have explained the Communities to the people but ended up confusing them further.

The Guide was produced, but with so many changes of mind and text by Mr Fogarty that people were tearing their hair out. Ironically in his prime, Fogarty had been deeply involved in Ireland's original accession to the EU in 1973 and, according to one of those great Hourican's myths, he was later described by Helmut Schmidt as one of the few people in Bonn in 1978 who actually understood the nascent theory of European and Monetary Union. But that was a different Fogarty to one now in charge: red-faced, embittered by Haughey's return and a fearful character for a timid Third Sec to come in contact with.

When finally printed, the Guide (or 'White Book') was given, en masse, to thousands of schoolchildren, for there are no better propagandists, and future Eurocrats, than schoolchildren and their teachers. In the book was a warm endorsement of Europe from An Taoiseach, Charles J Haughey. Having opposed the Single European Act (SEA) while in opposition Haughey had performed the usual U-turn in power and was enthusiastically endorsing the SEA, just as he was doing with the Anglo-Irish

Agreement. Fianna Fáil had abandoned those neutralists who felt that the SEA was a diminution of Ireland's much cherished neutrality — Ireland being the only member of the then Twelve EU members not also a member of NATO.

Early on, the Department began the process of 'blooding' me in the more general arts of diplomacy. By having me sit in on a Diplomatic Corp dinner, for example, or putting me in a top hat and tails for a Presentation of Ambassadorial Credentials in Phoenix Park. But the best training was probably a spell of being Duty Officer.

Duty Officers (D.O.s) are essentially night cover for the Department. Thus more junior members of DFA staff (from any Division) were appointed for a week at a time to represent the entire Department outside office hours. Back in 1987 we were issued a pager so as to be contactable outside the office. Later, this was replaced by a mobile phone. It's now almost quaint to think back to when the bleep would go off in a bar or café on a crowded Saturday afternoon. People who knew you assumed an emergency — a revolt in Central Africa perhaps. 'Yes, Yolima, but how many are on the streets?' you'd shout into a nearby phone, keeping up the image. In reality it was more likely to be bleach-blond Mrs Murphy and her family needing emergency passports to go to a 'family funeral' in Fungerola.

The pager was set off by one of the Gardaí, who were always on duty at the DFA reception outside office hours. Within their glass security box, the Guards were effectively DFA's switchboard after six and it was they who relayed the calls. A good Garda could save you trouble by judging the real emergencies and handling some of the queries themselves.

But sometimes the page could be about something more exciting. On my very first evening, Brian Keenan, the Beirut hostage, was rumoured to have been released and I had to go to Rathmines Garda Station to call the

Embassy in Baghdad. I was in one of those cubicles usually reserved for arrested suspects, the walls scrawled with nicknames and anti-cop graffiti. Our Embassy in Beirut had closed and Baghdad would investigate. Baghdad was familiar with Keenan's situation, his relatives and his more curious friends, including a man who gave me the home phone numbers of Sheikh Fadlallah and Nabih Berri, and insisted I call them.

"You'll find the Sheik a most interesting man," he said pompously. Given that the last time I'd seen the Sheik was in a documentary called 'Sword of Islam', standing on a podium condemning Israel, Russia and America, while prospective martyrs ran around in circles, with blood streaming down their foreheads, I thought it was a conversational pleasure I might pass up.

But I made umpteen other calls, after which it was clear that Keenan had not been not released and that this was just another Beirut rumour. In fact, Keenan wouldn't get out for another four years. There was a strange atmosphere around the Keenan kidnapping, not helped by rumour, and counter-rumour, coming from Beirut. But also there was the continuing criticism of DFA for not doing enough for him, which we felt unfair. One Ambassador was nearly killed helping him. Even our original action of breaking into Keenan's apartment and discovering his Irish passport was an unusual and daring gesture.

So high was Keenan on the agenda, and so doggedly was the matter pursued with Gulf and Arab states, that later, when he was released I heard people say with an edge of disappointment, 'That's the end of one of our big bilateral issues'. The Keenan kidnapping had given Ireland ongoing high-level access to the Iranians and others, which it otherwise mightn't have had. Meetings which, by the by, would also discuss construction contracts, beef exports and votes at the United Nations. A chilling insight into the *realpolitik* of issue-building.

It was the same with another issue which erupted on me one Friday night, with no warning. This was the conclusion of the Tribunal into the British killing of three unarmed IRA suspects on the Rock of Gibraltar. At 7 p.m., the Tribunal came in with an amazing verdict, effectively clearing the SAS. Almost immediately the phones started hopping, with calls of bitter complaint and queries from journalists looking for an official reaction. 'You must be very busy' a reporter from the London *Independent* said and I said 'Absolutely, we've been swamped — people are very angry'. The next day's *Independent* quoted an Irish official on 'people being very angry' and, worse, the curious fact, that the Irish Government 'still had, as yet, no reaction'. Which was true but it wasn't the way the Department might have put it. It was a early lesson on the perils of saying anything to the Press. A lot of Duty Officer calls were from the press, but they were always routed to the home phones of the Press officers.

What was interesting was the reaction the next day when the Gibraltar verdict was digested. "Fantastic" said the officials in Anglo-Irish and elsewhere, rubbing their hands. "Now we've got a stick to beat the British with for the next few months"

"Next few months — next few years!" corrected someone else, confident that the legendary stubbornness of the British on these matters would mean years of foot-dragging, just like the holes they dug themselves into over Bloody Sunday and the Guildford Four. And sure enough, the Gibraltar crisis escalated with the British Government banning a TV inquiry and then Thatcher fighting with the House of Commons over it. It was like the *realpolitik* of Keenan's capture; the real beneficiaries of such events were the officials who made hay over them for the years to come.

As Duty Officer in Iveagh House on a Saturday, you might have to partake in some of the little rituals of diplomacy, like receiving a man from the French Embassy, in a blue blazer and shiny black shoes, coming in to deliver a *démarche* about the shelling in Beirut. The French were backing the Christian warlord, Michel Aoun. Indeed the French were backing all sorts of rascals. Bringing the Emissary into the Chief of Protocol's room, I sat on one armchair while he sat in another and orally delivered his country's great concern about the Levantine situation — pausing occasionally to check the shine on his shoes. All done, he handed over the *démarche*, stamped with sealing wax and decorated with ribbons, and then left, his salary earned as a diplomat in Dublin. They were somewhat silly, these old diplomatic rituals, but given that the French had founded many of them, they were not going to let them die.

Beirut came up a lot while I was Duty Officer. On another occasion, during intense shelling, I had to make contact with an Irish woman stuck in the midst of it. Later, I described it to a friend in radio, who then rang up the woman and got her to talk on air, with the cracks of gunfire in the background. Duty Officer affairs were normally confidential but talking about this case was harmless enough and the publicity helped the woman's situation.

Mostly, however, the work was dealing with passports or Consular problems. The Consular section would tip you off on Friday about cases which might arise; an arrest in the Philippines, political turmoil in the Congo, an illness abroad, an advance of funds. You would also consult with Protocol about possible overflights — official permission for foreign planes to fly through Irish airspace. The planes were usually British, thus the sensitivity. Often these could arise unexpectedly and the Department of Defence would call you for permission, which you'd have to give on the spot, especially if it was an RAF Nimrod coming in on a rescue mission.

Events began almost immediately on a Friday night, so you'd go to Hourican's and wait for the pager to go off. Otherwise, you'd find yourself coming into Iveagh House at all hours. You would try to handle things at home, which, armed with all your Directories, you sometimes could — you were often just a conduit, after all — but often you had to go in. It was strange coming into Iveagh House on a Saturday or Sunday afternoon, the building eerily empty and — in winter — the garden full of snow. Or coming in late at night and seeing all the empty desks and the telex machines clacking away — for, of course, it was a working day at Embassies abroad. You were supposed to check these, especially the Confidential fax from the Anglo-Irish Secretariat in Belfast. And the Coreu traffic, upstairs in Political Co-ordination. The Coreu was a circular telex system between EU members and the main mechanism for European Union drafting of political statements and initiatives. The 'Coreus' arrived into the Communications Centre (Comcen) in the basement of the House, and were then sent upstairs in glass tubes, speeding along an air-vacuum pipe, like something from the Second World War. You could hear the rattle before they arrived.

If they were urgent, Comcen would call you. Because of the different time zones and decoding requirements, there were always Comcen people on duty, right through the weekend, taking telexes from around the world. Lined along the wall were wooden pigeon holes, with the names of all the different missions; a magical parade of desert kingdoms and tropical cities — Khartoum, Kuala Lumpur, Tokyo, Lagos. You'd press a bell and a girl appeared behind the perspex security screen — Hey, Duty Officer! — and passed you out the immediate telexes. The secure ones from Belfast were in envelopes, with the date and time written across the seal.

If something was urgent, you'd call the Third Sec for that desk, and if unavailable, work your way upwards. If it was very important, you'd call an Assistant Sec and interrupt their Saturday afternoon. To get to the Minister, you'd call the Private Secretary. But Ministers would often call you directly, as would TDs, looking for information and favours; a constituent in trouble abroad or an emergency passport. They also called about US visas, a big issue in the late Eighties. Officially the US Embassy didn't entertain representations, but there was some leeway. However, this leeway was so over-exploited, especially by certain rural TDs, that the Americans ended up shutting it down.

Deep in the cold basement of the House, beyond Comcen and the wine cellar, was the tiny Duty Officer's room. Its debris reflected the ad-hoc nature of the job, with a different Third Sec every week, handling different crises, resulting in a desk strewn with Post-It stickers and phone numbers. Because the room is only used 'after hours' it is always locked and the cleaners can't get at it. Hence the bin was constantly overflowing with empty Coke tins and biscuit wrappers. And a half bottle of Jacobs Creek on top of the safe. Not from the wine cellar — Jacobs Creek, *please*! — but from a Christmas party past when a couple wandered down there for a bit of romance.

On Consular issues, the Post-It notes had the factual coldness you'd expect from officials under pressure, and accustomed to relaying tragedy. Rome — 'Mrs X not expected to live', Toronto — 'poss. suicide, don't mention to family', 'YZ sentenced to eight years, drug running, Bangkok'. It was like an Interpol blotter and brought home the other side of our supposedly benign diaspora. Sometimes you'd be amazed, almost impressed, at the scams Irish citizens got up to around the world; sanctions busting in Africa, credit card forgeries in the US, drugs in Turkey. Images came to mind of jungle airstrips and drugs being loaded onto Learjets by boozy ex-pats. Or bank accounts being opened in the Cayman Islands.

On the wall of the duty room were lists of mortuary chapels and undertakers, and police stations abroad. Sometimes a lot of calls had to be made to track a situation down and as you sat there, waiting for an Embassy or hospital to call back, the Garda would ring from upstairs: 'I'm putting the kettle on — do you want a cup of tea?'

The D.O. Manual gave instructions on how to break bad news: who to tell first, what phrases to use, when to call them. Often, it was just a matter of finding a form of words, like so much else in this job, like writing speeches, or drafting an agreement. There was little enough practical help you could offer: in its absence, the art of diplomacy was to try and find a soothing and effective form of language.

Informing people about any death was difficult, but suicides, obviously, were worse. Until a definite picture emerged, there was a vacuum of desperate speculation into which you could only drop bits of information. In one case, a student had left his clothes on a bridge in France and gone missing during high floods. The floods suggested an accident but the clothes, with money still in the pockets, suggested something more deliberate. Whereas the mother was hopeful, the father wasn't. And then I spoke to the guy's roommate who said that yes, the guy had been very depressed. Usually the nature of being Duty Officer meant that when your stint was up, you had to leave some cases unresolved. In this case, however, after a few weeks I got a call at my desk from the current D.O. 'The Y family wanted to thank you for all your help. A body was found.'

You are also responsible for telling Embassies in Dublin, and their Duty Officers, about the death or imprisonment of their nationals. When a Panamanian tanker pulled into Cork with bodies on board I had to tell the Philippines Embassy that two of their nationals had been killed in a fight. A trickier situation was when nationals from Communist countries like Cuba or the Soviet Union tried to defect at Shannon. In these cases, more serious forces came into play which I will describe later.

Calling abroad, you'd get a chance to catch up with your colleagues, and see what weekend life was like in Copenhagen or the weather in Ottawa — useful research for a future posting. 'Mademoiselle Irlandaise — yes, I watch her very good,' the concierge told me when she answered the home phone of an officer in Paris. Suddenly I had an image from a dozen French novels, of the black-clad old lady in the apartment block, peeping out from behind the curtains. But you'd also catch up with some curmudgeonly, older colleagues who didn't want to stir themselves, a risky attitude since any suggestion of not doing your best could rebound badly. These situations often involved citizens in serious circumstances and if things went wrong you might have no comeback. Worse still, the media could get hold of it, or a politician.

The old Civil Servant adage that 'if something went wrong it was your fault, even if it wasn't your fault', was often borne out. If a officer was accused in public, the Department often let it pass, even if he or she was completely in the right. The objective was to shun such publicity — and, horror, a possible slanging match — at all costs. Some of the public knew this, and exploited it, trying to catch you out verbally and make you lose your cool. 'I want your senior officer,' they'd say, upping the stakes, and you'd have to stonewall them. These were the people whose sole purpose in life seemed to be to test public servants; cranks and oddballs and those high-blood pressure types who couldn't accept even a minimum of officialdom. Which was a pity really because they only ended up making life more miserable for themselves.

Most of the disputes concerned passports, which the D.O. could issue over the weekend. Ostensibly, it was an emergency service to facilitate people whose passports were lost or out of date and who needed to travel urgently due to a death or illness abroad. Or who were doing serious business abroad; a quaint hangover from the days when 'foreign investment' was a sacred mantra. And then there were the emergencies, unfortunate people coming in numb with shock and about to fly to New York to bring home a son killed in a car accident. Or visit a sister who was a nun, suddenly dying in Africa. But the system was widely abused, with people discovering just before their holidays that they had no passports. Some Third Secs were famous for their refusals but most of us ended up issuing. A family going on a holiday was a sort of emergency after all, and you didn't want to see people stuck.

In theory, the service was entirely at the discretion of the D.O., but in practise you might find other forces coming to bear, like phone calls from TDs or mandarins pulling strings. Ireland is a small society, with a strongly personalised political culture and it is no accident that our Duty Officer system, with its passport facility, was almost unique among European countries. There could be consequences for not helping people. Arguably this was a good thing, however, and a happy contrast to the sod-off bureaucracy of larger countries.

The reason for caution was, of course, security. You were always torn between the desire to help someone and the fear that they could be a chancer, trying to get a second passport, or even a first (in certain circumstances a more dangerous event). For this reason, emergency passports were always restricted to six or even three months and, before you issued, you checked all their documents and looked up the Stop List. The Stop List, kept in a safe in the D.O.'s room, was a big thick book of people not to be issued Irish Passports. The list doesn't distinguish between people who owe the Department £50 and a serious drug-running criminal or paramilitary. Sometimes, if you looked up a famous gangland or IRA name, you'd find not only their name but an entire family. The list also includes the children of separated parents, about whom there was a custody dispute — this was a very sensitive issue for passports. Each year, the list seemed to get bigger.

The Irish passport, which is relatively uncommon and politically neutral, is a valuable commodity, and especially useful in Africa or the Middle East. During the Irangate saga in 1988, the US National Security Adviser,

Robert McFarlane and Ollie North, secretly flew to Tehran on Irish passports, said to have come from a batch stolen in Dublin in the mid-Eighties. A few years later, Kevin McDonald, the Passport Officer at our Embassy in London, was caught selling them to North Africans and others, partly through post-nuptial citizenships. (The law has since changed and such citizenships now take seven years.) For a cash payment, unscrupulous Irish citizens would marry foreigners and then dissolve the liaison as soon as their nationality was passed on.

Some of them felt they were helping refugees and, indeed, it is ironic that this was one of the means by which young Irish illegals got to stay in the US — with our blessing. However, in London the racket had become so brazen that couples came straight from the Registry Office to the Embassy, with the confetti still in their hair, so anxious were they to apply for a passport. A passport had replaced consummation, in terms of post-marital panic. It was even suggested that, with regard to some Algerian prostitutes, the aforementioned McDonald was having sex in the Embassy itself, a glamorous role for the Office of Public Works furniture: almond-eyed Modigliani ladies stretching out in lieu of their missing paperwork. It also made up for the arriving 'newly weds' who appeared to have dispensed with such activity.

As Duty Officer, you could do your business from anywhere, and most of us have fielded queries from nightclubs, dinner parties and the top of the 45 bus. Likewise, if you got really browned off traipsing into Iveagh House, just to issue passports, you could take some blank ones and safely issue them from home, using the official stamp and ink pad. One fellow told us how he got out of his girlfriend's bed in Rathmines, to issue passports to some priests going to Israel. Hailed back to bed, he re-enacted the scene from the Sixties Czech film, *Closely Observed Trains*, where the railway clerk playfully stamps his girlfriend's buttocks, except in this case it was with the imprint 'Éire-Ireland', and, of course, 'Restricted' around her nether regions. Through the window, he could see the departing priests getting into a taxi.

3

'Our good friends, the Iraqis'

Dinner in the ballroom was a different type of training. Protocol section would often call you to make up the numbers at a dinner or function. 'Bodies were needed' and you were the diplomatic filler. My first one was the Annual Diplomatic Corps dinner, with the Papal Nuncio, Alibrandi and then US Ambassador, Margaret Heckler sitting beside the Minister, Brian Lenihan, at the top table.

The drill for these large dinners is short and brisk with the State delft, and its little golden harps, pulled away almost as soon as they're left down. You wouldn't want to be hungry and get caught talking. The French lady didn't complain, being used to these *nouvelle* occasions, which are really only pretend dinners. The smaller, more intimate dinners, upstairs in the Minister's dining room were quite different, sometimes stretching on into extra brandies and sing-songs. Indeed, I remember seeing the debris of the tables at the EU Summit lunch in Dublin Castle and noticing that only the Ministers and Prime Ministers actually ate. Their officials were too nervous to take a mouthful.

In general, then, the dinner was not a relaxing affair, especially since we also had at our table Dermot Gallagher, the Assistant Sec of Anglo-Irish, and his wife, Maeve. Dermot Gallagher deserves description here. Or 'Dag', as he was known, from his initials scrawled at the top of important documents; you were supposed to feel honoured when an Assistant Sec had seen your note. Unless the initials were 'CRF' — Christopher Robin

Fogarty — and it was scored with angry red lines. These acronyms became people's nicknames; the 'DOD' — Declan O'Donovan, who was head of our 'bunker' in Northern Ireland, the Maryfield Secretariat. Or 'DD' (pronounced Dee-Dee) — David Donoghue, an energetic Counsellor on the North. Or 'AA' — Anne Anderson, the head of personnel.

A coming force in the Department, Dag would go on to achieve great success as Ambassador in Washington where he had a major involvement in the Peace Process. He was part of the 'cute hoor' tradition of DFA, and proud of it, mocking the pretensions of South Dublin, as he saw them, and cutting through the intellectual twittering of the more rarefied mandarins. Thankfully, I never worked with him and therefore could afford to be mildly irreverent, for, in front of the more able seniors, it was much worse to show weakness or servility. You were supposed to be up for a ribbing.

A well-groomed man with a sort of doll's face of unchanging expression, he had a way of tilting his head when he spoke and staring at people. "What do you know about all that?" he'd say to some nerdy character prattling on about Nationalism. Or if he told you a story and you said, "Oh really", as I had a habit of doing, he would seize upon it and say "'Oh really' — that's a real Foreign Affairs expression", as if Foreign Affairs was something he was in by accident, a middle-class academic culture that he was trying to change.

"But you're Foreign Affairs, Dermot," you'd reply weakly. 'For all your man of the soil, "real Ireland" heritage' — you felt like saying — 'your kids go to the poshest of private schools and will probably become more Southside Dublin than I could ever be.' It was the same with other people in DFA, who made a great virtue of growing up with the 'curlew's cry' and the 'belt of the hurley' when what they really wanted was the house in Dublin 4 and the values that went with it.

In fairness, Dag was proud of his West of Ireland background and specifically his beloved Leitrim, for which he always looked out. Someone once said that, if Ireland was ever dismembered, Dag could become the Shevardnadze of Leitrim. As part of the Anglo-Irish Agreement, a North-South Canal was restored which went through Leitrim — a project I would later work on — and so anxious was Dag on its behalf, that the British Secretary of State, Tom King used to refer to it despairingly as 'The Gallagher Canal'. When Leitrim, amazingly, made it to the All Ireland semi-final of 1991, Dag was on the front of the *Irish Independent*, playing hurley with his son. Back for the Match, boy!

Robust images like these negated the more tweedy air that was perceived to have developed in the department under Garret's FG. A probable Fianna Fáiler, Dag got on well with Haughey and even better with Albert Reynolds, who thought he was the bees knees. And with Bruton, too. He was the master diplomat; tough and flexible, and very focussed. He had amazing energy and later, during the Peace Process, he would phone Dublin from the US at such incredibly early, and late hours, that people reckoned he could only be sleeping four or five hours a day. The other reason he called so often, was that by then the Secretary Noel Dorr was about to retire and Dag probably had his eye on the top job in the Department.

The other substantial part of my training related to the Presentation of Credentials. My first exposure to this was in this case of the Iraqi Ambassador, based in London but accredited to Dublin.

Basically, I had to get into a full morning suit with grey tie and black top hat and accompany the Ambassador to Áras an Uachtaráin to present Credentials to the President. Also formally attired, were the Chief of Protocol, Thelma Doran, later Ambassador to China, and her Deputy Joseph Brennan, later, ironically, the equally hard-working Protocol person at the Áras under President Robinson. The event was full of pageantry. In the Jury's Hotel forecourt, an Escort of Honour was formed, consisting of a cavalry motorcycle detachment, and as the Ambassador emerged there was a bugle salute. After this, the motorcade hummed its way along the Canal up to Phoenix Park.

This was the start of my love affair with motorcades; the thrill of the sirens and blue lights and the side streets momentarily blocked by police outriders. Or, in this case, army outriders. Onlookers reactions were always interesting, and sometimes you'd see the expletive-ridden annoyance as Concerned Citizens dreamed up another letter of protest to the Papers. 'Oh, be glad of a bit of glamour in your capital,' I felt like telling them. Going past Rathmines Bridge, I even saw someone I knew and I almost wanted to shout out the window. But there were also the looks of admiring curiosity as people glanced immediately towards the flag flapping on the main car's bonnet.

In Protocol, they kept the pennants of all the different countries, wrapped in crêpe paper, just as they kept full-sized flags to fly over Iveagh House, when visitors were in town. There was also our own flag and sometimes, at dusk, you'd see a Messenger climb out onto the roof to take it down, his foot precariously on the balcony, just like that famous picture of the Soviet soldier hanging his flag over the captured Reichstag.

There was an quasi-religious protocol for the National Flag, advising how it was to be flown and not draped and how it must never be allowed to touch the ground. If it did, it was desanctified and had to be destroyed immediately, to which some of our far-off Missions said 'Sod off, we've only got one and it's almost ruined already'. Often the cotton material was not up to the tropical or desert heat and distant Embassies would go through flags as quickly as they went through thin-skinned diplomats.

Protocol was an interesting area, divided into two sections. Protocol I set up all the dinners and lunches, booked hotels in Ireland and abroad, and arranged gifts for visitors. The Chief of Protocol, for example, accompanied the President on trips abroad. For the Third Sec, it was an ever changing roster, with the Indonesians one morning and the Japanese the next. You quickly got to know your Irish politicians. You also got to know your foods and wines, with a wine cellar in the basement which had to be pleasurably re-stocked and a catering back-up, run by Mrs Landy, the Housekeeper. You also had to know the city's posher restaurants and jiggle their services about, so they stayed up to scratch.

It was a busy job and sometimes when we came down to leave each evening, we'd see the Protocol people in the hall, still hanging about, their real work only beginning. The job fine-tuned your curtseying skills, the introductions and little bows so important to certain visitors.

Protocol II was a separate section which dealt with Embassies in Dublin, a job of constant soothing and pandering. Despite (or perhaps because) of the fact that foreign Embassies are legally foreign territory, their whims and building plans were a sensitive matter. The US Embassy, for example, is a monument to paranoia and perceived conspiracies, with cement-heavy flower pots to deter suicide bombers and a unhealthy desire to find out the names and occupations of the surrounding neighbours.

Sometimes such paranoia is rewarded. The Iranians were very pleased with their new Embassy in Blackrock — even if the reinforced railings didn't exactly go down a treat with the neighbours. At one stage, the Embassy was in danger of becoming one of their biggest missions in Europe, what with the terrorist-related restrictions elsewhere (those aforementioned suicide bombings). But, amazingly, they then discovered that among their neighbours was an old Iranian royalist from the Shah's time. They couldn't believe it: indeed it was a remarkable coincidence. Alarmed, they called out someone from

Protocol to take a look, bringing him up to a balcony and saying, "Look, Look, he could launch a bazooka rocket from over there!" The officer had to do his best to persuade them that an inter-Iranian feud was unlikely to break out in leafy Blackrock.

Meanwhile back in the Phoenix Park, the Iraqi motorcade drove past some grazing deer and pulled into the Áras, the gravel crunching underwheel as we approached the large white house. Inside, in the reception room, then President, Patrick Hillery, was standing beside the Secretary, Mr Dorr, and a very still Minister of State, Terry Leyden, who looked as uneasy as I did in a top hat and tails.

Again, there was an elaborate ritual, as the Iraqi Ambassador handed over his Letter of Credence. While he and the President nodded heads and spoke at the centre of the room, the rest of us were mutely arranged in a sort of star shape. Four Aide-De-Camps stood behind the President, facing us, while, on our side, facing them, were the Iraqis, our Protocol people and some anonymous aides. It was like a seven-a-side before kick-off. The Secretary stood perfectly still, like a tailor's dummy, but Leyden looked increasingly uncomfortable, as if he was holding his breath.

The ceremony over, the President did some introductions and gave us a little tour, showing a line of previous President's heads. Then the Ambassador went outside and inspected a Guard of Honour, accompanied by the Irish Officer in Charge and Brigadier Khamis, the beefy Iraqi military attaché. When we set out that morning, I had the Brigadier as my escort. Me and you, Brigadier. Looking at his medals, I was mindful that a colossal war with huge casualties was now taking place with Iran and that the Brigadier was probably glad of the respite.

Coming up the Canal, he enquired about the spire of the Royal Hospital Kilmainham. I said it was an old soldiers' home, which didn't seem to please him. I guess retirement in Iraq is not an option. 'Used to belong to the British, now gone,' I added and he beamed suddenly, clenching his fists. 'Yes, the British,' he said, 'finished, gone!" This seemed to please him no end, but I hadn't quite meant it in the general sense.

I'd have preferred to escort the Ambassador's wife, had she come along. With her chunky gold jewellery and strong calves, she was in that sexy 'mature woman' bracket that gets young men excited at the start of their careers. Watching her in the hotel, fussing over her husband's top hat, I imagined her vaguely bored in a hot foreign posting, and looking for a bit of (youthful) action. What would the Iraqis do if you threw the leg over? Throw the rest of you over, I suspect. Also in attendance, were the good-looking, pampered kids; clearly the Iraqi diplomatic corps were drawn from the local elites. But there were also two ropy looking characters, young Iraqis resident in Ireland. They muttered something about being students and it reminded me of the Libyan 'students' in UCD, very flush with cash and surprisingly active on behalf of their home regime.

After the Credentials, the Iraqis held a reception in a rooftop lounge at the Berkeley Court. It was a revealing gathering, with lots of builders, meatpackers and Fianna Fáil backbenchers milling around the room. A white haired man was introduced as a representative of the PLO. Iraq was a key country for Irish trade and investment and, in a stirring speech, a man with a strong Cork accent said we must support 'our Iraqi friends in the their brave struggle'. Privately, however, many people were quite content that Iran and Iraq were embroiled in a war which was giving continuous construction work to both sides, not to mention training for doctors, nurses and engineers.

The Ambassador thanked everyone, and the room applauded — except for the Brigadier, who was tucking into the canapés. Piquantly, I would see the Ambassador again, four years later, when he turned up at the UN at the height of the Kuwaiti crisis. He had since become Ambassador to the United States. A more difficult job you couldn't imagine and according to the US TV networks, Al Mashrat, a genial, mild-mannered man, was regarded as something of a wet — as many Iraqis must have been — and was allegedly being tailed by Iraqi agents just in case he might defect. It was chilling stuff. NBC showed pictures of Al-Mashrat walking around the UN, and apparently being followed by shadowy men in the background, his 'protection'. It made me wonder what had happened to the Brigadier. Or to the vivacious wife and her kids, and how they were bearing up under the pressure of the Gulf War and the sanctions which followed.

The large turnout for the Iraqi Ambassador Credentials should not have been surprising. On the trade front, Iraq and Ireland were closely linked, most notoriously through the export of beef which would prove so controversial later on, with allegations of fraud and of favouritism by Fianna Fáil towards just one producer, Larry Goodman. At the Beef Tribunal itself, many Foreign Affairs officials gave evidence, including Pat McCabe, Ambassador to Iraq, and John Swift, our head of Foreign Earnings, and there was satisfaction that DFA came off better than other Departments, such as Agriculture and our old 'friends', Industry and Commerce. But it was ironic too that the original Goodman deal was actually signed in Iveagh House, with the Iraqi flag flying overhead, an unusual honour. By this time, Iraq's war with Iran had become particularly savage and had spilled over into incidents abroad. Thus, on arrival, the Iraqi officials were amazed at the lack of security at the airport: on the way into Iveagh House they kept looking over their shoulders for Iranian snipers. 'What a shame,' growled a particularly cruel officer, 'if the only fresh meat we send back to Iraq will be themselves'. A tasteless but surprisingly prophetic comment, given that much of the Irish beef sent to Iraq turned out to be old and often barely edible.

These visits meant that I spent a lot of time over at the Taoiseach's Department where of course the Iraqis were always welcome. There was (and is) a substantial overlap between ourselves and the Taoiseach's Department, especially on the Protocol side. But also on EU matters, after Haughey rearranged the handling of European affairs in defiance of the brandy-fired Grey Door missive. As a result, I ended up as something of a glorified messenger boy, carrying documents between the two Departments, not the role I had anticipated at the interview process. Thus I saw a lot of the duck pond in St Stephen's Green and of my more senior colleagues returning from the Dáil or from other Departments, with briefs and speeches under their arms. My colleagues ribbed me that Sean O'hEigeartaigh and Wally Kirwan, of the Taoiseach's Department, were now as much my Counsellors as Noel Fahey.

This was before the Taoiseach's Department moved into the present Government Buildings on Merrion Row, with the courtyard fountain, the modern paintings and the sweeping staircases.

Back in 1987, however, the Taoiseach's Department was through the oak doors next to the Natural History Museum on Merrion Square, with its stuffed animals and prehistoric elks. Inside, an atmosphere of respect and fear pervaded the place. Even from cursory visits, it was quickly apparent that certain people were in favour and others weren't. The corridors were deserted, except for the poet, Anthony Cronin, the Taoiseach's Cultural Adviser. Another excision of 1987 — the Taoiseach had pretty much replaced his Department's Arts and Culture Division with just one man in his corduroys and moccasins.

Inside, a small elevator brought you up to a long corridor with big wooden doors on either side. It looked like Kilmainham Jail, with numbers over the doors. At the

end of the corridor, there was a double set of dark wood
doors — 'Private: Taoiseach's Chambers' — and
sometimes I had a giddy impulse to just burst open the
doors and go "Waheey, Charlie!" Somehow I resisted
temptation, instead loyally taking my documents back to
Harcourt Street and my proper masters.

The atmosphere of the Taoiseach's Department is
affected by the personality of who's in power, and has
become increasingly so, as the Department expands and
accumulates advisers. When Haughey was in
government, the place was crisply clean and no one
loitered on the landings. With Reynolds, it was the same,
although with more of a relaxed 'can-do' air to the place.
But when Bruton was in power, it was felt that the
discipline diminished. Messengers whistled and the
security people were sullen and sluggish.

Still, such informality meant that you could hang out
with the Taoiseach's people and go down to their coffee-
house to have a gossip about our masters. Because of its
size and intimacy, Department of the Taoiseach was
extraordinarily hands-on and a young Principal Officer,
the equivalent of a senior Third Secretary, could find
himself doing a one-on-one briefing with the Taoiseach,
or even sit with him and qualify his remarks to, for
example, an Alliance Party delegation. It was an access
that, at times, a more deserving TD could only dream of.
It also offered an insight into official thinking. I remember
some time later, an officer expressing great alarm at a
conversation he'd had with an equally young politician,
destined to be made an adviser to the Taoiseach on
Northern Ireland (he has since become a TD in the west of
Dublin). 'I spoke to him, at length, in Dublin Castle and
it's really dangerous,' said the official. 'He has all these —',
he shook his hands like Al Jolson, ' — ideas!' There was a
despairing pause. 'We have to stop him.'

'New kid on the block,' agreed another fellow,
chewing a pencil. 'He has to be stopped.'

'Eamon, will you tell (the related officers) to call us immediately.'

'Will do,' I said, suddenly feeling very mature.

4

The Soviet Desk

In 1988, after a year in the EU/Economic Division, I was sent over to Political Division in Iveagh House, to work in the Eastern Europe section, or 'the Soviet desk' as it was generally known. It was a welcome change. Rather than collating briefs, I was writing on politics in Eastern Europe and making contact with my equivalents in EU Ministries. We were up in the roof of the House with the Minister's chambers immediately below us. If you jumped hard enough, you could knock some ceiling plaster into his china tea cup. Across the corridor was the Minister's constituency office, about to undergo major expansion with the arrival of the new incumbent, Gerry Collins.

With Brian Lenihan's health in continuing decline, he was moved to the less onerous Department of Defence and replaced by Collins. A tough and smiling Limerick man, some of the press dubbed him 'Smirker' Collins before his dedicated travelling, especially in the Middle East, earned him the more elaborate sobriquet, 'Collins of Arabia'. But however far he travelled, home base was what mattered and Lenihan's political office appeared modest compared to the entourage of helpers Collins brought in. Apparently, he ran one of the biggest constituency machines in the country and, late into the night, you could hear the photocopiers pumping out Minister's statements on everything from the UN to Development Aid.

One evening, a new Third Sec was being shown around the different rooms with their wall maps; Central

America, the Middle East — areas of special interest to Irish foreign policy. 'And, in here, is the most important area of all,' said a jaded officer, indicating a large map on the wall. But the newcomer didn't recognise it and had to squint a bit closer. 'Limerick West,' came the reply. It was the Minister's constituency.

In our own office were the maps of Eastern Europe and the Soviet Union. After years of darkness, some of the towns were about to light up like bushfires — Vilnius, Timosoara, Leipzig — small conflagrations which would engulf the systems whose structures had already weakened. I couldn't have spent a better two years at this desk. 1988-1990 were, of course, the years Communism fell and the fact that some of the key events occurred during our EU Presidency in the first half of 1990 only added to the excitement.

In the two years, the desk was turned upside down. When I arrived, volumes of Soviet books and journals were packed neatly into corridor shelves, a dense jargon from which optimists tried to understand the new light of glasnost. If there was any possibility of change, it surely would be slow and incremental. Yet by the time I left, the system had completely collapsed. In retrospect the demise of Communism appeared inevitable. The writing was on the wall. The analysis we did was divided into economic and political and the economic assessment said one thing — this system is not going to hold out very long. However, this did not seem so obvious in 1988. The Eastern Bloc was stuck in time but it also seemed resilient and adaptable, despite the changes. Each week, onto our desks came the same official propaganda about combine harvesters and the education of smiling infants, not to mention the endless heroism of World War II and those strange hand-tinted portraits of leaders and dictators, now much older than their photos.

And yet we pored over these documents searching for clues of change. In the dull pages of the *Soviet Weekly*, the presence of a rock band — a long-haired rock band! —

might signal some thaw, some tolerated moment of rebellion. Likewise, statistics and speeches were studied for signs of productive fault lines. There was no shortage of material, from think-tanks, dissident groups and exiles organisations, those shadowy groups which lobbied hard around the UN General Assembly and often overlapped with displaced royalists. Or, shadier still, the sort of unsavoury right-wing organisations which re-emerged with the break up of Yugoslavia.

More immediate news came from the wire service machine, which sat in the copier room and permanently pumped out information. Newspapers and magazines were also trawled but, increasingly in the 1980s they had to be treated with caution, given the sometimes alarmist and sensational coverage. This was especially so in the right-wing UK press — a tautology, in those days — which were more content in describing the evils of the system than in telling us if anything was going to change. A more reliable and accurate picture could be got from the European media, or better still from our European partners.

By 1988, it was obvious that there was going to be movement and hitherto-skimpy files began swelling with papers and analyses. For some Kremlinologists, the pace was of change was bewildering, even disappointing. As part of our ongoing training, Personnel Section often organised occasional talks by invited outsiders such as the foreign editors of newspapers or diplomatic historians. One such was by a former long-time official, regarded at that time, even internationally, as something of an old Russian hand.

But he was also a bit of character who had been working on a major study of the Soviet Union to which he had just recently put the finishing touches. And then Gorbachev came along and started changing things. Jesus, Gorby, could you not have waited? A hasty postscript would have to be written, but, as glasnost gave way to perestroika, it was clear that a major rewrite was required.

Before long, it was obvious that the whole contemporary premise of the book had collapsed, and our beleaguered author must have felt like joining those student leftists who flew out to Berlin to protest that the Wall be put back up!

The changes in Eastern Europe were happening apace and the main EU response to developments was the Coreu system, the closed telex system between the twelve Foreign Ministries. On a daily basis, draft documents and statements would come in from the Presidency and members would give their views in French and English, the two working languages of the EU. Given the nuances, you would need to know your French.

The telexes had different status. 'Diffusion Restrainte' meant confidential, whereas 'Immediate Desk by —' implied it should be seen by a certain time. In the German Foreign Ministry, this was taken literally and it meant someone had to actually be there to receive it. Careless upgrading and you could ruin a German Third Sec's evening. Coreus came in on Latin America, the US and Africa but the majority were on the ever-active Middle East and, increasingly, Eastern Europe. A folder of all Coreus was passed around which everyone could read and it gave a good oversight of EU diplomacy. If a country hadn't come back with alterations by a certain deadline, it was presumed they accepted. Naturally there were furious rows and dogfights over drafts. The French cannot possibly accept the language on the Lebanon. The Greeks want a certain word changed. As I was to discover, it was all about language.

The Greeks were especially awkward, particularly on East Europe. When the Bulgarians expelled thousands of ethnic Turks in 1988, the Greeks tried to block the EU moves to help them, on the basis that some of the Turks might end up being 'settled' on Cyprus. The Greeks seemed to think only of themselves and, for them, Turkey was an obsession. So awkward and *non-Communitaire* were the Greeks that their attitude was used as a reason not to also allow in the Turks, a perverse analogy which I am sure would have enraged the Greeks!

The most serious use of the Coreu was a *démarche* on behalf of the Twelve, a protest letter handed in by a Head of Mission, usually the Presidency, which demanded a reply. To those who felt that, in an age of increased communications, Ambassadors had become no more than human decorations for their country, the mechanics of *démarches* and EU co-ordination had given a new lease of life to the world of diplomacy.

As well as the orthodox means of communications, Member States had access to information which they would pass amongst themselves. Much was shared in the context of European Political Co-operation (EPC). EPC was the system which co-ordinated the Foreign policy systems of the twelve. In reality, this meant seeking consensus by very subtly whittling down differences. If this sounds like a diminution of sovereignty, it certainly was. I was not squeamish about the purity of Irish neutrality — although later at the UN I would come to see its value — but I was still astonished by this continuous shredding of policy positions to reach consensus.

After considering Coreu traffic all week, the main business was done at EPC Working Groups, held in Brussels each month and attended by a Counsellor and First Secretary. The Working Group on Eastern Europe — there were also Groups for Latin America and the Middle East — would consider a seven item agenda, based on the most live and ongoing issues in their area. Their conclusions, smoothed over through the Coreu system, would then be sent to Copol, the EU's Political Committee, whose recommendations would then be considered at EPC Ministerials and nodded through by Ministers.

Copol was thus the key committee. It was made up of the Political Directors of the twelve, who were usually the Assistant Secretaries, or the equivalent, in their respective Ministries. They also met once a month.

Our Political Director was the Assistant Secretary of Political Division, a tall and weathered Cork man called Pádraig Murphy. He was an impressive figure, with amazing energy, strong drafting skills and an eerily calm demeanour no matter what the crisis — and during the Irish EU Presidency in 1990 there would be many. Because of the Gulf War in 1991, Murphy had to stay on as Political Director, after which his subsequent posting as Ambassador in Bonn must have seemed like a holiday.

After each Copol, everyone was called down to Murphy's room to hear him go through the substance of what the Political Directors of the twelve had discussed and agreed. His wood-panelled room, the old Library, was one of the finest in the House, with windows, including an oriel window, looking down on two sides of the garden and a large wood-carved chimney piece with a scene from Homer's *Iliad*. Around the big polished table, the Counsellors and First Secretaries would collect. Third Secretaries were further down the table, or sitting behind. Each time Murphy finished describing a discussion on Korea or the West Bank, he would flick the piece of paper down towards the First Sec who would slide it on towards the Third Sec — literally, paper pushing.

Murphy would go into some detail about discussions, so you got a picture of the skulduggery and horse-trading among the twelve not reflected in the official minutes. But these debriefings were also bonding exercises, dry-run get-togethers for the coming Irish Presidency of the EU. Murphy would always finish by appealing for briefer Briefing — 'and economics, ye always forget the economics' — recognising perhaps that it was now economics which was driving the political changes in Eastern Europe and elsewhere.

There is always a battle regarding briefings, between the mandarins who know that the Minister wants a two-sheet summary (one sheet, in Albert's case) and the nerdy experts who insist on providing a small booklet, full of fascinating but useless detail. 'Remember what a Minister has to read every day,' warned Murphy. 'Material from us, from Economic Division, and from Anglo-Irish, plus his papers for Cabinet. He's got constituency and party matters and he could also be sitting on one of the Parliamentary Committees. And he's got to meet delegations and prepare for those. He also has to run this Department — nuts, bolts and Embassies. For goodness sake, boys and girls, keep it brief.'

On this basis, Murphy was constantly rewriting the stuff sent to him: speeches, speaking notes and draft letters to the public. In the absence of Counsellors and First Secretaries, away at Working Groups — or permanently, due to cutbacks — stuff would go directly to him from Third Secs. And sometimes he would say, 'Look, just make the decisions yourself,' which surprised us. We were generally so resigned to having our prose rewritten that we mightn't have really made the effort.

He particularly rewrote PQs; Parliamentary Questions or questions in the Dáil. PQs are probably the most important articulation of foreign policy. Even more than speeches, they are regarded as specific descriptions of position and their preparation threw everyone into a sort of panic. Photocopiers were commandeered as drafts and re-drafts were tagged into folders.

Replying to PQs was an art in itself. The idea was to say as little as possible, as one Agriculture Civil Servant foolishly admitted to the Beef Tribunal. We had to protect the State from overly inquisitive TDs and there was no point in being garrulous and volunteering information. Looking over my shoulder at the green screen of prose I was preparing for a draft reply, my First Sec would say 'I don't like it already — there's too much text!' Instead, there was a great amusement taken from a Westminster PQ which got passed around. An opposition MP had asked a long and detailed question, enquiring if an overall situation would be such given various hypothetical criteria — to which the Minister replied succinctly, 'No'.

However it would be hard to get away with that. Generally, you said that 'the Minister was aware of concerns', 'reviewing developments', and 'monitoring the situation'. That was a great one for Eastern Europe — 'monitoring the situation'. Again, the EU became the lazy template for all crises, the kick-for-touch in moments of ambiguity. It was a habit which would cause understandable frustration for people who wanted more specific explanation. 'I will refer the Deputy to the EU position/recent *démarche*/Statement of the Twelve.' European Political Co-operation would become the reference point for the whole of foreign policy, not just for Ireland, but for other countries as well. At the UN, the Italians lazily prefaced almost every statement with 'As the Presidency has already stated.' But for Eurocrats such cap-doffing was a very welcome development.

Some PQs were disallowed or postponed, or put down as Written Questions which was fine because it meant there were no Follow-ups. For the tricky thing with PQs were the Follow-ups, when the Minister was on his feet and the questioner would try to get beyond the bland reply to catch him out. Like when Brian Lenihan was once continually pressed on possible Turkish membership of the EU. 'Repeat the Above, Repeat the Above,' was the instruction on his folder and so he repeated once again 'that the situation was being continually assessed and that Turkey, at present, was not in line for membership of the Community.' But eventually, perhaps bored with the official mantra, Lenihan airily added 'And sufficient unto death, the evil thereof.' To which the mandarins could only cry, 'What?' But not the Turks who were furious at this perceived biblical slur and saw in the words 'death' and 'evil', a fatal blow to their EU prospects.

To anticipate the shifting nature of a Deputy's follow-ups — usually, the same question asked four different ways, or for as long as the Ceann Comhairle will allow — a page of Possible Supplementaries were tucked in behind the Reply in the Minister's red folder, along with a

Background Note. The Minister's folder was usually red, to distinguish it from the green ones held by the mandarins. But because the red one was also the 'working folder' — to be eventually filed away in Registry — it often got held on to by the Private Secretary, and a green one given to the Minister. It has then happened that the Minister has ended up accidentally delivering an earlier or amended text — or worse still the 'real' reply, meant only for the Political Director.

Thus, Albert's famous excuse during the Harry Whelehan debate that he had not been given the correct folder. We assumed he was dumping the Civil Servants in it, but in fairness, given the confusion of the moment, it was quite possible that he hadn't been given the file with the most up to date, loose-leaf papers. PQs, by their nature, are usually 'live', and designed to trip up, so mandarins could be changing the replies up to the last minute. It was also important to keep the folders closely guarded from Opposition Deputies. Ambitious (and troublesome) backbenchers have made productive inroads by finding the 'real replies' inside a mislaid folder.

A few hours after Question Time, the Minister's Office received the 'blacks'; raw carbons of the stenographers accounts, which people would excitedly go over and get for their sections. Cleaned up, the replies would then appear in the Dáil Debate booklets, the Oireachtas Hansard, and thereafter be quoted ad nauseam in a thousand letters to the public on this particular subject. 'As the Minister told the Dáil on 5 May.' Along with EU Statements, this was the other monotonous hymn sheet to sing from, convenient when an individual or substantive reply could not be risked.

There were also the Jesuitical twists for which officials were famous. Asked repeatedly to recognise the sovereignty of Lithuania, we said we couldn't because we had never not recognised it. Which was true — Ireland had never formally recognised the annexation of the

Baltic States into the Soviet Union. In reality, of course, we completely recognised it — de facto but not *de jure* was the way the PQs put it. Along with our fellow European States, we were afraid to formally recognise Baltic independence because it would offend the Soviets. This desire not to upset the Soviets at a time of their own internal change would continue to have an interesting implications for the Baltics later on, such as during the Dublin Summit. (It was the same, later, with the massacres in Chechnya, conveniently ignored by the West because we desperately needed Yeltsin as Russian leader.)

Another slight of hand was on Raoul Wallenberg, the Swedish diplomat who saved thousands of Jews in wartime Vienna by issuing them with temporary visas. Wallenberg was rightly regarded as a hero and it was assumed that in chaos of the war's aftermath he had fallen into Soviet hands and been killed or transported back to Russia where he subsequently died in a prison camp. This was the Soviet version and most people accepted it. However, rumours persisted that Wallenberg was still alive and that the Soviets were too embarrassed to admit it. Alleged sightings had taken place in Gulags and an amazing amount of people wrote in urging us to do something.

The Labour Party put down a Dáil motion urging that he be given Honorary Irish Citizenship for his efforts — a honour which would strengthen the chance of his being discovered. Given that he hadn't been proved dead, it could be given to him *in absentia*. However, the relevant section wrote to say that he couldn't be given such a honour, because there was no proof he was alive and we can't issue a passport to someone who's dead. And that even if he was alive we wouldn't know how to reach him to tell him, it being necessary to gain his consent to the issuing of Honorary Citizenship.

I thought this was ridiculous and suggested that given that the visas which Wallenberg issued to save people's lives were fake, it would be more than ironic if we were to decline him honorary citizenship on the basis that he hadn't 'met the necessary criteria'. But the officials got annoyed, telling me that Irish Citizenship was not something that was given out lightly. At that time, only five people had received it; Tip O'Neill, for being a supportive Irish-American, the Beits, for giving us their paintings, Chester Beatty, for the same, and Tiede Herrema, for enduring a high profile kidnapping. And then there was the other reason, given with off-the record brusqueness. 'He's fucking dead, face up to it,' said a senior cynic. This was the same macho man, mind you, who loudly proclaimed that Brian Keenan was 'brown bread'. There were a lot of these doomsday types around.

On citizenship for Raoul Wallenberg, it was a neat fix. In the end, the debate was postponed and the proposal was shelved. But the sightings continued, and even after Communism had gone and a new Russia in place, people still couldn't accept that Wallenberg was not alive somewhere in northern Siberia. His case had gone from legitimate concern to outright conspiracy theory.

5

'Peaceful Co-existence'

On the Cold War issue, many officers were still of the 'peaceful co-existence' mindset, which was that there were two naughty superpowers, and we, reasonable neutrals, were in the middle trying to get them to be nice to each other. The US would have to learn to get along with the Soviets who, given a bit of understanding, might turn out to be not that bad really. I thought this was a somewhat cowardly and selfish attitude, but later at the UN I saw that for many countries it was the guiding principle in foreign relations. Don't rock the boat.

Or there were the 'sneaking regarders', people who were sceptical about all negative reports coming out of Eastern Europe, and regarded them as 'US propaganda'. Of course, at the time, some of the most strident anti-Communist views were held by Reagan and Thatcher, provocative figures in themselves, but one would have thought that those who spoke loudly about human rights in Latin America or South Africa, would also make a fuss about abuses in their own continent. Instead, they derided the Radio Free Europe booklets which we regularly received. 'Oh, but they're all CIA,' they'd say, without any evidence. And as if the abuses they documented weren't already well-known; people shot trying to flee the GDR, or the villagers forced into systemised complexes in Romania, and compelled to have five children per family.

But there were deeper reasons for the ambivalence. Many people had a grudging admiration for the Communist social system. If it didn't provide individual liberties — not a problem for Irish people who grew up in the Forties and Fifties — it was at least more equitable, they would say, and provided education and housing. It appealed to the strong social aspect of Irish nationalism and republicanism. The general Irish public took a much dimmer view of life under totalitarianism. Letters flowed in about refuseniks, dissidents, and the suppression of cultural rights. Particularly popular were issues with a historical/political parallel with Ireland, such as Poland or Lithuania. Or a religious connection through Catholicism. It is the same with East Timor, or before that, the Philippines. But this happens everywhere; a cursory look at the Italian or Spanish papers shows that the foreign issues which most matter are the ones to which a country is linked through ethnicity, colonialism or religion. Thus the high profile of Northern Ireland in the European media.

The file titles showed Irish priorities; 'Plight of the Clergy in Czechoslovakia and Hungary', with separate files on Cardinal Mindszenty, imprisoned for eight years by the Budapest authorities and who then spent years in refuge at the US Embassy. 'Sounds like Henderson,' someone said of a colleague who'd been stranded abroad for years. Other files concerned the (Catholic) Hungarian minority in (Communist, formerly Orthodox) Romania which, at two million, was one of the largest minorities in Europe. Hungarian officials, impressed by the Anglo-Irish Agreement, came in to research getting a similar mechanism for their own people. God love their optimism for this was at the time of Ceauçescu. The nomenclature of older files had a cautious, almost theological feel to them — 'Question of Recognition', 'Attendance at National Days', 'Status of East Berlin — Implications for Protocol', 'TASS Coverage of Events in Six Counties' (later changed to 'Northern Ireland'; a glasnost of our own). But such nuances — *de jure* but not de facto' — were more than academic. A divided Germany was always seen as a parallel for our own country, a fact of which Haughey and others were mindful when we so warmly endorsed German Reunification. After which, all the GDR files would soon be packed off to the National Archive for good.

My desk was actually 'Eastern Europe/CSCE', since half the work was concerned with the Conference on Security and Co-operation in Europe (CSCE). This was the follow-up process to the Helsinki Agreement of 1975, where thirty-five countries (all of the European States and the US) had signed up to an ongoing process of co-operation in the economic, social and cultural fields. They also promised to engage in confidence-building measures, such as disarmament and human rights.

The process was supposed to overcome division in Europe and assist democratisation but detractors attacked it as a sell-out which accepted the Communist domination of Eastern Europe. It was probably a bit of both, but mostly it was the former. Indeed the whole thing had the quality of a charade. What was particularly galling was that after the fall of Communism, the CSCE tried to claim the credit, just as the EU did by citing its own wonderful disunited example. At most, the CSCE had a niggling effect. In relation to human rights, for example, there was a mechanism, through which one State, or States, could demand an explanation from another regarding certain behaviour. Although often ignored by the subject country, or given a bland reply, it did have a nuisance value which produced results, such as the release of Soviet scientist, Andrei Sakharov, or an end to the harassment of Czech playwright, Václav Havel, and so its existence gave heart to dissidents.

The disarmament side of CSCE was even worse. Continuous, painful drafting went into developing mechanisms and areas for gradual disarmament, and then it would all collapse because the Bulgarians had changed their mind about some missile silo. For Ireland, disarmament was a major issue. Having originally put it on the UN agenda, we pursued it doggedly in other fora.

The Disarmament Section shared our room, each of us having different parts of the CSCE. Along the walls were books on missiles, *Jane's Defence Weekly* and files on previous conferences, the arcane data of weekly changes in position among the thirty-five States. The Disarmament talks were almost continually in session, usually in Geneva, and people had built their careers on them.

'This peacenik gravy train is coming to an end,' the people from the Asia section would taunt. 'What are you going to do now?' The snail's pace arms reductions were suddenly being swept aside by the unilateral cuts of the East Europeans. But the 'peaceniks' were undeterred; 'ethnic tensions' were providing new work. The work of the disarmers was never done and the Irish would rid the world of weapons.

Meanwhile the Soviet Desk also kept files on Irish based 'friendship societies' whose activities were carefully noted, especially the trips to Moscow or East Berlin. The Embassy in Moscow would report that an Irish delegation had arrived and, unsurprisingly, had made no contact with the Embassy. People may find such monitoring sinister but it was easily picked up information; the 'Irish visitors' would probably have appeared in *Pravda*. During the controversy over the Presidential candidacy of Mary McAleese, and the quoting from leaked DFA memos describing her attitude to Sinn Féin, there was public surprise that Departmental personnel would report so intimately on conversations and meetings, but that was our job. We were supposed to be constantly watching.

The obvious subjects would be the Workers' Party and the Irish Communist Party, but there were many others; study groups, academic partnerships and those easily misled artistic types with a grudge against their own culture. A major anxiety was that the Soviets and others might try and stir up trouble on North Ireland but, ironically, the Workers' Party did us a favour here. Since their bitter split with the more republican Sinn Féin they had changed, virtually at a stroke, the Soviet's hitherto militant attitude towards 'The Ulster Question'.

Some of our people were scathing about these Irish supporters. I remember being at a Czech Minister's reception in the Shelbourne, with Tim Corcoran, a large, gruff-voiced Counsellor, with a little Colonel Sanders beard. 'A lot of these fellow travellers are being flushed out now,' he said, contemptuously, as we looked around the room. He was amazed, as I was, by the number of well-wishers at the reception but what really got him was some twittering lecturer fellow who started telling us about the exaggerated unrest in Czechoslovakia. (The protests were just beginning.) 'It's only students,' he said, 'the industrial workers are very happy with the system.'

Later, Corcoran went on a fact finding trip to Romania, in the midst of the people's revolt. It was late December 1989, and only days before our Presidency, and Corcoran had to step in as a last-minute replacement on an EU troika team. Arriving at the airport, the whole place was under gun-fire and Corcoran had a heart attack. Eventually, he was flown out of Bucharest, but a few months later he died, his death included in the Daily Press Summary to all Missions as was customary for an officer.

The Czech reception was for a visit by one of their 'Ministers of State', including a meeting with our 'Minister of State', Sean Calleary, whose title must have pleased them. We often got Calleary to meet these visitors if the Minister couldn't. He was the ideal junior minister, offering no threat to the high profile Gerry Collins. Generally, such meetings were about trade imbalances and investment, but we sort of forced Calleary to raise the matter of democratic protests with them. 'You realise, of course, that there are some concerns here ...' muttered Calleary, but without any great conviction. 'Hey, troubles in the kitchen, troubles in the kitchen!' laughed the Minister and his shiny-suited advisers, but with even less conviction. They were like used-car salesmen, but you could see they were sweating too, fearing that their days were numbered.

The shift in the political landscape was obvious on these visits. When the Hungarian Foreign Minister and his party arrived, their demeanour and language made it clear that they wanted out of the Warsaw Pact as soon as possible. Nods and winks implied that though they used the proletarian-speak of Communism, even perestroika Communism, they were really only going through the motions. Even their clothes were changing.

Indeed especially their clothes. When the Soviet team arrived for Political Consultations, many of them were now in designer suits and Italian shoes, the spoils of travelling abroad for Communism. These Consultations were annual meetings between Foreign Ministries, but without Foreign Ministers — an ideal situation, really. Two teams of officials, in our case headed up by the Political Director, Pádraig Murphy, would get together and discuss a range of international issues. Facing Murphy was a then quite well known Soviet politician. For of course, in their system, the mandarins *were* the politicians. So Communism did have its advantages; an entire nation ruled by Politburos of Dermot Gallaghers and Noel Dorrs.

These Consultations were a serious note-take for a Third Sec and, for a while, I started falling behind. One of the younger Soviet officials, who through the whole discussion kept fixing his cuff links and examining the face of his sparkling new Rolex, looked at me blankly as I scribbled to catch up. And then smiled, as if to say, 'None of this really matters, does it?' And he was right; it meant fuck all. In fact, when the report went up the line, it didn't even return, gathering dust on some senior's desk before being thrown into a file somewhere, unamended.

I also took notes at Farewell Visits by departing Ambassadors, which in those days, for those countries, had a strange and unspoken poignancy. On 21 June 1989, the GDR Ambassador made a Farewell Visit. 'That's definitely a farewell call,' said someone ruefully. But a few days later, the Yugoslavian Ambassador also said his goodbye, a much sadder and potentially explosive farewell, although we weren't to know that at the time.

Eastern Europe also impinged in a direct fashion in the shape of people seeking asylum. This occurred more than one might expect, since Shannon airport was a major stopover for Aeroflot flights to Cuba and South America. It was all quite exciting. A call would come through that some East Germans or Bulgarians had legged it through the café at Shannon, or had (literally) jumped ship somewhere, or had defected from a basketball team and were now in a Garda station in Limerick quoting the Helsinki accords. The whole immigration system has since become much larger and more organised but back then asylum seekers really were dissidents, or 'wantaways', whose dramatic flight from their country was a political statement, with serious consequences.

The asylum drill was relatively straightforward. An immigration official would interview them and send us a report. We would consult with the relevant international body, the UN High Commission for Refugees (UNHCR) and then give a political instruction to the Department of Justice who were ultimately responsible for immigration. Happily, on asylum cases, Justice almost always abided by our direction. This was just as well, for they themselves usually took a narrow, unsympathetic approach. Also — without being snobbish about it — decisions were taken by some very low-level officials who would freely give their opinions in dismissive, disparaging tones: 'You can't have these people coming in here, making their curries'; 'Oh, they look like a lot of troublemakers, alright.'

The only positive aspect to this was that once you developed a friendly straight-talking rapport ('How's it going? What's up with the Chelsea?' and other blather) you were able to quietly guide things through and influence the officials concerned. I have to admit I pushed through a few borderline cases, especially when there was a clear humanitarian case. In one case, two Irish girls I knew had done Marriages of Convenience with Poles, to help them get out of Poland and work in Britain. When the Poles came to have their papers renewed, I happily pushed them through, regardless of whether the Poles were 'living' in Ireland, or still married to their 'wives'. On many cases, you might have to argue with the Justice officials to bring them around. It often depended on what official you were talking to. As the file went up the line, some refugee's future might be entirely dependent on each officer, swinging one way or the other.

In general, Justice was a terribly bureaucratic and conservative Department, happy to shroud itself in anonymity. In some cases during phone conversations, their officials wouldn't even give their names to us — fellow Civil Servants. For years, Justice was the only Government Department which wouldn't put their name on their building and they used to have a public lobby so infamously hostile that supplicants were reduced to tears. I stress this because Foreign Affairs had to deal with them on so many issues; immigrants, citizenship, international treaties and, of course, Northern Ireland. Perhaps such tight-fisted obduracy is to be expected from a Department which, over the years, has also dealt with the police, film censorship, prisons and abortion. 'Screws and Screws,' as someone put it. Inside their grim, school-partitioned building, they seem to get to every Minister, no matter how much a politician goes in determined to change things. For years, Gerry Collins had been a Justice Minister before he came to us.

It was thus with pleasure that we could tell Justice 'we've consulted with the UNHCR about the Russians, and they are to stay in Ireland.' On international issues, and many other issues, Foreign Affairs had last call. (Part of the antipathy towards DFA from the rest of the Civil Service, as well as our perceived lifestyle and 'intellectual' image, was the ease with which the Government would allow DFA to overrule them.) On asylum cases, we might also ignore the advice of UNHCR. Though they were on the liberal side, the UNHCR could also take a narrow, legalistic position; no clear evidence of torture, etc. At this time, however, the pressure on Eastern Europe regimes was often making it temporarily worse, not better, for their citizens, especially in places like Romania and the GDR. Thus, whatever about the harassment they were fleeing, to be sent back now would be to incur almost certain punishment and, on this basis, we recommended that they stay. This was particularly the view of the Political Director, Pádraig Murphy, to whom the file usually went for a final decision. Nor did the countries concerned necessarily take it lying down. The Soviet Embassy on Orwell Road was particularly re-active. On one occasion, two Russian sailors jumped ship in Cork harbour. But almost immediately one appeared to have been dragged back on board, or willingly went back on board, having changed his mind. We didn't know which, because we couldn't speak to him. Cleverly, his friend went directly to the media (My advice, off the record, to such people was always to 'go to the media'. After publicity, its harder for them to send you back. Or go to a TD, and then the media.) The Soviet sailor's picture duly appeared in *The Cork Examiner,* but his account of his friend being 'dragged back on board against his will' was a bit unconvincing. The ship now needed to leave the harbour. Should we insist on interviewing the chap who had gone back/been forced onto the ship? It would certainly be raising the stakes.

It was summer and there was no one around. The Counsellor and First Secretary were away at EU Working Groups in Brussels. The Minister was travelling. So I had to consult with people from an adjoining section and directly with the Political Director in his ornate office. Behind his large desk, with the subdued green lampshade, Murphy was sympathetic but could see the dilemma. A major incident would be created if we refused permission for the boat to leave, before we'd interviewed the sailor. 'This is obviously very serious,' said Murphy, 'I'll have to talk to the Taoiseach.'

'Right so,' I said and, a few hours later, Murphy called from Malahide Castle, where, ironically, a reception was being held for Daniel Ortega, the visiting leader of Marxist Nicaragua. 'I just spoke to the Taoiseach,' he said and he quickly summed up the elements, suggesting that Haughey was as sympathetic as he was and had mulled long and hard on it. 'However, there's nothing we can do. The ship should be allowed to leave.'

'OK,' I said and informed the relevant authorities in Cork.

On another occasion, a Russian had absconded from a visiting trade group in Dublin and was now staying in a refugee hostel. We discovered that later that night people from the Soviet Embassy had been sitting across the road, in a car. It seems they'd hoped that if the chap went for a walk, they could kidnap him, or at least talk to him. The Russian had applied for asylum and it made us think we must have someone valuable. The next day Sergei, the senior official at the Soviet Embassy was on the phone, protesting strongly about the situation and about our interference in the matters of Soviet Citizens and their welfare. They wanted to talk to him, but we said that wasn't possible. Again, a lot of people were absent and the First Sec on the Disarmament side, Michael Collins, (now Ambassador in the Czech Republic) who was familiar with the Soviets, had to deal with Sergei. It was an impressive performance. Sergei said he wanted to talk to the Political Director, but Collins said it wasn't on. Murphy, otherwise up to his eyes, didn't feel the need to be dragged into these situations, the parameters of which were now clear. Clauses from the Soviet constitution were quoted in retaliation for the Helsinki accords. Sergei muttered all kinds of threats and, by now, he wanted to see the Minister, or even the Taoiseach. Again, Collins stonewalled him and told him that wasn't possible.

Eventually Sergei suggested that the Soviets sit in on a meeting the Department was having with the defector. 'That won't be possible either.'

By this stage, we just sat in Collins' office and watched while he took call after call from the Soviets, but mainly from Sergei. In front of him was a ledger on which he was meticulously recording the time, duration and details of each call. It was a bluffing game, especially because it was Friday evening and Sergei knew that Duty Officers would soon be involved. But it was also like a lover's spat. 'No, that's what *you* said. I don't care … It's not possible … I'm putting the phone down *now* …' And then moments after replacing the receiver, Collins would point to the phone and sure enough, it would start ringing again. It was Sergei once more, badgering with a mixture of cajolery and threat. 'I'm now proceeding to the Taoiseach,' he declared, but we knew he wouldn't. To do so, and not succeed, as they undoubtedly wouldn't, would create a loss of face.

In the end, Sergei relented, and the Soviet asylum-seeker stayed, travelling on to the US. Most asylum seekers didn't stay in Ireland but went on to somewhere else, usually Germany or the US, which had an open door policy for citizens of Communist countries. Things got back to normal and Sergei later turned up in our ballroom for a cultural affairs reception. 'Sorry about that,' he told Collins and others.

'It's okay, Sergei. Will you have a drink?'

A few months later we had to work with Sergei under completely different circumstances. It should have been much better state of affairs — the visit of his Premier, Mikhail Gorbachev, in April 1990 — but Sergei was not a big fan of Gorbachev and, over dinner one night, he frankly admitted how disenchanted he was with the changes Gorbachev was introducing. He and his parents had given their life to the Soviet system and now, under Gorbachev's changes, it was all about to unravel. Undemocratic and unworkable as Communism was, there were a lot of people like Sergei who genuinely supported it.

In essence, the Gorbachev visit was just a stopover at Shannon Airport but the event got elevated into a full meeting with the Taoiseach and his Ministers. The *Irish Press* even styled it a 'Summit'. People mock this elevation — Gorbachev was on his way to a real US-USSR Summit — but such political opportunism had to be applauded. What would otherwise have been a quick stroll through Duty Free and a chance for Gorby to stretch his legs was transformed into an 'historic face-to-face' encounter. (Famously, Albert Reynolds tried to repeat the trick with Gorbachev's successor, Boris Yeltsin, but Yeltsin was sadly unable to get off the plane.)

The biggest problem with these visits was liasing with local sensitivities. On this occasion, the entire Clare County Council wanted to be on the tarmac to greet Gorbachev — hearing this, the Limerick Council wanted to do likewise. Firm instructions had to be sent from Dublin to put people in their place i.e. the terminal building. County Councillors and Mayors are the bane of Central Government, as I discovered later in Anglo-Irish.

The only concession to the locals in Shannon was that Raisa Gorbachev was taken to Bunratty Folk Park to meet children dressed up in 19th-century clothes and sitting on old schoolbenches — and quite a Stalinist vision it must have made. But Raisa enjoyed herself, as did Mikhail who was in ebullient form. What a shame then that Gorbachev thought he was still in the UK. At the round-table meeting — the so called 'summit' — Haughey spoke about our problems with Britain, hoping to get a bit of sympathy. 'Yes, but you share the same monarch,' said Gorbachev, meaning the Queen.

There were blank looks all round on the Irish side; this man was supposed to be well-informed. 'Not since 1922,' said Haughey, gritting his teeth.

'Ah,' said Gorbachev, unfazed, 'you threw that off sooner than most!', This drew even more puzzled looks, possibly because the interpreter's 'most' sounded like 'us'.

Happily, for all concerned, Gorbachev's gaffe never went public (until now).

6

EU Presidency 1990

The changes in Eastern Europe, which I was monitoring, gave our EU Presidency in 1990 an added dimension. The Presidency was a defining moment for DFA. Our last Presidency had been five years previously and the next was six years away by which time, in any case, centralisation of EU power structures had seen much of the action shift to Brussels. In 1990, however, in the context of European Political Co-operation (EPC), Dublin was originating language and leading the drafts on the EU response to the fall of communism. In these pre-Maastricht, and pre-Bosnia days there was an ebullient and hopeful ad-hoc air of improvisation to the organisation. Meanwhile, the debate on European Unity was led by powerful, driven figures like Mitterand, Thatcher and Kohl. For us, it was hard work, with late nights and constant redraftings but it was also great fun and we knew that if we acquitted ourselves we could get the postings we wanted in the summer.

Haughey too was enthusiastic. The Eurosceptic had turned Europhile and with his innate grasp of politics as theatre, he laid on a grand show. He even availed of the confusion in people's grasp of European titles to award himself the ludicrous title of 'President of the European Communities'. In fact, it was his faithful Foreign Minister, Gerard Collins, who as Chairman of the Council of Foreign Ministers, could more accurately be construed as something of an acting 'President'. However, there was already the ambitious Jacques Delors, as President of the

European Commission. Thus by the time the Summits came along, Collins was pushed firmly into the background. Not that it mattered. By then, he'd built himself a high profile through foreign travel and was well established in his 'Collins of Arabia' mode. Radio shows cruelly mocked his Limerick accent as he name-checked his mainly Middle Eastern friends.

Initially nailing his colours to the environmental mast, Haughey said that Ireland's would be the Green Presidency but it quickly became clear that this was going to be the 'East European Presidency' or more precisely the 'German Unification' Presidency. This was fine with us since in addition to the standard Summit held during a given Presidency, we also had an extra one in March, almost exclusively devoted to the other eleven EU members giving their 'permission' to West Germany's absorption of its de-Stalinised Eastern rump.

At the Dublin Summit, however, the 'reunification' was fairly one-sided. The newly elected GDR leaders were given only Observer Status and were whooshed out the door when *Les Douze* got down to their serious business behind the microphones and mineral water. '*Schnell*! *Schnell*!' shouted an official as the East German leader, De Maizierè, dallied too long on the Dublin Castle steps.

With regard to German unity Haughey, in contrast to the more cautious attitude of Thatcher and Mitterrand, was supportive, as were most Irish people, who saw the parallels with Ireland. It was an attitude for which Kohl was very appreciative and, six years later, in an address to the Dáil, he was still thanking CJ. Indeed, his gratitude was evident in the TV pictures as he arrived at Dublin Castle. Stopping on the Battle Axe Landing, he asked about a tapestry overhead. Bursting into laughter, he all but gave Haughey a high-five. By contrast, the others trudged up slowly. Thatcher turned around wearily and asked 'Where's Douglas?' as you would of a dog.

Haughey, of course, was in his element and stood in the Throne Room, at the top of the stairs, ready to greet the guests. It was like he was welcoming them into his own home, which is probably how he saw it. Later, during the press conferences, he dropped their names like they were old buddies, 'As Jacques has said,' 'Helmut and I'. He was particularly fond of Mitterrand and seemed to have modelled himself on him, particularly the mid-distance gaze and the imperious little walk with the arms at the side; the 'Mitterrand roll', as it was known.

Such pomposity was perhaps excusable because, alone of the twelve, Mitterrand was also a Head of State. As such, he wanted to be in the last car into the Castle Yard. Unfortunately, Thatcher had the same idea — the 'sceptic' arriving regally late. (At the 1985 Summit, a farcical situation arose with Thatcher's car hiding around the corner on Dame Street while Mitterrand's was at the top of Christchurch, each waiting for the other to go.) In 1990, they both got their way, since Thatcher was already in the Castle, having stayed there overnight for security reasons.

With Haughey, as with Mitterrand, there was a sense of 'history' and 'occasion' and the Taoiseach took great interest in the protocol detail, inspecting all the paintings and insisting that only the King's Silver be used for the lunch. The menu card was changed to include wild Irish salmon, and wild mushrooms. Everything had to be wild in that *faux* Chieftain windswept-and-interesting way which CJ affected. He even had the European leaders brought out to his house in Kinsealy for dinner; an audacious gesture, especially when he borrowed the treasured Derrynaflan chalice from the National Museum and put it on display in his dining room as if it was a family heirloom. The Premiers could look at it while they dined. 'Ah, Charles — you found zis in ze sea?'

Such gestures impressed the Europeans. In terms of Summitry, Haughey had the same mindset as Protocol, which was that the triumph was in the detail and a little style went a long way.

He even extended it beyond the Castle. City roads were repaired and flowers appeared. There was even a new pavement outside Le Coq Hardi. And, in the style of Ray Burke's famous stunt of getting trees planted on a housing estate the day before an election, and then having them removed the day after, Haughey got spotlights put on the statue of Wolfe Tone (sculpted by my father) on St Stephen's Green. But after the Presidency ended, the lights failed and the founding father of Irish Republicanism was back in the darkness.

Early on the first morning of the Summit I had to go upstairs to a plush room in the Castle where CJ was preparing for the big day. It was like being backstage at a Sinatra concert. The maestro was pacing the room slowly, waiting to go on. Around him, in atmospheric silence, sat the senior officials; Noel Dorr, Pádraig Murphy, Dermot Nally, the Secretary to the Government, and Pádraig O'hUiginn, the Secretary of Department of the Taoiseach.

They were the cream of the State's Civil Servants but they were saying absolutely nothing. There was still a great sense of fear and intimidation around Haughey and the mandarins seemed suddenly very human in front of him, the way we did before them. 'Thank you,' said Pádraig Murphy, when I handed him some papers and, at the sound of a voice – any voice – Haughey's gimlet eyes glanced over. And then glanced away again. But there was a mutual respect too. They had now had three years to get used to Haughey, three years since that Grey Door protest.

Inside the meeting, Haughey needed the mandarins, as did Gerry Collins. Even more so. Collins could not go 'on the hoof' and had to be tightly scripted. At one stage, Pádraig Murphy slipped Collins some speaking points when he got stuck chairing the meeting. 'I'm sorry but what is the Chairman reading from?' asked Van De Broek, the Dutch Foreign Minister, puzzled that Gerry's lengthy contribution appeared to be from a document. Murphy was always slipping the Minister torn bits of paper.

Murphy himself was at the top of his form at the Political Directors meeting. Colleagues, watching from translators booths, came back raving about his Chairmanship, a bit gushing perhaps but basically true. Murphy was by now a veteran of EPC issues and, with a sure hand, was able to drive the meeting through.

Dublin Castle, 1990, was possibly the highlight of Haughey's career and it is ironic that in the same venue, in 1998, he would have his come-uppance when a Tribunal revealed his finances. Ironic too how many of the other leaders present in 1990, also suffered from subsequent scandal, almost all in the same 1998-99 period. 'All political lives end in failure,' said Enoch Powell but the falls for some of these figures were particularly ignominious. In Spain, Felipe González was alleged to have set up paramilitary units to deal with Basque separatists. In Greece, Papandreou was continuously embroiled in scandal. In France, the reputation of Mitterrand, Haughey's hero, was damaged by revelations about his Vichy past and an illegitimate daughter. His Foreign Minister, Ronald Dumas, meanwhile, has recently been on trial in a typically French scandal, involving neo-colonial activity in Africa, secret donations to Elf Aquitaine, a mistress in Paris and some much discussed luxury underwear.

Even Helmut Kohl had the end of his career blighted by revelations about secret political donations. One charge even links him to a donation arranged by Mitterrand, which gives colour to the remark by former Italian Premier, Bettino Craxi, that European unity actually required such large, forceful and even, in Craxi's view, ruthless figures like Kohl and Mitterrand to see it through. (Craxi's remarks were made in Tunisia, where he was holed up to avoid corruption charges at home.) About the only Premier who left relatively untarnished was Margaret Thatcher, who was deposed only a few months after Dublin. In a way, Summits, and Europe, were her downfall and it was while at a CSCE Summit in

Paris that she met her end. With her party scheming against her, Thatcher didn't know if she'd return as Prime Minister. Such is the cruelty of political life. By then, I was in the US where it was the November Holiday. Coming into the UN the next morning, a British delegate cried joyously 'It gives a new meaning to Thanksgiving Day!' A lot of them were glad to see the back of her.

But by far the worst revelations to affect major figures at the Dublin Summits concerned — surprise, surprise — the Italians. Their Prime Minister, Andreotti, whom Haughey referred to, so admiringly, as 'a wily old fox', was on trial in Rome for nearly two years for large scale corruption and Mafia involvement. In Dublin, he was accompanied by his Foreign Minister, Gianni De Michelis. With his large, big bellied frame, hook nose, TV-screen glasses and long, lank, black hair, he was one of the most colourful figures at these Summits. A nightclub fan, he had apparently written an expert guide to European discos and was a sex symbol to Italian women. There is no accounting for the tastes of European women. The only thing I got off De Michelis was a strong whiff of body odour, both in Dublin and later at the UN where, as fellow letter 'I's, we had to sit close to the Italians. Each time De Michelis waddled past, doing the 'where's the restaurant?' shuffle, he left such a lingering odour, that you felt like buying him a deodorant. But not to worry. Within two years, De Michelis was up on corruption charges and was soon to discover the joys of all night prison discos.

In Dublin Castle, I was put working on the Press side, a welcome respite from Political Division where, in the context of European Summits, a Third Sec would sink to the lowest form of pond life. For the Presidency, the Press Office had expanded and integrated with the Government Information Service, and a Special Office was developed involving Fianna Fáil's legendary Press Secretary PJ Mara, and his assistant Eileen Gleeson. In a brazen move, the veteran political journalist and Haughey defender, John

Healy, was made a Press Officer, despite his ill health. 'That man is talking into his chin,' said a Finnish journalist. 'Chin' or 'gin'; either was applicable.

In the refurbished Press Centre, a busy office was presided over by our nattily dressed Michael Forbes, a lively and popular character, known among Irish hacks as 'Forbes of India', because of the way he spoke fondly of his former posting. Dealing with the foreign media was good fun. There were over 2000 journalists — 2000! — an astonishing multi-ethnic and multi-lingual concentration. You had to marvel at this experiment known as European integration. Many hacks were from wannabe EU States, Scandinavians and Austrians, checking up on what they might soon be joining. There was among almost all the journalists a healthy scepticism about the EU, especially among the UK media, which reflected their government's ambivalence, but also among US 'commentators', who strutted about jealously mocking an event which didn't involve them. What they loved was exchanges like when someone said aloud, about a Japanese crew lined up for accreditation, 'Come on, these guys are a bit of a sideshow to all this.' 'I'm sorry,' shot back their English interpreter, 'but for these guys, *this* is a sideshow!'

The defining feature of Summitry, and peace talks, is the hanging around. For officials, it meant trying to look busy and carrying bits of paper, and, for the media, it was the same. Either they retired to the Marquee on the back lawn, and availed of the food and drink, or they hung about in the Press area, hunched over their laptops or gathered in polyglot huddles speculating about what would be revealed to them anyway in the next hour or so. In the news vacuum, given the confusions of language and Chinese Whispers, rumours were flying around. Many people ended up standing by the Press Association and Reuters machines which, pumping out information from offices in London, could tell them more about what was happening in the room next to them than the people outside it.

Briefings, chaired by PJ Mara, were held to tell people that nothing had happened yet, but they were rather empty affairs, with Mara saying things like 'nothing on that yet, Una' and 'I'll get back to you on that, Tom'; little in-jokes which might wash with a home media but not with journalists from German TV, *Le Monde* and the *Wall Street Journal*. 'Who is this guy?' demanded a Dutch woman, loudly, and others agreed. Mara meant well but you cannot dally with the European media.

And yet, despite the big European themes, when the Conference doors opened, it was national issues the Premiers got questioned on. Like a bad rain cloud, each Government was followed to Dublin by the domestic stories breaking back home; each hack pack was like a small microcosm of its country abroad. Interesting too were the different responses. González took all the questions on the hoof, as did Kohl, standing in the corridor, surrounded by microphones. But Haughey took none and glided away, a tribute both to Haughey's aura, and Mara's control, but also an indictment of the then Irish media for accepting such treatment. Instead, they went to PJ for snippets.

The British too had their control mechanisms, such as at Thatcher's press conference when her Press Secretary, Bernard Ingham, sat on the podium beside her, and directed the rotation of questions from the floor. The two Dublin meetings, for example, confirmed the Delors Report laying down the agenda for the all important Inter-Governmental Conference (IGC), on economic and political union, to be held in Maastricht in December 1991. Fierce negotiations ensued as Thatcher resisted these moves towards European integration and, afterwards, St Patrick's Hall was crowded for her press conference, with the first six rows of seats filled by British journalists, eager to ask questions.

Down on the floor, Michael Forbes and Catherine Aylward, from our Press Office, stood in the aisles, like game show hosts ready with the microphone. But even though it was obvious that the BBC or Channel 4, with their hands in the air, were next, Ingham would direct the boom to someone else, such as say, the pro-Tory, anti-EU *Telegraph* or *Sunday Times*. This way the Tory media would ask the first questions but in a supportive and positive way, much like a tame backbencher in the Commons. Finally, begrudgingly, the mike would get passed to John Palmer of the *Guardian* but, with the sting taken out of the issues, Thatcher could then patronise him; 'Oh, John, we've gone through that already.'

Thatcher was in defiant, crackling form. Asked if she'd heard what Delors had said earlier — that 'if God had deliberated for as long as they had on European integration he never would have created Adam' — she said, 'Yes, I heard what he said, I was in the room.' After the laughter subsided, she added, 'And I was thinking, what a better job God did the second time around when he created Eve!' She also had some withering things to say about Kohl who had earlier given a gung-ho press conference, muttering stuff about 'the river that cannot be stopped'. It was the beginning of that post-Wall German restlessness.

What was interesting was the crowd Thatcher drew, not just officials and journalists, but everyone; kitchen staff and porters. She was a celebrity, a legend in her own lifetime, crossing the Castle Yard in her blue suit and big silver hair. When she made her Eve remark, the girls from Easons — Easons had set up a shop for the Summit — exclaimed 'She's great, isn't it?' and others agreed. It was amazing. Thatcher was supposed to be a hate figure. And this was Ireland too, with whom she'd had such an ambiguous relationship, letting the hunger strikers die and yet signing the Anglo-Irish Agreement.

The second Summit coincided with the World Cup, which made for an interesting distraction, especially given Ireland's unexpected success. On the Summit's eve, a press reception was held in Trinity College, a lavish affair with lots of food and drink but at the request of some German and Dutch journalists, a TV was installed so they could watch the German-Holland match. A grudge encounter always, this one was particularly so, with Rikjard, the Dutchman, spitting at Rudi Voller, after allegedly receiving racist abuse. Both players were sent off and a heated exchange erupted at the reception. 'Gentlemen, gentlemen!' pleaded Michael Forbes, 'the Summit hasn't started yet.'

As the tournament progressed, so did the Irish team and media pictures appeared of officials and Gardaí in Dublin Castle trying to crane their necks around corners to get a look at the many TV monitors showing the games. The Europeans got into the atmosphere, with a crowd assembled in the Marquee to watch the matches, all except the French who sulked because they weren't in the tournament. Indeed, such was the fever outside in the streets that the foreign journalists wanted to go out and capture it. Some TV crews went to the RDS to film people who were watching the Big Screens 'as if they were there'. The cynical hacks, of course, loved the fact that for the Irish people (or for any people, as they pointed out) a sports event in Italy had more impact that a European Summit in their capital.

The high point was our 2nd-Round tie against Romania, when, after 120 minutes, the match went to penalties, at exactly the time the Premiers were concluding their meeting. It was the end of the Summit and this was the only meeting left. Haughey, chairing it, realised what was going on — a useful official was listening on a Walkman — and, mindful of his priorities, he cut the proceedings short and went out to speak to Tommie Gorman of RTÉ, telling him how pleased he was about the Irish success. Meanwhile, in the Marquee, at the front of the crowd, the heavy set John Healy was pictured leaping into the air — or trying to leap into the air — at the sight of Dave O'Leary's penalty. It was a nice moment and probably his last public appearance, since a few months later he died.

The Summit came to an end, and with it, Ireland's Presidency. People drifted to the Marquee to watch the tournament's next game, England vs Belgium, appropriate given the day's political events — 'Come on Brussels!' Or sat around outside, enjoying the warm evening air. In the deserted Press centre, there were only a few last journalists, meeting deadlines. And the various Japanese crews. In an amazing neurosis of competition, one would not leave until the other left. What broke them, or some of them, was the distribution of gift packs. The packs, now a tradition of the Presidency, included music CD's, videos and a side of smoked salmon (that staple of Irish diplomacy but this stuff was 'wild', just the way Charlie, and Terry, liked it). The secret weapon, however, was a bottle of Jameson, which, for some reason, the Japanese opened immediately and began sipping at.

The Japanese love whiskey but apparently cannot hold it too well, and sure enough, while other hacks were still working and looking for documents, two Japanese journalists reappeared at our counter, giggling and wondering if there were any more gift packs. Before long, they were transformed into a backslapping gaggle of laughter, with one fellow crashed out on the fax machine, falling asleep. European journalists looked on drolly, almost with satisfaction. Despite our differences, there was a sense of camaraderie among the Europeans, and a sense of spirit which occasions like this, and the World Cup, engendered.

It was a shock then, when news came through that the Provos had bombed the Carlton Club in London. It was such a desperate, 'Don't forget about us' gesture. Journalists went back into action. 'Well, there's a news story,' said Conor Lenihan (now a TD, but then a radio reporter) and he sprung out of his seat in search of PJ Mara. 'PJ, what's the reaction?' 'For Jaysus sake, Conor, I've only just heard.' Others, however, refused to let it disturb things and went on with their evening. Some officials were furious, knowing that the bombing, and its venue (no one was killed), was calculated to outrage Britain and embarrass the Republic on the day of its EU Summit and World Cup success.

But business continued and we got on with our socialising. Needless to say, through the hard work, and play, of the Presidency, there was much bonding and romance. Foreign officials and hacks offered love tokens. A colleague received a piece of the Berlin Wall from a smitten broadcaster. 'Sure, that's only a bit of concrete from Werburgh Street!' said Forbes dismissively. Home-grown relationships were firmer, even including a few eventual marriages between Civil Servants and Gardaí. There were hundreds of Gardaí around for the Presidency and it was appropriate that, later that night, when we'd had our fill of the Castle, we borrowed a limo and went on to the Garda Club on Harrington Street where we partied until the wee hours.

Haughey now prepared to fly out to Italy for Ireland's next World Cup game, against the host team. But after the splendid pomp of the Summit, he was quickly brought back to earth by DFA. Literally, since, at Rome airport, he was left sitting in his aeroplane for nearly half-an-hour before Ambassador Robin Fogarty showed up. Yes the same Robin Fogarty of the rebellious luncheon session in the Grey Door.

Fogarty's excuse for the delay was one every Civil Servant would cherish; he 'was busy at his desk'. After the match — a 1-0 defeat to Italy — Haughey went down onto the sideline and got so carried away with the celebrations (yes, celebrations — this was Ireland after all) that he drifted in under the stadium and got lost.

When the Ministers in the VIP Box rounded on Fogarty about their missing cars, and missing Taoiseach, the unflappable Envoy merely waved them away. Minister Ray Burke then got angry and allegedly began snapping his fingers. Mortally offended, Ambassador Fogarty drew himself up to his full height. 'How dare you!' he said, staring at him. 'How dare you come here and speak like that!' Burke was speechless and, when the incident was later gleefully recounted among diplomats and Civil Servants, Fogarty became a hero. But he paid the price; his next posting was to Switzerland, which he hated.

7

Tehran or Toronto:
The Postings Lottery

Within DFA there is, obviously, great anticipation about postings and about the Wheel of Fortune aspect which decides one's fate. A sheet is sent around to those picked to go abroad, on which they must number their preferences. These are permutated by Personnel Division and then presented to the all powerful MAC, the Management Affairs Committee, comprising the Secretary and Assistant Secs. The MAC then sends its decision to Government. Understandably, the MAC spends most of its time discussing Ambassadorial postings and it is these which concern the Government. The Cabinet is not generally going to concern itself with Third or First Secs (although you'd be surprised).

In my year, the postings for Third Sec were Canberra, Ottawa, London, Brussels, Berne, Stockholm, Tehran, New Delhi, New York and San Francisco. It is quite a list to absorb. You have to think of all the possibilities, all the permutations. After which, you put your preferences, from one to eight, in the boxes after the cities. It is a bit like a PR voting ballot and just as precarious in terms of what you get. If you're lucky, you might get your 1st choice, but usually you got your 3rd or 4th. It is an extraordinary lottery. People who've set their heart on Buenos Aires can end up walking the ice-glazed streets of downtown Helsinki.

Some people put their first choice second or third on the basis that you'll never get you first choice. And, of course, people would be mindful of what other candidates were seeking and how likely they were to get it. There was a theory that maybe you should put your first choice last and work upwards, such were the vagaries of the system, but this was to impute a cynicism in the Department too ingenious to carry through. (It apparently dates from a rumour that a few years back some departing mandarins decided to make a humorous and childish farewell to Iveagh House by giving candidates the postings they least wanted.)

In such an arbitrary atmosphere, one chap in Harcourt Street, opened a book on the postings, with people betting on each other's destinations. But Personnel took a dim view of such frivolity, feeling that it reflected badly on the procedure. Another joker pinned up a cartoon depicting the MAC flinging darts at a dartboard. The dartboard was divided into different cities and the darts had people's names attached.

In fact, the Department has to perform an extraordinary balancing act here. It has to decide who could get on with whom in a certain Embassy and, more importantly, who could get on with the Ambassador — or the Ambassador's spouse. Or who was more suited to lobbying to Washington as opposed to getting people out of jail in Bangkok. But there was also politicking within the system. Ambassadors or Counsellors destined to go abroad themselves, could lobby to have favourites sent with them, and others excluded.

The latter might be doing someone a favour, for there's nothing worse than working with an Ambassador you don't like. Faced with a tyrannical Envoy every day, more than one diplomat has embraced the local culture with gusto; not so easy when the local culture is Chinese or Iranian. In which case, that affair with the French Ambassador's wife — or, in my fantasised-about case, the Iraqi Ambassadors wife's — might seem like the only liveable option. The sad story was often told of a beleaguered officer in one of our far-flung Embassies who collared the visiting Minister at the airport and said 'Minister, get me out of here — this place is making my life a misery!' Sadly, the Minister, otherwise having his arse licked by the selfsame fawning Envoy, was singularly unimpressed and ascended into the clouds without even glancing back at the diminishing figure on the tarmac.

In such situations, Personnel back in HQ suddenly seems a long way away and they're just not interested. Once you go, you go. They have enough on their plate. Unless you really start going mad and have to be brought home early. Or unless an Ambassador is truly being difficult, such as in one posting, where the Third Sec concerned had to be granted a sanity-saving transfer to another capital.

So the choice, before you leave, can be a tough one. For me, however, it was simple. I didn't want a diplomatic capital, which ruled out Canberra, Ottawa and Berne, or London, which was too near, and involved dealing with Irish prisoners or British journalists. Brussels was also too near and, besides, I'd had enough of *Les Douze* and their dreams of European Unity. As for New York, I'd have loved it, but it was to be filled immediately and there was no way my section would release me.

No; instead I was set on India. A complete change of scene, a new culture, a chance to finally write those sprawling classics on the bamboo veranda with a gin in my hand. Any officer I spoke to who'd been posted there had loved it. Forbes of India, naturally, but also my Counsellor, Noel Fahey. They seemed to go dewy-eyed at the memories and fondled with the little Buddhist knick-knacks on their desks. (People always had souvenirs of postings on their desks — mariskha dolls, American police badges, a thigh bone from the Congo.)

So India was put down first, and then San Francisco. But Forbes himself had put this down and would probably get it, having worked hard in Press section. This was another factor; well placed and hard-working Third Secs, like Press Officers and Minister's Private Secs, would almost certainly get their first choice, and deservedly so.

However, another way to get your choice is to make a pre-arrangement with another officer intent on the same posting, especially a hardship location where it might be difficult to get a combination of people wanting to go. One night, in a Dublin pub, I was approached by Cathal Mac Gerailt, a small red-faced Mayo man better known as 'Napoleon' because of his diminutive stature, aggressive approach and imperial sense of humour. Napoleon asked if I had thought about going to Tehran.

'Tehran?' I must say, I hadn't.

We were standing in the back snug of Doheny and Nesbitts, a strange place to consider a drink-free posting. If I wanted Tehran, I could get it, he said, which was probably true since nobody else was going for it. Napoleon was about to go there as Head of Mission, and he thought that, I was just the man to help him. I was flattered.

'Come on, you're not in Foreign Affairs so that you can go to places like Geneva or Paris,' he said dismissively. 'You can go to them any time. Try Iran. Wild, unpredictable, completely different. There's a challenge for you. Eh? Something truly different.' He gave me a vigorous wink, like he was selling a horse.

I told him I would think about it and I did. It had an insidious appeal. It followed my own instinct in dismissing some of the European postings. Iran: the very name suggested exotic danger and an alien culture. Ancient Persia. And there was a career element. Iran was still quite isolated. With a bit of daring and initiative, one could build a few bridges for Ireland — and the West (ah, the fantasies). As a hardship posting, you'd have very good leave, in an interesting area, and you'd be out after two years, after which you could practically name your next posting.

I consulted with ex-Iranian veterans. One of them was an dreamy character nicknamed Methuselah whom I found sitting in a dark room staring into his green screen. 'Ah, Iran,' he said and immediately went into a reverie about its beauty and tranquility. I don't know what had happened to Methuselah — he had been a long time seeking promotion — but perhaps Tehran had something to do with it.

He spoke of it with a glazed look. Recreating the old souk at dawn, he described the happy banter of the Jewish carpet dealers, an image somewhat at odds with my own image of Jews in Tehran, which was that they were either very, very quiet — or very, very dead. As for alcohol (wink, wink) the diplomats were all busy making home-made hooch. Why, the Dutch Ambassador had concocted the most extraordinary moonshine in his bath. Such resourcefulness probably explained why Napoleon had no problem going there.

'Ah, but I can't go into it all now,' said Methuselah, indicating a speech on his screen. 'Come back when you think you've got it. Then, I'll give you the real story,' he said widening his eyes and smiling mysteriously.

Such statements only whetted the appetite. Perhaps there was a deep magic in these places. I thought of Joseph Conrad and Bruce Chatwin, of cobalt blue doorways which led down side streets to strange worlds of ritual and denial. And, there was also Napoleon himself, a lively terrier-like character who might be good crack to be on a posting with. At present, he was in the Maryfield bunker in Belfast, from where he came to Dublin for uproarious bouts of R&R. Thus, his appearances in hostelries like Doheny and Nesbitts, usually full of spin doctors, hacks and other Civil Servants.

To complete the picture I dropped into Personnel to read the Post Reports. Post Reports are detailed accounts of Postings: the culture, the living standards, the place to hire a car. They were often quite flowery but could also be mundane, as if written for children. 'In New York, it is cold in the winter ...' Well, no kidding. The Iranian one, however, made interesting reading. It didn't detract from Methuselah's sense of mystery. Far from it. At the time of writing, there was virtually no mixing with the natives, no Westerners to meet, except other diplomats, absolutely no alcohol and a brand of pop music and cinema which rarely strayed beyond the 'greatness of Persia' and the 'glorious death of the martyrs'. Bizarrely there was skiing. But it was segregated. An image came to mind of all these women in black chadors flying down the slopes.

Suddenly, I wasn't so sure. Could I really hack such reflective solitude? These were the spring years of my life and I wasn't going to waste them away for the Irish Government. Also, contrary to Methuselah's 'deeper understanding', the place didn't necessarily grow on you. Other Iranian veterans said that, if anything, the natives could become more remote and impenetrable, and just plain arrogant, taking pity on you because you remained decadent and unsaved.

I sent a note to the Secretariat in Belfast (an Iran of its own, really; perhaps Napoleon enjoyed these isolated outposts) thanking him for considering me but regretting that, on balance, I was 'an outgoing, social sort of person' and I didn't think I'd suit Tehran. Maybe another time. Maybe when they desegregate the skiing. Napoleon said nothing and I presumed he understood my reasons, but a year later he turned on me in a New York bar. 'So you thought you were too social for Iran, then, did you?' he snapped. Such an attack made me glad I hadn't gone with him.

With the note sent, I felt a huge relief and concentrated instead on India and twilight images of garden parties and finely calibrated prose being chiselled in the purple dusk. I was set on Delhi, and my choices thereafter were almost indifferently selected, accepting that whatever way the dice fell, so be it. However, on the morning we sent in our forms, I still put Tehran quite high. Delirious with one of those pleasant tequila hangovers after a hard night in Rathmines, I put it No 4, just for old time's sake. 'No 4?' said someone amazed, 'you'll get it! Everyone else has put it last.' I had hoped that, after my note, Napoleon would have found a more willing volunteer, but I was now worried. Perhaps I might get to make that moonshine after all.

The announcement of Postings creates major excitement within the Department. It usually happens on a Friday, in the afternoon, so that people have the weekend to absorb the shock and the perpetrators can escape. This hasn't prevented them from being accosted in the pub where everyone retires to after the postings have been announced.

Personnel inform people by phone, but advance warning is usually given by the clerical staff who've seen the paperwork. Candidates stay by their phones, leaping to hear in what far-flung part of the globe they will be spending the next three years of their lives. The procedure is often complicated by people ringing to tell their colleagues the news, so clogging up the lines for other announcements. Now, with e-mail, messages can be flashed across screens — Lu Thornely to Brussels, LJ Duffy for Stockholm — which both heightens and dampens the suspense. For, of course, once you see someone has got Buenos Aires, it means you won't be going there and your heart sinks. But then you notice that that bastard, Graham, is off to Beijing and it lifts again.

Some people can't stand the suspense, or the agony, and just leave the building. Apocryphal stories are told of officers not getting certain postings because they weren't at their desks. 'Ah, to hell with it, Mary, give Rome to Donnelly instead.' The delays can be seem phenomenal, with many false D-days as the MAC gets bogged down in fights over the Ambassadorial slots.

When the postings do kick in, however, the pub is an extraordinary place, a piece of human theatre rendered especially vivid if the Counsellor and First Sec postings are also announced — forty or fifty people on the move, both ways. You see someone in the corner stunned that they're going to Tokyo rather than Rome, while others cheer their unexpected allocations. Older, wiser diplomats come over full of advice, or encouragement, consoling officers who will have just phoned their spouses and kids to pass on the shock. Moments of sudden rebellion erupt, with people saying they won't go, or that they definitely won't stay away for three years. But they always go. And they always serve out their three years. (Or almost always; there are some famous, audacious reversals, with officers deploying their full diplomatic skills to get a posting decision changed.)

By mid-afternoon on the Friday, I was getting worried. People were getting their postings and I had heard nothing. I lost Delhi early — no more sun-drenched mornings and servants fanning me in four-poster beds — and its disappearance was sharpened by the thought that I might get the as yet unallocated Iran posting. Segregated skiing was rearing its black-covered head and suddenly I foresaw a return appointment with the dreamy Methuselah in his darkened room. Jesus.

The phone rang. It was the personnel officer, launching into the formal prelude, 'I'm just ringing to inform you of the decision ...' The officer concerned, like a civil servant from the de Valera era, was rumoured to believe the foreign allowances were too high and that the whinging dips could as easily survive on an egg and crusts. 'And we've decided to post you to New York.'

'New York?' I was surprised.

'Yes, the Consulate there. I know you didn't give it a high preference ...'

Apparently, it wasn't to be filled immediately and they were holding off until the autumn. 'That's great,' I said, 'thank you very much.' New York; I hadn't thought about it, but it was a promising prospect. I was to be Vice-Consul of Ireland in New York, an elaborate and intriguing title which I felt I could live with.

As the officer spoke, a message flashed across my screen — 'Fitzgerald for Tehran'. The man who'd drawn the cartoon of the dartboard had been bulls-eyed by the MAC. This was another factor that determined people's destinies, it was joked; punishment postings.

Then, I got more good news. While in New York, I would also work at the United Nations, helping out during the General Assembly session and operating out of our Permanent Mission there. Having cheated the cutbacks to gain entry to the Department, I was about to be their beneficiary. Each year, the Department usually sends out a supplementary team for the UN session, but it was now cheaper if people were already on the ground, in the US. The session is held for about three months of each year (Oct-Dec) and, by the end of my time in the US, I would have done three sessions, in tandem with my time at the Consulate. The best of both worlds.

'Forget India. It's gone now,' said Forbes, who, as expected, got San Francisco, but who was also being seconded to the UN. 'Come on, we'll have a bit of crack in Manhattan.'

So I wouldn't be going to Tehran, but in a strange twist, neither would Napoleon. Iran had become a priority again and the Government had decided to hold off sending him, so they could dispatch a full Ambassador. Napoleon, a Counsellor, would have been Head of Mission. But not full Ambassador, which usually constitutes Assistant Secretary level. These distinctions were important, especially to someone like Napoleon. Not only was he bitter at not getting Tehran, but he would also become increasingly sour about not getting the full 'red hat', to use the common ecclesiastical metaphor for Ambassadorship. Hard and all as he worked — and Napoleon worked very hard — the Department would appear to have decided against promoting any more *bon viveur*, party-hearty figures to Ambassador, especially after some of the unfortunate publicity concerning such figures in the early Nineties.

In the weeks before departure, I did the usual preparations for a Posting. There was the transfer of belongings, which, in my case — a single young man in rented accommodation — was not a lot. Generously, Personnel offer an advance on one's impending Foreign Service Allowance, to facilitate the purchase of clothes, silverware and other accoutrements necessary for life and entertainment. One girl, upset with her grim posting, defiantly spent it all on farewell dinners in expensive city restaurants. Luckily, I had no language to learn, but others went on cramming courses. First Secs lined up for positions in Moscow or Tokyo would have already undertaken long courses, just as people destined for tropical climes could now be seen breaking in safari suits, and skirts, around St Stephen's Green.

To help me make purchases while in the US, I was given a tax-exempt card, issued by the US State Department and entitling one to tax-exemption on all purchases over $50, important in America where there are taxes on everything. The duty-free aspect of diplomacy is something which is much used, and abused, and even in our own service people were constantly driving new cars across foreign borders and buying hi-fi systems for friends. While in New York, hapless Irish illegals, pressed me to purchase cameras and computer systems for them, so they could avoid the big tax mark-up. (They were being cruelly denied legal status so why should they be paying tax?)

In tandem with my regular passport, I got a diplomatic passport, with which you could sail through any control unhindered. I also got the all-important Diplomatic Immunity card, which states that 'the bearer shall not be liable to arrest or detention'.

Diplomatic Immunity is a famous concept, much abused and therefore much pilloried in almost every country's media. In theory, a diplomat can commit any offence and walk free, unless their State agrees to forfeit the immunity. In New York, it infuriated the press since it meant that Embassies could run up huge unpaid parking fines, the greatest offenders being, predictably, the Cubans and Syrians. But it is probably a necessary concept, and apparently dates from the time of Peter the Great when the first people to be strung up, in event of a conflict, were the resident Ambassadors. (Not always a bad move, really.) In some regions, things haven't changed and its absolutely imperative to have it there. But, of course, there are the controversies, such as the Libyan Embassy siege in London in 1981, when a policewoman was shot and the alleged killer walked free. When Kevin McDonald was caught selling passports in London, the Irish Government waived his immunity so he could be prosecuted. McDonald was not actually a diplomat, but was covered by the same principle. Thus, the CD plates which he cheekily placed on his sports car.

In theory, anyone who is with a diplomat at the time of an offence, can also avail of the immunity, a fact which my friends would constantly remind me of, when we were out on the razzle in late-night New York.

Section II

United Nations

8

The World in One Room

I arrived in New York on a Sunday, the same day as the Minister, except he was on the Government Jet. The General Assembly (GA) was opening the next day and he was coming out to deliver the Government's statement and do all the UN business, an annual event which Ministers always enjoyed.

I'd been to New York before, on a student visa (J1), and it was strange to be back; the humidity, the colourful hoardings and the cab driver taking me to the wrong hotel. It was supposed to be the Plaza 50, but he took me instead to the green-glass UN Plaza Hotel, a more salubrious place which faces the UN and is host to Gulf sheikhs and the EU Ministers' Lunch. It was a common mishap and I was quickly redirected.

The marble-walled Plaza 50 was a 'long stay' hotel with cellophane-wrapped fruits in the rooms and a sign-in policy after midnight. The doorman was a dour old Irish man, a Fifties immigrant, who seemed to resent our high-pitched comings and goings. 'Sign here,' he'd say like Dracula's butler and a gnarled hand would point to the white clipboard.

Across the street was the San Carlos Hotel, where delegates used to stay in the 1950s. Later when we were coming home from the bars on Second Avenue, Michael Forbes used to give his 'San Carlos' speech, denouncing the conservatism of some of the stuffed shirts we had to work with and extolling the praises of Conor Cruise O'Brien and Máire McEntee, who apparently began their illicit affair in the San Carlos. He was a Counsellor, and married, and she was a First Secretary. She was also the Tánaiste's daughter. It caused a Departmental scandal.

Indeed, it would later cause a international scandal, when O'Brien took a non-Western stand on the Congo crisis, and the Western press exploited his 'domestic' situation. But what impressed many civil servants was the reaction of her father, the crusty 1916 rebel, annoyed not so much that she was having an affair but that, in running away with this man, 'she had left her desk' — a cardinal sin for a Civil Servant. Michael thought that such high-spirited adventure was the way to go and scaled the railings outside the Plaza 50 to make his point.

It was a passionate speech which perhaps had some basis in fact and later a Trinity Professor, who had once been a young delegate, told me of long nights of 'high jinks' in the San Carlos with the Swedish contingent. For the moment, I had the wrong idea, for the 'high jinks' meant drinking, of which there was plenty; on arrival, the Deputy Permanent Representative John Burke, took us aside and offered fatherly advice about eating properly and not 'gallivanting' too much. The Civil Service has a cautionary attitude to drinking anyway and, in fact, during my time at the Mission, I was to see at close hand the deleterious effects of free and endless boozing. As for the other sort of 'high jinks', one of my more amorous colleagues, one Virgil Johnston, was determined to find out all he could.

After I dumped my bags at the Plaza 50, I joined Virgil and three others in a Chinese restaurant. There were a number of us out for the session. Eamon McKee sporting a red beard was up from the Embassy in Washington. Virgil was out from the Dublin HQ as was Michael Forbes who was on his way to San Francisco. The party was completed by Vanessa Singleton, with her Rosetti curled hair, who had come to the UN Permanent Mission from a South American embassy. We were a complement to the staff already at the Mission. After our meal, we joined our older colleagues in Jameson's bar on Second Avenue. Jameson's was to become our late-night rendezvous point. The Minister himself wasn't there, of course. He was back in the Omni Berkshire Hotel on Madison Avenue, where his entourage were staying. The Omni was co-owned by Aer Lingus and directly opposite the Consulate.

Where the Minister stays in New York can be a tricky subject, ever since Dick Spring stayed in the Waldorf Astoria in 1992, rather than the less expensive Fitzpatrick's Hotel. One could see his point; it was closer to the UN and more private. But the negative publicity arising out of his decision was considerable — Labour had come into power in 1992 with a no-frills aura — and years later there were still jokes about it. For us, it was ridiculous; a Minister comes to New York to pursue high profile relations for the State and all the press can talk about is the hotel he stayed in. But that's the optics of modern politics, for you.

Our UN Embassy, officially known as the Permanent Mission (PMUN), was on the eighteenth floor of a skyscraper on Second Avenue. Actually, the address is 1 Dag Hammarskjold Plaza, in honour of the former UN Secretary-General, but you couldn't say that to a New York taxi driver. There was a bust of Dag outside the building next door, surrounded by a fountain. It looked the image of the PD Leader, Des O'Malley, which always gave us a laugh when we passed.

The Mission itself was a large, comfortable office, as befits the mentality that top resources must be given to 'our UN mission'. There was a story that Haughey once arrived into it, half-an-hour early as was his wont, putting everyone off their guard; 'He was just — there,' recalled a typist afterwards, like it was the Holy Ghost. On noticing that the typewriters were a bit out of date, Haughey announced, in a regal gesture, 'you shall have the Wang'. And so the PMUN was one of the first Missions to be computerised.

At one end of the Mission was a large room where the visiting delegates were put at separate desks piled with paper. The Ambassador seemed perpetually suspicious of the 'extra bodies' he had got for the session and, sensing the tensions that already existed in the Mission, we kept our heads down, staying in our back room and making occasional forays to the water-cooler to get the news from home. Most Embassies have their divisions, as I'd discover later in Washington, but the PMUN was notorious and, as the officers changed, the rancour and old tensions seemed to be passed on, a little like the UN itself.

Our Ambassador — or Permanent Representative — was one of the old-school diplomats, a tall, silver haired man, only a few years from retirement. Although he had a distinguished Charlton Heston demeanour, someone also described him as 'like a hulking Garda Sergeant from the 1950s', creeping up on you in the UN and asking you what you were doing. In this spirit, Forbes would ring us up on the phone and do the Cork accent, 'Who's been robbing the apples?' He was an impressive figure, a former lawyer, one of whose most famous achievements had been to take the British Government to the European Human Rights Court for their use of 'torture' in Northern Ireland in the 1970s.

In general, the Ambassador left us to silently get on with our work. He was really only interested in the Ministers. Ambassadors are generally only interested in Ministers, which is as Ministers like it.

The DFA principle that training is 'on the job' continues on a posting, where you are expected to have absorbed in advance the ritual and protocol. Some of us were fooled by the informality of Napoleon with his laughter and his irreverent stories. But we might better have watched the Deputy Perm Rep, John Burke, a man of almost monastic circumspection and clipped sentences. Senior diplomats can be extraordinarily vain creatures. The Ambassador was, after all, 'His, or Her, Excellency' and expected to be treated as such. You did not disturb them unless you absolutely had to with the result that much of the time you were expected to virtually divine what they might be thinking. Well-groomed himself, the Perm Rep also expected a strong sense of decorum around the office and UN buildings.

There was a good buzz in the opening week of the UN General Assembly, due to the presence of the Minister's team. In the boardroom, the Secretary and Political Director worked on the Minister's Speaking Points while beside us, the Press Officer manically drafted replies to breaking news stories in Ireland. Meanwhile, we absorbed our drafting instructions and read through the many UN press releases and documents before going off to our respective committees.

It was the Committees that made our presence — the 'extra bodies' — essential. Forbes was on the Second Committee, with the Deputy Perm Rep, Vanessa was on the Third Committee, handling Human Rights, and Eamon McKee was on the Special Committee, which mostly dealt with Palestine. Other PMUN officers , such as Virgil Johnston, worked on the Fifth Committee, which oversaw UN finances and budgets. Meanwhile, we all put in time on the equally fractious Sixth Committee which dealt with international law, and where he had the eagle-eyed Ambassador sit in for occasional company.

Meanwhile, I was in Plenary, or the actual General Assembly itself, which would eventually vote on the work of all these Committees but which was otherwise a forum for lengthy debate and for the Opening Statements of the Member States. Thus my job was to sit and listen and keep the seat warm for the Minister. I also had to watch out for the occasional snap votes and for any sudden references to Northern Ireland, also a rarity but at one time a not-uncommon tactic for Third World countries anxious to embarrass the British.

At 9.30 in the morning we all headed for the UN. The Minister, over in the Omni Berkshire with the

Ambassador, would come by car, but the rest of us would take the short walk along the Raoul Wallenberg walkway. 'Your old friend,' said the Political Director, remembering the Honorary Citizenship proposal.

Down on the streets, we joined company with delegates coming from other Missions, their laminate passes twinkling on silver chains. Two-tone suits, turbans, African costumes; we were unmistakable, as we walked towards the river and the great glass structure of the United Nations. It was like something out of a science fiction movie – 'The Day of the Living Diplomats' or something.

Camped along route were the different protestors, kept well back with their flags and loudhailers. Diplomats usually passed without making eye contact, but I found it hard not to look. Protests are always interesting and here, off First Avenue, were some of the most oppressed and disenfranchised of peoples: the Kurds; the Iranian Bahais; the Kashmiris waving their saffron flags; the stoic faces of the Mayan Indians. Some of the causes were exotic or truly 'lost'; exiles from discredited regimes, or Royalists hoping to turn the clock back. With Communism fading in Eastern Europe, plucky old ladies in fur coats re-appeared on the streets to demand the return of long forgotten monarchs; King Zog or Prince Michael of Romania.

The big protests were those which coincided with large ethnic groups already living in New York, or the US, like the Poles, Albanians or Colombians. There were regular protests by American Jews both for and against Israeli Government policy. One morning, loads of ultra-orthodox Jews appeared to protest against the visiting Israeli Premier and his policy of making Hasidim Jews go into the army in Israel. It was an amazing sight, thousands of black-clad Hasidim, with their long beards and fur lined hats. It was like something from another century, but it was also very New York.

Eamon Delaney

Stepping into the United Nations compound was like stepping into the past or more accurately, like stepping into the future, as the future used to be envisaged in the 1950s, when the world was full of concerned optimism and the UN needed a building as grand and modern as its mission. Overlooking the East River, the organisation's headquarters is a dramatic structure, with its General Assembly rotunda and its sheer, green-glass Secretariat. Around the perimeter fence, hang the multicoloured flags of its members.

Beneath the rotunda, school groups and tourists file in to see 'Peace' displays and exhibitions on the Environment with lots of pictures of indigenous farmers and smiling international children. In the public lobby, a piece of moon rock is on display and a model of the Sputnik hangs from the ceiling; gifts from the two superpowers who kept the UN enlivened but also enfeebled. In the Rothko Chapel, plaques are erected to UN representatives cut down during their missions, like Count Bernadotte and Dag Hammarskjold, who died in a mysterious plane crash in Africa.

Upstairs, in the delegates lobby, there was an almost quaint atmosphere, with the zinc escalators, plastic signposts and the old wood and white leather armchairs donated by the Scandinavian countries. This retro style was not entirely intentional but rather reflected the extent to which the UN was, and is, strapped for cash. Some of the Western powers, tired of the organisation's perceived ideological bias during the Cold War, simply didn't bother paying their dues.

Thus the decor, and some would say the thinking, has stayed in the era in which it was built. Compared to the EU meetings, for example, with their digital noticeboards and TV monitors around every corner, there was an almost old world charm to it — indeed a whole world charm. For here were all sorts of peoples on all sorts of time scales. Watching the delegates passing in African costumes and sheikh's garbs, one had the feeling of time

111

standing still, a sense heightened by the appearance of delegates from Communist countries, squeezed into shiny grey suits with the shortened sleeves.

It was just like the Hitchcock's *North By North West*, with its famous UN assassination scene. In it, foreign diplomats sit around a big room, waiting for something to happen — actually the Delegates Lounge, with views of the 59th Street bridge through the window — while, in the background, the tannoy system is paging people; 'Mr Vrinitsky, please go to your Mission!' When the main character, Thornhill, flees the UN he is dwarfed by the huge Secretariat building and he disappears against the scale of Grand Central Station. Thornhill is fleeing from a murder for which he is wrongly blamed — a metaphor for the United Nations if ever I saw one.

The retro, old-fashioned atmosphere also recalled the old days of the Irish foreign service. The days when the UN was the major focus of a country anxious to build on its independent profile, when the Department would send out a team of four or five Ambassadors for the session and not just a bunch of Third Secs. Indeed, the Minister would be here for weeks; Frank Aiken used to stay for the whole three-month session, sitting in on Committee informals for lengthy discussions about disarmament and meeting other politicians who'd made the transition from guerrilla to bureaucrat.

In the 1950s there were Cold War tensions to be tackled, the 'emergence' of Africa, all countries working for Peace and Harmony, and children of many colours holding hands in the sunset. And Ireland in the midst of it all, demanding the admittance of Red China, initiating whole programmes on Arms Control and calling for an end to conflict. After each session DFA would produce a handbook of the highlights which members of the public would buy, anxious to see what we'd voted on and ever-vigilant for any diminution in our neutrality. I used to come across the handbooks, hundreds of them, out in the stables of Iveagh House, lying on the dusty shelves next to speeches of former Taoisigh and the no longer kosher Anti-Partition leaflets.

The pictures said it all. The delegation in the chamber consulting dramatically behind the nameplate; the Minister, Seán McBride, with Conor Cruise O'Brien on his shoulder. What a combination. Or Freddy Boland, as President of the Assembly, breaking the gavel while trying to stop Khruschev from banging his shoe. Or Liam Cosgrave enjoying a light moment. Perhaps the aftermath of the time he reportedly asked the Israelis and the Arabs if they couldn't 'settle the matter like Christians'. Ah the good old days.

Nowadays, at most, the Minister might pop out for a few fast days (hours, sometimes) between Anglo-Irish face-offs and EU Ministerials, his mind more focussed on Brussels and Belfast than on Brunei Darussalam. Indeed, with *chers collègues Européen* in town, it was a handy occasion to get the Brussels business done, as would happen, a year later, when the French public rejected the Maastricht Treaty. The Twelve EU members suddenly had to meet in response, an emergency assembly which almost overshadowed the theoretical main event, the UN General Assembly's opening. This rightly caused resentment among those lesser countries not involved in Europe's internal squabble.

As the focus shifted to Brussels a new breed of diplomat had emerged; technocrats, with an Economics or Law background and not just the traditional History or English degree. Operators, close to their political masters. Around the Mission, you'd see the old types in their plain suits and prescription glasses, saving the pennies and full of phrases like 'the joker in the pack' and 'the litmus test'. They'd kick off their shoes in the office to scratch away at a few speeches, while the technocrats were fighting each other for the Minister's ear and telling him exactly what he wanted to hear. They were more like political handlers and, in the modern context, probably more useful.

Past the security guards and their trusty blue rope, I stepped into the General Assembly chamber where I would sit each day listening to speeches. It is an extraordinary room to walk into. Indeed, it is probably one of the most extraordinary rooms in the world — mainly because it virtually *is* the world.

It is an enormous, slightly inclined amphitheatre with rows of benches bearing the nameplates of the countries of the globe. All the benches face the podium, with its marble lectern so familiar from the famous speeches of the past. Overlooking the chamber were booths in which sat translators and TV crews and at the back of the chamber were the public galleries, usually frequented by schoolchildren, tourist groups or those publicly concerned types who go around New York visiting courts and libraries and writing to the papers. More organised observers also appear, as I was to discover; groups of people who stand up and shout during appropriate moments in the speech they appear to have 'accidentally' happened upon and then leave, en masse, to be bussed back to the Cuban Mission.

Beginning with one picked out of a hat, all the countries are each year seated alphabetically, according to their English spelling. To find my seat I just had to work the alphabet backwards from K, past the beautiful Jordan with her big trestle of hair, until I found Ireland, over on the west side of the Assembly, between Iran, Iraq and Israel. The 'hot' corner.

I shook hands with the Iranian and Iraqi delegates, who barely spoke to each other, and then with Israel, who the other two wouldn't even look at. During the Iran-Iraq War, the Irish delegate had to speak to both if he spoke to one, for fear of showing diplomatic preference. 'Ireland at the UN — between Iraq and a hard place' was how one newspaper put it. On the practical side, of course, construction, hospitals and beef interests were tied up in both countries and it wouldn't have done to be partial.

As I pulled into my seat, the Iraqis were still smiling, glad that someone was being friendly to them. They were the bad guys right now but even after the whipping they would get from the Western Allies, they still came back, year after year, refusing to offer up their weapons secrets. Beside Israel, Italy was checking his fingernails, but the Lebanon, behind me, was empty, as was a lot of the chamber. It got crowded for the Opening Statements and towards the session's end when elections took place and the work of the various Committees was voted on. Otherwise, you might not see some countries for days, when they'd make fleeting visits. The EU States were always here, however, or were supposed to be.

Michael Forbes came along the carpeted aisle and warned me Collins would be here in two minutes. A former Press Officer, he could almost time the Minister's footfall.

As the room filled up and clusters of delegates gathered behind their country's nameplates, I looked around at the colourful scene. In front of me was Guatemala; two old men with two young women, all bursting into Latin chatter when El Salvador comes over to say hello. Some of the Central American diplomats had been here for years; presumably recruited from the four per cent who ran, and owned, these countries. Needless to say, with 164 countries, there were all kinds of dubious types floating around; spies, retired guerrillas and the children of dictators sent to New York to further their 'foreign studies'. It was also a popular 'R&R' for military people who'd just come through a bruising, and often ugly, experience for their State.

A case in point was a large burly man at the Libyan desk who used to read the newspaper so brazenly — you were not supposed to read newspapers in the chamber — and made such strange throat-clearing noises that the neighbouring Japanese felt compelled to complain. Until they discovered that his previous occupation at home had been killing people. I mean, literally killing people and having them strung up. They decided not to press the point, although I understand that the delegate, who was semi-literate even in Arabic, and short of temper, caused great consternation later on when delicate drafting was in progress at the Third Committee.

I looked up: through the green glass panel on the east side, I could see the Minister and party approach. It was a great moment in Departmental choreography. The Minister, in front, looking around with feigned quizzicality, while at his side, was the stooped, monkish figure of the Secretary, Noel Dorr, and the tall, aloof person of the Political Director, Pádraig Murphy. At a distance behind was John Kirwan, a tough Dubliner brought in from Justice to protect Collins from DFA. A demanding Private Secretary to the Minister (PSM), he also saved the Department from a lot of the Minister's tantrums and acted as a good buffer zone. Behind him was gruff little Napoleon, tossing his head like a terrier. They all carried black cases, except for the Minister. The PSM carried the biggest case.

It was like Gerry's Gang striding through the schoolyard, all brought up short suddenly when Gerry stopped to greet an old friend — the Hungarians, or the Kuwaitis, for whom Collins was especially supportive in their hour of need. A hand massaged the sheikh's elbow, like he was a pleading constituent. And then Gerry resumed his stroll, and the gang all craned their necks forward, trying to hear what was just exchanged.

'Good man,' said the Minister, as I hopped out of the seat to give it to him, and the Secretary nodded and got into the co-pilot seat beside him. 'Are you looking after the living?' said the PSM, with eyes widening, and he took in all the countries around him.

A gavel sounded. The President of the Assembly had taken his seat and was about to begin the meeting. The first speaker would be the Foreign Minister of Romania. 'One of the old crowd in a different suit,' grumbled Collins, with a flick of the head. 'Here, give us that ...'

Briefs were pulled from cases and papers shuffled. The Minister pushed aside the day's press cuttings from Ireland and went through the important faxes from HQ, holding up for perusal the cryptic cables on the latest 'talks about talks' on the North. Dorr gently drew his attention to certain underlined sentences, but the Minister seemed content to draw his own conclusions. 'Bunch of lousers,' he said, although whether he was referring to the British, or to his own officials, remained unclear. In the seat behind, Pádraig Murphy was busy revising Gerry's speech, scheduled for delivery the following day.

After a while, the Minister gave a signal. 'Time to meet the Algerians,' said Collins, turning around, and as he rose they all followed, leaving Virgil and I in the seat. We watched the procession of heads leave the chamber. It seemed a bit dramatic. But then we noticed how other countries behaved, positively peacock-like, strutting through the Assembly with even more delegates.

(It was refreshing then, a year later, to see the new delegates of Albania stride in with all the ceremony of a bunch of bookie's runners at Shelbourne Park, black leather jackets flapping and Mexican moustaches twitching; any one of them could have been the Minister searching for his seat. 'It's over there!' they pointed. But that was next year. This year, it was still very much the old crowd in the old suits.)

The Minister was meeting the Algerians in the Chinese Lounge, an interesting place at the back of the chamber. Basically, a two-tiered lounge area with white leather seats and smoked glass tables, in the opening week it was a scene of frenetic activity as countries used the Lounge to hold quick fifteen minute bilaterals — an ideal form of hob-nob while debates were on in the chamber. Usually the bilaterals coincided with some lobbying objective, such as a regional dispute or a canvass to get elected to an international body. Or just as a form of friendly catch up; Ireland, for example, was sought out as a non-NATO guide to EU thinking.

However, there weren't many seats in the Lounge and you had to get in early to hold them. Thus, you'd have a dozen sleepy Third Secs dragged from their beds at dawn and dispatched to the Chinese Lounge to 'hold the seats'. The Lounge became an interesting free-for-all in international co-operation, with people jostling for seats and swapping them among their partners. Passing them amongst themselves, the EU States kept out countries like the ASEAN group. 'Fuck 'em,' said Napoleon, 'they can meet in the UN Plaza!'

However, Virgil got us all in trouble when he gave his seat to the Afghani delegate. Basically because he fancied her. 'I felt sorry for her,' he said, 'her own seat was taken by the Russians.' Napoleon was unimpressed. 'What the fuck are we doing, giving our seat to the Afghans?' Nor did we get it back. The girl's Afghani bosses handed the seat on to the Armenians, and thereafter it disappeared into some kind of Caucasian cycle.

The bilaterals were sit-up-sharply time. Later on, when you got to know the delegates on a more human and irreverent basis, it was interesting to see them in the Lounge, switched into 'the mode'. One minute, you'd all be sitting around being ironic and cheeky and then, suddenly, someone's Minister would approach and they'd jump up like puppets, whipping out pads and pencils, offering seats and doing the introductions.

Next up on the podium, was the Foreign Minister of Costa Rica, speaking in Spanish, so we put on the big white earpieces for translation. All the seats had such earpieces, with the option of five languages (French, Spanish, English, Russian and Chinese) and a volume control which could be turned all the way down during the really boring debates. The translators overlooked the chamber and usually closely followed a previously supplied script, although when some of us listened one year to the French translation of our Health Minister's relatively straightforward contribution to the disabled debate, they feared for how the intricacies of other issues like our Northern Irish policy must be coming across in Beijing.

The opening statements of almost all countries were identical and one could easily swap chunks and even pages from one to the other without anything sounding different. Like, who isn't 'concerned about the environment and the rain forests'? Who doesn't hope for 'an end to world hunger and a narrowing of the gap between North and South'? Who doesn't 'urge an end to the Middle East conflict' and hopes 'the parties will engage in dialogue'? 'Motherhood language', it was called; as in, who could be against motherhood?

International conflicts were addressed. Not necessarily the worst or most problematic ones but those which concern the UN. Thus, the Palestinians are big news, and the Kurds are not. And there was, of course, a major focus on the newly breaking conflicts, which in this session was Iraq's invasion of Kuwait and the deteriorating pre-war crisis in Yugoslavia.

And yet despite the similarities in rhetoric there are huge differences. In fact, as soon as you look around the room, a number of basic truths strike you. The world is more black (and brown) than it is white, the world is more Asian than it is European and the West is a minority against the rest. Later, when the recorded votes are flashed up on the scoreboards, this is glaringly obvious — the green lights of the West, and like-minded countries, are a tight, predictable little sprinkling set against a sea of red lights, or at best orange abstentions, for the rest of the world. It made me appreciate the solidarity of the EU. But it also made me appreciate Ireland's neutrality in spite of it.

In fact, on some votes, such as the popular left-wing resolutions emanating from African or Asian countries, you would see just three red lights on the screen, the UK, US and Israel voting against. Israel always supported the US and, with the Tories and Republicans in power in the UK and US respectively, there was a marked tendency to take a stronger stand on some issues than the orange abstention lights of the more left-leaning EU.

Admittedly, this was beginning to change by 1990 as formerly Communist countries entered the family of the West, often with a vengeance, gleefully voting against those Third World countries who had happily supported the previous regime. In addition, by 1991 dictatorships and juntas were being replaced by democracies and so were beginning to engage in a more mature type of voting than the old days, when even right-wing regimes would support the Third World just to stick it to the West. Nevertheless, it was a stunning piece of isolation for the West and made one wonder what it must have been like in the bad, old days of the Cold War. Although having said that, the real power base at the UN lay in the Western-dominated Security Council.

Still, as a grand talking shop, and as a forum where matters can be at least raised, the General Assembly was a necessary and important arena. It is the only international body which even the most cynical of despotic countries take half-seriously and where sworn enemies sit down together. Or even sit beside each other like Iran, Iraq and Israel. Better jaw-jaw than war-war, as Churchill said, even if the jaw-jaw is often just an airing of grievances rather than an attempt at genuine dialogue.

By 1990, the stock of UN was in the ascendant after relative successes in Cambodia and Afghanistan. A so-called New World Order was about to ensue and the UN was to play a central role — Iraq being the first country to test its mettle. With the break-up of the Soviet Union, and then of Yugoslavia, a whole bunch of new Members came in filling up the blank seats at the back. Statehood was an amorphous and constantly changing thing; Czechoslovakia splits and we all move down a seat, Germany unites and we all move back. Inspired by the new spirit of internationalism, smaller and smaller countries wanted to join. In 1991, it was Liechtenstein. A year later, the Marshall Islands and Micronesia. I almost expected *Mouse on the Moon*-era Peter Sellers to walk in with the delegation of the Duchy of Grand Fenwick.

As it was, there were countries here I'd never heard of and which I'd be hard put to find on a map. Saint Vincent and the Grenadines — it sounded like a reggae band. And, in the spirit of 1950s ska, they even looked like one. Vanuatu, it sounded obscene. There were three Guineas — Guinea, Guinea-Bissau and Equatorial Guinea — each from a different continent. Other excellent names included São Tomé and Príncipe, Burkina Faso and, our old friend, St Kitts and Nevis. (To help with orientation, we were issued with a floor plan, which ever ready Virgil was already putting to good use by circling with a pen those 'countries' which caught his fancy.)

And then there were the countries with Observer Status, the ones literally waiting in the wings on a sort of subs bench at the side of the chamber, with just one delegate each. In this limbo group, we had Monaco, the Holy See, which had lost most of its temporal power, Palestine, which didn't yet exist, and Cyprus which did but which was divided. As was Korea and, since neither of Koreas recognised the other, they had postponed the chance of getting a seat each. This official invisibility even went as far as the Koreas not being named on the floor plan. Instead, they were put on the subs bench, with the Vatican between them, presumably to stop them from leaning over and slapping each other.

Also on the bench was Switzerland, adhering to its strict policy of neutrality, (although it would ultimately join in 1996). A seat each was also given to international bodies like the Organisation of African Unity, the League of Arab States and the European Commission. I was not the only Irish delegate in the room; the EU and Holy See were often represented by Irish people. Indeed, in the early Nineties, a large number of Irish people represented the EU abroad. Sometimes they, and Irish people in the UN, came and joined us in Jameson's.

By day, the Vatican delegate, a red-faced Kerry priest, would come over to the Irish seat for a chat. He was always looking for GAA scores and the news from home. Because I had to face towards the podium, while I talked to him, it sometimes looked like he was hearing my confession. I could see the other delegations nudging each other. Ah, there's Ireland getting advice from the Vatican. After he left, the Italian would give me a reassuring nod; we're in the same boat. But Napoleon felt that the priest was outstaying his welcome and would make brusque body movements which told him to get lost. 'Don't let that fellow hang around here,' he said sharply and I could suddenly feel the anti-clerical resentment of a generation older than mine.

By now, Gerry and the Gang had returned from their encounter with the Algerians, joined by the Vanessa and McKee, who had come in from their Committees. There were now so many of us that we had to take some of the Israeli seats, as they had earlier taken ours, a reciprocity which gave rise to mild jokes about 'invasions' and 'occupied territories', jokes which did something to temper the mood of their Foreign Minister, David Levy, who stared at Collins, remembering him from a recent ill-tempered EU Troika trip to Israel.

Collins was oblivious. He was Collins of Arabia, after all, and he barked at his gang for papers and instructions. 'Where's my brief? What time do I meet the Vietnamese?' Collins was a combative figure, in part as a defence mechanism against the smart-aleck mandarins, whom he knew had such controlling instincts. But, in this, he was at least a solid and reliable figure and, compared to other ministers, there were no gaffes or sudden, wayward initiatives. He also had that curious habit, akin to a mobster from another era, of turning rank on its head and being complimentary to serviles like myself and other Third Secs. 'You're the only one doing any work around here!' he'd say and go on to berate the seniors in front of us, an awkward moment which we could be punished for just witnessing.

No more than when they were being berated the way Napoleon was now. Collins was quizzing him about the schedule and Napoleon was dithering. Collins knew Napoleon from our Northern Irish Bunker in Maryfield and there was no love lost. 'Well, are the Hungarians before or after?' asked Gerry.

'Eh...' hesitated Napoleon, leaning forward, while the others leaned well back. 'Buck it! Do you know anything at all?' said Collins loudly, and he ostentatiously turned to Dorr for clarification. Napoleon reddened; dressed down in front of his colleagues, not to mention the Israelis and Guatemalans. The Iraqis were watching too but they'd be used to this sort of stuff.

When he wasn't making lively remarks and studying his brief, Gerry was on the look out for Ireland's friends. 'I'm going down to talk to Genscher,' he'd say and he'd get up suddenly and go down to the congratulate the newly united Germany. Germany had been officially reunited the day before at the CSCE Conference. (It is customary for the Foreign Minister to be congratulated after his or her speech but so many people clamoured to congratulate the Germans that the President had to ask for calm in the Assembly to allow the hapless Zambian on the rostrum to be heard.) Usually, on these forays, I would get a tap on the shoulder to go after the Minister. Like a tottering child, he must not be allowed to wander unattended.

Collins successor as Minister, David Andrews, was even more prone to these wanders around the chamber. In between bilaterals in the Chinese Lounge, he would announce that he was off 'for a cup of tea' and throw the schedule-obsessed officials into a panic. I was sent after him but, when I caught up, Andrews told me not to worry. He seemed to enjoy putting those boys on edge. Now that he was Minister, he resented being 'controlled' by officials and wanted to offer initiatives of his own, such as a later UN speech on Somalia. By contrast, Collins kept tightly to his brief, which made him ideal for the Civil Servants. However, the only problem with a politician with few ideas is that it gives incentive to ambitious officials to compete for his ear. Or in this case, his speech. And there was usually a bit of a dogfight for the General Assembly speech.

Much of it had to do with personalities. Personal relations have a lot to do with shape of a speech; competing personalities who might have fallen out over something trivial such as a posting or a conversation in a pub will then struggle over language which could mean the difference between Ireland condemning Iraq's invasion of Kuwait or merely criticising it strongly; differences which can have quite different impacts on the people targeted.

Of course, in the fine-tuning of language, the key factors are always those of ideology and policy, but the desire of a mandarin to make a personal impact may be the final determining element. Thus, in New York, we had the overlapping and sometimes quite different drafting skills of the ultra-cautious Dorr, the equally cautious but more direct Murphy and the user-friendly, sound-bite oriented Press Officer.

Such infighting thrived on idleness. The fact that so many mandarins were here, sitting behind the nameplate in New York, when they would usually be hyper-busy in their rooms at home, only encouraged them to put their ladles in. They were also sitting behind each other, and so could comment on each others drafts almost before the ink was dry. But the real struggle was with the people who weren't there at all; the sections back in HQ sending out references which 'must go in' or 'must come out', depending on a changing international situation. On this occasion the most notable of these was Dermot 'Dag' Gallagher, in Anglo-Irish Division, who wanted to insert some tough language on Northern Ireland about the behaviour of the security forces there, as well as an update on the chances for political progress.

But when his draft language arrived it was too long, taking up a whole two pages of an eight page speech. The others weren't happy with this, and neither was the Minister who didn't want awkward references to the North to spoil his international moment, his one big opportunity to get expansive on the New World Order and geo-political trends.

There was also the existing sensitive theology about how the question of the North should be addressed at the UN — which was basically hardly at all. There had been a time when the North was constantly raised at the UN and other fora, but this had ultimately only bored foreigners already well aware of our historic quarrel.

The Security Council did discuss the North when the conflict re-ignited in 1969 but with Britain sitting alongside its Western Allies as Permanent Members, discussion on this torturous inter-European dispute was not something which the Council wanted to get into. Constantly raising the issue also gave the impression that we were continuously at war, which was not the impression the South wished to give when it was trying to develop itself as a modern State and attract jobs and investment. By 1980, Haughey, briefly, and then Fitzgerald realised that the only way to get progress on the North was to engage with the British rather than keep shouting at them in international fora.

Any doubts about the merits of this approach were dispelled by watching other States raise their bilateral disputes, which they did with great gusto in the opening weeks — a bitter series of exchanges which enlivened the homogeneity of Members' Statements. There were harsh words between India and Pakistan over Kashmir, between Greece and Turkey over Cyprus and the Aegean, between Colombia and Ecuador over land, between Hungary and Czechoslovakia over a dam and ethnic minorities, and between Armenia and Azerbaijan, over minorities also. The attacks produced replies which in turn provoked counter replies. The whole business was greeted with a collective groan, especially the more familiar disputes where the language hadn't changed in decades.

Not raising Northern Ireland was thus a sign of maturity; you have the ability to think beyond your main grievance. One of the reasons why Greece is treated with such impatience in the UN, and contempt within the EU, is that it never stops talking about the Turks and about Cyprus.

There was a stridency of language to these attacks, and an old style nationalism, which Ireland, at least officially, has fought hard to get beyond. And it is surely significant that after all the bluff and bluster, which gets them nowhere, many of these States, like India and Pakistan or Greece and Turkey, are only now sitting down and working out their problems through negotiation and settlement.

Having said that, Northern Ireland was still mentioned — very much so. Before the Peace Process, the UN General Assembly speech was regarded as one of the major opportunities abroad for summing up the situation and for mentioning those specific aspects which needed highlighting. The rarity of their mentions meant that, when they came, they had a more telling effect, especially if they were those sticks which the British, through their legendary stubbornness, had given us to beat them with, such as the Gibraltar débâcle or the then continuing lack of enquiry into Bloody Sunday.

Usually, the overall reference was couched in the 'peace-speak' which I would later become more familiar with when I worked in Anglo-Irish Division. Basically, the Irish Government was 'working with the British Government, and the main political parties in the North to find a framework which would satisfy all sides and provide the basis for a lasting peace'. The statement would also deplore violence of all sorts but would criticise the injustice and discrimination still prevalent in the North. It might also be useful to mention issues such as the apparent 'shoot-to-kill' policy of the security forces, or the continuing incarceration of the Birmingham Six.

There was, thus, a balance to be struck, but for this General Assembly, the speech had become something of a struggle, with Dag back in HQ reluctant to whittle down his language, and the mandarins out here saying there wasn't enough space. Meanwhile, the Press Officer was complaining about the delay, since he wanted to pass advance copies to the Press, both here and in Dublin. Also, as often happened in the UN, the Minister's time slot was drifting away. Due to overruns caused not least by those recriminative exchanges on bilateral disputes but also by the sycophantic bursts of applause which greeted others, the schedule had fallen way behind. Already a few States were being bumped on to the next day, sending Collins further into tomorrow afternoon, and even into the evening. 'Save your scratching,' he told the mandarins toiling away on his statement, 'we won't be getting out of here for a while.'

The next day, the time slot for Ireland's statement continued to slip away as Ministers and Premiers basked in the applause they wouldn't get at home. The President of the Assembly was not the most effective of Chairmen. Indeed, he was quite an eccentric character, with jokey rulings from the chair and a deep, guttural manner of introduction which was quickly mimicked by the younger delegates. Especially when he began introducing countries by their wrong names — the potential for confusion here was ample.

After lunch many of the delegates became much more friendly and effusive and the changes in some between morning and afternoon was often staggering. Clearly it was more than a prawn sandwich they were having in the Delegates Lounge.

As the afternoon became evening, the Chamber began to empty of its Ministers and more senior diplomats. 'At this rate,' said Collins sourly, 'the only people listening to me will be fifty bored Third Secretaries'.

Particularly disappointing was the four o'clock threshold, which meant he had missed the nine o'clock TV news at home. The Press Officer concentrated instead on newspaper coverage and the next morning's radio shows. Where once he, or she, was purely a 'spokesperson', the Press Officer has now, with the new spin culture, become a more pro-active position, talking up some 'stories' and bargaining with journalists to get others 'killed'.

The struggle for the speech, meanwhile, resolved itself dramatically, when in an apparent fit of pique at not being able to keep in all his language on the North, Dag dropped his reconciliation stuff, rendering the text much more critical of the British than one might have expected. Gerry rose to deliver and, we watched, stiff-backed from our little desk republic, as he made the long march to the podium.

As Collins spoke from the UN podium I could see the CG 'checking against delivery' and nodding his head appreciatively as Collins ended each paragraph, as if the Minister reading in public was some kind of major achievement.

By contrast, his successor, David Andrews, was wont to abandon the prescribed text. In 1992, his speech was almost entirely devoted to one issue, the famine in Somalia, from where he had just returned. The speech was hard-hitting and critical of the EU, especially the Commission, about whose bureaucracy and indifference in the region, Andrews was scathing. With its stark and emotional language, Andrews' speech was also a departure from the more generalised references to famine usually made by Western countries, including Ireland. It was, in a sense, a brief reassertion of Ireland's traditional role of highlighting hunger and injustice abroad, a role undermined by continued movement towards European Union and the synchronising of Western opinion.

Andrews' speech didn't discriminate in its targets for it also attacked African countries, and specifically Somalia's neighbours, for not doing enough about the situation. As the speech concluded, our Ambassador from Washington, who had come up for the occasion, asked me to go down towards the Somalian desk and check on their reaction.

Quietly, I crept down the aisle to check, but the seats were empty; the Somalians had left and the Ethiopians were at the bar. Not being able to feed their own people was a way of life for these countries, as was holding some of the most sumptuous receptions in the UN and travelling around in the biggest cars. It was a joke around the UN; the smaller the country, the bigger the car. (Or, the smaller the country, the longer the speech.) Each morning, as we came in on foot, we would see some of the Africans arriving at the Delegates Entrance in their sleek black limos, although their Missions were only a few blocks away. Doors were opened, and in they walked, proud and sullen as peacocks, content that no suppressed dissident or tame parliament in their own country could ever touch them.

When Collins finished his speech a mob of officials and VIPs descended on him to congratulate him. Even the Holy See managed to get in amongst us, an image somewhat at odds with the our new-found desire to keep them at a pluralistic distance. Eventually the Minister withdrew, followed quickly by senior mandarins, Ambassadors and the Consul General. It was such a sudden movement of 'follow the leader' that the General Assembly floor was truncated by a line of dark-suited Irish officials. The 'goods train', as Napoleon described it, was leaving the chamber with the carriages periodically shunting as Gerry stopped to receive handshakes from the Moroccans and 'my good friends, the Kuwaitis'.

Afterwards Gerry was taken by officials to his favourite downtown restaurant, Astis, an Italian joint on 12th Street with a flashing red neon sign outside and singing waiters inside. 'Astis!' he insisted, whenever they tried to suggest perhaps some other 'interesting French place'.

After the Minister went to bed, his senior officials joined the permanent UN crowd in Jameson's on Second Avenue, along with errant Semi-Staters and journalists. Wherever the Minister goes in the world, be it Tokyo, Buenos Aires or Addis Ababa, the senior squad always expect the respective Mission to come out and party with them.

Jameson's was at the heart of a cluster of Irish bars on Second Avenue, between 44th and 48th Streets, a midtown party zone which always had a floating traffic of idle suits and out-of-towners. In the evenings, you'd see young office workers in the windows of cheesy cocktail bars raising a toast with Happy Hour daiquiris. Later, on Consulate duty, I would stop off here as I came back from Irish-American dances in Queens, the bridge returning me to the stomping ground of new Irish immigrants and feckless young professionals flush with money.

The Ambassador didn't join us in the pub; nor did the Secretary or Minister. Collins didn't mix much with the Department socially and even pretended to frown on the late night revelry. There was a story about him in Washington coming back early from a private dinner expecting, with almost childish delight, to find the mandarins passing around the brandy, only to burst in and find them working, surrounded by their papers.

However, the Minister must have muttered the venue to his foreign colleagues for one night someone found the Dutch Foreign Minister, Van Den Broek, wandering along Second Avenue and looking for the pub — 'Mr Collins said that you would be here.' Other Missions frequented this Second Avenue stretch, especially the Australians and New Zealanders who would go there to watch the televised cricket and rugby games. For us, it was just pure chat and mimicry. In revenge for his humiliation at the hands of the Minister, Napoleon would do impersonations of Collins and the more servile officials, sending us all into laughter.

The stories of Ministers' spouses when they're abroad were part of DFA folklore — the husband who wanted an entire museum re-opened on a Sunday, or the wife who wanted all the carpets changed in an Embassy. One had to be careful not to laugh too much at this kind of thing but, unlike in Hourican's at home, the fact that you were now abroad, and experiencing such behaviour, gave you a new status and thus a certain latitude in the eyes of the senior mandarins.

Napoleon particularly warmed to younger diplomats, testing them with questions, anecdotes and punchlines so obscure you'd have to be a sophist to work out the joke. 'That is the joke!' he'd say, spluttering into laughter. For Napoleon, it was the best time of the year, living it up with the visiting delegates.

Unfortunately, Napoleon wanted it to go on and on, and later he would keep up the fun without us, befriending some of the dodgier African delegates and getting a new team together for the Second Avenue pubs. 'Drinking with mass murderers,' was how one colleague harshly put it, although in fairness, such socialising gave Napoleon invaluable contacts. It was also an understandable respite from the long hours he put in, monitoring the Security Council debates on the Balkans and Middle East. (Napoleon was always on the watch out. At one stage, the EU countries had a barring order on meeting Iraq, but convinced that the French would break it — the French were so distrusted among EU colleagues — Napoleon, at the behest of the Spanish, asked me to keep a close eye on them.)

Our senior people had that ability, common in Irish life, of being able to stay up very late, drink heroically and yet remain very much together. Often, they were defusing, or burning off adrenalin. But the younger of us had still to learn these skills. One night I got lost on the way back to the hotel and walked in the wrong direction.

I was over on the Westside and a young fur-coated woman approached, gripping my hand and asking if I'd like 'to party'. 'No thanks,' I said but, in taking my hand, she'd also taken my watch. Cleanly; I didn't even notice it go. When I discovered the theft, I wobbled back to confront her, eventually finding her standing outside a café with a bunch of hyena-faced men, who just laughed at me.

Instead, I stumbled into a cab but I was short of money so when I got back to the hotel, not only did I have to sign in but I had to ask Dracula's butler, the startled doorman, to arrange a loan from reception. I paid it back the next day, of course, but it registered on my hotel bill: months later, in an impressive display of retrospective accounting, Accounts branch sent me a letter asking why I'd borrowed five dollars from the Plaza 50. I told them I got lost in a taxi but resisted telling them the rest of the story. Nor did I tell the person who had given me the watch, an ex-girlfriend, that I had lost it 'to a hooker in New York'. Even if she accepted my innocence I don't think she'd be pleased to hear that it was now sitting on the wrist of some Manhattan pimp.

The next morning, we were all in the Mission, preparing for another day. The mandarins, busy fine-tuning briefs and statements, acted as if nothing had happened — as if we hadn't been skulling pints at four a.m. But the younger ones were suffering and I could see Eamon McKee holding his temples and trying to keep the headache at bay, as I was. Meanwhile, it was another big morning at the General Assembly, with Foreign Ministers and Prime Ministers floating around, whilst in the Chinese Lounge Vanessa and Martin were holding the seats.

Often, the Chinese Lounge bilaterals fell through. A Foreign Minister may be suddenly unavailable and the roster is filled by another country. Bilaterals can also fall through for more dramatic reasons, such as a political crisis at home. It was one of the features of the General

Assembly, that with so many Premiers and Ministers away in New York, there was bound to be mischief at home. Many's the ruler who has made a fine and stirring speech, only to come off the podium and discover he has no country. It was a bit like one of those Royal Weddings or funerals in London where, by the ceremony's end, some part of the Commonwealth was in revolt.

With sudden changes in bilaterals, new Speaking Notes had to be hastily drawn up. 'Quick, what do we know about Uzbekistan?' the Political Director would say, turning around in the seat. With his pen at the ready, it was a flattering consultation, but it also put you on the spot. 'Uzbekistan. Well, it's big ...' said Michael, half messing, and I duly offered some dimly remembered details from the Soviet desk.

Strange trade-offs were raised in bilaterals. Seeking our support for their election to the Board of UNESCO, the Turks mentioned their co-operation in helping us recover the Beit Painting. 'The painting has still not been returned!' wrote an official on the fax from HQ, 'but we'll vote for them anyway.' All kinds of horse-trading went on to secure votes There was a story that Israel, pressuring Sri Lanka not to support an Arab-led resolution against them had made convenient mention of the fact that, for years, Sri Lanka was being supplied with artificial limbs by Israel, who were specialists in the art after decades of war.

The implication was clear. Sri Lanka should now help out Israel or all those victims of the Tamil Tigers lacking arms and legs will have to get themselves wheeled around Colombo. The story is probably apocryphal but it sums up the grim mixture of politics and humanity which is the United Nations.

While the Minister and gang went to their bilaterals, McKee and I stayed in the seat, nursing our hangovers. We were in giggly form, a giddiness enhanced by the sight of so many important faces in the room. For the General Assembly is not just Foreign Ministers and

Premiers. Every few years, a country would send its Number one, so we got a fair few Crown Princes, Presidents and Queens. From Africa and Asia, came Sultans and heaven-descended monarchs, forced to explain themselves to a room full of barely attentive bureaucrats, a prospect which, paradoxically, seemed to fill them pleasure. Ah, the world stage.

My hangover really kicked in after an over-excited Danish colleague came over to tell us about how his Foreign Minister's party had gone hooking for bluefish off Long Island. It was an interesting story but the man was so animated, that I suddenly needed a break. 'Baby sharks. Have you ever fished for baby sharks?' he cried and I could see McKee staring at him through bloodshot eyes.

I slipped out to the Chinese Lounge. Surprisingly empty, the ASEAN group were in conclave, so I sat on one of the big white armchairs to steady myself. But not for long. Suddenly, there was rush of people towards me. It was the Israelis and the Egyptians, Foreign Ministers David Levy and Abu Mousa, followed by a battery of photographers. Usually the media is excluded from the chamber, but due to tensions, these two hadn't met for some time, and there was considerable interest.

I quickly vacated the seat but unfortunately just as I did so, I let off a horrible Guinness-matured fart which lingered stubbornly around the seats that the Egyptians and Israelis were sitting into. I had visions of next day's newspapers in Cairo and Tel Aviv showing pictures of Mousa and Levy with noses more wrinkled and disdainful than the occasion merited. One could almost hear the Middle Eastern sceptics in the cafés; 'You see Ahmed, look at their faces — they are not happy with this peace process.'

Suddenly, from behind an alcove, I could see Gerry and the gang bowing and curtseying to the Vietnamese and I quickly got back to the chamber, where the newly elected President of Nicaragua, Violeta Chamorro, was on the podium, resplendent in a white suit. Ms Chamorro finished to applause and a sort of half-hearted standing ovation. It was hard to tell. So many people were getting in and out of their seats anyway, arranging bilaterals and preparing for their own speeches. Amongst them were our Minister and mandarins returned from their bilateral meeting in the Chinese Lounge. They would be leaving that afternoon.

With most of their work done, the Minister and his party relaxed a bit. There had been good press coverage of Collins' speech and tonight he would be on the TV news in Ireland. Right now, he was preparing for the EU lunch at the Omni Carlton and the always welcome chance of a chin-wag with Genscher, Ordonez and the rest of *Les Douze*.

However, he had not been in such good form earlier and, seeing the hungover condition of some of the officials, he badgered them with even more intemperate demands. Napoleon again came in for public stick; 'Jesus, you smell like a brewery,' he said, waving him away. But mostly, he was only having a joke.

Collins also complained about the Press Summary, which was given to all officials each morning. The Press Summary is a daily one-sheet synopsis of the Irish newspapers and radio, done early in the morning by the Third Secretary in Press Section in Dublin and sent to all missions — it is an important instant fix on the stories in Ireland. Usually, it shows the hand of whoever compiled it, and, for some time now, this one reflected the racing interest of its bow-tied compiler, Ben Whitty, an avid form-studier. Thus, before the GAA scores and soccer, we got the winners at the Curragh or even more obscure race meets in the midlands. It was a bit of fun, really. But not for the Minister, who now had the time to go through the summary pedantically and at length.

Eventually his annoyance passed and Collins sat back and enjoyed the rest of the speeches. He was much bemused by the walkouts, when delegates left their seats to show disapproval of a speaker. It was very common gesture in the chamber, especially in our corner. 'So you're away then?' he said to a delegate who didn't wish to have his rude departure so explicitly recognised. Some walkouts are supposed to be discreet.

'Excuse me?' asked the delegate.

'I said, you're off then?' said Gerry, as if he was chatting to someone leaving a bar counter. He smiled as he said it and, behind him, some of the mandarins were sniggering.

There is, of course, a whole art to sitting in the chamber, and leaving it; the different types of walkout, the weak or strong handclap, the reduced presence behind the nameplate. In the opening week, the impact of walkout was muted relative to their effect later on when the place settled down, but it was still quite a conspicuous choreography. For example, two delegates might walk out and two stay. Or rather than leave the seat completely empty, you could have just the Third Sec; 'the worst kind of insult,' said the Ambassador with a little laugh. Ha, ha. The other trick, used by some of the Arab countries, was to leave a delegate sitting on one of the back seats, as if he'd just plonked down there by accident and wasn't in control of the nameplate.

But the EU countries stayed in their seats for all the speeches. About the only thing they walked out for was lunch in the Plaza, and seeing Genscher and Van De Broek rising from their seats, Collins gave the signal, 'Right, lads, it's time to go'. Vanessa, myself and McKee were left behind the nameplate. Uffe Elleman Jensen, the Danish Foreign Minister, passed us, followed by a train of flunkeys. 'More bluefish?' whispered McKee to our friend, but the usually garrulous Danish delegate shot us a dark 'I'm too busy to talk now' look.

Later that afternoon, US President George Bush addressed the assembly, giving his famous 'New World Order' speech, but by then the limos were ferrying Collins and party to the airport. Back in our Mission, empty desks were strewn with abandoned texts and everyone could breathe a little easier. 'Right, to Jameson's!' shouted Napoleon to an immediate chorus of agreement.

9

Horse-trading on Human Rights

The next day, there were speeches by more heads of Government and Foreign Ministers but within a week the General Assembly had settled into its normal pattern of long, monotonous debates about specific issues and me sitting on my own behind the nameplate. The novelty had worn off and a certain kind of boredom descended, relieved only by looking around and by surreptitious reading of the newspaper. You were not allowed to read newspapers in the Chamber — excepting our Libyan friend whom people were too scared to stop — and so delegates would smuggle in photocopies.

Despite the colourful characters and the often historic speeches, the General Assembly is famous for its boredom. I remember watching John Pilger's searing TV documentary *Cambodia in the Year 10*. After the pictures of malnourished children, Pilger damningly showed footage of the General Assembly during the Cambodian debate. 'And what are the Australian delegation doing during this important debate?' he asked, sarcastically and the camera would pan to the Australian desk. 'Oh, they're reading the newspaper. And the Americans … oh, they're asleep,' and the camera would show some bloke nodding off. Pilger was using the delegates' behaviour as a metaphor for international indifference on Cambodia.

I shared his outrage until I went to sit in the GA for three sessions. The Cambodian debate lasted for about eight hours, with dozens of countries trooping up to express the pious hope that the relevant parties in

Cambodia could negotiate a settlement. Who could blame the Australians for pulling out the crossword? (Or the New Zealand delegates for drawing up their All-Time Best Cricket 15?) Besides the Cambodian debate was riven with hypocrisy, for it was the bizarre 'even-handedness' of the UN which had sustained the Khmer Rouge as a negotiating force in Cambodian politics and resulted in that country's seat being left empty. But only a few brave countries were prepared to address this in their speeches.

One time, I was chatting to the Liechtenstein delegate when a Kuwaiti turned around and glared at me; we were 'talking' during the Palestine debate. His reaction was nonsensical given that some delegates practically gave each other high-fives during serious debates and the hugging and kissing Central Americans fell upon each other in a Latin frenzy whenever they met in the aisles. No, this was just Kuwait 'getting back to normal'. After the Gulf War, when the Kuwaitis had got their country back, and killed thousands of Palestinians in the process, they wanted to show that they were back 'being concerned' about Palestine again, just like the rest of the Arab world.

In fact, the Palestine debate takes up to three days; 'debate' being a rather glorious name for a series of almost identical statements attacking Israel which, ironically, they do not recognise as actually being in the chamber. And if that is not enough, there are three more General Assembly debates on Israel. The issue of Palestine takes up to 20% of the GA's time, while the situation of the Kurds, for example, gets none. No wonder Ed Koch, Mayor of New York wanted the UN moved out of the city, especially when it passed the infamous 'Zionism is Racism' resolution (reversed in 1993).

And, whatever about Cambodia, the Palestine debate is surely the pinnacle of hypocrisy. For the Gulf States in particular, the Palestinians are a useful political football. They bleat on about the issue and yet their own record on the Palestinians is appalling; refusing them citizenship, keeping them in refugee camps so as to sustain the problem and regarding them as a radicalised threat to their own oligarchical regimes. It comes as no surprise to hear that most of the funding for UNRWA and other Palestinian support agencies came not from the rich Gulf States but from the EU.

Some of the accusations were rich indeed. We had Mauritania, which had legalised slavery, attacking Western countries for their treatment of refugees. Or Iran talking about the Group Areas Act in apartheid South Africa — this from a theocracy which had executed thousands. The South African issue was particularly rich in hypocrisy; indeed when Mandela was released and a commitment to free elections made there was almost a sense of disappointment and even panic on the part of some nations. 'Jaysus, he sounds worried,' said Napoleon, listening to one of the African speakers. Not only would the age-old whipping boy be gone, but a new South Africa would be an indictment to the corruption and division in the rest of the region.

It was particularly important to have someone's else problem to point at, especially if the problem was the West's. Nor need there be any sense of proportion. 'Hey, it's like the 1930s again,' said the jolly Guatemalan obscurely one morning, 'we should all be wearing those little hats!' I had no idea what he was talking about until I realised he was referring to the racist attacks in Europe, and particularly in Germany, which the *New York Times* was predictably comparing to the 1930s. The *Times* gave the issue wide coverage and, even within the cocoon of the UN, it showed the vice-like grip of that paper on the city's middle-class chatter. (Later, at downtown parties I would hear whole chunks of *NYT* coverage and opinion coming back at me over a cocktail glass.)

Of course, the racist attacks in Europe were appalling but it seemed strange to get a ribbing about it from the delegate of Guatemala, which had tortured and killed thousands of its own people. But that didn't matter. What was important was that it was 'making the news'. Ha, ha, you're on the front page. In his speech to the General Assembly, the German Foreign Minister, Klaus Kinkel, recognised this and forcefully listed the huge numbers of immigrants then entering Germany, numbers which would put the rest of Europe, including Ireland, to shame.

The disintegration of Yugoslavia was a great opportunity for non-European countries to wag their fingers and, granted, the crisis was to Europe's shame — and to the EU's shame — from beginning to end. But there was something about the way the phrase 'ethnic cleansing' was used repeatedly in every speech by delegates from countries which had been carved out of ethnic cleansing that made one suspicious. Ethnic cleansing: they couldn't get enough of the words. And then you realised that it wasn't so much the practise, as the fact that it was named, which made it so offensive and which provided such a wonderful stick to beat the Europeans.

The Yugoslavia crisis had a strange effect on other states, especially the European ones. I asked one of the Greek delegates about the situation in Macedonia.

'I'm sorry, I don't know what you mean.'

'You know, the situation in Macedonia.'

'There is no such place.' she said, staring at me and then I remembered that the Greeks had a policy of not recognising Macedonia because they considered it part of their country. They wanted the ex-Yugoslav bit to be called Skopje, after its capital. This was the official policy, but I didn't think that their delegates were going to keep up this nonsense.

'Okay, the other Macedonian part,' I said, 'the part in Yugoslavia.'

'I am sorry,' she said, like an automaton, for this still wasn't good enough. 'I don't where you mean. I must go now.' When she got back to her desk, she looked over at me, as if to say that was a performance, and we all know it was, but I am not going to blink.

Later, when the GA wasn't in session, I helped out on the Committees, where the hypocrisy was even worse. The Third Committee dealt with Human Rights, but the whole basis of the Committee was bargaining over language. Because consensus was needed, resolutions would get watered down to nothing, just like at the CSCE, except, instead of thirty-five countries, you now had the whole world putting its oar in.

Suffice to say that half the countries in the room didn't really appreciate the concept of human rights and found the Western preoccupation with the idea quaint and worthy. Countries like Iran and Indonesia just didn't understand why a Government would want to give up the idea of having a controlled press and the right to throw people into jail when it wished. Indeed, they found it almost decadent that a Government would abandon such responsibilities.

Instead, they would use the old Soviet-bloc trick of talking about Social Order and Economic and Social Rights, which are not really rights at all. In fairness, they really believed in these concepts. It's okay for you, they'd say, to talk about people having 'uncensored access to computers', but we'd like to get computers for our people in the first place. The West already had most of the world's resources — in 1990 it was about to launch a war to secure its oil supply — and with such luxuries they could afford to sit back and lecture others on the rights of free association and assembly. Our people are so hungry, one delegate said, that if we let them demonstrate freely, they'd pull down the Government!

There was so much horse-trading about resolutions at the Third Committee that there was a continuous hubbub at the back of the room, which delegates from other Committees found intriguing. People were constantly getting up out of their seats and making hand signals to draw each other away for quick consultations. It was like the Ballinasloe Horse Fair except instead of brown mares and ponies, it was Draft Resolutions (DRs) on Cambodia or Eastern Europe.

It is the sort of culture which suits gregariousness and personal relations and I am convinced that this is why the Cubans had the extraordinarily high profile they did. Of course, it was their mission to use the UN as much as possible, as it was for all the Communist countries — making hay while the Americans and others arrogantly ignored it — and they were constantly on the move, cajoling and persuading whereas the more wooden North Europeans would sit there silently, wondering why support for their resolutions was being eaten away. The other interesting thing was the degree of respect the Cubans got from other South American countries, even the right-wing ones. Geographical and ethnic loyalty transcended ideology. The Cubans were sticking it to the gringos and the other Latins respected them for it.

By contrast, the Western leaders, the Americans and the British seemed to have no sensitivity at times. From bitter experience, the Americans had learned to carry a big stick and speak quietly but the British seemed to speak loudly and carry no stick at all. It always amazed me how unreflective the British diplomats were of the British people and culture I knew and liked. They were to a man "clubable" Sandhurst types, white and male, with an air of academic disarray, a bookish doggedness, with which they looked down their noses at everybody.

They would constantly intervene in debates with the most pedantic and arrogant of observations — it was a sort of 'we're on the look out for you UN types, don't you worry'. They also had a really annoying habit of often waiting until the last minute, just before an item vote, and then voicing objections. They did this in the General Assembly and it pissed off everybody. The behaviour of such individuals affects how a country is perceived. There is, after all, an art to diplomacy, but the British didn't care. Neither did they seem to realise that their methods were doing the very opposite to what was intended, and losing them support.

Before a DR can be canvassed around the floor, co-sponsors for the resolution have to be assembled and a draft agreed, usually on the basis of language suggested by the lead country. Once the DR is circulated, other states can join in and co-sponsor, as they wish, or they can drop out. With the draft in circulation, a related battle ensues for its language to be toughened or watered down. The country which is the subject of the DR will obviously be alert and will canvass against it, or better still, get other countries to do so. Sometimes the connection between the subject country and the countries working on its behalf can be tenuous and unexpected.

In the case of the EU and likeminded States, the lead country initiating the DR language, was the Presidency, which in Autumn 1990 was Italy, and at one stage we had great difficulty getting a DR on the human rights situation in Iran. At an upstairs meeting, the young Italian who chaired the meeting was perspiring and had loosened his tie, a rare fashion *faux pas* for an Italian diplomat. He was obviously under a lot of pressure. It was clear that, behind the scenes, the Iranians were leaning on the Italians to water down the DR, if not withdraw it altogether. The situation was made more difficult by the fact that the DR was based on the report of the Special Rapporteur (SR) of the UN who had visited Iran and made a fairly damning report. There were now suggestions that the SR may have gone too far, or 'beyond his brief' as it was put, a charge that drew great umbrage from the British and Dutch who wanted to get tough on Iran.

Words were haggled over and phrases bandied to and fro, with delegates saying they would have leave the room to get new instructions. Almost all the discussion was in English — the French attempts to have it fifty-fifty at EU meetings was a losing battle — and since I was one of only two delegates with English as a first language, I kept getting asked for new and more precise phrasing.

One of the words the Italians wanted to change was a reference to 'accounts' of atrocities which they regarded as too strong, but the Dutch thought that the replacement of 'rumours' was too weak — it almost made the SR's sources sound like speculative gossip. I suggested 'reports' which was gratefully seized on.

'Ah, yes, reports. Reports is the one,' said the Spaniard, 'this way it can be either true or untrue!' But I don't think that was the SR's point.

At least this resolution was eventually passed. The one on Myanmar collapsed, much to the embarrassment of its Swedish initiators and other likeminded countries, including most of the EU.

Since 1988, Myanmar, formerly known as Burma, had been under the ruthless control of the military who ignored the overwhelming election victory of the opposition Democratic Party led by Aung San Suu Kyi and outlawed them.

Myanmar was a tricky one for countries such as Australia and New Zealand, who blow hot and cold on the issue, for fear of upsetting the Asian countries in their region with whom they live and trade. China is also very sceptical about Western agitation on the matter. Again, as with the Cubans in South America, ideological differences wilt in the face of regional or racial solidarity.

However, an interesting group had gathered in an upstairs room to co-sponsor the DR, including many East European countries. Democratisation was suddenly back in vogue — Nicaragua and Chile had just turned — and those countries who'd come through the process were anxious to help others. At one stage, the Panamanian delegate gave a spirited contribution on why they were supporting the DR, mentioning the way Noriega had tried to cancel the election results in Panama but how with 'some difficulty' democracy had triumphed.

She didn't mention that 'some difficulty' had involved an American invasion, but her listeners didn't mind, perhaps because she was young and very good looking.

(Inevitably, on Virgil's floor plan, the Panama seat had been ringed and re-ringed, as had its occupant — to no avail.)

'Absolutely!' said an old guy listening to her speech and we all agreed that Panama was a very good example of stopping dictatorship.

'How does Ireland feel?' asked the Chairman.

'Ireland is in complete agreement,' I said and the Panamanian girl gave me an appreciative smile. (Mental note; must ask the Ambassador about our position.)

However, it all turned sour quick enough. We had about three meetings on the DR and each time there were fewer people in the room — the co-sponsors were being got at, as the Asians canvassed. Realising the haemorrhaging of support, the Swedes watered down the resolution, but it was too late. By the third meeting, even our Panamanian friend had mysteriously gone missing. Such was the collapse, that even the media knew what was going on, which was most unusual for a Third Committee DR, and at our final meeting, a chirpy *New York Times* reporter was hovering outside the door, waiting to write the story of 'the Western collapse'.

It turned out that Myanmar had good friends in the region and on the Assembly floor. Theirs, after all, was an 'internal situation', not involving a neighbouring country or an ethnic group, and the realisation was, that if today it's Myanmar being verbally attacked, it could be someone else tomorrow.

The most chilling example of *realpolitick*, however, was on East Timor. Indonesia is a former Dutch colony, while neighbouring East Timor was formerly Portuguese. Since 1976, however, the Indonesians had occupied East Timor, often brutally, and so when the Indonesians routinely abuse the inhabitants, the Portuguese valiantly try and speak up on their behalf. So too, to a lesser extent, do the other Portuguese-speaking countries. Portugal and its former colonies have one of more interesting and eclectic informal groupings; Brazil, Angola, Surinam and

Mozambique. It is a benign form of co-operation, which proves that in the UN, language and post-colonial links, are the other great unifiers along with geography and religion.

By 1991, the situation had worsened in East Timor and a videotape had emerged of a massacre in Dili. The tape showed the impact of the camera; atrocities are committed all the time but only with a video, or actual news footage, can the impact be brought across. The Dili video has since become famous but this was its first exposure in the West, and delegates were invited by the Portuguese group to a special showing upstairs in the UN.

The video was disturbing stuff. A hand-held camera records a East Timorese rally being broken up by gunshots from Indonesian soldiers. The protestors are pursued down a dusty road and you can see people dropping while in the background, you can hear the soldiers still shooting and picking people off.

There were gasps and sighs in the room as the events of the video unfolded. 'It's like Sharpeville,' said one delegate.

But what was amazing was the attitude of my Dutch colleague, sitting alongside. At first, he watched the video with vague disinterest, even fixing his tie, but then, as people gasped, he watched with agitation and even mild confusion — what's all the fuss about here? A diplomat's face, in such a situation, can express a whole national outlook. As can his body language for, just like at the GA, the bored delegate suddenly got up out his chair, collected his papers — with a little thud to gather them — and almost jauntily walked out. On the screen, the video was still running and the soldiers were shooting away.

I couldn't believe it, and neither could others. But later, we heard that the Dutch were quietly — very quietly — canvassing against the video on behalf of the Indonesians. It was the usual line; the video was only one 'source' and could not be trusted, off-screen there were other 'agitators', possibly armed. And there was the 'wider picture'; if East Timor regained independence, the whole of Indonesia could unravel and that's not something that anyone wants.

It was an interesting revelation about the EU, that its Member States still bat on behalf of their former colonies. It was also the case that, in terms of forming EU policy, the other States usually defer to whichever Member State had formerly been there. Thus the Spanish talk about South America, the Italians about Libya, the Portuguese about Mozambique. This prompted doubt about the veracity of the information supplied by former colonial masters. Britain, for example, would always speak on India and this really pissed off some of our people who'd been posted there. Not only did they find Britain's assessment predictably self-serving, but it was usually gleaned from only one part of the political establishment. Or it was just plain wrong. It was often easy to forget that the EU was an ex-colonials club, but old habits clearly died hard.

The Dutch stance on East Timor amazed me, however, perhaps because the Dutch have this idealistic, laid-back image, with their liberal politics and their Coffee Shops — although clearly this is only one aspect of the Netherlands mind set. One day, at the back of the Third Committee room, I asked a younger Dutch delegate about East Timor. He didn't deny that they had a questionable if not reprehensible view of the situation there. 'But that's incredible,' I said, bluntly.

'You know, it's funny,' he said, after a pause, 'when I was a student in Amsterdam I used to go on big marches about East Timor, and collect petitions. But then I joined the Foreign Ministry and my views had to change.'

'Just like that?'

'Just like that,' he said, shrugging, and he gave me that laid-back smile.

10

A Walk in the Garden

Sometimes I had to escape from it all and go for a walk in the UN Garden, the concrete and shrubbery arrangement which overlooks the East River and overhangs the FDR Drive with its continuous traffic rumbling underneath. Looking across at the old warehouses and tied up rowboats of Queens, I felt that that was the real world, compared to where I was. It was also where I'd soon be going since many of the Irish-American functions that came with consular duty were held in Astoria, just across the 59th Street bridge. Late in the evening, through the big bay windows in the Delegates Lounge, you could see the lights crossing the bridge, and the red neon Coca-Cola sign glowing in the dusk. New York was always out there.

Unfortunately, here too in the Garden one was confronted by more of the UN's hypocrisy, or more accurately, that of those Member States which had contributed sculptures. Obvious symbolism abounded; bronze doves and children holding hands. A muscular piece of social realism, courtesy of the now defunct GDR, depicted a man dramatically beating his sword into a ploughshare. 'More like a metaphor for German unity,' said Vanessa. Slightly better was a sort of child-like space rocket, made out of bits of old US and Soviet missiles, their rivet lines and military markings still visible.

Best of all, however, was the huge knotted gun near the front of the building. It was like something you'd see in a student bedsit — 'Stop the violence, man' — but in its

149

rubbery coyness it was also slightly surreal, like an image from Dali or Magritte. And vaguely sexual. 'There's something for you, Virgil,' we told him one morning, in honour of our libidinous colleague. 'Put a knot it.' But not everyone was as irreverent and, as we laughed, a group of Nepalese delegates were smilingly posing in front of 'The Gun' and proudly holding up their necklace laminates: We Are Delegates. Unfortunately, they misunderstood our Freud-inspired laughter and afterwards we had to buy them coffees to repair any damage that might have been done to Irish-Nepalese relations.

The donation of art was popular and throughout the buildings were gifts from dictatorships and Arab sheikdoms, much of it clearly lifted straight out of museums and donated without any sense of accountability to their countries. It was no surprise that some of the most elaborate and expensive of gifts came from the poorest and most repressed of States. There was no gift from Ireland but given the embarrassment over the donation of Harry Clarke's windows to the UN in Geneva, I suppose we didn't want a repetition. The stained glass windows, with their beautiful depiction of the 'Diarmuid agus Gráinne' folk story, had to be withdrawn when de Valera and his joyless officials noticed that Diarmuid and Gráinne were naked. Today, the windows are in a private collection in Texas.

One of the most recognisable gifts was a large carpet version of Picasso's *Guernica*, fittingly put outside the Security Council, which meets to prevent, or institute, war. Along the corridors were other gifts, some in glass boxes, behind which you could see delegates napping on sofas. At first I was amazed by the number of people nodding off, but I forgot, of course, that for these people, naps and siestas were a way of life, just as going to Jameson's was for us.

Likewise, the endless cups of coffee, for which delegates would go to either of the Lounge areas, or downstairs to the Viennese Café. Gifts were not just art and treasures; in the style of the Swedes and their Chinese Lounge furniture, the Austrians had donated a small, open-plan café, which was always busy with haggling delegates and great hoots of multinational laughter. This was another cultural difference. While the quiet Europeans frowned and sipped their cappuccinos, the Caribbeans and Africans were slapping knees and swapping high-fives.

The café was known, ironically of course, as the Waldheim Café, in honour of the former UN Secretary General. Amazingly, he was still well respected here, despite the unmasking of his Nazi past. In fact, UN people were quite defensive about him. His bust was still in the public lobby and, in the bookshop his smiling face was among the postcard portraits of former Secretaries-General. Naturally we bought a few to send back to surprised friends, some with the addition of a Hitler moustache and the 'Order of the Oaks' medal which Waldheim received from the Nazis for his 'outstanding work' in the Balkans.

Sending the prank cards wasn't as easy as it sounds for they had to be posted from the UN. This being international territory the UN had its own post office and its own stamps and it was part of the fun for visiting delegates to send postcards to friends and family. I had to post the Minister's cards. Of all the postcards in the shop, Collins went to the International Flags Series and picked out six pictures of the Irish tricolour. No pictures of Kalahari bushmen for him. The man was a patriot and no mistake.

The people at the UN post office had the same grim and humourless approach as the rest of the UN staff. The UN staff were famous for their moodiness, a vast bureaucracy collected from the countries of the world and working for a organisation which, they felt, was underfunded and under-respected. They particularly resented us, the Visiting Delegates, and with good reason. When we weren't badgering them for more documentation, they saw us in the company of mass murderers, swanning from cushy meeting to ice-chinking reception.

This resentment was especially palpable when you went over to the Secretariat building. Going up its many floors, you'd come upon antiquated offices and faded posters of international children. On the ground floor, there was the big UN restaurant or canteen. The food wasn't bad but around you were the sullen and frustrated faces that you'd see in any large organisation, bitching about factions and internal tensions. In the General Assembly building, by contrast, there was the luxurious Delegates Restaurant, looking out over the East River. Or, the reputedly luxurious. In fact, as is often the case with these restaurants, with their ostentatious chefs and their cornucopias of fruits at the centre of the room, the food was usually heavy and creamed. But it was where the Ambassadors and the Ministers and their families came and as such it had prestige. You had to make arrangements to get a table, fighting with a fussy maître d' at the door.

To avoid the prospect of having some former torturer beside you, flambéing his pork, we went instead to the sushi or Thai places on Second Avenue. You'd go mad if you didn't a least get out of the UN at lunchtime. Appropriately enough, Napoleon was fond of the Sans Culottes, a down-home French place with salamis on the table, but he got annoyed when I wouldn't top up on the wine. I never drink at lunchtime and I didn't want to encourage him to. But I felt bad about it later. It was like I was stepping around a child. We also went to Kate Kearney's, an Irish bar and one of his favourite haunts, from where he would shortly be directing his voting strategy and drafting statements. 'So, Eamon,' he said, one day, to great laughter from the seasoned drinkers, 'do you want a drink or do you want a slap in the mouth?'

'Eh, I think I'll have a glass of Guinness,' I said. Jaysus.

Socialising inside the UN was done in the Delegates Lounges. The South Lounge was really just a bar beside the Security Council, often to be seen on news coverage when political figures stop at the railings to give sound-bites as they go into the chamber. But the North Lounge, down near the General Assembly, was more impressive, with people sitting around on leather sofas and smoking, always smoking. This is the one which featured in *North by North West*.

Our Ambassador was often to be seen prowling around here, a strange figure when seen from afar, with his hunched shoulders and a permanently suspicious expression. In keeping with the Mission's schoolhouse atmosphere, we used to run if we saw him and scarper back to our Committees — he didn't like people being away from their seats. At one end of the Lounge was the all-important bar, but, at the request of one member, the Iranians, it had recently been screened off, adding to my sense of relief at failing to get that posting in Tehran.

Upstairs in the Secretariat Building was the Press Centre, which we would drift up to each evening to get the latest news. By its very nature, it was well placed, especially since many of the big stories, like Bosnia and Iraq, were happening right here at the UN.

The Centre issued daily press releases. Thus, not only did we get the texts of all statements but there was also a summarised round-up, nicely subbed so it could be slipped into our weekly reports. Little wonder the Plenary Delegates spent their time in the GA doing the crossword or writing postcards, or in the case of a Canadian delegate, sketching. One of my Irish predecessors apparently finished her Masters Degree in the seat. The other delegates must have thought she was fierce busy when they saw her scribbling away.

Again, in the Press Centre, there was that anachronistic atmosphere, with red lights flashing on big white phones and long tables with — incredibly — manual typewriters on which the hacks could tap away.

Many journalists used the centre as their New York or even US base and there were a lot of foreign agencies and TV networks. The journalists were either those old style Walter Cronkite-types with bow ties and seersucker jackets — 'So exactly what is happening in Ireland, young man? — or the stripy-shirt types out from Fleet Street, loudly proclaiming their sulphurous opinions but better crack than their diplomatic counterparts. Next door was the Chinese News Agency, with grinning propagandists sucking on non-tipped cigarettes and tapping at their Remingtons.

The Press Centre was also responsible for the continuous TV coverage of the General Assembly which it showed live on monitors. Handy, for it meant that you could see exactly what was going on while you were away. If, by some bizarre chance, the matter of 'British-occupied Ireland' was raised by a mischievous Arab State, you could race back to the chamber for a reply.

The cameras were an ever present feature in the GA and you sometimes forgot they were there. They generally focussed on the podium and the speaker, but they also took in the supposedly absorbed reactions of the assembled delegates. The camera at the back contented itself with fish-eye views of the room, but the cameras on the balconies roved at will over the delegates below, highlighting perhaps a gaggle of Arabs reading a girlie magazine or a lone Asian picking his nose. Consequently you had to be careful. The bored cameramen with time on their hands were determined to make the most of the few angles open to them. Their favourite was when a country was being attacked from the podium. Close in on the subject for facial reaction, the camera would frame the familiar tableau of stoic Ambassador, frowning No 2 and hunched Press Secretary, already scribbling the response. When South Africa was condemned, as it endlessly was, the camera would dwell on the South African seat which, as of 1990 had been empty for the last thirty years.

I was particularly prone to this kind of coverage since Ireland was stuck between Iraq and Israel, countries to which speakers constantly referred, usually in negative terms. Each time Iraq was denounced, the cameras would zoom in on the Iraqi delegates — who sat there, nonplussed, twirling their worry beads — and then pan back with a long view of the half-roused Iranian and Irish delegates on either side.

The footage was not just for the archive, but was sold on to networks for their daily coverage. Thus, later in the hotel, we could watch ourselves on CNN, or bits of ourselves (our shoulders, usually) when the Iraqis were being condemned. Uncertainty about where the footage ended up instilled a sort of paranoia about the cameras. Thus some delegates were convinced they were being singled out. At first, we thought that the suspicion of one Polish chap was just a hangover from his old days at home — Woijech was one of the new 'dissident turned diplomats' — but then we noticed that the camera did seem to prey on him a lot. We concluded that this was motivated by the inordinate amount of time he spent brazenly checking out the passing female delegates. It was as if the cameraman had it in for him, or for the UN — his hated employers — and wanted to show the reality of delegate harmony. This occasionally led to surreal television news footage: Argentina would be attacking Britain over Las Malvinas and suddenly we'd have a gratuitous shot of Poland, grinning inanely, as Afghanistan passed by. In the context of the news report, the shot would make no sense at all.

The real goal was not to fall asleep, something which happened with extraordinary regularity in the GA, and not just after a heavy lunch. One morning, I came in and saw the delegate from Equatorial Guinea with his head flipped back. Ah, no, not a poisoning. Not in my first week. But a droll Belgian made a signal, 'He's asleep — don't worry, you'll see lots more of it around here.' But it was morning, why was he asleep? I could only presume he'd been at some Equatorial Guinea Disco the night before, or perhaps he and the other three Guinea countries had gone out and had a big Guinean piss up. But sleepiness affected us all and even the most senior officials dropped off on occasion.

It's easy to be overly cynical about the laid back atmosphere, or about the UN itself. Despite the criticisms frequently levelled at the institution, it's important to stress that the faults of the UN are really those of its Member States who won't support it enough and who horse-trade over its honoured commitments. This is hardly surprising. Countries behave like this not because they are faceless, bureaucratic institutions but precisely because they behave like human beings; human beings at their worst, driven by self-interest, expediency and opportunism. Yet when the UN fails because of this, the Member States then blame the organisation. The triumph and downfall of the UN is that all of humanity is represented there. To achieve meaningful results every country needs to be there but achieving consensus in a 'tent' this big is exceedingly difficult. It is not the UN that is at fault. In theory, the UN is a fantastic organisation. It is the countries themselves who hold it back.

One evening, for example, I was strolling back from the press centre, when I met Kristen, a young American, who'd just returned from doing famine work for the UN in Somalia. She wanted to hear the Somalian debate and asked me to show her where the General Assembly was. But listening to her descriptions of the famine, full of idealism and wonder, I was fearful of what she would find in the General Assembly. 'The Somalian people don't want pity,' she explained, 'pity to them is weakness. They just want something done. Somalian people look you in the eye and say "all my family starved to death".' She nodded ruefully. And yet she loved her work, and loved working for the UN. Not just here in New York, but 'in the field' thousands of people were working, all around the world. Her next job was with UNWRA in Gaza. By way of response, I said that we'd devoted our entire speech to Somalia. She knew that and knew about President Robinson's interest.

'You'll have to sit over here,' I said, when we got inside the Chamber, and after we said goodbye, I could see her getting into an observer seat and putting on an earpiece. All around me delegates were slouched in their seats and twirling worry beads. It was late and my thoughts drifted as I looked high up at the ceiling spotlights. I thought about the famine workers in Somalia, Blue Helmets in Cambodia and UN trucks speeding through the worst of war zones, winning grudging respect from even the worst of tyrants. The reputation of the UN waxes and wanes but the world would be a sorry place without it.

As a group of delegates, we had a few social forays; 'New York events' like going to Little Italy, for a night of singing and slagging. Or the Wollman Memorial ice rink in Central Park, where Vanessa had gone with her Danish paramour but where the rest of us spent our time clinging to the rails.

'I've never done it before,' chorused the German and Austrian members of the group; only for both of them to reveal themselves as perfect skaters with twists and twirls. It was a game between them, neither of them wanting to show their cards too early. A German and an Austrian who hadn't skated — come off it.

We also went to each other's receptions but they were quiet affairs with diplomats tottering around canapé trays. Also, because of the strange, divisive atmosphere in the Mission, there were functions you wouldn't hear about, or which only certain people would go to. The personal intrigues at our own Mission seem to match those between the different States. Nor should one underestimate the potential for international and domestic intrigues to coalesce. That's when you're really in trouble, with people 'stealing' work, as I saw later in Anglo-Irish, and spoiling each other's contacts. The other fascinating thing was when malcontents in different Missions hooked up and formed a sort of multilateral grudge group, with great potential to mess up foreign policies.

For example, no one at the Mission told us about the party to celebrate Cuba's Independence, which Vanessa and I went along to in the Cuban Mission, that besieged Third Avenue block surrounded by a police cordon and wire cages. (Just what is it that Cuba brings out in the official US psyche?)

Despite the boycott of the US and others, there was a big crowd in the room, but then we noticed that they had also invited the UN doormen and the girls who worked in the café. 'Ah, so they're boosting up the numbers,' said someone, 'just like their "audience" in the GA. That's a bit desperate.' But, checking our snobbery for a moment, we thought, This is Cuba, they're socialists, after all. Why wouldn't they invite the UN staff? In fact it was refreshing to come to an actual party instead of a diplomatic reception; with salsa music and the Cuba Libre rum being doled out with the chopped pineapples. George, the Bronx-born GA doorman, was in animated discussion about baseball with Diego, the Cuban No 3. In any other circumstances, it would be 'those goddamn Cubans'.

What we didn't know was that the EU was also boycotting the affair — a low-key boycott, not explicitly done, but part of the continuing isolation of Cuba intended to force them into democratisation. It showed the bullish thinking of the time. 1990; the Berlin Wall was down and Castro can only have a year or two to go. But, over a decade later, Castro remains very much in charge. And the boycott seems to have subsided.

As we walked around the room, mixing with South American diplomats and left-wing Americans, Vanessa whispered through gritted teeth 'there are none of *chers collègues* here'. It was true. There were no other EU States. Except the Portuguese delegate who also didn't know there was a boycott. 'Don't worry, we didn't see you,' we said. 'I didn't see you,' she replied, laughing, and we decided that because none of our other EU colleagues were here there was no one to report on our attendance.

Towards Christmas, the Third Committee had its party in La Maganette on 3rd Avenue. Again, the music was salsa and merengue. There was a happy recognition at UN parties that the music should be from South America, or better still, the Caribbean. The party was good crack. On the dance floor, the stiffer Europeans were 'getting on down', but true to form, the blue-blazered British delegates stood in the corner talking only to each other. Some of the Africans, however, had turned into fairly flash characters, with their Hawaiian shirts and black suits.

Certain delegates were getting romantic, building on relationships started on the GA floor. There was even a 'love across the barricades' affair between a Greek and Turk. They were like a movie couple, handsome, popular and very shy. But they had to go softly given their countries' mutual antagonism. The Greek was going so softly I thought he might lose the girl, especially given the efforts of Woijech, the oily Polish delegate who was trying to ruin things. But, under cover of darkness, they clung to each other like a naval frigates to a disputed Aegean island. Incidentally, political differences didn't prevent warm personal relations. The contrary perhaps; conflict creates familiarity. The Pakistani and Indian delegates were always hanging out together, having a laugh at their political masters.

Our own Virgil was less successful in the romance stakes and had more or less given up on the General Assembly group who had turned out to be a more conservative group than he had expected. The glamorous, Hermes-scarfed Afghani proved too austere for even a cup of coffee — perhaps the dreaded onslaught of the fundamentalists in her own country was having an effect — while an Australian he'd been flirting with, now had a boyfriend 'flying in from home'. And that's a long way to fly. Maria, the husky Guatemalan in front of us, was very friendly. But she was also a daily communicant and a member of Opus Dei. Her gold crucifix, tantalisingly dangled over freckled cleavage, seem to ward off Virgil, vampire that he was.

The Guatemalans were an interesting group. One of their delegates, a slightly outrageous young man, said he was kept in New York 'to keep him from getting into trouble at home'. A camp sort of fellow, Pedro was a popular figure in the GA for his irreverent attitude which I considered refreshing until the day I asked him about the human rights situation in Guatemala. He gave me a blank smile; he didn't know what I was talking about. It was the old 'there is no Macedonia' syndrome.

I had just come back from Guatemala where I had been struck by the beaten nature of the people, especially the Indians, who seemed to live in abject fear of officialdom and the army. Reddening, Pedro told me that he still didn't know what I was talking about. I must be mistaken. He smiled at me like I was a bit simple. But further questions, provoked a defence so mechanical and unconvincing — 'Communist propaganda', 'terrorists' — that clearly there were other reasons why he'd been here for fourteen years. Really, he was the ideal diplomat, all the better with his sham-liberal veneer. In a room full of smooth talkers, he fitted in perfectly.

The smile was taken off his face, however, when out of nowhere, Rigoberta Menchu Tum, the Guatemalan human rights activist, was awarded the Nobel Peace Prize. It was the talk of the UN and her face was on the cover of *The New York Times*, the same paper Pedro had quoted so smugly about those neo-Nazi attacks in Western Europe. The reaction of the Guatemalan delegation was a mixture of deep embarrassment and forced pretend 'celebration'. 'You must be delighted,' we said and Maria agreed that it was a wonderful achievement for the peoples of Guatemala' — bland diplo-speak was already co-opting Rigoberta's prize. 'It's great Pedro, no?' Wincing, Pedro replied that 'Yes, it was a recognition of some of our problems' and then he gave us that tight little smile, which basically said, would you please fuck off now and stop goading me.

11

Gulf War

Early every Friday morning, we all met in the Embassy, or Mission, to review progress. At the request of the Ambassador, everyone attended and gave little spiels about their week. By now, the Committees had completed much of their work and drafts of resolutions were being brought into the GA to be voted on.

Most resolutions were just nodded through. Just as no one was going to argue against 'Motherhood' issues, no one was going to vote against them; world hunger, the environment, peace studies. But, as in the Committees, the tussle for language and amendments continued right up until the end and if a consensus could not be achieved the Draft Resolution (DR), and often its separate amendments, are put to the vote.

Voting is done through the panel on every desk, just under the nameplate; a green button for yes, red for no and orange for abstention. The colours appear accordingly, next to the country's name on the big scoreboard overhanging the podium. It was here, as I've said earlier, that 'the West' shrunk to a little trickle of lights. Strategy often played a role in voting. Although everyone was supposed to press their buttons at once, some left it until the very last second, thus gaining the advantage, important in the Arab world, of seeing other countries' votes first. Or else they wanted the attention of being the last green light to pop up on the screen.

Some colours change in front of your eyes as countries realise they've hit the wrong button. Or have decided to switch votes at the last moment; those artificial limbs for Sri Lanka. There were stories about delegates waddling in from the Delegates Lounge, and accidentally voting the wrong way. Although the procedure sounds simple, such is the conveyor belt of items, that you have to pay close attention. A country could, for example, support a cluster item (a group DR) but abstain on one of its parts. And all the time, there was the poker game of DRs being suddenly withdrawn or amended. The object, basically, was for the Committees to sort all this out before the DRs reached the GA.

On a human level, delegates helped each other out. If someone wasn't in their seat, their neighbour could hit the button for them — not an easy arrangement in our corner. Such surrogate button-pushing was also done to show a country was in the house. Sometimes if a button didn't work, or was a bit faulty, the country concerned went apoplectic, especially if it was order-freaks like the South Koreans. From the back of the room a cry would come and small men started jumping up and down. You'd think had a rat had run across their desk, or a bomb was about to go off in downtown Seoul. With a great show of seriousness, the Mediterranean Chairman would halt the proceedings and send down George and the other UN Security Guards to take a look.

In the same way that States could absent themselves from the chamber for a speech, they can also absent themselves from a vote to make a point, or avoid embarrassment. Or just sit back and not press any button. If a vote was really contentious, a roll call was requested, with each country taking it in turn, alphabetically, to shout their 'yes' or 'nyet' into a microphone. It is a strange feeling to hear your voice carrying through this famous crowded chamber, announcing 'Ireland says Yes.' Only to be outdone by Napoleon, breaking the boredom of a roll-call vote by piping up with a 'Sí, Senor'. It got a great laugh; Napoleon, an old Madrid hand, had a strong bond with the Spanish-speaking delegates.

At the end of the session were the elections; for the Security Council, Ecosoc, UNESCO and all the other UN bodies, including the Chairs and Vice-Chairs of the next session's Committees. This is where the real fun begins, with most of the votes taking place through Secret Ballot.

The polling brings home the extraordinary duplicity of the UN's members. After relentless canvassing, a country may have assembled a healthy vote, only to see it collapse in a secret ballot. Countries assure you of their support, only to go in and vote for your enemy. It happened to us when the Ambassador went up for a second term on the International Law Commission (ILC). Perhaps he shouldn't have gone for it. It may have seemed greedy that Ireland, a small country, was going for the ILC again, but he had wide support to do so. After energetic canvassing, we counted and re-counted the promised votes. It was in the bag and the Mission was going to celebrate.

The day of a big vote is extraordinary. Everybody is in the chamber. Equatorial Guinea, the Marshall Islands; all crowded into their seats. It sometimes took a few rounds to complete an election and, with all the different ballots taking place, there is frenetic activity as delegates run around trying to keep people on board and do a last minute canvass. Third Secs even stand nervously in the aisles to prevent people from going to the loo, or taking a phone call. 'Where are you going, you're supposed to vote for us.' It was something I hadn't seen since student elections.

Senior diplomats can invest their whole reputation on getting their country elected to something (as do some Ministers). For Security Council membership, a country's campaign can begin two or three years before the actual poll. Think of what that can do to a State's foreign policy in the meantime. The New Zealand delegates said that after they were elected, they found it hard to stop campaigning, such was the momentum.

On the day itself, the vote exposes the rawest of human emotion, as elections always do. For a successful country which hasn't been expected to do well, there is a great cheer, especially if it is a popular neutral like Sweden and delegates all around will rush over to offer congratulations. But for the losers, who had really expected to succeed, there is only despair, embarrassment and even, sometimes, tears. And there is recrimination. The candidates are usually put forward by their groupings — the ASEAN group, or the WEOG group for Western Europeans. But when the sums come in, the unlucky candidate will know immediately that their supposed supporters have broken ranks.

In our case, with the ILC vote, it was immediately apparent that Ireland was going to have problems. Our first vote looked OK, but by the second round it was obvious that there was a serious falling away in the support promised. A sudden tension fell over the seat, as some people got near the Ambassador, behind the nameplate, while others moved away, distancing themselves from impending defeat.

One of us stood by the West Wing exit, supposedly to prevent those delegates from leaving who were expected to vote for us — a fruitless exercise, as it turned out. But also because the Ambassador was getting signals from someone inside the election office about how it was going. The signals were not good and you could see that the senior officers were almost reluctant to pass on the numbers to the now-smouldering *His Excellency*. Nor was the situation helped by The Holy See coming over and jocularly offering to 'say a prayer' for us. Napoleon told him to piss off.

In the end, prayers were not enough. In fairness, the Ambassador was gracious in defeat and took it quite philosophically. But it was extraordinary to look around the room and think that all these countries had lied to you. Their promises were cast-iron guarantees which they knew we had totted, re-totted and relayed back to HQ.

We weren't sure exactly who'd let us down but we did know, for example, that Australia, firmly behind us at the start, had withdrawn their support for an unknown reason. Because they told us so before the vote. It was embarrassing for them, especially as we shared the same building and, worse, the same elevator. They asked for it to be kept quiet but of course we told the Kiwis who gleefully passed it on. The rivalry between New Zealand and Australia is not to be underestimated.

Sometimes Ireland got votes it didn't want, like from Iran or the Arab countries. Indeed Ireland wasn't even a candidate, but Britain was, and it was done just to piss them off. Such occurrences were less frequent that in the past, but it still happened occasionally. One evening, late into the night, the British were struggling to get elected onto something they thought would have been a shoe-in. We were on about the sixth round of balloting and as I returned from voting — you had to go down to the side of the podium to vote — I passed the British delegates who were, by now, well-pissed off. 'You'll probably get a vote,' said one of them sourly, 'you usually do, when we stand. From Libya or one of those people. Iraq, probably.'

The alacrity with which the UN/Western Europe responded to the Iraqi invasion of Kuwait was striking, especially compared to the later weak response on Bosnia, the other big issue of my time at the UN. Of course, Bosnia was much more complex but in the case of Kuwait there were two other crucial factors: oil and timing.

As regards timing: if you are going to make a controversial move in international diplomacy, do it while the rest of the world is distracted. In the week that martial law was declared in Poland in 1981, Israel annexed the Golan Heights. While the world watched Romania in revolt in 1989, the US invaded Panama. (The US media even tried to piggy back on the alleged similarity — 'End of Two Dictators' — when in fact Noriega, bad and all as he was, was in no way comparable to the vile Ceauçescu.) In the long summer of 1990, however, nothing else was happening, beyond Western States congratulating themselves on the emerging 'New World Order', on international democracy and the upholding of the rule of law. Then Iraq rolled into Kuwait. It was the most public and brazen act.

By the time the GA opened in September 1990, the countries of the world were queuing up to condemn Iraq. Again, there were States who were themselves hardly squeaky clean — and countries occupying other countries with less substantial 'historical claims' than that advanced by Iraq with regard to Kuwait — but that didn't matter. Almost every country mentioned Iraq in its speech and very few were prepared to do them any favours, although many of the Arab countries sought to balance the issue by trying to focus on the 'Israel question', as if we didn't have enough of that already.

On the floor, however, it was a different story and, among delegates, there were an extraordinary number of 'sneaking regarders' for Iraq, and for the fact that they were able to stick it to the international community and, in particular, to the US. And then hold out. There was little respect for Kuwait among other Arab countries, or indeed for any of the Gulf States. Delegates would whisper 'Bahrain is a British creation, you know — a banking arrangement for a ruling elite.' Syria and Iraq may be rogue states but there was a feeling that at least they were in some sense egalitarian and built roads and hospitals. They were police states, but they were populist.

Watching the way the Kuwaitis preened around in their flash suits and Rolex watches, one could understand where this attitude came from. They seemed less like patriots eager to go back and fight for their country than idle rich kids waiting to have their Porsches returned. Far from this feeling diminishing as the Western Coalition was formed, it got worse. The Egyptians, in particular, were scathing; 'our soldiers are over in the desert waiting to free Kuwait, and possibly die in the process, while the

Kuwaiti Royal Family are living it up in the Cairo nightclubs.'

The Iraqi invasion was, in particular, an offence against the UN. One can kill and torture thousands of your own people, but take an inch of your neighbour's land and the world may step in. Obsessed with borders and territorial treaties as the UN was, this was a reminder that the main causes of international disputes were land and borders. Which is understandable; if all the States who complained about their neighbours in their Opening Statements were to act on their impulses, the world would be up for grabs.

Sitting next to Iraq, we were awe-struck by the way they absorbed the world's condemnation and blandly looked at their watches. Perhaps, at most, twirling their worry beads if the going got rough. They spent much of the time furiously writing responses and rights of reply. At times, they wrote the replies in advance of hearing the condemnations. They would then read out what they'd hastily written, without clearing it with anybody, an impressive case of delegated sanction. But a daunting one. If we slipped up — late for a vote, erroneous language — we got carpeted by Napoleon and, after persistent offences, a small note might go onto our file. But, if these guys slipped up, it could mean fresh missiles and sanctions and a hanging by Saddam Hussein. Even if they didn't slip up, it could mean a hanging by Saddam Hussein. We used to wonder how they lived with such pressure. Even the Iranians sitting beside them seemed impressed.

The Iraqi delegates were OK people and far more personable than the Iranians, or, at times, the Israelis. For most people, the Iranians were the most chilling people in the room. There is something slightly reassuring about a mass murderer who is, at least, chummy and takes a drink, as Napoleon will tell you. But the icy Iranians sat there motionless, with apparent disdain for the rest of the UN. Every Iranian speech began with an invocation to

'Allah — the beautiful, the most merciful' and proceeded into a denunciation of just about the rest of humanity. Mind you, by comparison with the other EU States, we got on quite well with the Iranians. Eamon McKee was quite flattered when one Iranian delegate told him, 'Everything you say, I report to my capital. They always want to know, what are the Irish thinking.'

In the GA, it was curious to see the Iranian reaction while Iraq was being condemned. This, after all, was their great rival, a country which had invaded them and tried to destroy their Revolution and yet here they were in defiance of the world, sticking it to the US, the Great Satan. But the Iranians, in their priestly collars (they never wore ties) showed little response and simply sat it out. Watch and wait.

Thus compared to the Iranians, the Iraqis were a bit of crack, talking about sports or shopping. They even warmed to Virgil's search for a girlfriend, suggesting the El Salvador delegate. 'But she's so big,' we said. 'Yes, big. Big is good!' they said in a refreshing antidote to the Western fixation with anorexic figures. Ah, the differences between States. One day, an Iraqi delegate told me about his weekend and about how he'd taken his kids to the Five Flags Adventure Park in New Jersey. For some reason, I found this unbearably sad. Iraq was being denounced from all quarters, a war was about to commence in which thousands would die, and yet here was the Iraqi delegate having a typical day out with his family. I imagined his kids playing with American kids who wouldn't know who they were.

Far from the delegates blindly following some whim of Saddam's, they became quite animated about their cause — Kuwait as the missing sixth province of Iraq — and drew a comparison with Northern Ireland, an analogy we resisted, even if we could see their logic. We feared they might start mentioning it in speeches, and try to embarrass the British, but nothing came of it. Instead, they had another Irish issue to ask about. 'I've been reading in our newspaper,' said a delegate, 'about this beef to Iraq scandal. What is it all about?' 'Oh, it doesn't matter. It's an Irish scandal,' we said, smiling and they seemed relieved to hear it was something they were blameless in.

At the next session, with the war over, and sanctions taking effect, the Iraqis would make a more official approach. Taking you aside for a one-on-one canvass, they would describe, again with great passion, the food shortages in Iraq, the cutbacks and lack of medicine. Hard to believe it was a situation which would last for another ten years. You often got these one-on-one approaches in the GA or Committees. After an earthquake in Nicaragua, their Third Sec, a friendly chap who joined us on our nights out, went into 'the mode', energetically describing his country's need for extra immediate relief. But it was fruitless. We had already decided not to support an aid increase. 'They've got enough already,' said a mandarin bluntly, referring to the funds sent in after democratisation. Another case of timing; don't let your natural disasters coincide with an existing aid package.

Of course, the Kuwaitis also saw us as their friends. 'Collins of Arabia' was effusive in his support of the beleaguered sheikhdom as indeed were most countries. Approachable though the individual Iraqi delegates were, there was still a sense of outrage at what they'd done; the wholesale invasion of a neighbouring State. The Kuwaitis produced leaflets which spared nothing in their depiction of tortured and dismembered victims. At one stage, in the Security Council chamber, they turned off the lights and put on a stomach-churning slide show with secretly filmed footage of executions, fuzzy images reminiscent of the Nazi killing of partisans in Eastern Europe.

The next time we were in the Security Council was for the final meeting approving Operation Desert Storm. For it was the Security Council, not the GA, which would give the ultimate sanction. It was one of the most surreal moments at the UN. The delegates had first choice on the observer seats in the room and the gallery was full, overflowing with people sitting along the aisles and cross-legged on the carpet. The media jostled in the glass boxes overhead while outside, TV vans and halogen lights were camped along the sidewalk, as they had been for the previous few weeks. Across the road, Kuwaiti exiles shouted their support while American and Arab students chanted 'No Blood for Oil!'

We were all there in the chamber. The Hermes-clad Afghani, the "Bluefish" Dane, with his more amorous colleague beside Vanessa, and, likewise, the Greek and Turk hoping their own countries would never come to this. It reminded me of the people who were said to have dined on top of the hill and looked down at the Napoleonic battles. The girl from Panama, who had supported so strongly the Myanmar DR and then disappeared, had even had her hair done. 'Yes, of course, a little trim,' she said with a serious face as she fiddled with the gold jewellery that all the Central American delegates were fond of wearing. The whole thing seemed extraordinary.

The Security Council were going to vote for war. That was clear from the arithmetic. But before they did, those who didn't support military action were going to give their side. Much as we disliked the Cubans for the length of their speeches (like their leader, they would talk for hours) they gave a persuasive, withering argument against military action, made all the more poignant by the fact that everyone knew the decision had already been taken and the cruisers and F16s were already being lined up. 'You tell us sanctions are not enough, that we cannot wait for them to work. But you waited twenty years for them to work in South Africa.' The Yemen also counselled caution, asking was there not some other way. 'Why the rush to war?' Such comments played on the knowledge that George Bush had upped the stakes for war, after Thatcher had virtually questioned his manhood.

Then the Iraqis spoke. Not the Foreign Minister. In a petty gesture, unworthy of their hosting of the UN, the US would not let Tariq Aziz fly in. However, Aziz came later, quite a sight to see, one seat away from us, denouncing the world's aggression towards his country. At the Security Council, the Iraqi Ambassador spoke, and he too had a powerful voice, which in rolling Arabic sounded particularly hurt and proud. The Council table is horseshoe-shaped and the Iraqis were put sitting at the end, called to account for themselves before the fifteen members.

Listening to Iraq, and to the statements of the US and UK, which closed the issue, and set the trigger for action, you almost thought that if you were a different person — or the person you might once have been — you would stand up and shout 'Stop all this, thousands of people will die because of your actions. This is the Security Council, established to solve conflicts, not escalate them. There must be another way around this.' But, of course, you didn't. You just sat there beside the Dutch Third Sec, and former Myanmar activist, and watched the grinding wheels of the Security Council take their course.

The other thing which sunk in watching the Security Council, with its bitter defiant rhetoric and its heart-stopping decisions, was what a different world you inhabited compared to this. Not just in the GA, but Western Europe and the EU. Looking at this cockpit of wild rhetoric and savage consequence, you were suddenly very glad you lived in a Europe of compromise, settlement and democracy. Although, ironically, Europe was about to experience its own savage and internecine war.

Around the horseshoe table, a show of hands let war proceed. The US media didn't show the images of carbonised corpses but some time later I saw the BBC documentary, *The Gulf War* and its series of jaw-dropping images; the silhouettes of Iraqi soldiers picked off on the infra-red screens of helicopter gunships, Iraqi policemen hung from the meathooks they had used for Kurdish suspects, ecstatic rebels rising against Saddam and then, most brutally, the same rebels, unsupported by Bush who had encouraged them to revolt, being bayoneted and killed as they surrendered. The Iraqi military happily filmed the rebels pleading for their lives. This was war, pitiless and desperate. This was the follow-on from the UN resolution, but it was also what happened when there was no UN at all.

And yet when I returned to the GA the following year, the same Iraqi delegates were sitting there. They had lost Kuwait, their country had been bombed, hundreds of thousands had been killed and yet there they were, twirling their worry beads and asking about the Irish Beef tribunal. War came and went but the diplomats, like their countries, endured. In many ways, indeed, their real work had only begun, for they now had to try and break down the international isolation to which their country was subjected.

Incredibly, this isolation continues today and, indeed, almost immediately the war ended, the focus shifted from Iraq's threat to its neighbours to its alleged stockpiling of weapons of mass destruction. It was interesting, however, that by contrast, nothing was said about Kuwait's failure to honour its pre-war commitment to introduce democratic reforms — a limited concession to the West, which had just fought an international war on its behalf. Instead, the Kuwaitis just went back to being the semi-corrupt kingdom it had been, just as Saudi Arabia, saved from the Iraqi marauders, did nothing to follow up on those tantalising democratic noises it had made about women's rights, noises presumably made to get American support behind them. If anything, the position of women got worse in Saudi Arabia, as did that of their long suffering immigrant workers.

Once the embarrassment of Iraq's invasion went away, the Gulf States went back to their traditional preoccupations, including the Palestinians, for whom they could never protest enough. But not before the Kuwaitis dished out their own punishment to the Palestinians living amongst them, killing more Palestinians in two months than Israel killed in four years of the Intifada. It was a massacre about which the Gulf States, and the UN, barely raised a murmur. Admittedly, the killings were because the Palestinians in Kuwait had, in general, backed the invading Iraqis, but given the manner of the revenge, with summary executions and disappearances, one would have thought that the international community might have raised a protest, especially since it had just fought a war there. But, instead, it said nothing. The following year, having washed the blood out of its execution halls, the Kuwaitis went back to denouncing Israel's treatment of the Palestinians. Hypocrisy, indeed. As our Political Director had predicted, working at the UN demanded a strong stomach.

Section III

America

12

Irish America

When I came back to New York after Christmas, I was at the Consulate, about as different from the UN as it was possible to be. Basically, we were dealing with the Irish community, and by extension, the Irish-American community. To give you an idea of the scope of this, in the last US census, forty million Americans claimed Irish descent, although thankfully not all of them have activated their heritage.

The Consulate was responsible for thirteen States, from Maine to Georgia — the Consulates and Embassy divide up America between them — but in reality our main concern was with the tri-state area of New York, New Jersey and Connecticut. The most pressing issue was the 50,000 or so Irish illegals. The poor economic situation at home had seen people emigrate in their droves in the Eighties and early Nineties, a political embarrassment for the Irish Government.

To deal with the illegals, and to assist in the ongoing efforts to get them legalised, a second Third Secretary had been sent to the Consulate. This was James McIntyre, a soft spoken chap who became our Immigration Liaison Officer. It was not an easy job. The illegals, often already bitter, had to endure a shadowy and complex existence in the US, and sometimes it required the fixing skills of a TD mixed with the sympathetic ear of a priest to help them.

The Consulate was a large office, then situated on the eighteenth floor of an old art deco building just off Madison Avenue in midtown New York. As well as James and myself, the officers comprised the Consul General (CG), the Deputy Consul General (DCG) and a Press Officer who worked to the Embassy in Washington. In theory, the whole Consulate was answerable to the Embassy, but in practice this was not always the case and, under the present incumbent, the Consulate would enjoy an unusual degree of independence.

The CG was an energetic character, an intensely ambitious and hard-working diplomat, whose energy added to the activity of what was already a busy office. The office issued a huge volume of passports, visas and citizenships, and it also had a busy social calendar. The CG was on the verge of getting promotion to Ambassador — 'the red hat is descending,' quipped Napoleon, using the common ecclesiastical metaphor — but he still saw no need to let up on our constant attendance at every dinner dance and community function; what is known at home, less than affectionately, as the 'Paddywackery circuit'.

Tall, with a trim brown beard and a sort of barkish Dublin accent, the CG sat behind his desk and described the Community in dramatic terms. 'Be nice to these people,' he told me on my first morning, 'and they'll be nice to you. But if you upset them, they can make life very awkward for you. Believe me, if you cut your own throat, they'll let you bleed and you won't stop bleeding.'

I thought the CG's language was a bit over the top. With his red braces and rimless glasses, I thought maybe he'd been in New York too long and that this Wall Street-esque 'do-or-die' thing had got to him. But when he stared at me I nodded obediently: I understand.

On cue, sirens sounded down in the street. 'It's a jungle out there,' said the Consul and he jerked his thumb toward the Rockefeller Centre and surrounding skyscrapers. 'But if you do well, you can do very well and then we can all do well with you.' This was one of his favourite sayings. An ambitious man, the CG was a dynamo of energy who was on a fast track in the Department.

'My door is always open,' he said pointing to the closed door. In fact, you were left to your own devices and before I had even left the room, the CG was on the phone to the former Governor, 'sorting out' something. He was always 'sorting out' something. He should have been a TD or a Minister rather than a Consul General.

The Deputy CG was also from Dublin but he was quite the opposite, a laid-back character, only a few years from retirement and very fond of the golf courses. He was also something of a storyteller and I'd met him a few times in Hourican's telling tales of his postings in Africa and his long years in the Passport Office in Dublin, an Africa of sorts where one was never heard of again, battling with the natives. Except these natives were our own.

And then there was the Press Officer, attached to what was effectively a separate office within the Consulate and who dealt with the US media in the South and West. It had a wide brief and worked to the Embassy in Washington. But such demarcations had a tendency to shift and, in New York, successive Press Officers, like Anne Barrington and Dermot Bragnan, had to be vigilant to protect their bailiwick.

Whereas most of the officers were male almost all of the staff were women, which is either a comment on the recruitment policy of the foreign service or maybe just a reflection of the job market in New York, since all of the staff were locally recruited and lived permanently in New York. Some of them had worked in the office for years and had seen it all, from deportations to scandal-embroiled celebrities, forced to beat hasty retreats to Ireland. In the same way that Civil Servants were the real Government, and not the politicians, so the real Consulate was, not its transitory diplomats, but the long-serving permanent staff.

Indeed, for years, the Department didn't send female officers to Consulate postings in North America, since the conservatism of the Irish-American community rendered them unable to cope with female professionals. Indeed in the past this chauvinism was another factor to be taken into account when postings were considered. By the late Nineties, however, this was changing and many of the Vice Consuls, and Consuls in North America were women.

The Irish-Americans also had a problem with non-Catholics and there was a famous case in Washington of an officer, a Belfast Protestant, having to be reposted because of resistance from the local community. One would think that the Irish-Americans would be glad of such admittedly tokenistic diversity, but as I was soon to discover they weren't always such a sophisticated bunch.

One of my first priorities was getting somewhere to live. The CG had said that his officers must live in Manhattan, 'close to the office', an agreeable stipulation, but I was more specific; I wanted downtown Manhattan, Chelsea or Greenwich Village. Preferably, the West Village. However, to satisfy regulations, and the concerns of Irish taxpayers who'd be paying for it, I had to go through the motions of checking out apartments in all areas, whether it be twenty concrete floors above 86th Street or on the west wing of a make-believe hotel in Murray Hill with a tasselled doorman and ivy-strewn fountain.

I saw a lot of tacky bachelor pads — a legacy of the Eighties — full of matt-black furniture and track lighting. In the Zeckendorf Towers on Union Square, built over a shopping centre and apparently popular with quiet Japanese businessmen and transitory British secretaries, I was shown around the 'extras' by a bejewelled young agent called Ricky, all hands and winks and glossy black curls. After taking me through a smelly gym with lots of young professionals grunting and sweating on bicycles and ridiculous contraptions called 'Stairmasters'- a quick wink directed my attention to some moving thighs, presumably part of the 'extras' — Ricky ushered me around the swimming pool and gave me a peek at the jacuzzi, where old boys gurgled like defeated lobsters, oblivious to the notice above their matted heads; 'Do not use if you have a pacemaker or artificial limb.'

As a tenant, I could take a guest here anytime. 'So it makes for a hot date,' said Ricky, with his hands outstretched. 'Hey, what do you say — come on, a guy like you?' But I decided not to be 'a guy like him' and pointing inexplicably to the pacemaker sign, I said it'd be a problem. 'Oh ...' he nodded, clearly puzzled.

I opted instead for the far West Village and a whitewashed loft on Hudson Street. High ceilinged, with a blond wood floor, it was on the 4th floor of an old printing building, now mostly populated by young professionals, media types and their pampered dogs. The area seemed quiet and leafy; a TD wouldn't balk if he visited it. In theory — and, in practise, with other Embassies — a TD, or even a Minister, could be staying with you, but it was most unlikely in New York. Still, the Deputy CG would have to come around and examine it. In less busy Postings, the Head of Mission actually comes around, leading to some great moments in Departmental folklore, as a fastidious mandarin is dragged off into the backstreets of some sprawling barrio, or in one case, into the heart of a red-light area, with the girls lounging around the doorway. 'Looking for business, sir?'

However, the Deputy CG seemed to like my area and was particularly taken with St Luke's Place, a location for endless fashion shoots and movie scenes. He also liked the roguish story that St Luke's was actually a section of the adjoining Leroy Street, but got named differently because the then Mayor of New York, a playboy character called Jimmy Walker, didn't want the embarrassment of his mistress living on the same street as himself. 'A sort of a Haughey thing,' he said, with a smile. Nevertheless, we were on the edge of a big gay area and I found myself having to steer him clear of neighbouring Christopher Street, where grown men in dog collars and leather bum flaps were strutting around, arm in arm. 'So Minister, which bar will it be tonight, the Wellhung Cowboy or the

Bulldyke's Lair?' I was worried what people might think if they saw the DCG walking around with a handsome young Irish fellow like myself.

In the end, I got the nod and HQ gave permission to sign a two-year lease. Irish tax payers would not have been disappointed. A large house-warming party was held, fuelled with diplomatic-priced liquor, which sold through the UN at $6 a bottle of rum or vodka. (For 'work' purposes, you understand. Just ask Napoleon.) The UN also provided party-goers in the shape of delegates from India, Nicaragua and Germany. Michael Forbes, then in San Francisco, couldn't make it but Eamon McKee was there, along with Vanessa Singleton and her now established partner, the Great Dane. Virgil Johnston was not in the mood, however. Unsuccessful in his amorous pursuits at the UN, he got lucky in the cheesy bars of Second Avenue, and hooked up with a gum-chewing girl from Queens who took him for a complete ride. But not in the happy sense. 'My brudders are wondering when you gonna take us out,' she told him, wagging an inch-long fingernail. But not 'us' in the cosy couple sense; 'us' meant the brothers as well. Typically, Virgil had over-talked the talk, and they now saw him as some kind of high flying Ambassador who was going to show them all a good time. We had a good time ourselves, however, and made such a racket that I had to leave the phone off the hook to stop the complaints. It was an uptight, yuppie building, typical of New York. There was a gym on the ground floor, and early in the morning, you could hear the sneaker squeaks and thumps of the glass racketball courts, as stress-hardened professionals let off steam before hitting the office. Sometimes coming back from a night on the tiles at five or six a.m., I would see them already up and walking their pampered dogs. I used to laugh. Life is too short.

Meanwhile, in my own office, it took a few weeks to get accustomed. The CG was right. It was a busy office. Each day began quietly enough at 8.30 a.m. when the girls dealt with backlogged passports, opened mail and sorted faxes from HQ (Dublin being five hours ahead). But come 10 a.m., when the public office opened and various shapes of customers came through the doors, suddenly the staff were running back and forth from copier to counter to get passports approved and visas issued.

It seemed like my most useful function in the first week was signing things. Perhaps even in my first year. Having worked at a text-heavy desk in Dublin, and then in a sitting position at the UN, I was now in a situation where I just signed things by day and shook hands by night — a bit like the Minister himself.

Mainly it was passports, visas and Citizenships, but there were also things like the Repatriation of Human Remains, which are always urgent; a dead body can't hang about. 'Human Remains!' one of the girls would shout to the back office, like they were on a police dig. These certificates enabled the body to be transferred to Ireland. It was ironic that while young Irish were coming out here to work, older emigrants, and even Irish-Americans, were fulfilling a life-long wish of going back to Ireland to be buried. Recently, however, such repatriation had taken on a sadder, and sometimes even sinister air, as we signed Certs for young lads killed on rushed building sites, or protection feuds in Florida.

The main paperwork was Citizenship which had become very popular in recent years. All it required was the proof of an Irish-born grandparent and you could get a green certificate. Signing them was like being a midwife and in one afternoon you could bring into the world more Irish citizens than a large-sized maternity hospital. Instant, virgin births: the Bishops would be proud of us.

Applicants for Citizenship were mostly older Irish-Americans, sentimental retirees who, in the autumn of their lives, now had the time and curiosity about their origins to want to have them legalised. Increasingly, however, younger Americans were applying, mindful that an Irish passport was also an EU passport and a virtual work permit for all of its countries. In a changing labour market, American youngsters were considering job options in their grandparents' countries, an interesting reversal of Ellis Island, eighty years on.

But even as a travel document, the Irish passport appeared to offer a useful, and uncontentious, travel document to those Americans who expected trouble if they used their US one. In terms of disguise, a fig leaf surely, for even if the passport was Irish, even the most dim-witted Arab cop or terrorist was going to spot the gum, the golfing slacks and the braying accent. Also the passport still had to state the place of birth, truthfully, as 'USA', although the clever ones had asked for the option of a passport in Gaelic, presumably hoping that any budding Abu Nidal would think 'SAM' was just another Leinster county and not the Uncle himself in a different jacket.

At first, it was annoying to think that all these people — foreigners — were walking around with the same passport as I had but that was before I saw the scams that the Irish were up so that they could strut around with US citizenship, or at very least the right to profitably reside here; the fake IDs, the 'sister's social security number', the Marriages of Convenience. So in a sense, it was fair swap, a few passports for lots of Green Cards.

Of course, it wasn't all plain signing. Figurehead I might have been, but half the purpose of my being here was to make the tricky decisions the permanent staff couldn't and already some difficult cases were waiting in the in-tray; child-custody battles, a suspected Marriage of Convenience and a request from a prisoner to be transferred to Ireland.

None of them were urgent, thankfully. The prisoner was doing life for murder so I figured he couldn't be in that much of a hurry for a window-barred change of scenery. Meanwhile the child-custody cases were already in legal proceedings, so the most I could offer was emotional support, which was the most I could offer in many distress cases, as I was regrettably to discover. The suspected Marriage of Convenience was of a foreigner to an Irishwoman to get her citizenship, and not other way around. The ones that were the other way round — of Irish people marrying to stay in the US — were well known to us, but they were the ones we didn't talk about. They were legit.

Problems in the public office, however, couldn't be postponed so easily. From overhearing the transactions of the girls at the window, you could usually hear problems coming. Passport applicants upset at the cost of renewals, or security delays, or who couldn't, or wouldn't, get a guarantor to sign their application form ('I've never been to a doctor and I don't have a bank account, so there.'). More seriously, Maidie or Jo would call me up to question someone they were sure was lying about a lost passport. After ten years of dealing with the customers, face to face, they had an uncanny knowledge of spotting the fibbers. The stories that don't add up, the passports 'lost again' in Atlantic City and the visa applicants from Asian countries who let slip something about having relatives in Birmingham, their Irish 'holiday' about to transform into settlement in Britain.

Over the next few months, I had to deal with irate spouses and bereaved relatives, not to mention the people who came in with no documentation at all. And very often, for fear that the people were being genuine, and they usually were, you had to forgo the bureaucracy and be flexible to facilitate them in times of stress. As with being Duty Officer, allowances had to be made. Aside from anything else, you didn't want them going home and getting onto a Minister or a TD about how they weren't helped out because they didn't have a little piece of paper or couldn't remember a guarantor's name. That was something every diplomat wished to avoid.

Thus, when a tall, young American came in with his mother and asked that his Citizenship be 'speeded up' so he could declare for the Irish basketball team before his eighteenth birthday, I was more than happy to oblige. The forms weren't filled out correctly but letters from the Irish Basketball authorities were produced informing Chuck Kelly about his Olympic 'prospects'. Thinking about the national soccer team's success, I was more than happy to cut corners. I didn't want someone saying that a bureaucrat in New York had stopped this young fellow from playing, and scoring, for Ireland.

However, controversial figures also applied, like Robert Chambers, the infamous Central Park yuppie killer. Passport applications are confidential and yet so nervous were the Consulate about possible publicity, that they wouldn't put his Prison-issued receipt on file. I thought they were being over-anxious. Prisoners, perhaps as a sick joke, are actually permitted passports and it wasn't our fault that a murderer was suddenly proud of his ethnic heritage. The Chambers case had shocked New York. 'That boy's Irish mother scrubbed floors to put him through College,' said the girls ruefully, aghast at such a warping of the American dream.

Much more intriguing was Patty Hearst, the former radical, who qualified through marriage to her former parole officer, a mild-mannered Irish-American. Her application was interesting given that, in a curiously vengeful attitude by the American authorities, she continued to be refused US citizenship. Personally, compared to how bland most modern celebrities were, I regarded Hearst as an iconic, almost historic figure: the cool-looking heiress, the Great American family (and *Citizen Kane* inspiration) and the flirtation with armed revolutionaries in the 1970s. Handing her the passport, I had to give her a quick talk on the responsibilities of Irish Citizenship and, as I did so, she fixed me with a clear-eyed gaze. As did the former parole officer.

There were some funny encounters. Not long after being released from prison in Ireland, where he'd been wrongfully jailed by the State for a train robbery, Nicky

Kelly came in for a passport. 'That'll be $20 please,' said one of the girls from behind the screen.

'Did you hear that?' said Kelly to his mate. 'They're looking for money off me now.'

However, you couldn't always be vigilant. One time, the solicitor and men's magazine publisher, Elio Malocco, popped in for a new passport, flustered and in an awful hurry. Only after he left, did I remember that he'd been in the news recently. I checked the Irish newspapers. Oh, dear. It turned out he was on the run from the police, having defrauded the *Irish Press* out of thousands of pounds. Still, unless specifically stopped by the police, even on-the-run fraudsters were entitled to passports. I decided against mentioning it to the CG.

Each morning, there was the never-ending variety of consular cases. People came into the public office looking for an Advance of Funds and wouldn't leave until they got the money. To release funds, the family must lodge similar monies in Ireland, with the Department or with a Garda Station. But some families didn't want to know. Or they'd say this is the fourth time we've done this. In London, to deter junkies, the Embassy gave out luncheon vouchers.

With responsibility for thirteen States, you didn't know where something might crop up. Arrests in Florida, or the death of an Irish national in Georgia. Tasteless arguments about demarcation developed among Consulates. After a plane with an Irish person on board crashed in Colorado, colleagues in California called us, claiming the deceased was their responsibility. They heard we'd been on to the Emergency Centre. 'But the plane came from New Jersey,' I said.

'Yeah, but it crashed in Colorado. Come on, the body's ours.' Usually they'd be happy to forfeit the responsibility but things were a bit slow out West and they wanted the distraction.

Such cases offered an insight into the loose way the American police dealt with fatalities, so much at odds with the professionalism suggested by TV and movie images. 'Hey, we got a woman lying down up here,' said a cop ringing from upstate Connecticut. 'Been here for a while, unidentified, and we thought, you know, she might be a missing Irish girl.' I thought the woman was lying in a cell, but it was a police morgue and the body was in a fridge. 'She's got, like, freckles and red hair and stuff.' Daunted, I checked with Consular Section but no such Irish girl was missing. 'Yeah, I suppose so,' said the cop, when I called him back, 'she's got, like, Russian tattoos as well.' Oh right, thanks for telling me.

Another time, an old Irish guy had died alone in an apartment. The scene was frozen until a next-of-kin, or a friend, could be contacted. Anxious to free up the apartment, the landlord faxed us the man's Irish birth cert which he'd found hidden in a jug. 'Oh, so there *is* a Birth Cert,' I said, 'Do the police know this?' 'Oh, sure' said the man. They just hadn't got around to the standard procedure in New York, or elsewhere, which is to inform a foreign mission about the death of one of its nationals. It made me think about those whereabouts letters and the lost monies in estate cases.

Ongoing cases cropped up, such as the disputes over child custody. In one of them, I told the man, an American, to write to the wife's family, stating that he was initiating legal action to recover his rights to the child. (She had just left for Ireland one morning with their daughter.) Now she had written back saying she didn't care; the Atlantic lay between her and him and the law would protect her. In this, she was right. The Irish Courts would look more favourably on her as an Irish mother, than him as an estranged foreign spouse, even though she had broken the law here. In the US, as elsewhere, family law is almost impossible to impose; parents would just put the kids in a car and switch States overnight.

'This issue won't rest,' said the man defiantly. He was a steel fixer and you could hear the toughness in his voice. But also the emotion breaking.

The other case was an Irish woman who'd left her husband, after he'd assaulted her again. She was crying and all you could really do was offer solace and try to calm her down. We often referred such cases to Project Irish Outreach, a Catholic Charity, which did tremendous work. In the US, you'd be glad of the long arm of the Church. But, sure enough, within days, the woman's husband got on, looking for her whereabouts and vaguely threatening us for 'helping her run away'. It was a tricky one, because you couldn't lie to the man, but you could hardly tell him where she was either.

'So, how did you meet her again?' I asked, sitting across the boardroom table from Rashid Shamen, a Bengali. Shamen wanted a visa to join his fiancée in Ireland but the Department of Justice suspected a Marriage of Convenience.

Irish visas are notoriously tough to acquire and when Justice refuses they don't give a reason. The defence is that Ireland was a back door to Britain, with no passport controls between the two countries. But it also had to do with 'protecting' Irish culture and jobs, an attitude which didn't stop Ireland from clamouring for visas when its own people went abroad, including, and especially, the US.

'She come in for soda. To shop. And I talking with her.' Rashid gave a crisp little smile. He seemed nervous but was not short on answers. He met Caroline in Woodside a year ago and he proposed to marry her and live in Ireland (at first) where he would work at computer programming. The last answer was important, for he would have to support himself. He looked very young. Not more than a boy. In fact, he was nineteen.

It was a crude technique, to ask the same questions again to see if he'd answer differently, but in the end, we recommended a visa and he went to Ireland. The irony was that Irish kids all over New York were doing Marriages of Convenience to stay in the US, one of the many scams employed until the visa amnesty came through. I'd even been to a Mock Wedding Party in the Sin É Café, in the East Village, where people were being advised on how to prepare for interviews with the Immigration and Naturalisation Service (INS). Basically, the sort of questions I was asking Ahmed; What's your father-in-law's name? What toothpaste does your wife use?

It was strange, really, because the Consulate was effectively helping illegals to remain undetected and evade the law, just as they were being helped to get to Ireland and back, by being issued with an Emergency Travel Document (ETD), surrendered at port of entry, which would not show that they were living in the US. Some emigrants hadn't been home in years, fearing they wouldn't get re-entry. The annual issue of ETDs went from a handful a year, to hundreds in the 1990s. It was ridiculous. It was like the 'Schutz Passes', of my friend Wallenberg, being issued to fleeing Jews.

The Americans knew what we were up to. How could they not, since the whole purpose of having a second Vice Consul, dealing with Immigration, was to offer such advice. But they turned a blind eye. Occasionally, they would deport people, but only if they'd broken the law in some other respect: thus we sometimes had the amazing sight of someone being brought into the office in chains and forced to apply for a passport. But, in general, the Americans welcomed the influx of white, educated, English-speaking labour. Why wouldn't they? The fortunate Irish thus got lenient treatment compared to the South American illegals, lined up at JFK for deportation.

But their situation remained difficult: Irish illegals were unable to open bank accounts, visit hospitals or get paid properly — ruthless employers exploited their twilight status. Many Irish people had built up their own businesses, got married and had American children — and still they were illegal. But, by 1991, the Morrison Visas began to improve the situation and the Consulate got involved with the notification programme, with boxes of letters all over the floor. Here too, there was great duplicity, since firm job offers were required. So many people were guaranteed 'jobs' by one particular East Village café, that a US Consular Official in Dublin exclaimed, 'Wow, it must be a really big place!'

But, like Japanese prisoners in the jungle, many illegals had spent so long hidden away that they were now afraid to re-emerge for fear that the scheme was a plot to catch them. Many of the first visas thus went to people in Ireland who had no intention of coming to the US and were only using them as a insurance policy if jobs elsewhere didn't work out. Subsequent tranches rectified this, but on the whole, the programme was quite under-subscribed.

By the mid-Nineties, the Irish economy was recovering and the immigrants were returning in droves. Older Irish-Americans who felt that subsequent emigrant waves — especially those in the Eighties — weren't playing the game had their suspicions confirmed. The younger immigrants were not interested in putting down roots but used the US as a temporary economic shelter. Having mocked American, and Irish, patriotism, they had earned their money and gone home to help Ireland become a high-tech Switzerland. Out in the Astoria Manor, meanwhile, the dancers doing the Siege of Ennis were getting older and more assimilated, cut off by the departure of immigrants who, in contrast to those who'd come over in the 1950s, didn't stay.

From the Consulate, we dispensed lots of information and had cupboards full of propaganda; on the State, its flags and its folklore. And on Northern Ireland, going right back to the 1950s (although our 'line' on that subject had been gradually modified, of course).

We also had to deal with other, more unusual requests and queries. True Paddywackery abounded. For his sister's wedding, one man wanted Irish coinage to emulate the 'dowry' depicted in *The Quiet Man*. A woman who lost her certificate saying she'd kissed the Blarney

Stone wanted a replacement. But there were also some very smart Irish-Americans, scarily competent journalists and academics, fact-checking articles on Samuel Beckett and the Brehon Laws.

There were also a lot of letters from cranks, conspiracy-theorists naturally drawn towards foreign Embassies and the UN. 'I am being held against my will in a Mental Health facility in Florida. I want to go to Ireland. Call me back.' The thing is you *would* call them back. That was the point about being a Civil Servant. And soon you'd be talking to a man about cameras inside the lightbulbs, bugging devices in his yoghurt and having to sleep at night with cardboard inside his jacket to prevent being stabbed by the CIA. 'Make sure its good strong cardboard,' you'd find yourself saying, as you got sucked into his mindset, 'corrugated cardboard is no good.'

A lot of cranks turned up in the public office, as did many older people, just for a chat, or to ask for the Irish newspapers. One visitor was a large, fast-talking woman in a red dress. She claimed to be a visionary and had spoken to Our Lady. The end was nigh and a United Ireland was at hand (I can't remember which came first). In an X-Ray photo of her knee — the X Ray was held up against the security window for us all to take a look — a leprechaun had appeared along with the face of Jesus, a combination too ridiculous to contemplate. The thing about cranks is that they quickly lose their novelty value and become simply chattering egotists. Yet the amazing thing about this case was that it did look like a leprechaun.

The woman's ambition was to carry a statue of the Blessed Virgin down Fifth Avenue on St Patrick's Day. As much for the crack, I told her to contact the Parade Chairman, the beleaguered Frankie Beirne, already under siege from the gays and the Mayor. Within days, Frankie's despairing Leitrim accent was on the other end of a phone line: 'Eamon, listen, we can't have people carrying statues. Really, we've outlined the regulations before' — a reference to the nineteenth-century Parade rules which barred all statues, moving vehicles and domestic animals, except Irish wolfhounds.

Far from being disappointed, the woman arrived in a few weeks later, quite triumphant because Mary had left a crown on her doorstep. She held it up to the window. 'That's fantastic,' I said. It was one of those plastic gold crowns which the Pakistani cab drivers carried on their dashboards, along with mint seeds and blue perfume bottles. 'I'm going away for a few weeks now,' she said and I wished her luck. God love her. Her life revolved around us, the Cathedral and an institution upstate.

We also got a lot of letters concerning Missing Persons and people looking for their relatives, the fall out of the mass immigration of the 1940s and 1950s which had dispersed so many. A lot of the 'Whereabouts' letters were related to Estate Cases and fortunes that might have been left by rich Uncles or Aunts.

It was sometimes a worth a shot. We reckoned that millions were lost to the Irish by immigrants not leaving wills. With relatives untraced, the money goes to New York State. On the whole, however, the scope for complication meant that the Embassy didn't get involved. And yet still the letters from the Surrogates Court arrived, often with just two addresses; a sub-Post Office in Ireland, nearest to where the deceased's family came from, and the Consulate of Ireland. And perhaps a last address in England for a vanished sister, also an immigrant.

Often, it wasn't just the money. Many of the letters, scrawled in biro on old Basildon Bond or hastily torn bits of school copybook, were clearly desperate attempts to make contact with long-lost loved ones. The information was sometimes speculative and ridiculously sparse. 'Last seen working in a bar in Woodside, now closed'; 'Came over in 1952, would be known to GAA in Philadelphia'; 'In Newark, I think, she married a Turk'.

New York was like a big black hole of missing relatives and friends. 'She's gone into the Pictures, they say'; 'He's after driving around Millionaires'. One woman sent in a faded photo of a son she was hoping to trace, standing smiling with a buddy on a steamer's deck. 'Don't mind the fellow on the left,' she added blithely, 'he was gunned down later on a sidewalk.' Mothers seeking sons or daughters were only too happy to share their concerns with the Consul General of the day. 'Sean wrote putting on the style about his fancy job, but I know he's drinking. He's ended up in bad company in that BOWERY,' one wrote in dramatic capitals. 'Any help you can give me, sir.'

It reminded me of those black-and-white photos Weegee took in the Bowery bars of the 1950s; all the celebrating yet doomed Irish faces looking up at the camera. In one shot, the bar is named The Stork Club in an ironic joke to a more upmarket version with same name uptown. Or on themselves. What would the letter writers back home think if they saw such pictures? There they are now in New York, laughing away. Anything can happen. Sometimes, after reading these files, I'd go down to the subway beneath the Consulate, deserted after rush hour, and listen to the squeaks, like ghost trains, in the darkened tunnels. The city was built on immigrants.

There were also more recent requests, genuine Missing Persons. I had to go around the restaurants in Union Square looking for an Irish model who'd run away from home. When you made contact with such people, they were often irate. How dare you hunt me down for my family! The long arm of the concerned State was unwanted. The US Post Office had a 'Missing Person-Last Address' office you could write to, but such was personal mobility in the US, that there was little they could do. Our advice to people was to put letters in the Irish weekly newspapers which, in terms of community, were the ideal bulletin boards.

The weeklies came out every Wednesday. The *Irish Echo* was the longest established, with coverage of the suburbs and other States. The *Voice* was a more recently founded rival with a younger readership, city-based and liberal. And finally there was the *People*, the IRA's paper; incendiary, revelatory and full of quaint phrases about 'Free State traitors' and '26 County puppets'. We were '26 County puppets'. The *People* was basically *An Phoblacht* but without the left-wing stuff which would offend their more conservative US audience. The Gulf War, for example, was gently stepped around.

The weeklies gave a good view of the Community, with articles on immigration reform, traditional music and the politics of groups like the Ancient Order of Hibernians. The social pages carried pictures of County Dinner Dances and fundraisers in Woodside, events I would soon be at myself. We had a useful but tricky relationship with the papers, who were wary of the Consulate. My over-exuberant enjoyment at judging the New York Rose of Tralee, for example — an amazing night, with people standing on chairs cheering the contestants — was gleefully described. It began with a po-faced description of the 'young man from the Consulate' — as if I was some class of a monk — and finished with me allegedly carousing across Woodside Avenue, arm in arm with two of the buxom contestants. 'Less of that,' said the CG eyeing me over the paper.

But it was hard not to get carried away, given the feverish atmosphere among the Irish. Every week, in the Social pages, you'd see the faces of younger immigrants, in Montauk and Sag Harbour, outdoorsy and tanned, or in the pubs and clubs at night, having the crack. The early Nineties generation, making money and hanging out with Americans. These were the people who were forced to leave Ireland and now they were going to enjoy it. Why wouldn't they be happy? They were the equivalent of Weegee's photos except these immigrants had come educated and confident, doffing the hat to nobody. The ads reflected the plenitude of labour not available in Ireland; building companies, lawyers and nanny services (New York yuppies were amazed to hear their children growing up with Irish accents). Or removal companies, owned by Israelis and staffed by Irish. If you wanted a removal company in New York, you thought of the Holy Land — Haifa, Hallelujah. A friend of mine working for one such got a T-shirt as a going-away present. 'Nice Jewish Boy', it read.

The weeklies had a lot of coverage of sports and the GAA but their coverage of Northern Ireland was obsessive. Letters from old codgers complained about the 'Saxon's crimes' and 'English oppressors' — language long gone from the lexicon at home. One lady complained about Richard Harris starring in *The Field*, when he had 'enjoyed' playing that 'villain Cromwell'. In the obituaries, you'd see the older generation passing away. Their life stories; the cops, the World Wars, the small time businesses in Red Hook, Albany, Waterbury, Hoboken. The photos showed their hopeful faces, a little more sober than those in the Weegee's Bowery photos, but no less wistful. Eager to get on.

When not in the office, we were often out in the airport. Airport duty is a large part of diplomatic life, not least in New York since both JFK and La Guardia airports were major route hubs. Consequently I was often helping politicians make the transit to some 'fact-finding mission' on the West Coast or an Inter-Parliamentary Conference in Caribbean. The inter-parliamentary business was one of most popular of junket activities — outdone only by the European Parliament version. While Ministers work hard, their backbench party colleagues are off in the sunny climes of Barbados and Australia, introducing themselves to fellow democrats.

The CG believed that all politicians were to be treated with kid gloves. This was never more true than when they were abroad. If things didn't go right, the Civil Servant was the first and last person to blame. The lower their rank, the more pomp and ceremony they expect. Ministers of State demanded more than Ministers, TDs more than Ministers of State and so on. Worst of all were the Senators who took advantage of American confusion over their role (in the US, Senators were major figures) to demand royal treatment. Sean Doherty, for example, when Cathaoirleach of the Seanad, travelled as 'the Speaker of the Senate', a much more glorious title to the Americans who were rolling out the red carpet for him.

Homeward-bound politicians were taken to the Aer Lingus VIP lounge at JFK, where they fell upon the Irish newspapers and desperately began phoning home to see if their seats were still safe. Like despots at the UN, there was no guarantee that some opportunistic would-be TD hadn't availed of their absence to undermine their position. Now, of course, with the Internet and mobile phones, they can check en route. Thus technology has eroded the power of the junior diplomat, for there was always a great pleasure in announcing 'Today's papers, Deputies!' to a group of feverish TDs and watching them all jump up like a bunch of starving dogs for the Pedigree Chum.

One hoped, of course, that the news therein was good, for woe betide the Civil Servant looking after a politician in a bad mood, especially if it's a Minister and party. Even at the best of times we had to be very careful, offering just the right mixture of formality and charm. More than one diplomat has been destroyed by being overly familiar with a Minister and often those politicians you imagine to be the most informal and down-to-earth are actually the most demanding of ceremony and attention.

For example, when Labour came into power in 1992, the raft of new faces they brought with them created some suspicion. With regard to some protocol matter they would consistently check previous practice: 'Is this what you'd do before?' First time Ministers didn't want to be treated any differently to previous Governments or to Fianna Fáil Ministers, their Coalition partners. In time, however, they mellowed out.

The ideal situation was to get politicians near retirement age, when they'd become more sanguine. By the late nineties, Des O'Malley, in his role as Chairman of the Oireachtas Committee on Foreign Affairs had become a staple of these trips, cracking jokes and asking Embassies for the racing returns from home. One late night in Warsaw, he was dared by a Civil Servant to sing 'Arise and Follow Charlie' the now discontinued Fianna Fáil marching song, and he eventually obliged — all the words. 'Oh, to have had a video camera,' said the First Sec afterwards.

On the whole, however, it was as well not to get too relaxed around travelling politicians. On the contrary, you had to be absolutely on your guard. One time, I had to meet some Parliamentarians coming in from Buenos Aires. Having 'overdone the networking', as they put it, they didn't wish to do too much talking. But as we drove into the city, they livened up and began asking probing questions. There are always one or two inquisitors on these trips, especially if they perceive you to be the 'typical Southside DFA type', who needs to be tested.

One chap kept asking me the GAA scores from the National League. Thankfully, it was a stretch limo and he had to ask me over the back of long seat, and six beefy shoulders, so I was able to bluff a bit and pretend to half hear him. 'Eh, I'm not sure how that one ended up … it was tight enough at the start.' When I checked the score later it turned out that the game had been cancelled because of poor weather.

Another guy kept asking me the landmarks as we approached Manhattan. 'And what about that one?'

'That's the Chrysler.'

'And that one?'

'The Citicorp.'

'Hmmm. I see, I see, I see. And tell me now, what's that over there?'

'Oh, for Christ's sake, it's King Kong,' I mentally shouted. It was like when I found myself out on the balcony of our UN Ambassador's residence, with Mrs Collins beside me, the Minister's wife. The Ambassador's

East End Drive apartment is amazing, a rooftop pad overlooking the East River on one side and the lights of midtown on the other. Quite methodically, Mrs Collins began asking me about every one of those lights. I suddenly found myself alone beside her as cowardly diplomats scarpered inside for the brandy.

Her husband was more impish. Taken on a Circle Line cruise of Manhattan, he quietly asked the guide beforehand to mention the Ambassadorial apartment in his narration. 'And up there we see the magnificent residence of the Irish Ambassador to the UN!' announced the guide, to a boat full of Japanese tourists as the Ambassador nearly jumped into the river. The Smirker grinned on contentedly.

13

Dancing for Ireland

The Social circuit was a large part of the job in New York and my first function was the Fall Dinner Dance of the County Louth Society. The County Societies — or P&Bs, Patriotic and Benevolent Organisations — were the lifeblood of the Community and over the next three years I would go to almost all thirty-two of them.

'Invest in a tuxedo,' the CG told me, 'you'll need it.' He was right. I would be in and out of the tuxedo almost every weekend. 'We should put them in the National Museum,' my colleague, James McIntyre used to say, 'they've seen more service for Ireland than some of those Volunteer uniforms.'

The protocol, and even the atmosphere, of these functions has not changed since the 1950s, and part of it was that the VIPs or people on the dais, or podium, would wear black tie. It used to be all the men at these dinner dances wore black tie — it must have looked like a penguin colony. People forget how formal New York used to be and, indeed, it is often the ethnic groups who keep up this formality, keen to show their respectability. Nowadays, however, people stare at you, sitting in a cab or limo, and assume you're a waiter, or part of a wedding band. One time I was going to Scarsdale for the annual dinner of the Friendly Sons of St Patrick. It is a huge gathering, a thousand people, all male and all in dinner jackets. Getting the train from Grand Central, I found myself among the Friday evening after-office crowd.

'Give us a song, Pedro,' they shouted boozily, 'how about "Mack the Knife"?'

Another time, at the Longford Dance, I left the room and wandered into the other functions. Usually, these Dances are held in large Banqueting Suites with other events — a Colombian wedding or a Polish reception — going on next door. Bored with the Irish dances, and, believe me, when you hear the Rose of Castlerea for the 150th time, you *will* get bored, you can always check out the other functions.

Next door to the Longford dance, there was an Ultra Orthodox bar mitzvah, with lots of bearded young men in black coats and women with long skirts and sleeves; clothing that was more than handy, for the central heating had broken down and the guests were very upset. 'Hey, there's one now!' someone shouted when they saw me, 'go on, ask him!'

With my tuxedo, they thought I was one of the waiters, or managers, and suddenly I was being barraged by complaints about the cold. 'What's he saying?' someone called out.

'He says he doesn't work here,' a man shouted back.

'No, of course, he doesn't,' was the sarcastic response. It was real New York; all hunched shoulders and protest. I explained that it was also cold next door, which was true. 'What, as cold as this?' asked another man, and when I said that no, perhaps it wasn't *this* cold, he said 'No, of course, it's not,' and shrugged. As if say, just our luck: the Jews get the coldest room.

Most of the dances were held in Queens and Brooklyn. Back in the 1940s, they were held in Manhattan, at hotels like the Roosevelt or the Plaza, with 2000 people in a room. But those *really* were the days of the Irish in America. Now the functions had gone with the communities, out to the suburbs, although often the communities had gone further out — Connecticut, Westchester — and people enjoyed coming back to places like Woodside and the Bronx where their parents had lived, especially with the recent rejuvenation of those areas with new Irish immigrants.

Astoria, just across the river from the UN, was a good example, a formerly Irish area, now populated mostly by Greeks and Yugoslavs. The Louth dance was being held in the Astoria Manor. Stepping into a café for directions — the Ghanaian driver hadn't a clue where we were — we were told by the local Croatians that we couldn't miss it. 'Many lights, many lights!'

They were right. The Astoria Manor is a large confection of black glass, mirrors, and piping white lights, like something out of *Goodfellas*. 'Very I-talian, I'm afraid,' an old biddy whispered at a later function, the 'I' painfully enunciated, in case they might be there at the Wexford dinner to hear her. I-talian, of course, meant Italian-American, as in muscle cars and big-haired Brooklyn girls, not the Italy of Roman ruins and stylish Lambrettas which Europeans were used to.

These venues, like the people, had changed little; places like the well-named Crystal Place in Astoria, or the Tower View in Woodside, with the F train rumbling overhead. Inside the Tower View, backlit photos of Glendalough and JFK in Ireland adorned the walls, hyper-real John Hinde images which harked back to an imaginary and idealised homeland. When I told Napoleon I was off to the splendidly named Kneers Golden Pheasant Ballroom in Woodside, he snorted with disbelief. He'd been there in the Seventies, as Vice Consul, fighting the 'crazies', as he called the rabid nationalists. He even recognised the names of the guests.

The king of venues, however, was Leonard's of Great Neck, out on Long Island. It looked like a wedding cake. A big Vegas-style arrangement with 'Leonard's' written signature-style across the pink-tiled frontage. Roof spotlights lit up the sky and you could actually see the beams from the highway. 'Follow that spaceship', I told an Indian cabby and I watched his eyes widen as we swung into a forecourt with a multicoloured fountain and white-gloved doormen who came down to open the car door. It was like arriving for the Oscars.

Inside were huge chandeliers, frosted glass and velvet cushioned panels on gilt-edged doors. Again, the place was catering for simultaneous events. Latino girls in powder-blue dresses, their escorts in purple cummerbunds, horsed around in the glittering lobby, while a family gathered noisily for a bar mitzvah. This wasn't the serious black-clad Jewishness of the city but a more suburban vibe; Jewish-Lite, with gum-chewing guys in pony tails and open silk shirts. Confusion reigned. As the piper led people into the Donegal dance, two kids in tie-dyed kippas joined the line, thinking it was theirs. 'Yo, come back here!' said their father, pulling them out.

Apparently, on one occasion, many years ago, the Sligo Society got the kosher dish, while the Jewish orthodox wedding sat down, appalled, to the fatty bacon and cabbage. But it was an ambitious kitchen. On another occasion in the Sixties, the waiters entered with flaming salvers — 'Here come the shish kebabs!' cried the MC — only to set off the fire sprinklers and send the drenched women running to the bathroom, their beehive hairdos disintegrating.

But back to the Astoria Manor. Inside the starlit lobby, I followed the Irish crowd up the grand staircase. Short-haired men with strong cheekbones looked suspiciously around them as they ushered their frowning wives up the steps. Big, square-jawed youngsters followed; the First Generation. It wasn't that they weren't going to have a good time. Rather, it seemed that they just wanted to keep a dignified air away from the boisterous, leather-tied Italians and cleavaged Hispanic girls running in and out of the other reception rooms.

Watching these glitter-clad creatures swish to and fro, I was tempted to investigate, but I veered instead for a verdant table behind which two old ladies were handing out green-sprayed buttonholes. A burly police bagpiper with calves like tree trunks was warming up to lead in the

VIPs. 'Ah, the new man at the Consulate!' the ladies cooed. 'Thank God you're here, they're lining up for the piper.'

'Good man, good man,' said the Chairman and he introduced me to the nervous Guest of Honour, a smiling Chaplain, and a citation-bearing representative of Mort Shulman, the local Assemblyman, who had to attend a B'nai Brith dinner and, sadly, couldn't be with his friends 'the Gaels'.

I exchanged some vigorous handshakes. And smiles, firm hearty smiles. I was learning to smile for my country. The Society officers were a mixture of American and Irish, but I noticed that they weren't young, and indeed of the stream of people going into the hall beside me most were over forty. The recent emigrants, the 'new Irish', were not joining the societies. Their absence was a story we were to hear more about.

The room was quite full all the same, maybe 400 or 500 people. Needless to say, there is big competition between the Counties for the most impressive turn-out, with the likes of Cork and Kerry fighting out a sort of Munster Final scenario, and getting the numbers up to a waiter-crippling 800.

I had arrived at the end of 'Cocktail Hour', where people mingle and fill up their side plates with hors d'oeuvres of pasta, sausage and chicken wings; normally meals in themselves, but here they were only starters. The Irish had taken to the American habit of eating at every available opportunity. Later, a dandruffed priest told me that it was because of the Famine. 'Food mightn't be here tomorrow,' he said, seriously, and he looked at me as if to say 'And neither might you.' But after a bellyful of these dinners and, more particularly, the long speeches which preceded them, I began to see the wisdom of such precautionary stuffing.

The piper elbowed up 'The West's Awake' and we followed him into the big reception room where the crowd rose and gave us a standing ovation, clapping us up onto the dais. I was slightly embarrassed. I saw people checking me out — the 'man from the Government'. Young women in silk dresses gave me the judicious once-over. Already bored with their escorts, I thought confidently. Or dragged along by their 'old country' parents to discover their roots. Hopefully, I could help them on that score.

Sometimes, at these dinners, you wait outside and when the MC calls out your name, you walk in waving — 'Eamon Delaney, the Vice Consul of Ireland!' — and everyone applauds. It's like a Hall of Fame moment at the Oscars. Tonight, however, we walked in single file, like the lining-out in Croke Park. There was a strict order too; the Guest of Honour, followed by myself, and then the Chaplain — State before Church — and then the various committee members, with their strange titles like 'Sergeant-at-Arms'. The dais, and the room in general, is decorated with balloons in the county colours, and the US and Irish flags. There is also a County banner, uncomfortably similar to that of the Orange Order and usually featuring one of the county's illustrious sons or daughters. The martyred Kevin Barry of Carlow or, for Roscommon, a tired-looking Douglas Hyde, despairing perhaps of the avowedly sectarian world of which he was unwittingly a part.

But even if they were cheesy, it was nice to see these banners later, coming up Fifth Avenue on St Patrick's Day, floating along against the bif stores and corporate glasswork, like out-of-place medieval pageants. By which time, you would know the Counties well and the banner-carriers might shout out a greeting, 'Mr Vice Consul, how you doin'?' And you'd wave back, a little exchange which usually brought a wry look from whatever moody Minister happened to be beside you. It was also nice because, despite being the biggest and most representative of Irish bodies, the Counties got a raw deal at the Parade, and were usually put to the back. This was because the Parade was in the vice-like grip of the Ancient

Order of Hibernians, the true dinosaurs of the Irish community.

The National Anthems began and everyone went absolutely quiet, turning to face the tricolour. The Irish anthem was first, sung in English but I don't know when I'd last heard it delivered with such gusto. All the words were sung out clearly and heads — young and old — moved from side to side in a sort of dreamy defiance, as if, come woe or weal, they really would 'man the Bhearna Bhaoil'. Particularly poignant was the line 'Some have come — from a land beyond the Wave', a reminder of those who had come, and gone before them, restless for the old country whilst living in the new.

For the new country, there was an immediate raising of hands to breasts; 'O'er the ramparts we came, by the twilight's last gleaming.' 'The 'dawn's early rise' was sighted with such conviction that it wouldn't surprise me if some of them imagined themselves to be back there right now at Fredericksburg, Iwo Jima or the Gulf of Tonkin. These functions were often peppered with decorated war veterans. During the Gulf War, the receptions were festooned with yellow ribbons, and best wishes were read out for the serving sons and daughters of members. As with the cops, Irish-Americans have had a heavy involvement in the military and some functions were even held in Legion Posts and VFW halls (Veterans of Foreign Wars). Seeing the Marine Flags on the walls and posters proclaiming 'These Colours Don't Run', you realised that this sort of patriotism wasn't something from the movies, or the redneck South, but a deep embodiment of American, and Irish-American, life.

With the anthems finished, the crowd noisily sat down again, as the MC, Tommy Smith, introduced the VIPs who stood and did a Reagan-like wave. Tommy was a football commentator in Gaelic Park in the Bronx and his introductions had the rushed quality of a Sunday game. I heard myself described as a 'new young man straight off the boat from Ireland': the magical 'boat' which no aeroplane can replace. 'From Dublin, but we won't hold that against him!'

The Dance Chairman reviewed a successful year for the Society. Speaking into his chest and uneasy with the attention, he thanked his wife for all her support and the crowd applauded. Beside me, the Secretary waited his turn, nervously clutching his speech. His hands were huge, stumpy fingered and callused. He had probably been a labourer or a stevedore, like many of the people in the room. The old blue-collar Irish, the ones who didn't join the army or police.

An elfish man with a long chin was introduced to a loud cheer. This was Frankie Beirne, chairman of the St Patrick's Day Parade, the largest parade in New York and, as Frankie was fond of telling the TV stations, 'the biggest parade in the world', a superlative that went down well in this most superlative of cities. Frankie had recently been involved in controversy, having excluded an Irish gay group from marching in the parade 'saying there was no room'. Less publicly he had also courted trouble by refusing to resign in the wake of a split in the parade's organising body, the Ancient Order of Hibernians (AOH).

The split, a classic old-style personality clash with no ideological or practical content, was unintelligible to most New Yorkers and indeed to many Irish-Americans. To the Louth Society, however, little Frankie, with a Leitrim accent so strong you'd think someone was holding his nose, was 'one of them' and they'd stick by him through thick and thin. He had seen off the liberals, the Mayor and *The New York Times* and now even his own organisation couldn't get rid of him.

Frankie concluded his fast and furious harangue of his opponents by calling for a 'healing of divisions' and modestly reminding the alert audience that it was only when the Irish were united that they gained any kind of freedom. And with a big grin, he said he'd see them all next year on fifth Avenue. (As it turned out, it wasn't going to be as easy as that. Rather than accept the gays into the Parade, the AOH threatened to cancel the entire event; when they took the same stand a year later, the issue ended up in the courts.)

After Frankie, I got up and said how glad I was to be here, bringing the best wishes of the Consul General and 'the Government at home in Ireland'. A little flushed, I sat down and noticed that people were still staring. They had seen so many Consuls and Vice Consuls come and go, 'Young Men from the Old Country'. For a moment, looking down at these worn and eager faces, I felt vaguely guilty that I was here among them all, these people who had had to leave Ireland and couldn't grow old there. I felt I was part of something that they had missed out on. Ireland had changed and they knew it. It had changed without them. It had changed in a way that had truly left them behind.

The Guest of Honour was then introduced, which unusually was not an older, business figure, but a group of young people, mostly from Louth, who had founded the Irish Immigrant Emergency Fund, a group set up to help bereaved relatives bear the cost of flying a dead body back to Ireland. The cost is expensive and, at one stage, Aer Lingus used to do it gratis for those in need.

One of their friends had apparently died after falling from a building scaffold and, when they had a whip-round to help, they were so impressed by the response that they set up a group to help others. It was a classic example of the community helping its own. In the bars of Woodside or the Bronx, there were posters up for these fundraisers, for a child's kidney transplant perhaps or for someone who'd lost a business in a fire.

Usually, however, the Guest of Honour was a prominent business or political figure. The cynical view was that this was done to pull in lucrative advertising for the programme and fill up the tables at the dance. But such figures had real worth, fêted as role-models and offering a good snapshot on Irish assimilation. Watched adoringly by his, or her, family and friends, the Guest of Honour would have their life story read out by the MC and, despite the diversity of the Irish experience, it was amazing how similar such stories were. Give or take a name or two, it usually went something like this;

'One of six children, he left Ardee in 1942 to seek his fortune in America. One windy Sunday in Gaelic Park, he met the lovely Katherine Griffin from Carna, Co Galway. It was love at first sight' (whistles from the audience) 'and they married shortly afterwards. They settled in Hoboken, New Jersey where they lived with their three lovely children; Nancy, now a nurse in Mount Sinai, Shawn, a lawyer, and very good on the tin whistle we hear, and Eileen in her final year at Mount Holyoke.'

If it wasn't Mount Holyoke, it might be Iona or Manhattan College. If Shawn wasn't a lawyer, he might be a banker or a Naval Officer. Often, the sons and daughters of cops wised up to the legal game, became lawyers and rose into the middle class.

Listening to all this, I would catch the eye of James Higgins, a droll chap from Dublin who took photographs for the *Irish Voice*. With his leather jacket and floral tie, his look would communicate the understanding that we were witnessing a different world, a time capsule of a community which no longer existed in Ireland — if it ever had. It was quite different to the world we would be experiencing later when we met up in the trendy cafes of the East Village.

Beside him was another photographer, for whom this was nothing unusual: Tom Forde, from the rival *Irish Echo*. With his older equipment and a huge nylon tie, cheery-faced Tom had been capturing generations of other cheery faces since the days of exploding zinc flash bulbs. Later, he told me sadly that he thought the new young immigrants had 'no social focus'; always sitting in pubs, whining. Woodside and the Bronx, nothing but pubs. Whereas, in the fifties, they went on picnics, played football and went dancing in the Jaeger House, real dancing where people dressed up in gowns and bow-ties. I was very impressed until I met one of his contemporaries. 'Bullshit,' he said, 'it was just the same. More sex, maybe, that's all.' I didn't catch if there was more sex then or now.

The speeches over, I was brought to the Chairman's table where I was introduced to some VIPs. On my plate, slabs of prime rib beef and 'two veg' awaited me; being dais-bound means you forgo the soup. Frankie Beirne extended a surprisingly long hand for man so short. 'Good laddie,' he said and his wife nodded, 'Welcome to New York.'

'I'm a good friend of your boss,' said a silver-haired man, whom I half-recognised. He was Jack Mooney, Grand Marshall of a previous Parade and, by the look of his topped-up Florida tan and pearly white teeth, still basking in the glow of this, the greatest honour the Community can bestow. Although in the case of Jack, the CEO of a beer company, it was something of an accelerated honour, since he'd stepped in with emergency advertising for the Parade's TV coverage when the excluded gays cleverly targeted the usual advertisers to withdraw.

Of course, it meant that the sober Parade had had to take on an alcohol endorsement. By 'sober', I mean, the marchers; the surrounding crowd is usually well tanked-up, which made the TV advertising sort of appropriate. But it also meant that someone like Jack arrived as a last gasp Grand Marshall, and this pissed off some of the loyal time-servers.

Jack asked about the situation with 'those young illegals' and I gave him the spiel about the upcoming Green Cards. As I did, I noticed some men at the end of the table eyeing me keenly, even suspiciously. They were wearing tuxedos and munching their beef but I hadn't noticed them on the dais. 'So when are the English going to get out of Ireland?' one of them suddenly asked.

'Eh ...' I was stunned. I'd been told to expect this but still, it was a bit blunt. He was staring at me. I immediately went into the usual patter about peaceful co-existence and the search for a settlement.

'Yeah, so will they be gone in five years or ten?' he asked and I had to broaden my patter. Needless to say, I got no support from the others at the table, except for the Chairman who muttered something about 'a time and place'. Mooney grinned at the tablecloth while his Florida tan took on a deeper flush. 'Well it'll be good when it happens,' said Mr Tuxedo and, just as suddenly, he and his mates got up and left. Then I realised; they were the band.

'Don't mind that stuff,' said little Frankie, 'I get it from them all the time.' Which was true. For all the trouble he caused other people, Frankie wouldn't let the IRA or their support organisation, Noraid, take over the Parade and the Consulate were grateful to him for that. The Republicans wanted placards and martyr posters but Frankie kept them to the one banner, the famous one, which read, as the man said, 'England get out of Ireland'.

'Won't you dance?' asked an old dear suddenly, her diaphanous fingers rising in a stranglehold, and I readily agreed. Out onto the floor we schoonered, Tuxedo watching us as we waltzed delicately to the 'bump-tish-tish' of the drummer keeping time with his chewing gum. But Tuxedo seemed to have mellowed and, closing his eyes, he suddenly summed a vision of the 'vales of Leinster', so green and magical that one wondered why any of these people had left it in the first place. Possibly, because, as the man once told the tourist 'the children can't eat the view'. England Out of Ireland, perhaps, but multinationals in, please.

I must say I was relieved. I had expected some fiery rebel ballads. But it was harmless stuff, nice old tunes I hadn't heard in years. In fact, I was to hear very few rebel songs at these dances. There was instead an emphasis on respectability and 'putting on a good show'. People were expertly dressed — even if there were some amazing 1950s fashions — and very well behaved.

For example, even though it was a free bar and people had paid $70 a ticket, I rarely ever saw intoxication at these events. They were still playing against the WASP stereotypes of them, in contrast to the new Irish — the Nineties kids — who had no such inhibitions. Or so the old timers claimed. 'And they don't know the dances,' one old lady told me, just as old Dominicans said their kids don't know the merengue. It was a New York story.

I was about to get my own chance to dance, when a girl pulled me out for the Siege of Ennis. 'Are you enjoying yourself?' she said and I said I was. Her name was Rosie and she played with the Women's GAA. She was also involved in the new Young Camogies, a split from the existing Camogie Association which reflected the tensions between old and new immigrants, as well as the Irish propensity for splits. The GAA, indeed, was one of the big Irish organisations in New York, and in North America. Their dinner dances were as large again as those of the Counties.

Rosie was a laughing girl with a mane of black curls and a cream beaded dress which clung to her big-hipped figure, like the one Marilyn Monroe wore when she sang for JFK. It's funny but even the younger Irish in this atmosphere seemed old fashioned, more formal than most of their contemporaries. In Irish-America, I saw an America many young Irish wouldn't see — indeed, many young Americans wouldn't see — but I also discovered an Ireland I didn't know at home.

'Get in line! Get in line!' said an stout woman as the accordion wheezed, ready to begin the Siege.

It was a dance I dimly remembered from school days in the Gaeltacht, a nimble arrangement, with two couples facing each other, stepping in and out and moving across and back, where they break to grab the partner in front and spin around wildly. Often very wildly until, the floor spinning, they break and grope blindly for the hand of their partner — ah, Rosie of the firm grip — and go back and forth one more time. Each couple, or both couples, then go under the hoisted arms of the couple opposite and come face to face with a new couple and do the whole thing all over again and so on down the dance floor. Instead of dancing with one woman, you dance with twenty and even with a man, although men dancing with men wasn't popular here. Not with Vets and firemen. And not after Frankie's speech earlier on. Girls on girls, mind you, didn't seem to be a problem.

With the dance over, we went to the bar where I had my fingers crushed by another round of energetic handshakes. On the floor, people were now jiving, another dance which made me regret the narrowness of my mainly urban upbringing. As I watched Rosie going through her paces with some handsome footballer, I thought of John Waters' book *Jiving at the Crossroads* and of how he had used the jive as a metaphor for the whole division between rural and urban Ireland.

Soon, I was brought around to meet Irish-Americans, who were full of questions. Where do you live in the city? The 'West Village' drew mixed reactions. It was a bit downtown and gay but it was also near the old Irish docking area of Spring Street and the detective HQ on Hudson Street.

Where are you from in Ireland? Dublin usually brings a groan, it not being regarded as fully Irish. Thankfully, I had my Galway hat to put on — having being part-reared there — as well as the counties of my mother and father, Cavan and Mayo. Like Charlie Haughey, I was from everywhere. Irish-Americans are obsessed by counties, in a way which doesn't exist at home, except for football and Dáil constituencies. Here, people got presented with marble maps of places like Carlow. Try drawing Carlow from memory. Indeed, so tired was our Immigration Officer, James McIntyre, of people exclaiming 'Oh, you're from Ireland — what part?', that he used to curtly reply 'All of me.' The other one was 'Where do you hail from, me lad?' Taking a step backwards, you'd shout, 'From over here!' But that was being too smart.

'Are you married?' was usually the next question, put either by mothers introducing their daughters or by the kind of guy who thought that to be unmarried in New York meant you were running around with everything in sight. There was a deep conservatism to this, of course, and later when I brought partners to these dances, Irish friends anxious to experience this culture first hand, it was inevitably assumed that they were girlfriends. By the end of it, people must have thought I was a right tart.

One friend was even described from the podium as my wife. 'I'm not his wife!' she shouted with a vehemence which surprised me, and everyone around. Later, when the 'gays in the parade' row was at its height, Gary, a sculptor friend, suggested that he come along in his white suit, with just a hint of black mascara. And perhaps a wink for the police bagpiper. That'd get them talking.

At one table, I was introduced to Kerry and Kelly, an eponymous hazard which illustrated a peculiar habit of Irish-Americans; giving their children Irish place names and surnames as first names. (The other was phonetic spellings of Gaelic names, thus Shawn and Sheela, and, of course, the names of patriots. I met more John Daniel O'Connell's and Robert Emmet Lee's here than I ever did in Ireland, the latter simultaneously covering the bases of Irish and American nationalism.)

Kerry and Kelly had the classic Irish-American look: the shoulder length hair, the pert nose and freckles. It's funny how the Irish-Americans seem to epitomise the old fashioned look of wholesome America. In the same way that the boys were invariably square-jawed and short-haired in that football hero way — and usually about a foot taller than their parents — the girls were like a refined version of the Irish Colleen, as if the health and wealth of America had turned them all into chirpy Peggy Sues.

There was a diner that James and I used to go to on Broadway called the Stardust, which had among its memorabilia, framed posters of the Subway Girls, a series put up in the late fifties of smiling 'New York girls', usually of Irish or Swedish ancestry, with a little blurb about what they did and why they took the subway. Later at a reception in the Brooklyn DA's office, I met this lawyer who exactly fitted the profile. 'You look like a Subway Girl,' I couldn't help telling her.

'That's what everyone says!' she cried in recognition. She even described how her Dad's friends, veterans and cops, would say 'Let me introduce you to my sons — my sons would love you.' But when she met the sons, they didn't love her at all. They wanted Californian blondes. America had changed. It was the fathers who loved her, because she looked like the girls they used to fancy when they were young, the girls of the 1950s. It was like those old men who bemoan the silicone excess of modern babes and recall instead the glamour and elegance of Ava Gardner.

I must say, right now I was keen on exploring the Fifties myself and I was about to hand over my telephone number when suddenly I heard it being called out over the microphone. I couldn't believe it. It was Tuxedo: in between 'Wonderful Wexford' and 'Galway Bay', he was now urging people to call the Irish Consulate to protest against the impending extradition from Ireland of Dessie Ellis, an IRA man wanted in Britain. The 1990s were breaking in again.

I was stunned. And so were the organisers who rushed down to apologise, saying it shouldn't have happened, nothing to do with them. I said it didn't matter and it didn't. I was having a great time; the food, the drink, the company and the music — notwithstanding the political opinions of the man who was singing it. And besides, most of the people in the room didn't appear to have taken in what the band leader was saying.

An Accidental Diplomat

However, content with his blow for Ireland and humbled by some browbeating from the Organising Committee — I could see the Sergeant-at-Arms waving the same — Tuxedo soon retreated to his music and, before long, he was launching into some old time rock 'n' roll. 'Come on Every-body!' he shouted, driven less by the desire to get the English out of Ireland and more by the wish to get everybody on the dance floor.

They responded too, including old-timers only too happy to relive their youth. And yet while Kerry and Kelly bopped away like Prohibition-era flappers, I noticed little Frankie and the wife, still waltzing back and forth at the edge of the dancefloor, as if nothing had changed.

On the way to the bathroom I peeped in at the other functions. The Italian party was rocking and the Hispanic wedding was getting smoochy, with young couples glued to each other in the disco-lit darkness, the boys in silver silk shirts, the girls in shimmering blue and pink dresses. The older folk were drinking rum in alcoves and getting into heavy conversations, wedding stuff, plans for the future and the past. Out in the street, the white horse and trap were waiting.

Back with 'the Louths', I found myself dragged into a ring where Rosie and her camogie friends had kicked off their shoes and were dancing barefoot. One of them, in a black cocktail dress, had a silver ankle bracelet shaking away on one of her brown legs. Very brown, tanned to her pink toes. It must have been a warm summer in New York. And I was glad I was here for it. Yes, this was definitely better than Tehran and possibly better than New Delhi. Those novels-in-progress can wait.

'Don't let it go to your head!' said a burly ex-cop. He meant the dancing, but also maybe the girls. 'Don't worry, I'm still finding my feet,' I shouted back.

'Sure, no bother to you,' said a woman beside him, 'Isn't it just like home.'

But that was the whole point. It wasn't *just* like home.

First, I'll take Manhattan ... Early days as Vice Consul of Ireland in New York, 1990.

Gorbachev at Shannon, April 1990. Haughey's tense expression might be because Gorbachev has just asked him if Ireland was ruled by a British Monarch.

European Summit, Dublin Castle, 1990. Foreign Affairs Secretary Noel Dorr (right) and Political Director Ted Barrington watch closely while Taoiseach, Charles Haughey, delivers an agreed text.

Dublin Castle, 1990. Haughey with his good friend, the Italian Premier, Andreotti (the 'wily old fox') and Foreign Minister, Gianni De Michelis. Andreotti later faced major corruption charges in Italy, while De Michelis was sentenced to four years in prison. Foreign Minister, Gerry Collins, is smiling on the left.

Newark, New Jersey. St Patrick's Day 1991. The Parade now goes through an almost entirely Black area.

'The most extraordinary room in the world.' The General Assembly of the United Nations, New York.

Me so crazy. A humorous moment in the Iraqi seat at the UN, 1991. Ireland is in the 'hot corner', seated alphabetically between Iraq, Iran and Israel.

Queens, New York, 1992. Keeping abreast of matters at the
Carlow Association of New York dinner dance.

With protestors against changes to Articles 2 and 3 of the Constitution in the
background, Dick Spring arrives at the Mansion House, Dublin, 1992.
'Lose the white mac' a letter writer suggested to the Minister.

A handshake too far. The collapse of the Fianna Fail–Labour coalition in 1994 created an unexpected challenge for the Peace Process.

The Forum for Peace, 1995. Sean Donlon, Northern Ireland adviser to Taoiseach John Bruton, meets Gerry Adams and Pat Doherty of Sinn Fein, while a grim-faced Sean O'hUiginn drops out of view.

A *Sunday Independent* cartoon gives an Orangeman's view of the 'Prince of Darkness', Sean O'hUiginn, head of the Department's Anglo-Irish Division.

Northern Secretary Sir Patrick Mayhew arriving at Iveagh House with Dick Spring, 1993.

Outside the scrum. The White House lawn, St Patrick's Day. Irish Ambassador, Sean O'hUiginn and Dermot Gallagher (in dark suits) wait while reporters question the Taoiseach, Bertie Ahern.

Battle-scarred but still standing. The Remembrance ceremony at Islandbridge in 1995 — my last protocol engagement.

The nearest thing to home was probably the Consulate itself, where we held many parties to which the Irish-American community would come. While most of our socialising was out 'on the circuit' we were host to a lot of receptions: launch parties for new books or Broadway shows, and grip-and-grin sessions for visiting Ministers. The CG and his wife were particularly interested in artistic matters which was timely given that there was then something of a Irish cultural renaissance in the city. But Pádraic Mac Kernan, our Ambassador in Washington, was apparently not too impressed by all this partying, possibly because it contrasted with the quietness of DC life, and at one stage he tried to curtail the number of receptions, on the grounds that the Consulate was a fire hazard. We thought it was ludicrous and, after obeying this stricture for a while, we went back to holding parties as before.

The receptions, held in the boardroom, were a bit of fun. But they were work, as well. James McIntyre and I had to meet all the people we met on the circuit, except now we were on home turf and couldn't escape. Such events honed the crucial diplomatic skill of mixing: the trick is to mingle among people briskly and firmly, without getting stuck or without being rude. Like in a dealing room, you had to develop 'brokers' ears so you could hear three conversations at once. Perfecting the 'another 45 coming' routine was also useful; looking over the person's shoulder as if there was a bus coming. i.e. trying to check out who else is in the room. James and I would rescue each other by saying 'Eamon, the Governor's office are on the line!' permitting an escape from the clutches of some longwinded sentimentalist, who were in fact often impressed by such interruptions.

The other escape was to go out to the balcony for a breather, where we had to tell people watching the sun going down on Park Avenue to take their glasses in from the ledge, because they could kill someone eighteen floors below — 'and the Irish Government was not insured for such an event'. I used to love announcing that. Another time, I found a sozzled couple freely making out. 'We're definitely not insured for that,' I told them, 'Here, get inside the drapes' And they nodded their thanks. The billowing drapes led into the CG's room.

Such dalliances were rare, however, for the crowd was generally quite old, a fact for which we rightly got stick. The invitation list had moss growing on it. It was the same in other Consulates and reflected the hiatus in immigration. The Chicago Vice Consul once demonstrated this for me, pulling out an old file for a 1950s de Valera visit then singling out the numerous individuals who would be coming to a Consulate function that night. Usually they were AOH luminaries, teachers, and people from City Hall and the Irish cultural organisations. Someone said the crowd looked like 'they'd been exhumed'. We tried to invite younger people, but the new Irish didn't organise like the earlier immigrants and were in any case wary of Governments and Consulates.

This made for a slightly self-satisfied atmosphere at Consulate parties which could be become nauseous. There was lots of 'It's great to be Irish' or, worse, 'It's great to be Hibernian.' Beefy American men and braying women would back you into a corner and, canapé in hand, tell you how important your heritage was. This tended to alienate the younger Irish, for there's nothing worse than being lectured about your nationality. Irish-Americans don't realise how much this offends the native Irish. Irish lesbians or atheists may not be their idea of the 'old country', but they should recognise that some such people actually come from there, unlike themselves.

The receptions were good crack. Usually a crew would go on afterwards to the Irish bars on Second Avenue, meeting up with people coming from the Broadway shows or from gigs or film launches. There seemed to be so much Irish cultural activity in the city at the time. Afterwards, you might go on downtown, heading into the graffiti-scrawled hostelries, still in your suit — always a provocative pleasure. After the Downtown Beirut, or a bar on Ludlow Street, you could find yourself at a party with East Village kids in prescription glasses, talking about how the CIA controls the weather.

'You're working for the Government?' a purple-haired girl once shrieked when I told her what I did. 'Sssh,' I whispered, afraid that her anarcho-syndicalist friends might have lynched me. 'But sure, its only the Irish Government,' I reassured her, 'It's only Smirker Collins.'

We also had a lot of contact with local politicians, especially on issues like immigration and the North. While the CG and the Ambassador were meeting people like Connecticut Senator Chris Dodd or the Kennedys, we were on circuit meeting the Next Generation; Joseph Crowley in the Bronx, or local Assemblyman Sal Albanese, sitting on the dais and speed-flicking through the County Journals, taking in all the names and checking for his own. Or Congressman (later Senator) Chuck Schumer declaring to a roaring hall in Bay Ridge that 'the Irish are coming back to Brooklyn, they're coming back to New York, and they're coming here to stay!' Schumer appeared to be almost in tears as someone described the building of the Brooklyn Bridge, and the Irish navvies who got stuck inside in the concrete.

It was real 'ye-boy-ye' stuff. Later, when I was in Washington, I'd see Schumer and feel an affinity. You always felt an affinity with New York when you were outside it. No city makes you a native so quickly. After only a month in New York, you were moaning about the subway, shopping for bargain vegetables in Chinatown and discussing the black activist, Al Sharpton, with complete strangers.

There was a particular affinity with Brooklyn. It may have been subsidiary to Manhattan but, with its brownstone neighbourhoods and ethnic rainbow it was the city's soul. Brooklyn was old New York. Its politics were also important, especially among the Irish societies.

For example, although AOH divisions were mainly about personality and ideology, there was also a big split between Brooklyn and the city. If a Grand Marshall came from Brooklyn one year, he, or she, couldn't do so the next. In the meantime, the Brooklyn 'vote' had to be courted.

I'd often meet Charlie Hynes, the famous Brooklyn District Attorney, radical on Northern Ireland but tough on high profile crime. 'Give my regards to the General,' he told me one night in what I initially thought was a reference to the notorious Dublin criminal. Instead he had an even cleverer man in mind; the 'Consul General'. At a reception for the Cathedral Club, the powerful Brooklyn Catholic society, I sat beside Hynes on a three-tiered dais. It was like the TV game show, *Celebrity Squares*. Or a party political conference, which, in fact, is essentially what it was, with the large figure of Bishop Moriarty of Brooklyn in sarcastic pre-eminence. In New York, the clerics were like old style pols.

Suddenly, Hynes was gone, his chicken untouched. 'He's got five of these things to go to every night,' someone said. Worse than myself, I thought, for in New York the law enforcers were also politicians, and the DA was an elected position. In 1997, Hynes ran for New York Governor, on the Democratic ticket, but he had to quit early for lack of money. The issue of election funding, by this stage, was getting out of hand.

One of the more moving events I went to was in Hynes' office in Brooklyn, in honour of Jimmy Madigan, an Irish-born schoolteacher who had been killed in Red Hook, a tough area of Brooklyn. Rescuing his kids from a street shooting, Madigan was himself cut down. His widow, a pale, elegant woman, sat stoically while tributes were read, along with poems and a powerful, spine-tingling version of 'Carrickfergus', sung by a children's choir of mixed races. Paul O'Dwyer, the legendary white-haired civil rights lawyer, spoke evocatively about the days when Red Hook was a big Irish area and how important it was that people still went there, as educators and social workers. There was a strong social humanitarian aspect to these old-style New York Democrats.

A more unusual event was a special concert in the Brooklyn Academy of Music to honour Martin Luther King Day. Again, it was part of the CG's manic desire that we went to everything, but it took us out of our ethnic ghetto and as such was much appreciated. Amidst all the songs and pageants, the MC welcomed the attendance of three consulates; Guyana, Haiti — and Ireland! At the concert's end, we all linked arms and sang 'We Shall Overcome'. Afterwards, as the light faded, a bunch of us crunched up through the snow-covered streets of Park Slope, past the beautiful brownstones, with the snow tinted pink and green by the surrounding neon. We passed the old Irish bars and slipped into a cosy neighbourhood diner where in the company of community workers and local activists, I whiled away the official holiday listening to political gossip and the stories of successive immigrants.

14

Greens Under the Bed

Each Monday, we would give oral reports on the outside events attended over the weekend. In general, the CG would do the power-broking events; Ireland Fund dinners at the Waldorf or 'working breakfasts' with the Tara Circle. The DCG would do the upmarket cultural stuff, like the Wild Geese in Greenwich, Connecticut or the Friendly Sons out on Long Island. James and I would do the more proletarian events, like police hops and County dinner dances.

It was a situation I was happy with. I preferred the authentic atmosphere and crack of the 'céilí and chicken' circuit than the more snobbish Wild Geese with their cut-glass world of Aran jumpers and poetry readings. In many ways, the richer Irish-America gets, the phonier and more self important it becomes.

But the CG was apoplectic when he heard about the Dessie Ellis stunt at the Louth Dance, only relaxing slightly when I told him about the Society's apologies and Frankie Beirne's support. His reaction showed the sensitivities for the Embassy and Consulate of dealing with the issue of Northern Ireland in the US context. Ironically only a few weeks earlier I had been asked to spy on the Dessie Ellis protest outside the Consulate. It was a Sunday and the office was closed but a small group had gathered down on the street, holding placards. Because I was not yet working at the Consulate (I was still at the UN) I would not be recognised and so could mingle in with the demo and listen to the speeches.

Bernadette McAliskey spoke and condemned the Irish Government for 'extraditing an innocent man'. McAliskey is one of more hardline people thrown up by the Northern conflict and people cheered. (Interestingly, Consulate files revealed that McAliskey herself was 'monitored' when she came out to the US as an spokesperson in the late Sixties, causing consternation among Irish-Americans by consorting with Black Panthers and other revolutionaries.) Unfortunately I was suddenly photographed listening to her, although thankfully the photo was never used.

And something else happened which gave me a start. 'Come with me,' said some heavy dude, grabbing my arm. 'Oh no, rumbled,' I thought. But then he began opening the trunk of a parked car. For a horrible moment, I thought he was going to pull out a mortar and take a pot at the Consulate. Instead he handed me dozens of copies of the *Irish People*, the IRA's paper in North America. 'Here, flog a few of these' he said, pushing them into my hands, it being presumed that I was an 'activist' like him. 'Eh … later,' I mumbled and melted away. I don't think Noraid would have taken too kindly to being infiltrated by the Free State. Nor would the CG have appreciated me getting quite so undercover.

The CG was paranoid about the Noraid element, or the 'radicals', as he called them. (Noraid was a shorthand for Irish Northern Aid, ostensibly a fundraising organisation for the families of IRA prisoners.) To understand such suspicion it's crucial to appreciate the great hold the Irish Republican movement has had over Irish-America, and by extension US opinion, and the hard job the Irish Government has had in winning it back.

Now, of course, with the Peace Process and US involvement in it, the whole scene has changed, but in 1990 there was still a strong hangover of the 1980s when the Consulate was pointedly not invited to some County dinner dances, or was heckled and booed at those it was asked to attend. Sometimes even assaulted. While the

British Consulate on Third Avenue was constantly picketed, the real venom was reserved for the Irish Government, an attitude straight out of the Irish Civil War. Of course much of Irish-American opinion dated from that time, and having been bolstered by waves of émigrés since then it was ripe for re-emergence when Northern Ireland erupted in the 1970s.

Let's be honest, Irish-American attitudes to the North have been hugely damaging to the relationship between Ireland and Irish-America, a fact which most Irish-Americans now readily acknowledge. To most Irish people, Irish-Americans have meant tour buses, shamrocks and unthinking support for the IRA. Perhaps it's always the way with émigré communities (the Greeks, the Cubans, the Jews). But it was a conflict about which Irish-Americans often knew little. For them, it was a straight fight between Britain and Ireland. The Unionist dimension, for example, was totally lost on them.

For us, it was particularly tricky, especially since we also had to deal with the British and their deliberate misinformation. Thus, by taking a reasonable, moderate nationalist approach, the Irish Government was caught between Noraid on one side and the British on the other. About Noraid, however, all Irish Governments felt the same. It is important to stress this because there has been a tendency, in retrospect, to suggest that in the past some politicians, and some diplomats, were unnecessarily tough in their attitude. Indeed, if anything, Fianna Fáil, as 'the Republican party', were tougher on Noraid. Telexes from the early Seventies show that Jack Lynch saw Irish-American opinion as dangerously sentimental and even potentially destabilising for the Irish State.

After the Archive Act of 1987, Embassies and Consulates were forced to return files they'd had for years; their contents demonstrated the consistency of Irish policy with regard to Irish-American Republicanism. Little had changed over the years. Preparing for the visits of Presidents O'Kelly (1959) and de Valera (1964), there were the same brooding references to 'radicals' and 'tricky' local politicians. Heckles were planned for and attempts made to control speeches. Nor was the Consulate shy about going undercover, back then, to spy on the radicals, just like myself mingling at the Dessie Ellis demo.

When Lemass, as Taoiseach, stayed at the Waldorf in 1965, a picket was mounted outside, with placards attacking him as a 'Sell-Out' and 'Traitor', just as there were when his son-in-law, CJ Haughey, stayed there in 1991. Looking at their grey faces and old raincoats, I wouldn't be surprised if they were same protestors, with Tuxedo in among them, striking up a tune. And yet they had a wind-chilled integrity too, just like the two old ladies in oatmeal coats and hairnets who, starting with Bobby Sands hunger strike in 1981, stood outside the British Consulate every evening (every evening!) for ten years, giving out leaflets and holding placards saying 'Time to Go'. The hunger strike had a major effect on opinion in New York and for years afterwards the British Consulate on Second Avenue didn't fly its flag.

The files also gave a flavour of relations with local politicians which were always interesting. When President O'Kelly visited in 1959, New York Governor Nelson A Rockefeller was reluctant to have dinner with him, not wishing to appear too closely aligned with the Paddies. But come 1964, and the gubernatorial election, he was more than keen and then President de Valera had to beat off competing invitations from Speaker of the State Assembly, Joseph Carlino and Senate Majority Leader, Walter J. Mahoney, both Republicans. The Consulate decided that the President should decline. This proved politically astute: Democratic candidate, Lyndon B Johnston won the Presidency by a landslide in 1964 and Carlino and Mahoney were voted out.

For diplomats, the rules on association with Noraid were clear. We were not to share a platform or dais with support organisations of the IRA. This was made clear in

1983 when Michael Flannery was made Grand Marshall of the St Patrick's Day Parade. Flannery was eighty years old, a tall, thin and ascetic man like something straight out of de Valera's Volunteer unit. Indeed, he fought in the War of Independence, where, as a teetotaller, he destroyed poitín stills, a piece of Republican puritanism which must have gone down well in Irish-America.

In 1983, however, he was also suspected to be a gun-runner for the modern IRA. The Government protested at this honouring of Flannery but the Parade organisers persisted. It was high stakes stuff. The community didn't believe that the Irish Government would stay away from the Parade but they did. It certainly got the message across. Unfortunately, it created a lot of bad feeling in the Community and people would still come up to me, a decade later, and say how hurt they were that the Irish Government had boycotted their party. But the bad feeling cut the other way too and many Irish-Americans felt that it was now time to end Noraid's use of their community as a cheerleader for the IRA.

The Flannery affair had been a turning point for both sides. It made me smile during the 'gays in the Parade' controversy when people asked me 'why doesn't the Irish Government boycott the Parade in protest?' 'Again?' I responded to them, 'Have you any idea of the trouble it caused the first time?' And anyway, the Government was never going to boycott the Parade, just because the gays weren't allowed to march. As far as the CG was concerned, we had no view on the matter.

After 1983, the Government attended the Parade but visiting Ministers and Consular officials would vacate the platform when the Noraid banners passed. Although Frankie Beirne had kept Noraid to their big 'England Get Out of Ireland' banner, there were still a large number of Noraid association banners, with their Lodge numbers and adopted IRA heroes, a fact which often shocked visitors from Ireland, who were not used to this up-front culture.

The *Irish Echo* and the *Voice* would mock our 'getting on and off platforms' — taking a constitutional leak, it was called — and found the Irish Government's behaviour quaint. But these people didn't have to live in Ireland and see the consequences of IRA actions. They didn't see the killings and the funerals and the crying children. To them it was just 'the Cause', something to be quietly celebrated in the back bars of Brooklyn, or in the umpteen whinging letters written to their papers.

After the bitter differences of the 1980s, the Irish State and Noraid learned to step around each other and things gradually improved. What's more the American public and in particular the Irish-American public, were starting to develop a better understanding of the complexity Northern Ireland. There were also issues on which the Irish Government found it was useful to work with the more radical end of Irish-America, such as in highlighting the darker side of British policy in the North — issues like Shoot-to-Kill, plastic bullets and (un)fair employment practises. On these issues, Irish-America had ready-made and impressive propaganda outlets.

We also had to accept that we were moving among people who felt differently about the North. In a community in which hardline views were not unusual, it was quite difficult not to fraternise with IRA supporters. As one diplomat said, you can't exactly go around the dancefloor, checking people's views on 'political violence' before you take them for a waltz. I mean, you'd be rightly stumped for the Siege of Ennis, with its multiple and changing partners.

There was also the problem that the State's neat differentiation between the Old IRA of the 1920s and the modern IRA, was so not easy to sustain in the US, where many of the old IRA had ended up. As indeed had many of the not-so-old IRA who'd been active in the forties, fifties and sixties. On one occasion, the CG attended the funeral of a Republican die-hard who'd been 'out' in the twenties, and a few times since. Expecting he might be called upon to speak, the CG suggested that he add a few words about the 'futility of violence and the need to pursue change through peaceful means'. 'If you do,' said one old crone, 'it'll be old Bartley in the grave and you going in after him.'

The CG quickly agreed that perhaps it wasn't the time or the place.

If they weren't attacking us, the Noraid types would try and fraternise with us and so, by association, gain legitimacy. There was a childish desire to catch us out, and squeeze into photos beside us. The Irish-American community knew our policy and yet they'd often try to have it both ways. Thus at the Longford dance I and much of the Committee were surprised by the appearance of Gerry McGeough, an IRA man famously captured on a FBI 'sting' video trying to buy weapons. This was the sort of stunt we most feared on the circuit and to make it worse, McGeough gave an incendiary speech, linking the events of 1798 in Ballinamuck, Longford to the ongoing 'war' in Ireland. Granted, the dais was dissolved before McGeough gave his thunderous speech but when I looked over, faces went sheepish and looked away. They knew they'd done wrong. At such times you feel awful, the Consulate man in the suit obliged to scold them.

We had to be ready for such surprises. One time, I came into the Tipperary dance, when I saw Mike Flannery, the legendary gun runner, up on the dais, or VIP platform, sitting in my seat, *eating my melon*! Embarrassed, the organisers pretended not to see me. And then said that they didn't know Flannery had also been invited.

Other encounters were more innocuous, like when someone came up to me at a benefit in Yonkers Raceway and told me about his visa problems. About to write down his details, he said, 'there's no need. It's all in here' and handed me a leaflet — 'Free Sean Mackin — Stop the Deportation'. It turned out that he was on an RUC suspect list back in Northern Ireland. 'Oh, right,' I said and my first instinct was to make sure I hadn't been photographed. But Mackin's approach was a legitimate one. Having never been convicted of any charge, he was simply on a suspect list, which had mysteriously made its way into the hands of Loyalist paramilitaries.

Then there were the moments you couldn't foresee, like my colleague, James, attending the St Patrick's Parade in Philadelphia. With its strong emigrant links to the North, Philadelphia had a reputation for difficulty but James was relieved when the Parade seemed more good humoured than political. There was even the bizarre sight of grown men dressed as leprechauns, with curly-toed shoes and false pointy beards, waving to the crowd. Then James heard some upcoming marchers singing what sounded like the World Cup soccer chant 'Ooh-ah, Paul McGrath, Say Ooh-ah, Paul McGrath!' Ah, the spirit of the World Cup. Standing at street level, he and the other VIPs went down to join them, shuffling in among the dancing marchers, until James heard 'Ooh-ah, up the 'Ra' (the IRA) and shuffled just as quickly back out again!

If Noraid were one of the difficulties we faced in explaining Northern Ireland in the US, then the other was the British with their misinformation and security 'briefings'.

One night we were in the British Consulate, on Third Avenue, for their 1992 Election Party. It was an extraordinary night, the staff shouting for Labour on the Big Screen and the suits rooting for the Tories. Whereas people in the UK were amazed that the Tories won, to us in New York it seemed amazing to even conceive of them losing, so used were we to their longevity and media domination. (It was also something I'd experience with Irish elections; being abroad, even in an Embassy, makes it difficult to see the full picture.) Televisions were set up in the rooms of the Consulate, a dull, institutional building, like so much of the British Foreign Service, and watching the late surge of Conservative Holds, I found myself sitting on the desk of an Information Officer.

Glancing over his shelves, I found the most amazing material.

It was on the North but it wasn't the usual line given in public. It described, instead, how Southern Ireland was 'soft on terrorism' and gave a strange potted history of Northern Ireland; of how the 1960s Civil Rights movement had been 'taken over by Republican Communists' and of how the vast majority of Catholics were happy with the status quo. It went back centuries, describing the casualties of the Famine as 'exaggerated' and stating that in 1916 'a minority of a minority of extremists' had 'hijacked the Nationalist movement' and staged a violent assault, subsequently 'rejected' by the people.

Mainly, however, it spoke of 'terrorism'. But it adopted that clinical apolitical tone, which people like former Israeli Premier, Benjamin Netanyahu, use when they want to deny a context, as if the IRA, the Baader-Meinhof and the Aryan Nation were all the same, as if 'terrorists' were some migratory bird which might pop up anywhere. The 'terrorists are madmen' perspective was (and is) particularly popular in the US, where 'Terrorism Experts' talk about the Middle East and nod sagely during TV discussions, so perhaps it is not surprising that the British should utilise such a strategy there.

But, in reality, it was an uphill struggle for the British, for US opinion was always going to see it differently. Too much so for our taste, perhaps; the PLO were demonised in the US but the IRA were like Afghan Freedom Fighters (although there's been a subsequent change of view on both subjects). But, in broader terms, the prevailing US attitude was obviously very satisfactory. Despite all their resources, and the so-called Special US-UK Relationship, and despite Britain's attempts to project themselves as 'honest brokers, mediating in a civil conflict of inter-ethnic religious strife', (some of the language contained in the propaganda I was now busy stuffing down my trousers) US opinion was always going to see the conflict from the Irish perspective. This wasn't just because of the Irish-American heritage, or even America's own colonial history. Rather because this is the way most of the world have seen the Six Counties conflict: the only difference was that the US actually voiced their opinions (and, in the late 1990s, got directly involved).

Back at the British Consulate, loud cheers sounded outside in the corridor — the 'Con Holds' were flowing now, as was the champagne — and, figuring the coast was clear, I stuffed a few more papers under my belt. I knew our Press Officer would be more than grateful for this 'confidential' briefing material. (Sixty per cent of the Press Officer's time in the US is spent handling the North.) Camouflaged by the surrounding drunks, I sort of walked stiff-legged to the elevator. By the window, I saw a woman staring out at Third Avenue quietly sobbing: five more years of the Tories.

In this context, it sometimes became impossible to moderate your thoughts on the North. At a launch of a new chapter of the Ancient Order of Hibernians in Scranton I took questions from the audience. Maybe it was the location, way up in the snow-bound Pennsylvania Hills, in an old mining town settled by Mayo emigrants, where so many young miners had lost their lives. Or maybe it was the warmth of the hospitality, inside a local hall, following by a lively dance. But I decided to depart from the script. After the inevitable speeches, one of the AOH bigwigs chaired a question and answer session. He was a hard liner on the North, which, predictably, was the subject of most of the questions. I started out with the usual language about the search for settlement and the need for Agreement. But, after a while, I just got impatient with this strait-jacketed language and spoke frankly. At the time, things were not good in the North, with continuing allegations about security forces collusion with loyalist gunmen, and general bad faith by the British on political negotiations.

I spoke about this and then went on to tell them that, really, no matter what agreements we had with the British, we could never trust them. That they were devious and arrogant regarding the situation and that many of them, deep down, still couldn't even accept southern Irish independence. I briefly tempered this by acknowledging the need to work closely with them, stressing that what was being pursued now was a peaceful, interim settlement which everyone could live with. But I finished by stating that partition was morally and practically wrong and the only long-term solution was for the British to completely withdraw. I could see the jaws dropping. I was also conscious that there was no press around.

The next day, a Sunday, I took the long ride back into the city, sitting inside the warm bus with the snow flakes hitting the window. Green destination signs passed us for places like Dublin and Moscow, and at one stage heavy snow forced us to briefly stop outside a town called Strasbourg whilst snowploughs cleared the road. It was deserted, but looking down its ghostly white street, I suddenly saw a Irish tricolour hanging over a shop and it almost brought a lump to my throat. I thought back on the weekend and about how far and wide the Irish had travelled and still kept a hold on the flag. 'Let's go!' said the driver, laughing, as snowploughs completed their work and the bus pulled out for the city.

I thought nothing more of the trip but a week later James MacIntyre came up to me and said 'I met that Jim Gibbons in Montauk.' Gibbons was the AOH bigwig. 'Jaysus, what the hell did you say to that guy in Scranton?'

'Nothing. I just spoke to them all about the North.'

'Well, it must have been something special. Gibbons kept saying, "That fellow has the right idea. Don't know about the rest of you but, by God, he's got the right idea"'

'Well, you know how it is, James. I was up in the hills. There was music, dancing. I suppose I went a bit native.'

15

Back to Ellis Island

In the early 1990s there were major changes on the Irish political landscape, and this affected our work in the US. In 1990, Labour Party candidate Mary Robinson became President, beating former Foreign Minister Brian Lenihan in a controversial contest. Partly on the liberal momentum of this, Labour won a huge vote in the 1992 election and formed a coalition government with Fianna Fáil (FF). In the meantime, Charlie Haughey was replaced as FF leader in February 1992 by Albert Reynolds. Sean Doherty's revelations that Haughey knew about taps on journalists' phones back in the Eighties, drove FF's coalition partners, the Progressive Democrats (PDs), to demand Haughey's resignation. And so, after years of heaves, Charlie was finally gone. However, the PD leader, Des O'Malley, would soon find that sharing power with Charlie's successor could be an even more uncomfortable arrangement.

We also got a new Minister. The Smirker was gone, mainly because of his infamous appearance when, far from smirking, he made his tearful appeal to Albert not to 'be bursting up the party'. Meaning, 'Leave Charlie alone and don't mind those PDs.' Which meant that when Albert got in, it was unlikely Collins was going to reappointed. And so it was. Poor old Smirker. I was almost in tears myself. In to replace him as Foreign Minister, was David Andrews, a long time opponent of Haughey and regarded as part of the old, 'respectable' wing of Fianna Fáil.

Reynolds first visit to New York as Taoiseach created great anxiety and senior officials had to check back to see that they hadn't offended him as a Minister. Curiously, having once regarded Haughey as the *bête noire*, DFA had got quite used to him, especially mandarins like Dag and Ted Barrington with whom he worked smoothly. (Barrington had even, at one stage, been tipped as a future Secretary to the Government.) Contrary to his reputation, Haughey respected mandarins. Reynolds, by contrast, was an unknown quantity. Active and go-ahead, he wanted to 'do things' which, God forbid, is always a shock for Civil Servants.

For example, Pádraic Mac Kernan, our Ambassador in Washington, was soon, on transfer to Brussels, turned into a heroic figure for going back to our EU partners and securing the abortion protocol to the Maastricht Treaty, an extraordinary concession which allowed us to opt out of any EU-wide abortion rulings. The issue, which had haunted Irish politics in the Eighties, was about to come back with a vengeance and, in the 'X Case', Reynolds would face his first major political test. In fairness, Albert had to address a backed-up political agenda — the 'social' issues, the North, the economy — and after the stiff pageantry of Haughey, he was a breath of fresh air. Unfortunately, the alacrity and stubbornness with which he pursued these issues, would also be his undoing.

The visit of a Taoiseach, or President, is always a major moment for a Mission abroad, especially in a high profile city like New York, but the focussed nature of the Consul General (CG) made it even more so. It was as if the nervous energy of the city had permeated his whole personality. Each morning, we all sat around to go through the three-day schedule, minute by minute. Car plans were pored over and, in the company of the Secret Service, who often sat in on our meetings, buzz-words were thrown about like 'frozen zone' and 'advancing the location'. The CG was also a great man for 'walking the ground', taking dummy runs up the baggage elevator in the Waldorf Towers, or marching along the famous steps in Columbia University where lounging students had to part for our official shoes. 'She'll be looking down this way,' said the CG, describing the way President Robinson would be standing when she received her Honorary Degree, next to George Stephanopolous, Clinton's spin doctor, and Susan Sontag, the academic.

Such reconnaissance was useful. For example, Reynolds was also to receive a degree, at NYU. ('His first' said a colleague disdainfully: with the new Irish, came new snobbishness.) NYU is built around Washington Square and after the conferring ceremony, Albert was to walk across the small square in his robes and go towards Ireland House, a renovated period building which was going to serve as an Irish Cultural Centre. To the applause of a small crowd of students and academics, the Taoiseach would cut the ribbon.

That the Secret Service accepted this arrangement was amazing since the Square is also a permanent encampment of Rasta hustlers and small-time drug dealers. Keeping themselves a few steps behind Albert, they let me go in front, shooing away the hobos and dealers. 'No, no smoke, no coke. Go away!' I said. 'Taoiseach, please, come this way.' One homeless guy even gave Albert a wave from under his cardboard box and, ever the politician, Albert waved back. 'A constituent from home, perhaps,' whispered a voice behind us, archly.

The pageantry of these visits is overseen by the omnipresent gum-chewing Secret Service, who, of course, are far from secret, checking rooftops, walking around in dark suits and crew cuts, and talking into their watches. Actually, we got on well with them, many of whom were Irish-Americans, recruited from other security forces. They found us a relief to deal with compared to other countries. Watching the way some States behaved at the UN, I could just imagine what they'd be like when their

Presidents were in town, not to mention the entourages of despots and dictators.

The priority for the Service was getting a Prime Minister or President in and out of the US safely. Once they were out of US air space, they could be hit with a missile for all they cared. Nor did Foreign Ministers matter. It was just the No 1s. But, in this, they were at least egalitarian and the same protection was extended to the President of little Cape Verde as would be to Boris Yeltsin. Little wonder dictators loved coming to this citadel of democracy. 'Do you think the UN would be taken as seriously,' a hack asked me, 'if it was situated in the centre of Africa, as the Africans pretend to prefer?' A provocative question, perhaps, but one worth thinking about.

Albert Reynolds flew in from Washington on the Government jet and we awaited him on an outlying stretch of tarmac at JFK. Our glossy black limos were bookended by the Pajero jeeps of the Secret Service, bristling with more aerials than an excited lobster. At one stage, two of the Service guys, opened a trunk and nonchalantly checked on an extraordinary panoply of weapons — shotguns, rifles, short-arm Uzis. The limo drivers nearly dropped their coffees.

'We got a wheels-up in Washington,' said one of flunkies, touching his earpiece, and everyone got 'into the mode'. The Government jet was in the air, and it wasn't long before it was sighted over New York. By the time it touched down, the limos had swung into position and everyone was quickly shepherded into their appointed cars. More jockeying. Promotions can be secured by an opportunistic mandarin hopping into the wrong car at the right time for the long ride in with a sympathetic Minister. But I noticed the Ambassador almost shouldering the CG aside and telling him to get into Car C.

At the signal, the convoy took off, led by a Secret Service jeep. Well, not quite led. A demarcation issue arose, and because JFK was under the control of the Port Authority, the whole convoy had to be escorted out of the airport by one of their green and white panda cars. The Port Authority is a body which takes itself very seriously and, in the 1930s, their chief, Robert Moses, even tried to make their official seal equivalent to that of the City and State. Following the green car meanwhile was a familiar sky blue police car of the NYPD, laden down with overweight, grinning cops. Sometimes the protocol of local policing was as absurd as that of diplomacy. Nor was the Port Authority in any kind of hurry. There was a sort of a 'Let's take it nice and slow here' attitude, like, 'We got an airport to run and we're not very impressed.'

Frustrated by the crawl out of the JFK, the Secret Service reasserted themselves on the highway, flashing their blue and red siren lights, and taking over a whole traffic lane. There is nothing quite like the buzz of this ride. In Dublin, it's a bit of fun, watching people stare at the wailing sirens, while others get annoyed, preparing angry Letters to the Editor. But in New York it is quite amazing; pure pageantry, the fleet of sleek limos rumbling along the freeway, picking up unhindered speed as the grey towers of Manhattan rise inexorably, deliriously, in the distance.

Unfortunately, this being New York, it wasn't all unhindered and the whole cavalcade was brought up short in front of a toll booth, where the boom stayed stubbornly down. I couldn't believe it. Our lights were flashing and the Service guy in the first jeep had his arm out, trying to wave us through. But no dice and the desultory toll clerk requested a ID card for examination. The Service guy was enraged, especially since it happened in front of us. It's all about vanity on these occasions; for the Prime Minister, for the diplomats and for the security.

New York brought a similar rebuff in the shape of its street life. Coming out of the tunnel at 59th Street, the first lights the traffic hits when it comes into the city, we were greeted by Squeegee Men, homeless guys who, uninvited, clean windscreens and then ask for change. Sure enough, an old bearded guy was on his way towards the stalled jeep. The Service man flashed on his blue light — off since the tunnel — but the tramp was undeterred, even when a megaphone voice, hidden in the radiator, shouted at him, 'Keep away from the car!' Again it was only when an ID was wearily produced, that the hobo relented and reluctantly stepped away, on to another car, filled with frightened tourists from Kansas.

The lights changed and the jeep, followed by us, angrily swung out onto the street, only to get immediately caught in a traffic snarl. And in a gridlock-buster, thus provoking a cacophony of horns and shouts ('Hey, asshole, get out of there!'). Welcome to New York. The Service guys told us afterwards that they hated the city. If the President, their President, visits Seattle or Austin they can shut the town down. In New York, you just have to live with it.

And yet despite their much vaunted image, they were surprisingly vulnerable. So opaque is the division between American life and movies, that the Secret Service have come to believe in their cinematic image, and exude an air of self-satisfied invincibility. They even dress like the movies. But, in reality, they're recruited from regular police forces and can be as sloppy as the rest of us.

When Albert arrived, for example, I had to bring a Diplomatic Box to the hotel and leave it in his Private Secretary's room, next to the Taoiseach's bedroom. Blithely waved upstairs, I passed the bedroom 'commandeered' by the Service, and equipped out with radios and weapons. Except, right now, they were more busy playing cards and eating large packets of tortilla crisps. When one of them deigned to check me, he didn't recognise my Diplomatic ID Card — 'you hotel staff?' Nor did he ask about the box. I mean, for all he knew, it could have been filled with high-grade semtex, instead of Waterford Crystal clocks for B-list VIP's.

The first visit of President Robinson in 1990 was an even more interesting affair. By now, Robinson was on the cover of countless US magazines, and arousing great curiosity. Her impact cannot be exaggerated, especially in the US. Put crudely, she was a great commodity for Ireland at a time when the country was more immediately associated with bombs and abortion. Which is probably why the normally conservative establishment (including Irish-America) rallied around her.

One joke was that people in the Department voted for her, and then they had to meet her. But this is too glib. Her opponent, Brian Lenihan, was a popular former Minister, and much of his old office were already eyeing up jobs in Phoenix Park. Lenihan's illness, and subsequent operation in the US, created a strong bond between him and Departmental people, as is evident from the number of DFA faces which appeared in his book *To Mayo and Back*. But most DFA types, conscious of the country's image abroad, would probably have voted for the change which Robinson represented. Diplomats can vote while abroad, and although it's a secret ballot, some smart aleck in HQ claimed that, since most officers voted on the spot, with their ballot on top of the envelope, it was possible, by holding the envelopes up against the light, to see the indentations of people's preferences. Which, in this case, were apparently mainly for Robinson.

Once elected, however, Robinson had a mixed relationship with DFA, a Department she had more contact with than others. She overlapped upon their issues and language — the North, human rights, foreign policy — and stories soon abounded of rows and disputes. Also, although putatively liberal, the DFA is at core an essentially FF/FG culture, inherently conservative and cautious, and Robinson's independent stance took some getting used to, especially for the older mandarins, so accustomed to being able to manage and script their political 'masters'. Almost arrogantly so. Robinson was wary and suspicious but she would need to be. For the first year of her term, Haughey was still in power.

There was also a bit of old-time sexism here. Whereas Haughey was admired for being tough and a great old character when he was being ruthless and imperious — firing instructions, firing officials — Robinson was seen as haughty and austere for doing the same. Arguably, it was the source of popularity for them both. As in business, the electorate like to be bullied and Robinson, like Haughey, knew that if she were to relax the strict protocol the gravitas and aura surrounding the Presidency could not be sustained. (The same goes for diplomacy, incidentally.)

For example, Robinson ordered that one Ambassador be kept away from her because 'he smelled of whiskey'. This was regarded as callous by his colleagues. But, in point of fact, he did smell of whiskey, and was regarded as an alcoholic. A nice story was told of how his Third Sec was grilled before the Secretary and ordered to tell the truth about the situation at the Embassy concerned. Touchingly, she tried to cover up for her Head of Mission. 'But Secretary, that's the weather over there, we often fall asleep at our desks.'

For Robinson's visit, the CG was again thrown into a tizzy of excitement and an impressive itinerary was arranged — Breakfast TV shows, a reception at Tavern on the Green and a call to the Tir Na nÓg Immigrant Drop-In Centre in the Bronx. For my part, I was to accompany Nicholas Robinson, her husband, who wanted to research some 18th century caricatures (Edmund Burke, etc.) at the Pierpont Morgan Library, a splendid other-worldly alternative to the hurly-burly of the main schedule.

I was glad of the respite for such visits brought out more of the madness that we saw at the Summits, with people standing around trying to look important, or carrying bits of paper and shouting, 'Sheila, you must see this.' Or clutching a mobile phone, then in their infancy (and still a badge of importance) and calling some Private Secretary in a crowded limo to tell her that everything was okay, a useless message which only served to have your name recited aloud amongst important people.

Meanwhile, the new Ambassador, Dermot Gallagher, up from Washington, hung around the lobby mocking this rigid-backed alertness, while, of course, contributing to it himself. And it deserved mocking. After all the luggage was taken in from cars some people making a TV documentary about the President asked could we do it again, with empty suitcases, just to get some 'road' pictures of the President 'on tour'. But the younger diplomats refused, reluctant to be caught on film, doing such demeaning tasks. Obviously, they preferred to be inside, off camera, getting picked on by bored mandarins, who were themselves, of course, only passing on the grief they were already getting from their political masters upstairs.

The highlight of Robinson's visit was a trip out to Ellis Island where the President was to unveil a statue of Annie Moore, the young Irish immigrant who left Cobh in 1923 with her brothers and became the first recorded person to come through this famous entry point, now a Museum.

I had already 'turned the sod' for the statue about five months previously, at a Saturday morning ceremony at the front of the island. Fearing a proliferation of statues on their sacred lawn — the first Jew was already being pushed for — the authorities later pushed Annie indoors, but at this stage she was still destined for outside, with the glass towers of downtown Manhattan across the water. I felt like a politician, spading aloft the pre-cut sod, and posing for the photographers. And for a TV crew; Erin Focus, one of the Irish cable television channels.

Afterwards, scrolls honouring our efforts were presented, along with US flags certified as having been flown over the nation's capitol on St Patrick's Day. So many flags were handed out that I imagined some guy spending the whole day on the Mall running flags up and down flagpoles. The Americans, of course, love these presentations, especially 'piece of the Real Cross' affairs;

the actual baseball, a piece of someone's desk, the chair they sat in, and so forth.

The sod turned, we went inside for the 'eats' and a wander around the Museum. Ellis Island is an extraordinary place, an atmospheric and poignant insight into the making of America. Photos and mementoes bring to life the whole flux of immigration and remind you of all the other ethnic groups, the Danes and Swedes and Syrians. Inside the hall, where once the emigrants lined up for processing, children wander among the displays, pressing buttons to hear the recordings of actual immigrants. And then move on, as children do, leaving the voices of the dead to talk on in the empty rooms. But, despite our numbers, there were frustratingly few Irish exhibits. The huge Irish influx came before proper documentation, or education, and many of their experiences went unrecorded, except in song or memory.

All the more poignant then to see in among the gleaming samovars and sparkling Czech jewellery, a miserable delft plate from Limerick, a piece of Carrickmacross lace or, most affecting of all, a well-scratched fiddle, lying idle when once it must have shook the boards of Bantry pubs, steamships and Hoboken floors. I thought of the wedding in *On the Waterfront* and the way Brando rescues Eva Marie Saint from a fiddle-driven frenzy. (Surely, the quintessential Irish-American movie; in one scene, we see a bar counter, corrupt dockers and a priest with a bloody nose.)

On the Museum walls, meanwhile, were anti-Irish cartoons; lazy, simian-featured drunks, bomb-throwing Fenians and a shocking image of scores of alligators crawling up American shorelines, with mitres in the style of snapping jaws. The Papists are coming! Such images made explicable the fierce defensiveness of Irish-Americans, with their long-held emphasis on education and teetotalism, and their desire to show patriotism by joining the military and police. It also explained their clannish need to form protective clubs and societies. And then perhaps keep down other immigrants, for not embracing 'American values'.

The unveiling of Annie Moore was going to be a big party, with Circle Line ferries bringing people out from Battery Park in Manhattan and Liberty Park in New Jersey. The former ferry owners were Irish and the service was being offered gratis. Such gestures were common among exiles. When de Valera was Taoiseach, an Irish-American once offered to buy us an Embassy building in Washington but the Long Fellow declined the kind offer.

The Saturday before, James and I did a dry-run from Jersey, taking the empty ferry across the bay. Wet-run, more like. Standing with the skipper in his rain sprinkled cabin, we took turns on the tiller. 'Get Liberty in your sights,' he told us, 'and go straight for her'. The skipper had previously worked on the Achill Island ferry, a nice association, as we rounded the southern end of Manhattan. Downtown was completely empty and you could see the city in all its mist-shrouded strangeness; a narrow-canyoned, sci-fi metropolis, but one with an aura of smugglers' coves along its shoreline, with broken-wood jetties and little fishing boats puttering out on a Saturday morning.

On the night itself, however, it was much more lively. Practically the whole community was invited to the ceremony, a unique cross-section of different groups, and we had good crack taking them out, with the boats almost colliding as they pulled in to berth. Disembarking, the crowd poured up the slipways; GAA, County Societies, theatre groups, the AOH and Friendly Sons. It was an interesting reversal, the Consulate bringing the Irish-Americans back to Ellis Island. And, for the first time, hosting the 'new Irish immigrants', the younger crowd from Woodside and the East Village, with their spiky hair and leopardskin hats.

With another Green Card lottery in the offing, a lot of them were looking for sponsors. 'These Irish-Americans are always banging on about their heritage. Well, it's time to put them to the test,' declared Gary, a sculptor, who was also searching for rich patrons to fund his work. 'Eamon, where's those Wild Geese? They've loads of dosh.' The cocktail bars, which had been set up around the hall, lubricated the mixing amongst the guests.

After a while, the President spoke. In retrospect, one can perhaps be sceptical about all those 'healing speeches' by Robinson (a custom continued by her successor, Mary McAleese), but at the time such rhetoric made a big difference. Especially in somewhere like New York, the heartland of the diaspora, and a deeply conservative one at that. When she called for a pluralist Irishness and a more liberal environment, I could see Frankie Beirne of the Ancient Order of Hibernians (AOH), shuffle uncomfortably. When she welcomed the Irish Lesbian and Gay Organisation (ILGO), who wanted to march in the Parade, the Consul General tensed his shoulders. The Áras had specifically asked for ILGO to be invited, after we had left them off the list.

The CG wanted nothing to do with the gay issue. Ostensibly a Sixties liberal, entertaining poets and supporting non-denominational education, he had, like many of his generation, been burnt by the 1980s conservative backlash, and had learned to live with the realities of Irish politics. But at times he seemed absurdly cautious. He wouldn't even respond to the letter ILGO sent him asking for his view on the Parade issue. When they rang him up one day to press him on the issue — they had come through on his personal line — he quickly changed his voice and said the 'Consul General wasn't available'. We were sitting in front of him. He shrugged and smiled; master diplomat.

After Robinson concluded her speech, there was jockeying as people pressed forward to offer their congratulations and get in front of the snapping cameras. AOH luminaries and local politicians eagerly shook hands with a President who had just excoriated them as being remnants of the past. There was also some interesting jockeying among DFA personnel. With officials here from the Consulate, Mission, Embassy and HQ, the scope for in-fighting and intrigue was immense. There had already been a dogfight over her speech. Interesting how many people thought Robinson's speeches were her own. If they only knew the struggle to which poor Annie Moore — the inspiration for the statue Robinson was dedicating — was subjected. A personal spat arose between two speechwriters over whether Annie Moore should arrive in America 'hungry and lonely' or 'vibrant and determined'.

The demarcation issue was complicated for, although the Embassy had overall responsibility for Robinson's US visit, she was now in New York, on our turf. You also had to factor in the President's personal team, including her adviser and formidable protector, Bride Rosney. Meanwhile, Dermot 'Dag' Gallagher, Mac Kernan's successor as Ambassador in Washington, was keeping a close eye on the CG and seemed taken aback by the high profile that the consulate had achieved in New York. As Ambassador, Gallagher got to introduce Robinson, but the CG sort of trumped him by hopping up on the platform to introduce the Ambassador. The introduction was so lavish that Dag found it difficult to complain about such upstaging. Truly, the Dag had met his match. The CG then remained on the podium while the Ambassador spoke, beaming away for the cameras.

At this stage, I was up on the balcony, with a vodka and tonic in my hand, and standing beside Napoleon, who was chuckling at his ambitious colleagues below. 'Look at the state of them!' he laughed. The Americans too got into the demarcation tussle with another dispute over territory. Technically, Ellis Island is the preserve of the US Coastguard and, jealous about their independence, they provided the Secret Service with more than a few headaches. At one stage, the Americans looked panicked; 'My God, all these Irish are drinking and are going to stay here.' But as dusk fell, people were drifting back towards the boats, everyone giddy and in good spirits.

The lights of the city were twinkling in the distance as we went across the bay, and you could see the usual snake of red tail-lights going up the FDR Drive. Below deck, a crowd was getting up a sing-song — old style Police Emeralds and East Village trendies comingling in music — while others were out on deck gazing up at the huge acidic green statue of Liberty, with her yellow lamp glowing. As the President's helicopter flew over, its green and red lights winking, an big ironic cheer was elicited from the high-spirited crowd.

As we pulled into Battery Park, the boats dropped their gangplanks, and people began disembarking. Seizing the moment, the CG and his wife rushed onto the dock and stood by the gangplank, shaking hands with everyone — and I mean, everyone — as they came off. 'Thank you very much for coming. Consul General of Ireland.' I couldn't believe it. So rapid and mechanistic was it, that they even shook the startled hands of a few tourists, coming off a Circle Line ferry. 'Hey, who was that guy?' a Midwestern man asked his wife. 'I dunno. Some kind of politician.' A technically inaccurate description but a effectively true one.

With the President's return to Ireland I had another hairy ride out to the airport, when the Secret Service guy, escorting us, and the Presidents belongings, got lost among the outlying hangars of JFK. I could have told him the way but they insist on taking control. 'Just follow me. Okay. Keep following me.' He was a young guy and it was his first job on his own, so he was understandably nervous. He was one of those clean-cut Irish-American guys from Boston — a sort of Dan Quayle lookalike, just out of college.

With the President leaving, the objective was to get the stuff on the Government jet so that when the VIPs arrive, the plane can take off immediately. The jet was parked by Hangar 26, on the outer edge of JFK. With its low redbrick buildings, ragged windsock, and grass cracks showing on the concrete runway, it was evocative of the old New York and the airport's former name; Idlewild.

And idle wild was our journey. Quayle was in the car up front, but the situation was not helped by my driver, a clown of an guy who kept shouting at an ice hockey game on his radio — 'Let's go Rangers!' — and enjoyed a game of cat and mouse with our escort, passing him at the lights and losing him as we came out from the city. Usually the Secret Service do background checks on our drivers so I don't know how this guy slipped through. He thought it was a hoot us being escorted to the airport and relished any chance of dropping him a block behind. 'I'm too clever for that College Boy,' he'd boast and he'd cut through a few side streets to shorten the journey. Now we had two people who thought they knew a faster way. 'Can't wait to tell my wife I was escorting the President of Ireland!'

'The President of Ireland's luggage,' I corrected him, gripping the sideboard. And then I realised. Of course; he's a last-minute stand-in driver. Louis, the appointed driver, had taken sick and this guy had slipped through without any background check. Naturally, he saw our escort as a licence to break almost all the traffic signals and most of the red lights, although he was disappointed that the Service guy wouldn't put on a more dramatic show. 'Why won't he put on his siren lights?'

'He will very soon,' I said, holding the door handle, 'or the police will.' At one stage, the plate windows of a burger restaurant loomed up so closely that I thought he was going to give new meaning to the phrase 'Drive-Thru McDonalds', with the diners fleeing from their Big Macs.

Eventually, we got to JFK. Having lost Quayle somewhere on the roundabouts, we saw him appear again, red-faced and panicked. It was then that he led us towards some empty hangars, clearly in the wrong direction — we could see the descending numbers; 21, 20. Suddenly, it began raining. Stopping his car, Dan Quayle jumped out and started jabbing at his mobile. 'He's cooking now,' said my friend. But I was 'cooking' too. The President's luggage; gifts, eighteenth-century prints, master plan for a UN take-over — they just had to get on that plane.

'26!' shouted the Secret Service man and, jumping back into his car, he led us to another hangar, behind which, we saw — thank God — the Government jet on the tarmac. The President would be here in minutes, and the step ladder was out. 'You run things tight,' said the Air Cadet inside the cockpit, already at the controls, with his helmet and headphones on. Down at the tail of the plane, a hatch opened and another Cadet's hands emerged to take on the boxes. It was like a scene from *Casablanca* or a drugs movie getaway. The last box, wet from the rain, slid from the Cadet's grip and almost came back on top of me. Toppled by a Diplomatic Box — it would have been too much. I pushed it back up and it went in like a basketball. The hatch closed.

Within minutes, the President arrived in a flurry of limos and flashing lights. We watched from a distance as the rain poured down. Protected by wind-blown umbrellas, President Robinson gave a series of little nods and shook hands with the CG and Ambassador. Up the stepladder and, after another hatch was firmly closed, the jet taxied and took off for Ireland. Thank God for that.

Then, a 'tok tok' on our window. Dan Quayle wanted to say something. 'Great stuff, guys. Listen, we, eh ...' He stood there, drenched, his eyes bulging. 'We won't mention this to anyone.'

'Of course not,' we said nodding firmly.

'He's boiling alright,' said our lunatic driver, as the sodden Quayle boy walked away and suddenly his mouth dropped like he'd just seen his beloved Rangers score the most amazing goal. 'Holy Fuck. Look at them guns!' The jeep's hold had just been opened and the Secret Service guys were packing away their weapons.

'That's unbelievable!' he said and, for a moment, I thought he was going to jump out of the car and grab one.

'Come on,' I said, panicking, 'let's get out of here.'

16

Protestors at the Gate

To understand the impact of Robinson's visit in 1990, it's important to recall the state of Ireland at the time. Now that the 'liberal agenda' — often referred to as if it was a conspiracy — is part of Irish society, it is salutary to remind ourselves of how things were. Divorce was rejected in 1986 (indeed was only barely acceded to in 1995), homosexuality was still illegal and it was a criminal offence to put the phone numbers of English abortion clinics in leaflets and magazines. *Playboy* and its ilk were banned, and people still protested about the presence of condom machines in toilets, even though AIDS had become an international hazard.

This anachronistic state of affairs was the subject of international curiosity. At the UN, delegates would come up and say, 'I believe your country does not allow divorce — this is fascinating.' And you would say, yes, this was the case but the matter was being looked at. What made it galling was that the enquirer was often from a country where people were stoned for adultery, or flogged for wearing lipstick. Thus, their enquiries didn't necessarily come with a disapproving air. Americans, however, couldn't understand it. 'The Irish are supposed to be rebels,' people would say, 'how do they put up with this?' 'This *is* a rebellion,' I'd say, a rebellion against secularism and Western materialism, before trying to get off the subject.

The most problematic issue was abortion. Granted all countries have problems with abortion. In the US, it is a emotive and explosive issue. But in Ireland the situation was made worse by attempts to copper-fasten an abortion ban in the Constitution. The vote to get it into the Constitution created a bitter and divisive debate. However, it was a hollow victory for, by putting in such an ambiguous ban — an exception was made if a woman's life was in danger — the Pro-Lifers had created a future loophole which made possible the very situation they hoped to prevent. In 1992, it did and it gave Ireland some of its most spectacular headlines around the world.

It was a Saturday and I was at home in New York when a friend called to say there was going to be a demonstration outside the Consulate. A fourteen-year-old girl in Ireland had been prevented from having an abortion in England. This was the 'X Case', and the girl had been impregnated by her father's best friend. Her family had taken her to England but when they alerted the authorities, hoping that an abortion might produce the necessary DNA to secure a conviction, they were told to return from England at once, before the termination was performed. Technically the State was obliged to do under the Constitution, but in a classic Irish example of an Irish response to an Irish problem, no one had believed that the law would be applied so rigorously. Now that it had been, people were up in arms.

I called the Press Officer but he said 'Ah, I think we'll let this pass,' meaning we won't react. We completely underestimated the depth of feeling, however. In no time, crowds had gathered outside the Consulate and were chanting the same slogan as at home; 'Let Her Go!'

This was grist to the mill of the new diaspora. This was very definitely the Ireland they had left behind, but it was also a situation they were determined to try and change, even from afar. Thus, the demos outside other Irish Embassies, especially in London. It was a sign of things to come. Back issues of *Hot Press*, the Irish rock magazine, would get passed around Sin É Café, and I would bring them into the Consulate as an example of the anger and frustration welling up at home. Likewise, the Diplomatic bag would include copies of the *Sunday Independent*, which was adopting a new tone for Irish newspapers; irreverent, iconoclastic, berating the Bishops and politicians. These were key years of change in Irish society and younger immigrants wanted to help the brave souls who were trying to reform things at home. Their networks of communication were impressive and, as with Republican groups, we noticed that in New York they were often able to get information quicker than we were.

With the X Case protest, the range of people who got involved was also impressive. Not just the usual faces who supported every cause. In the *Irish Voice*, we used to see the same people protesting about immigration and Votes for Emigrants, or for Joe Doherty, the IRA prisoner fighting deportation to Britain. Remarkable how many middle-class kids rediscovered their nationalism in the far-off hothouse of New York and then abandoned such agitation when they got back to Dublin and the full complexity of the situation was again evident. But this protest drew in all sorts; professionals, nurses, waitresses, accountants, people from Woodside and Tribeca. Many of them were people I knew. In fact, almost all my Irish friends were on the protest.

And yet despite this, I still attracted suspicious dirty looks, and even abuse, when I went over to Brownies that evening, in the East Village, where people had collected after the demo. Granted, I was collecting leaflets from the bar counter, to take away for examination. And, also, of course, I hadn't been on the demo. But I still found such hostility strange, as if I was a lackey spy for the unfeeling State.

Later, I would end up helping them, and faxing them the various political statements from Ireland. This wasn't irregular, since the Government had decided to back the girl, and her family, against the Constitution, effectively attacking the very laws it had introduced, at the behest of the people who had supported these laws.

But the suspicion of the demonstrators was probably justified for we represented the fudge culture which they had come to despise, as exemplified the next day when I brought the leaflets into the office. There was an almost disdainful attitude as officials corrected the protestors' statement as you would an exam paper or a draft speech; 'this isn't exactly true'. Clearly, it hadn't the polish or the smooth precision of a Government press release. Possibly because it was written in a state of outrage at this treatment of a fourteen-year-old victim. The officials also took a dim view of the Guinness rings dried into it; the leaflet had been taken off a bar counter, after all. This suggested frivolity, apparently, but I thought it was the opposite. It linked the young protestors into the whole culture of Irish life. Through Guinness rings, they were at one with the old people they opposed. As with anti-Vietnam protestors, their antagonism was not 'unpatriotic', but actually a most profound and troubled form of patriotism.

The dispute was an embarrassment to the Consul General and upset the whole image we'd been trying to project of Ireland as a happy, content little place and we its New York representatives. Now the CG and the Irish political establishment were hoping that the Supreme Court would reverse the decision of the lower Courts and let the girl travel. Because of the complete evasion of legislative responsibility by politicians in this area, echoing the evasion of the people, the Courts had become, by default, the legislators. Albert, in fairness, took a practical can-do attitude and let President Robinson make a long holding statement, which was masterful in its lack of provocation or anger. The fourteen-year-old girl, meanwhile, remained anonymous, a storm breaking over her head.

But in a more general way, the X Case brought home the whole sham of Irish public life, the hypocrisy and cowardice of Haughey, especially towards the Catholic Church, and the ineffectuality of Garret FitzGerald, and his Constitutional Crusade. The net effect was to create an absurd world of make-believe, even for the politicians themselves. When Charlie McCreevy visited New York, he brought along his partner: McCreevy had become Minister, under Reynolds, and they were like kids, enjoying New York. Her name was also McCreevy but this had been achieved not through remarriage (which at the time was, of course, impossible) but through changing it via a deed poll!

At least it partly solved the problem of how she should be described on the itinerary. Unlike Bertie Ahern's partner who we wondered if we could refer to at all. Agonised Press officers sucked on pencils and debated the modalities of description. What were we like? And yet the CG could nonchalantly describe the Manhattan apartment of an Irish cleric's girlfriend, a genuine scandal. Of course, it was the unmasking of another Bishop, Eamon Casey — again with a Tri-State based partner — which dealt a decisive blow to the whole Church-based conservatism. 'It'll never be the same again,' said Mairéad, in the passport office,, as we all crowded around that morning's sensational Press Summary. And it never was.

By now, the people that I'd seen that Sunday in Brownies had formed a group and acquired an office. As well as picketing the Consulate, they bombarded us with phone calls, hitting all the different numbers. 'Hello, hello, I wish to register my protest.' Calls came in from all over the East Coast, many orchestrated but many spontaneous too, prompted by the considerable news coverage. It was surreal, all these phones ringing. It was like we were under siege. And then the fax machine started flapping out faxes of protest; 'I wish to voice my disgust …' Particularly disturbing were the personally worded messages coming in from New York politicians usually friendly to the Consulate.

At least it meant a respite from the endless enquiries about Citizenship from retired Americans, although a few of these still doggedly got through. 'Is this about the abortion case?' said Marie, wearily lifting another receiver. 'Why no, it's about our Irish passports!' said a stunned grandmother in Florida.

The Action Group was supported by the Women's' Action Coalition (WAC) and other New York organisations. This 'foreign involvement' was alleged to show that militants were behind them, as if it mattered. The same argument was used against the Irish gays. In fact, the gays got frustratingly little support from New York gays who, with AIDS and workplace discrimination, had more to think about than marching down a wind-whipped Fifth Avenue with a Parade of red-faced bigots. However, the involvement of WAC and others did lead to tensions within the Action Group, and an attempt to get Catholic Pro-Choicers involved, so as to widen its appeal, was resisted by the more secular hard line elements.

By now, we were on the Group's side, and even the CG had lightened up. Once he heard that the Ambassador in Washington had gone out to meet the protestors on his doorstep, the CG felt he could do likewise and a three woman delegation came in to present their case. In my three years in New York, the Gay and Lesbian group were never allowed near the Consulate, but this group were regarded as 'very constructive', led by a 'very presentable and well spoken' merchant banker. She wore a suit so she got in. It was so predictable.

Among all the protest calls coming in, you'd hear voices you knew. 'Sarah Owens, is that you?!' I said, recognising a girl who was quite involved in the downtown arts scene.

'Sssh. Keep talking, Eamon. CBS are filming me.'

On successive evenings, the protest grew until Madison Avenue was blocked off and TV crews and reporters jostled for pictures. They were, by far, the biggest demos outside the Consulate since the North erupted in 1969 and it became impossible to work, what with the phones ringing and chants coming in the window. 'Not the Church, Not the State, Women will decide their fate!'

The street corner was directly below the CG's office. He was now in high-drama mood, and while he sat compiling despatches for HQ, I had to go out and count the heads. Unfortunately, with vertigo, I got dizzy each time I looked over the balcony, and felt I was going to throw myself off. Perhaps, in the style of some self-immolated Czech dissident, it might be interpreted as the ultimate sacrifice, a dramatic blow for a more tolerant Ireland. I envisaged a traditional street renaming in years to come, with President Robinson coming along to unveil a plaque in my name.

It took a few looks before I could get an idea of the numbers of people, what with the mingling of heads and the spumes of steam coming out of the sidewalk. 'Eh, its about 600!' I shouted in from the balcony. '600. At least 600,' said the CG, writing, 'even 700'. The CG was happy to bump up the figures.

But my headcount drew the attention of some of the protestors. 'Look they're spying!' someone shouted and there was a roar, followed by a shrill of whistles. And then laughter. The mood had lightened, as progress was anticipated. Later, as I emerged with briefcase and ducked down into the subway, to heckled laughter, I envied them their sense of cause and camaraderie. I felt like I'd just come out of the East German Embassy or the Mission of a Latin American dictator.

The next day, the Supreme Court came out with their judgement. The girl should be allowed to travel for an abortion. Her life was in danger, because she had threatened to commit suicide, an interpretation which was greeted with relief by Pro-Choicers. The protests ended and we went back to work. But a few days later another demo sprung up outside the Consulate; three old people silently holding placards. They were Pro-Lifers, holding foetus pictures and inflammatory anti-abortion slogans. 'President Robinson's Message to the Unborn —

Drop Dead', said one, in a weird use of modern street talk. But, in every other respect, they were a throwback, like those ladies in tweed coats and hairnets who stood outside the British Consulate.

'Get rid of them,' I was told, brutally. The protestors were directly outside the building's door. 'Go on, get the police, if necessary. Just get them away from there!'

It was clear that when the shoe was on the other foot, short shrift would be given to the opposition. Whoever that opposition was.

17

High Season

The three months up to St Patrick's Day are the busiest on the social calendar, with a mounting sense of excitement as March 17 approaches. Such is the congestion of receptions, launches and dinners, that a tight Consulate schedule is organised delegating functions to different people. From the posh Ireland Fund at the 21 Club, to the 'set-ups' and sodas of a Christian Brothers hall on Flatbush Avenue. Everything is packed into this period — Greenwich Hibernians, Suffolk County Police and the ominously titled 'Wall Street Friends of Tara.'

In this period, you didn't just dine for Ireland, you ate for the Government and danced for the well-being of the State. Sometimes, you could get two or three County Dinners a night, the Kerry and Galway dances running simultaneously in different rooms in the Astoria Manor, with Mayo across the road in the Crystal Palace. Just to be different, Sligo and Donegal held theirs out in Leonard's of Great Neck. Given the logistics of getting from place to place quickly, I'd often travel with James Higgins, who was taking photographs for the *Irish Voice*. James had one of those big old Yank-tank gas-guzzlers, a 1970s' Thunderbird, with seats so low you could hardly see out the window.

On my corkboard at home, I pinned up the withering button holes from various dances, flowers sprayed with green dye and tied with silver ribbons. Next to them were the Holy pictures I got from older people in return for helping them out on consular cases. 'Wow, that's so cool,' my American friends would say, thinking it was some kitsch Catholic thing, like the way trendies in the East Village buy those bodega prayer candles.

'It's not supposed to be cool,' I'd say snappily. A heathen at home, in America I rediscovered, if not religion, then my defensiveness about Irish Catholicism. (In the US, I discovered another source of grievance for Irish-Americans, the extraordinary anti-Catholic feeling which still lurks in the American psyche.) My ironic friends usually went quiet however when they saw the souvenir US flags and induction scrolls for the Retired Detectives Association. 'Hey, what's all this about?' they'd wail, querying my endorsement of the same 'fascist' cops who had assaulted protesters on Tompkins Square.

'Good friends of ours, the police,' I'd say smugly, 'they keep us informed on the activities of the Irish illegals.' (Not true but good for a wind-up.)

Around this time, there were also the various St Patrick's Parades in the regions; Philadelphia, Atlanta, Mahopac, Pearl River, Scranton and many other towns. A big Parade was held along Prospect Park in Brooklyn, which was multi-ethnic and more fun than Manhattan. Generally, however, all the Parades were a variation on each other; high school bands, police cadets and large-girthed 'revellers' in Aran jumpers. There was little of the spontaneity and colour of the Parades at home. Out here, the celebration of ethnicity was a grim old business.

In Newark, the Parade still went through the old downtown area, now completely black with only the bar names still Irish. A defiant gesture, perhaps, or else a heartening signal that America's first urban proletariat was still in touch with its original metropolitan centres.

These events were invaluable as an insight into the US heartland. In Garden City, Long Island, there was a big parade which adjourned afterwards to the Irish Centre in Mineola, a white-fenced wooden hall where we all had steaming bacon and cabbage followed by a cracking céile.

On one level, it was like the Galway Gaeltacht in the 1970s, but it was also like the wedding scene in *The Deer Hunter*, with couples, young and old, twirling around in a boisterous celebration of blue-collar America. Just as intriguing was the Parade itself; fire engines and stony-faced soldiers, and lots of societies like the Rotary Club and the Elks. And the Kiwanis; a sort of Freemason outfit where businessmen went around with strange little tasselled hats on their heads. The whole thing was like something out of a David Lynch movie, or one of those slow motion alternative rock videos which play on the pastel weirdness of suburban American life.

Sensing my alienation, the priest beside me on the platform offered a swig of whiskey. 'Here, you'll need it. Keeps out the cold.' It was often cold or raining at the Parades, a fact which always reminded me of that most audacious of ideas from our Civil Service; the proposal to move the date of the national holiday from March 17 to mid-summer. The idea was also intended to facilitate the Lenten abstinence, something which didn't really matter anymore, as the hip flask of the priest testified.

The sense of community at the Parades was almost suffocating. As well as war veterans, whose subsequent lives seemed to be defined by the time they had spent in Vietnam, there were about ten different forms of police and resident Committees, all marching past with ridiculous pomposity. It was so different to the more relaxed approach in Ireland, where the Parades were a bit of crack. There were no children's floats here, no papier mâché puppets or humorous skits on politicians. Instead, we had citizen militias, brandishing their guns and walking past in tigerish combats. Adults acting as young boys. Suddenly, you could see how people might take to the hills in Montana and start swearing vengeance on the Government. Suddenly too, you could see why American cultural rebellion, when it did occur, was so savage. It would have to be. I mean, what would it be like to grow up gay here? You'd probably just board the first Greyhound into the city.

The New Jersey Irish Festival, held at the Garden State Centre in Middleton was similarly revealing. Attended by over 15,000 people, it is one of the biggest Irish events in the region, but with those kind of numbers we are talking about a very diluted form of Irish-America. These were the 'third or fourth Generation' that the Consul General had described when we first met and whom I couldn't imagine. Now they were before me, the obese, spandex nightmare that so many Eurosnobs talk about. In a large field, overhung with the smell of fried food, gaudy stalls were selling candy floss, Gaelic trinkets and really bad Irish folk music. The link between these people and Ireland was tenuous at best, the equivalent of a tartan biscuit tin for a Scottish-American, of which incidentally there were many here. It seems that down the line in America, the Scottish and Irish thing gets a bit blurred.

It was thus kind of shocking that the only actual Irish people here were tending the Noraid stall, selling IRA key fobs and bodhráns carved by prisoners. They were also selling t-shirts with 'IRA Rocks London', like you'd have for a touring band except that the gig guide was a list of actual bombings. Some of the concerts were 'cancelled'; the ones that didn't go off, ho, ho. American browsers thought they were hilarious. They hadn't the first clue about Northern Ireland. I was kind of hoping they might buy the t-shirts and then wear them in London, or even in Ireland. When the stallholders heard my accent they straightened up suspiciously; an Irish person. And yet there was a strange integrity to them too, standing there, ever hopeful, with their miserable prison art. They looked like they were only in this candyfloss world out of sufferance, because they needed support from anywhere.

Suddenly, a burst of gunfire. In the field next to us, lines of soldiers were marching on each other. A re-enactment of the American Civil War. Apparently, the only war fought on US soil since Independence has become a popular hobby among fully grown men, who regularly dress up in the grey and blue uniforms of the Union and Confederate armies. A weird smile came over the Noraid stallholders, as they watched these bank managers and air-conditioning salesmen shooting at each other with blank bullets, while being cheered on by the hotdog-eating tracksuits.

But the highlight of the Festival was the raising of the World's Largest Tricolour. I kid you not. The huge flag was packed into an accordion fold on the ground. The ground, alas — it should never touch the ground! I should have read them the Consular Instructions. At the whistle, a powerful cherry-picker crane lifted up the flag, while a bunch of us VIPs, and lucky people from the crowd, rushed in to help unfurl it. The operation was riven with accidental symbolism. Two of the Noraid people were at the orange end and were almost smothered by the cloth, while I was similarly enclosed by a fold of green, and had a small panic attack. In fact, the whole thing was quite dangerous; at one stage, a gust of wind sent the hem of the flag swinging backwards, slapping some of the lycra-clad lifters to the ground. Perhaps it was annoyed at this travesty of Irish culture.

The main St Patrick's Day Parade is of course in New York City and, after all the expectation, it's actually quite boring, a militaristic display of cops, soldiers and high school bands. And people carrying exciting banners like 'Con Edison Emerald Society No 6'. It was once memorably described as having all the grace of 'a funeral at a fast pace'. Except that it is noisy, the sounds provided by police bagpipers and Republican flute bands, visiting from the North. Drummers beat their drums with the same resolve, and purpose, as Orange bands in the North. We are here to stay. We are not going away.

The noise perfectly captures the Irish-American attitude that by walking down Fifth Avenue they were really sticking it to the WASPs, the same impulse which led them to build a huge Cathedral on the Avenue, outside which the marchers stop to be blessed by a grinning Cardinal. The whole thing smacks of triumphalism. Feeling besieged and resentful, the marchers almost scowl at the bemused crowd.

The lack of integration contrasts with the parade in Ireland, or in other New York events like the West Indian/Caribbean Parade in Crown Heights, Brooklyn. Crown Heights is a *real* Parade, a carnival-like atmosphere with children crowding around steel bands on flatbed trucks and Mardi Gras outfits swirling out onto the sidewalks, where older people stand around jerk chicken stalls, drinking plastic cups of rum. Not to mention those South American girls in diamanté pantsuits, grind-dancing on top of PA systems. (Blimey!). That was not something one was likely to see on 5th Avenue.

No, siree. No such exuberance for the Ancient Order of Hibernians (AOH). The rules famously forbade floats, dating from the Victorian Paddywackery of the nineteenth-century when O'Connellite Nationalists put on a floral procession that would have given Cecil B DeMille a run for his money. For the same reason, all animals were barred except 'the faithful Irish wolfhound'. Apparently people used to bring in their goats and cattle and try to sell them. (In fact, the nineteenth-century Parade sounds like a bit of fun.) The anti-float regulation meant that all wheeled vehicles were also barred. In 1991, the same year the gays were first excluded, this law was also used to exclude children in wheelchairs! Sometimes you felt that what the AOH really needed was a course in Public Relations.

This was especially evident at the beginning of their dispute with the gays, many of whom were young activists from Ireland, with a background in Republican or women's issues. Media-savvy, they knew how to play to the city's vigilant press, while the grey men of the AOH tightened their jaws before the camera and said 'No Comment'. It wasn't that the media were unsympathetic to the AOH. Far from it. People were weary of the endless agit-politics of the city's gay community. But images like the Grand Marshall's aides, in their ridiculous top hats and tails, turning their backs on the Mayor, made the AOH look like something out of the last century.

Ostensibly excluding the gays because there was no room, the AOH suddenly had to change tack when the City offered policing for an extended Parade. The AOH should have been straight up and said that the Parade was a Catholic, semi-religious event, as the gays well knew. Of course, the equation of Irish with Catholic was, in itself, objectionable but Irish-Americans weren't conscious of such sectarianism. A compromise emerged when a liberal, city-based section of the AOH (Division Six) let the gays march with them, but for this gesture, they were later expelled, only adding to the Order's divisions. Politicians, sensing which way the wind was blowing, marched with the gays. This was not without incident: New York's black Mayor, David Dinkins, had a half-full beer can thrown at him. He said it reminded him of Montgomery, Alabama. Tensions were high.

The following year, the gays wanted to march under their own banner and, with the AOH attitude toughening, the gays resorted to the Courts. Turned down, they appealed to the Supreme Court. The saga went on and on. Unable to march, they lay down in front of the Parade at 42nd Street, and were hauled off into police vans. It was a real old New York ding-dong which brought out the best in tabloid headlines. 'Gays Get Their Irish Up', 'Dinkins Catches an Eire-ful Over Parade', 'Irish Stew on 5th Avenue'. The latter was a reference to a 1993 arrangement whereby the gays marched before the main Parade, offering the possibility of what another paper described as a 'right old donnybrook by the Park'.

The row also drew out some typical conundrums. The American Civil Liberties Union supported the AOH and their right to exclude. So did some gay groups, who feared that forced inclusion could allow a homophobic group to get into the Gay Pride Parade. In Boston, where a similar dispute was underway, there was already talk of the Ku Klux Klan applying to march in the Martin Luther King Parade! And what of the PLO in the Israeli Day Parade?

People were humorous about it. 'Sure gays have been marching down the Avenue for years — many of them in uniform,' someone told a stunned crowd at the Astoria Manor. Or as someone else put it: 'Give the AOH a chance. These guys have only just come to terms with heterosexuality!'

But there was bitterness too. For seeking flexibility, Police Commissioner Ray Kelly became 'Gay Kelly'. His stand was regarded as especially treacherous because he was Irish-American. The paranoia was almost quaint. Likewise, publisher Niall O'Dowd got stick because his newspaper *The Irish Voice* had supported the gays. O'Dowd's real crime was that he had written an Op Ed piece for *The New York Times* which was regarded as washing the dirty linen in public. O'Dowd pointed out that not only were gay groups marching in Parades in Ireland, but in Cork their float had won a prize.

'We don't care what happens in Ireland,' a woman told me bitterly. 'Over there, they turn the flag upside down, and do what they want. But over here, it's more serious.'

The dispute, and the siege mentality it created, was another reason for staying away and, on the day itself, many people, especially the downtown crowd, remained in their own area and held parties. A side benefit of the CG's ambition — with the Minister in tow, he went to everything, from the profile-building Mass to the Mayor's breakfast — was that it gave the rest of us the day off. Just as well, for the other reason you wouldn't go to the Parade was that you were usually sleeping off the night before, which is when the real crack was had.

On St Patrick's Eve, the whole social scene came to a climax. There was a good buzz around midtown with receptions in the hotels and pubs. A lot of people came over from Ireland, but again there was that backslapping atmosphere — it's great to be Irish — except now it was being engaged in by the Irish themselves. Or there was the opposite, a sort of witless mockery of Irish-Americans which tended to make Consulate people like myself — who after all spent the rest of the year with them — quite defensive. 'There's more to it than plastic shamrocks,' you told them but, as befits such sophisticated tourists, they were too busy getting carried away with the liberal licensing hours.

Journalists came out from Dublin, doing colour pieces and looking for gossipy stories. The CG told us to be careful about being quoted. A previous Press Officer had got into trouble when he was asked by a TV crew, where was the best place in the city to spend St Patrick's Day. 'Chinatown,' he replied curtly.

But another experience was more interesting, possibly because it befell a smooth Eurocrat we knew, who was usually the essence of precision. Carried away by the revelry in a Second Avenue Bar, he gladly obliged when a book was passed around in which revellers were asked to write their highlight of St Patrick's Day. 'My highlight,' wrote Mr Smoothie, 'is coming out of an Irish bar and seeing a big black mamma with "Fuck Me I'm Irish" written on her chest.' Alas, the book belonged to a journalist and the comments duly appeared in print. There was consternation and old Smoothie had to sweat a little more for the hitherto certain promotion.

For more innocent reasons, the CG also had to sweat for his 'red hat'. Just before the festive week, the news came through that he'd been promoted. He was going to Iraq as Ambassador. Except that with Saddam Hussein still holding out on the West, and with EU States still keeping their Baghdad Embassies closed as a protest, he was unable to actually get there. The CG would spend another year in New York. 'The fate of one wily fellow is tied to another,' chuckled Napoleon, whose own St

Patrick's Day consisted of hauling African diplomats into Kate Kearney's tavern. And leaving them there.

My own season in America concluded not far from there, up on a fairy-lit rooftop, overlooking Second Avenue. Indeed, we were right above Jameson's, our regular post-UN haunt. Some Limerick people were having a party and a heaving crowd had come in from Woodside and the Bronx. Up the long stairs, the walls were decorated with green bunting and St Patrick's beer signs. The same decorations that Irish-Americans wrote about to the Consulate, suggesting we protest to the beer companies about this 'ethnic-stereotyping'. Excuse me, but had any of these people ever been to a St Patrick's Eve party?

Tonight, no one cared. Next to a life-sized cardboard figure of Kathy Ireland, the Budweiser girl, was a poster of Mary Robinson and signs saying, 'Gays, Cripples — all are welcome'. At midnight, guests were given a full Irish breakfast, followed by green jello shots, laced with vodka. Gary, the sculptor, was wearing a lime-green wig and waved down jauntily to the Teamsters and boozy firemen in the street below. The East Village crowd were here in force and, against the din of thumping music, stories were exchanged about Green Card interviews and 'fake employers'. Mocking it all, a Belfast girl spoke loudly about her 'British heritage' and opened her blouse to flash a t-shirt — 'Proud To Be A Prod'.

'Drop the 'A'!' shouted someone, to which she responded with two fingers. It was definitely a more raucous and lively atmosphere than the dinners in the Waldorf.

Almost too lively and I had to go out on the roof for a breather. Leaning back, I looked up at the Citicorp Centre with its illuminated roof entangled in clouds — that's how close to the heavens we were. And yet sometimes, if you are high up, on a balcony on the West Side or in Chelsea, you can look down over the Village brownstones with their aerials and endless wooden water towers —

just as if you were looking down over some darkened village in a valley.

What an amazing city, I thought, and what a lucky person I was to have come and experienced it in this way; twenty-eight, single, and supported by the generous Irish taxpayer. It had been tremendous posting after all, one which would stay with me forever. Tehran might also have been amazing but who can tell? Such is the lottery of the foreign service. Perhaps I might have become a dab hand at the segregated skiing. Instead, I had developed a deep affection for New York and even for our much maligned cousins, the Irish-Americans. Now, whenever I hear the 'Rose of Castlerea', I always think of a brightly lit room in Astoria, and the dancers, young and old, moving back and forth in a timeless configuration of exile and continuity.

I went back inside for a shot of whiskey; Bushmills, at the insistence of the Belfast girl. Over a few more, we got into a big discussion about politics and life and exile, but it was a struggle against the increasing volume of the music. 'So,' I said, getting closer. 'Does Ulster still Say No?'

'Ulster Says Maybe,' she said with a smile.

I spent most of my last few months in the US at the Embassy in Washington DC, briefly replacing a First Sec who had returned home for the Talks on Northern Ireland, or the 'Talks about Talks' as they were known then. The First Secretary concerned, Tim O'Connor, was an old North hand and I was told that he was going home to 'help the SDLP to talk to each other'. Appropriately, he is today based in Armagh, as the Government's Joint Secretary in the new North-South Body.

In Washington, O'Connor had been on the Commercial side and my job could not have been simpler. I was expected to mind the desk and 'keep an eye on things', reading the commercial newspapers and various reports and attend occasional nod-along meetings. I was not expected to make any new contacts, which might complicate matters. The Embassy was split into Political and Commercial sides, or floors, and inevitably there was rivalry between the two. The Ambassador, Pádraic Mac Kernan, was not overly busy; nor was Ireland, in this, the last year of George Bush's administration, high on the US agenda. All would change when Clinton became president and the National Security Council became involved in the North, but in 1992, one senior Irish desk officer at the State Department, could be described as someone 'who got through the entire *New York Times* every day'. Nor was our own Embassy particularly busy and, after the hectic pace of New York, it seemed like a holiday.

Each morning, I'd walk from Georgetown Harbour Mews where I had an apartment, to the Embassy on Massachusetts Avenue, a pleasant journey through Foggy Bottom and DuPont Circle, the streets confettied with fragrant cherry blossom. Because of the high humidity, I couldn't walk too fast, or my Brooks Brothers shirt would break into a sweat, an apt metaphor for my DC interlude. The Embassy was located on Sheridan Circle, a leafy roundabout which also gave its name to a round table group comprising the Semi-State Bodies and other Irish institutions in the city. Outside my third floor window, below the flag and harp was the corner where in 1974 Orlando Letelier, the exiled Chilean opposition leader, was killed in a car bomb by Pinochet's agents, almost certainly with US collusion. It is the only such outrage ever committed in the nation's capital by a foreign regime.

Beside us, were the Romanian and Egyptian Embassies, where they seemed to be continuously washing their cars. Or standing around. As someone said, much of diplomatic life was 'watching and waiting'. Along Embassy Row, many of the buildings were constructed in the architectural style of their countries; a white-walled hacienda for Mexico, a pagoda for Thailand and a cube of black glass for Sweden. The British Embassy was a huge gated compound which housed over 700 people. '700 people?' I exclaimed, thinking what a lot of potential for misinformation. 'What do they all do?' I asked a British official. 'I have no idea,' he replied firmly, 'and I'm certain, neither do they.' The US-UK military connection was a contributory factor, however, as it was for the Australians who also had a very large Embassy.

Our own Embassy was a fine building, originally owned by the Kellogg family, with large balcony windows and a sweeping interior staircase, adorned with paintings and sculptures on loan from the National Gallery. (Such exhibits were in circulation throughout all Embassies and residences.) The Ambassador's residence, in the North West of the city, was a possibly even finer building, with gravelled paths and a cut-stone, outdoor swimming pool. Hanging in the living room, was a large portrait of Hilton Edwards and Micheál MacLiammoir, the famous gay theatrical couple, which I found appropriate given the half-gay nature of our foreign service, but also ironic given the then illegal status of such lifestyles at home.

The main issues on the Commercial side were the GATT talks and European agricultural subsidies, which were often at the centre of angry press conferences called by American farmers in the National Press Club. Meanwhile, the normally efficient EU co-ordination seemed chaotic; often only eight of the twelve turned up for talks in fellow EU Embassies. Despite the fact that these were ostensibly important get-togethers, the Italians and Greeks hardly ever showed. When they did their elderly representatives were often surprised when they saw me enter the room. The already youthful reputation of our foreign service was here exaggerated by my temporary substitution for Tim. I should stress again that, compared to us, other foreign services seemed almost Jurassic. At meetings of the Consulates Association in New York, a body which represented the city's foreign Consulates, we were by far the youngest people in the room. It was perhaps for this reason that our ambitious Consul General, along with his trusted Deputy, got elected to run the thing. The CG should definitely have been in politics.

My other activity was assisting our exporters in the US with 'paperwork', especially with agriculture and often in dodgy circumstances. (Irish beef, it seems, will be the end of us.) The Embassy was also responsible for Mexico, where our exporters seemed to be in even dodgier territory. But we weren't averse to pulling strokes ourselves, including trying to get the US to break the customs pre-clearance they'd given their soldiers returning from the Gulf, so that they could go shopping at Shannon where they'd been stopping over in their thousands. The US pre-clearance was a strict arrangement in keeping with America's desire to keep the whole Gulf operation as above-board and fluent as possible. Our move then was an outrageous piece of opportunism which must have breached all sorts of protocols. We even went into the State Department to pitch our case; the Americans listened with bemusement and then firmly said no. 'Well, that was worth a try,' said my senior colleague afterwards as we drove back up the Mall in the limo. 'Worth a try,' I repeated, shaking my head. What were we like?

We'd even reminded them of the fact that we'd allowed the US to refuel their planes at Shannon, en route to the Gulf, but the Americans were looking for a bit more than that. In any case, by this time many Americans thought we were about to emerge out of our military neutrality and I had a bit of fun when I went along to a massive arms fair, wearing the name tag; 'Ireland — Civil Government'. It was one of these classic US conventions, where you ask a simple question about some multi-finned rocket launcher, and an unblinking man, in a uniform, gives you a long, robotic answer. 'But, of course, sir, your country is neutral,' he added. 'Yes, but Europe is changing and Ireland with it,' I said, fixing him with a look. 'I get you, sir, I get you loud and clear,' he said, his eyes popping, and he quickly began bringing me through missile parts and various explosive capabilities. He clearly thought — 'These guys are starting from scratch: great new customers.' By the time I left, I think I had given tentative agreement to an entire surface-to-air missile system and I could imagine the apoplectic rage of the neutralists back home. But I was only having a bit of crack.

On the Political side, downstairs in the Embassy, I encountered Eamon McKee again, who'd been at the UN with us. He was busy working Capitol Hill where, on the issue of immigration, the Embassy had secured a major success with the Morrison visa program, providing visas for the Irish illegals. (McKee even ended up marrying an aide from Morrison's office.) Eamon's Counsellor, Brendan Scannell, was one those rough diamonds in DFA, a trove of anecdotal wisdom and advice. With his strong Kerry accent — 'Y'arrah, that's the way of it ... ' — he had a way of cutting to the core of a situation and seemed to be always 'fixing' things. It was he who later encouraged me to take a career break from the Department. He was also, in DFA folklore, the man who 'saved Haughey's life' when, on the way to South Bend, Indiana to receive the traditional honours that Notre Dame University bestows on various Taoisigh, Haughey took ill and was laid up in bed with a incredibly high temperature. With his workaholic instincts, Haughey was determined to go ahead with his schedule and Scannell had to virtually tie him down. Politicians liked Scannell and he constantly had people staying with him. 'What are the FitzGeralds like?' I asked him after he'd been host to Garret and Joan. 'Ah, they're nice people, but they're not in the real world.' Later, when he was Ambassador in Israel, I asked him about the tension between Sephardic and Ashkenazi (European-origin) Jews. 'It's like a fight between two Kerry tinkers,' he said, 'and, if you intervene, the pair of them will turn on you.' Which is about as good a description of Israeli society as any I can think of.

There was also a Press Officer in Washington to whom the Press Office in New York was technically answerable but, as we all knew well, New York was a long way away. I could now feel the tensions between Embassy and Consulate up close in the form of suspicious glances and constant denigration of my New York colleagues. And yet when I returned to Manhattan, sporting an Annapolis tan, I was regarded as having enjoyed myself too much 'down there', and incurred equal suspicion.

In a sense, the relationship between the Embassy and its largest Consulate, in New York, mirrored that between Washington, as the political capital, and New York, as the 'real' US capital. But if New York was polyglot and messy, Washington was a proper capital in the elegant, old world sense. With its clean, cream-white buildings and spacious lay out, you felt you were truly at the heart of an Empire, for good or bad, and everything seemed to be tinged with the strange nostalgia of recent history. Familiar institutions were in close proximity; the Justice Department and the Treasury, FBI headquarters, the Supreme Court and the White House. Stretched between the Capitol building and the Lincoln Memorial, was the long grassy Mall, with its reflecting pond and surrounding monuments, the imperial architecture softened by the picnics and football games to which the Mall was constantly host. Of course, almost all the political and institutional life was situated in the North West of the city, with the rest of the city an often violent hinterland, rarely seen, except later when we went to night clubs in the predominantly black areas of South West and South East (although we personally encountered more violence amidst the menacing frat-boy culture of Georgetown University). As befits such an Empire, its civil service was truly huge and visits to the Department of Agriculture, for example, revealed a labyrinthine bureaucracy of Gogolian proportions, with endless rooms of miserable-looking clerks. So much for the 'less Government' promise of the Republicans.

The city at this time was in an odd mood. The end of the Cold War was an unexpected triumph, but there was a sense of regret that the dramatic days of bipolar intrigue were over. It was perhaps for this reason that the Gulf War celebrations seemed so over the top, and an interesting postscript to the debates I'd witnessed at the UN. It began with a Victory Parade down Pennsylvania Avenue with absurd, goose-stepping soldiers and Stealth bombers flying over, after which thousands of people descended on the Mall to check out the assembled military hardware. The Mall was usually such a pleasant sight when seen from a ground perspective, with kites flying and rows of volleyball nets, but now it was cluttered with missile batteries, scud launchers, tanks and gun tents. Basically, all the things I'd seen at the arms fair except here it was part of a family day out, with kids clambering inside gun turrets and peering through telescopic sights, assisted by their loving mothers, while proud Dads were encouraged to try out the latest M16s by gum-chewing soldiers. Perched on top of a tank, a square jawed soldier told a rapt audience that 'This here unit, wiped out eleven tanks of the Iraqi enemy.'

'Was there anyone sitting in those tanks at the time?' we asked loudly, knowing how one-sided the war was, and we nearly got lynched.

We were being mischievous but it was hard not to be and the surly defensiveness of the crowd suggested that they knew how disproportionate this outpouring was for a hi-tech war. Around the field, telling stories to their families, were picnicking groups of boozy soldiers, clad in those brown desert fatigues so associated with that war but which seemed ridiculous here, given that most of the soldiers had hardly been out of military base. What they were celebrating instead was the long history of the US military and the great relief that they might finally be getting over their Vietnam complex, or 'body bag syndrome' (although a later reluctance to use ground troops in Bosnia or Kosovo would prove that this wasn't entirely the case).

A reminder of this syndrome stood on the Mall, in the form of the black wall of the Vietnam Memorial, with all the names etched on it, and against which daily scenes of personal melodrama were played out. Camped nearby, on an almost permanent basis, was a tent belonging to some long-haired Vets, who were convinced that their buddies were still being held captive somewhere in the jungle and were handing out conspiratorial Missing in Action material. I saw the black silhouette MIA flags familiar from Irish-American functions in New York.

Despite such displays, the city had a good-humoured atmosphere, which I found relaxing after New York. There was a huge floating population of young interns, lobbyists and staffers, working in Congressional offices and the Senate, or in the various think-tanks and institutes in the city. There were also lots of 'out-of-towners' and I met a much broader range of Americans than I would in New York, especially from the South and Mid-West. Washington was also a big University town, with Georgetown, GW University and black colleges like Howard, all of which added to the outgoing atmosphere.

The Embassies also mixed a good deal together and there was a lively crew at our own Embassy, especially on the secretarial side. Our weekends would begin over at the Australian Embassy, which had its own bar and a Friday evening 'social', a strange 1950s-style colonial throwback with men standing around in army uniforms or shorts and women in hairdos like Queen Elizabeth, whose portrait hung on the wall. There was also a large map of Australia but a Tasmanian friend of ours was so upset at the omission of her island that she got up in her denim shorts and carved it into the wall; a stunt which resulted in our exclusion for a while. After this, we would go on to barbecues in Bethesda or Chevy Chase and come back into the city at midnight, ending up at the busy intersection of the Adams Morgan crossroads, a beehive of interns and staffers, buzzing in and out of bars like 'Cities' or 'Heaven and Hell'. Nor did the city seem to change; years later a long article on 'Monica Lewinsky's Washington' opened with a description of Cities bar, where the interns who were denied entry 'gathered outside, cluttering the pavement like starlings'. In my own time, the Lewinsky-type access to power was plausible too, and high-spirited staffers seemed to be constantly swapping scandal and telling stories about their political masters. Not so much Beltway chatter as below the belt shenanigans.

I often met up with Bob, an Irish friend, who usually had a merry bunch of aides and starry-eyed political workers with him. By day, he worked in Ted Kennedy's Office and in the evening he stayed at Hickory Hill, the Robert Kennedy estate in Virginia. Ted Kennedy was a major figure in Washington, almost a President by default for liberal Democrats, with a huge legislative machine and a large office. It was like a replica of DFA, with an almost equal number of people on the Asia or Africa desks or on issues connected to Ireland. His interest in Ireland was obvious with photos of former Taoisigh on the walls and framed versions of the same 'Legalise the Irish' posters that I saw in Bronx bars or East Village cafes. Bob and I went over to the Hideout, Kennedy's private retreat, high up on the left side of the Capitol dome, with porthole views back up the Mall. We had a bit of crack, whistling at the girls below and hoping to get into the next days *Washington Times* (notoriously anti-Kennedy) with the headline, 'New Sensation — Girls Wolf-Whistled At From Teddy's Lair!' The controversy over his nephew, William Kennedy Smith, was all over the media at the time.

In the afternoon, we'd go out to Hickory Hill, which Ethel Kennedy had kept like a shrine to her late husband, Robert, and his brother John. In the living room, I sat in the seat RFK used as Attorney General, next to a flagstaff from JFK's Oval office. On the walls were pictures of the

Kennedy children along with, again, pictures of visiting Irish politicians. In the back garden, we took a dip in the sky-blue outdoor pool, familiar from those colourchrome home movies which recalled the glamour and easy optimism of the early Sixties. Afterwards, we took Ethel's vintage convertible and went back into the city, driving past the nearby CIA headquarters in Langley, the proximity of which was always a boon to conspiracy theorists. With the top down, we inhaled the cherry blossom and far-off briny sea. As we came over Arlington bridge, I was glad to see that the Mall had been rescued from the militarists and returned again to the kids flying kites and the volleyball. We parked by the Potomac River, which was filled with sailing boats, and watched the sun go down behind the Lincoln memorial. 'This,' I thought, 'is the life.'

When I returned to New York, my posting to the US was up and I began to prepare for the return to Dublin. Just before I finally left, however, I paid a last visit to South America. While in the US, I had tried to travel as much as possible, including trips to the West Coast and Latin America and I decided to do one more. On your travels, you'd often look up fellow officers and a lot of DFA people took 'busmen's holidays' by staying with each other in foreign cities. In the part of South America I was going to, there was no Embassy, but there was an Honorary Consul. 'Look him up. He'll be good for a lunch,' I was told and that he certainly was.

I was always curious about the Honorary Consul system. Basically where the State has no Embassy or Consulate, we are nominally represented by a local worthy, who is willing to do the job for next to nothing and is issued with a flag, escutcheon (official harp on shield) and a bunch of passports for emergency purposes. Essentially, they do it for the prestige, or because of ethnic ties, and the post is usually taken up by a local business person, with trade links, or a well-placed ex-pat. Thus, for example, Michael Smurfit is Ireland's Honorary Consul in

Monaco, or has someone do it for him, while Tony Ryan the air tycoon, used to represent Mexico in Ireland. Other examples include barrister Gerard Danaher for Croatia and socialites, and Gerard and Clodagh Kean, for Chile. There is a minimal annual fee and they keep fifty per cent of the consular fees, but, in most cases, there is little consular work, and the job generally involves meeting visiting ministers or a wandering diplomat like myself.

However, some Honorary Consuls are called upon to do trojan work; while I was Duty Officer back in Dublin, I discovered the value of some of our own representatives, like a priest in South Africa who, as well as constantly challenging the apartheid authorities, did amazing work issuing Irish passports (this was before we had an Embassy there). Or the representative in Thailand who was constantly bailing out lost hippies and Irish drugs offenders, a task which also frequently fell to Our Man in Bombay, the splendidly named Robert W Leybourne Callaghan, who had chambers at the Royal Bombay Yacht Club in Apollo Bunder.

We even had Honorary Consuls in the United States itself to cover those regions beyond the reach of our Embassy and Consulates. However, such appointments are made by the Minister, not the Cabinet, and in the US we suffered the aftermath of a previous Minister who made a series of 'death-bed' appointments just before he left office. Predictably, some of the appointees, often Irish-Americans, were a bit disappointing. Unfortunately, however, once an Honorary Consul has been appointed, it is very hard to get rid of them. A previous Honorary Consul in Pakistan, for example, ended up taking a court action against the Government to prevent his removal.

It was a similar case which made me curious about the system. Talking to Michael Forbes, on the phone from San Francisco, he let slip that he had to go down to South America to 'find an Honorary Consul'. What do you mean 'find him'? I asked, but he wouldn't say any more. In DFA, there were secrets that people kept from each other and no amount of persuasion would get Forbes to elaborate. Later, it emerged that the Consul concerned had gone gaga and Forbes had to go down and — like a Rebel in the burning GPO — rescue the flag and harp, not to mention the bag of passports, now overrun with lizards and stained with the wax of a burning witch-doctors skull. (Okay, I'm exaggerating but you get the general picture.)

When I arrived in my own, quite different, South American country, the Honorary Consul was away sailing, but his Deputy agreed to meet me, and took me over to their office, a tiny room down some back streets with a picture of President Robinson on the wall and a Remington manual typewriter on a battered desk. Outside, chickens were running around but I was a bit too tired to take it all in. As with much of South America, the city was high above sea level and I was suffering from a combination of altitude sickness and the celebration of my birthday the night before. For the first few days, one is supposed to avoid drink, cigarettes and coffee, but unfortunately I embraced all three with gusto. Thus, when the Consul told me we were going for a big three-course lunch in a bullfighters' restaurant, my heart sank. Below dead animal's heads, and with the heat baking away outside, a jolly waiter served up a succession of heavy, creamed dishes and fortified wines. In any other circumstances I think I would nodded off straight into my main course of sticky ribs but what kept me alert was the extraordinary views of our Acting Consul.

Ostensibly a mild-mannered, middle-aged man, with his pink face and white hair, he looked like a priest who'd been away in the Missions too long. And, indeed, he told me that he hadn't been back to Ireland for an incredible eighteen years. He couldn't live there 'because of the growth of Communism,' he said, pouring me more wine.

'The what?'

'The influence of the Semi-State bodies,' he said, and the general expansion of the Public Sector, as he started railing about the lack of individual enterprise and the socialist influence of the teachers, the media and the Church. By contrast, he praised an African country, which he'd recently lived in, and done business with, which he said was now running 'very smoothly'. But there'd recently been a coup in this country and democracy was suspended. I felt I had to put this to him but he replied bluntly that there was 'no point in having democracy, if the people aren't educated.' He then softened this to suggest that more of both would be welcome — *eventually*. Although he hadn't been back to Ireland for a long time, he seemed to be very up-to-date on events, getting material from Iveagh House, and said he was most pleased by some of the recent changes in economic policies.

After dinner, he asked me if I would accompany him back to the old city. He had to buy a few cartridges. Sure, I said, remembering the old Remington, but once outside, hit by the daylight and the postprandial brandies, I felt very, very tired. 'You're grand,' the Consul assured me, in an accent which hadn't changed in eigtheen years. 'Come on, we'll walk quickly.' And off we went through winding back streets and cobblestoned lanes, until I didn't know where I was. At one stage, I was bent double, gulping for air, when he pointed out the sheep's bones embedded as decorative setts in the ground. 'Vertebrae bones,' he explained and I nodded; great idea. Rising, I was hit by a sickly smell of frying and what looked like a small dog being turned on a spit by a toothless street vendor. I gazed at it in nauseous wonder and the vendor cried 'El rato, el rato!' Right, fine. 'The rats in the jungle are very big,' explained the Consul; mindful of the sticky carcass in my stomach, I replied that I didn't doubt it.

We went down another street, where a bunch of empty coffins were standing outside a sweetshop. 'Opposite the hospital,' noted the Consul, pointing across the street. 'In South America, people are very up-front about death.' As, indeed, was our Consul who went on to dismiss the primitive medical facilities. 'Most of the patients are going to die anyway,' he said, nonchalantly tapping a coffin. 'So, why not. Ah, here we are!'

We were in front of a gun shop, with rifles and shotguns in the window. 'Yes,' he said, noting my surprised expression, 'cartridges for guns. I like to let off a few rounds during the night, just to keep thieves away.'

'Not thieves at the Consulate,' I stuttered.

'No, no,' he said, putting me at ease. 'I have a little smelting operation out in the jungle. We're smelting for gold.' And then with a big smile — the first time I'd really seen him smile — he quickly whispered 'There's loads of gold in this country. Tell nobody!' And in he popped to the gunshop.

This is *unreal*, I told myself, thinking it was definitely time to go home; to the hotel, to New York and to Ireland. The poor Secretary, Noel Dorr; has he any idea what the Department is like on some of its outer margins?

Back in New York, the process of withdrawal was well underway. 'Is everything going back to two dimensions?' a colleague asked, who was facing a similar withdrawal herself. It was a good description of the way the West Village and in-tray correspondence began to recede. I said my goodbyes and attended a few farewell barbecues held by friends. I held a few parties myself, just to use up the duty-free drink. Not that there wasn't more coming with me; such diplomatic perks were fully availed for the return home. As was the transfer of belongings, amongst which I managed to include a few computers and some sculptures. At JFK, the Aer Lingus people with whom I dealt with on everything from the transfer of bodies to the visits of politicians said their goodbyes and bumped me up to First Class. As the plane soared, I looked down at the lights of the city, at the glowing bowl of Shea Stadium and the coastal port lights of Long Island, and thought, my love affair with this city is only beginning.

Section IV

Northern Ireland

18

Bugs and Shredders

When I returned from the US I was put into Anglo-Irish, the Division dealing with Northern Ireland and relations with Britain. Along with the EU Division, it is probably the most important part of the Department. It is one thing dealing with the political situation in Sri Lanka or Poland, it is quite another when it is your own country, where a state of war has existed for the last twenty years. Everything involving the State and the Northern part of the island came through this Division, although in a curious overlap which had implications for the Peace Process later on, the Taoiseach's Department is also involved.

The Division has grown in leaps and bounds. The largest leap was in the early Eighties in expectation of a major agreement arising out of the two Government's Anglo-Irish Studies. But such a prospect was oversold by an excitable Brian Lenihan and CJ Haughey, and Thatcher lost her nerve. Nonetheless in 1985, the Anglo-Irish Agreement was signed and the Division grew again in the expectation of new political progress. But they hadn't reckoned with the ferocity of Unionist opposition. These sudden increases in personnel would later create awkward promotional bottlenecks in the Department, just as did the sudden increase which followed our EEC accession in 1973.

The Division structure was effectively determined by the Agreement. On one side, were Political, Economic and Social Affairs, and the US. Significantly, US-Irish relations were in the Anglo-Irish Division. On the other side were Human Rights, Cultural and East-West affairs. East-West was the euphemism given to British-Irish relations, including the Irish in Britain. It also handled the British-Irish Parliamentary Body, a non-executive 'talking tier' of the Agreement, which was really just a dining club but effective nonetheless. Why wouldn't it be, given the dining prelude to the Agreement itself. Like many Tories, its long standing co-chairman, Peter Temple Morris, arrived in Ireland as a mild Unionist and apparently left seeing the wisdom of a United Ireland. He even deserted the Tories for New Labour some time later.

On the other side was Security and Legal Affairs, which worked closely with the Department of Justice. Justice also had people in Maryfield, the Government's Secretariat in the North. Meanwhile, the International Fund for Ireland was downstairs, operating as a unit on its own, dispensing money in the Cross Border area and fighting off the demands of local politicians and 'deserving causes'. From time to time, the Division also created new units, think-tanks and temporary research sections, set up to serve the ongoing Talks process and to dream up new schemes and models to tackle the Overall Problem, and build on the Irish State's 'foot in the door'.

The Division is in a modern hospital-looking block, built onto the back of Iveagh House. The two buildings are linked by a long carpeted corridor, looking out onto garden graced by a statue of Abraham Lincoln, strangely appropriate given the man's role in another difficult North-South relationship. A coded security door leads to the upper floor but the main entrance is through a caged staircase known as the Golden Gate, accessed by a man inside a glass box pressing a buzzer, a replication of the box at the Department's front entrance. The back entrance is via Earlsfort Terrace where, in the yard, trucks were almost permanently parked, doing on-the-spot shredding of some of the huge amount of documents the Division produced.

There is a manic, and competitive, desire to record everything on Anglo-Irish matters and such papers will be a boon to historians of the future should they ever be released. But the dangers of such inscription were revealed later with leaks in 1993 and 1997, both of which had major implications for, respectively, a British-Irish agreement on the North and the Irish Presidential election. Typically, it wasn't Civil Servants who leaked but politicians, or more likely, their spin doctors or advisers.

Civil Servants were too conditioned by the culture of security, with shredders in every room. As well as the commercial shredders in the yard, some officers had mini-shredders attached to their desks, so they could shred as they went. Faxes to Maryfield were sent by secure fax, or sealed diplomatic bag, and phone calls were by secure phone where you pressed a button to scramble the line. Despite this it was always assumed that the British were listening in; the main target of such security measures was thus to prevent penetration by the Provos or Unionists.

The British would bug anything they could get their hands on. In the 1980s our Embassy in London was so badly penetrated they couldn't even use electric typewriters because the British could decipher the noise patterns of the golfballs. So letters were typed manually, driven to the airport and given to the pilot to take to Dublin. In the 1990s it was still assumed that GCHQ were listening and Seán Ó'hUiginn, the head of Anglo-Irish, would talk to the Ambassador in Washington in Irish and recite, *sotto voce*, the children's poem, 'M'Asal Beag Dubh', just to have a bit of fun with the moles.

The Maryfield staff rotated every week and each Friday, you'd see the black cars in the yard filling up with paper. Escorted to the Border by the Gardaí, they went the rest of the way with the RUC. Maryfield was just outside Belfast, surrounded by large fields. Sometimes they went by helicopter. Cars and routes were often changed. By now, the threat had reduced from the dark days of the late Eighties when a loyalist mob was almost permanently encamped outside the gates, along with George Seawright, the Scottish loyalist, who sat in a caravan and ominously took notes of the car regs going in and out. Seawright was later shot dead by the INLA.

The staff lived permanently in the school-type building and didn't leave the compound. But they compensated with a lifestyle of wining and dining which became almost legendary. Thus, Gerry Collins' jibe to Napoleon at the UN, 'is the drink not as good as it was in Maryfield?' The parties became famous and were soon an attraction for the softer elements of Unionism, which was half their purpose. Typical Free State diplomacy; win them over with hospitality. For the staff, the giddy partying was understandably escapist, given the mob at the gate. It was a classic neo-colonial outpost, a besieged foothold for the Free State in Northern Ireland, except now the roles were reversed.

The social offensive was particularly active under Declan O'Donovan, a tireless 'North' expert, *bon viveur* and more recently Ambassador to Japan. The epic dinners he held each evening after the 1992 Talks — Maryfield was the Irish team's base — became the stuff of folklore, mainly because the in-fighting, story-telling and intellectual bullying therein were far more daunting than anything seen earlier in the day with the Unionists and British. O'Donovan was a democrat and made sure that all of the staff could sit down and watch these brandy-fuelled combats between combative mandarins. Such jibing, of course, was only a relief from the frustration elsewhere; the bruising 1992 Talks.

The Loyalist threat, meanwhile, never went away. In fact, it got more specific. In 1994, the UVF named Departmental officers as legitimate targets and, in 1997, even in the middle of an IRA ceasefire, the Loyalist Volunteer Force gave the Maryfield staff forty-eight hours to leave Northern Ireland 'or face the consequences'. The threat, naturally, was ignored. But everyone was encouraged to join the Life Insurance plan. This was mainly aimed at the 'Travellers', officers who went to the North undercover meeting people who were best met incognito (see below). In the event of a tragedy, the compensation wasn't very much and black jokes abounded about its only merit being that it might free up a few promotions.

It was only in 1998, with the Good Friday Agreement, that Maryfield was finally wound down, although I am quite sure that its mechanics, and paperwork, is still clunking away somewhere in Dublin. (How ambitious the Government had once been about the Agreement was revealed to me later when a colleague showed me a secret file, concerning buildings in central Belfast, which the Government had purchased under an assumed name. For reasons of security and practicality, they were later sold on, and the paperwork conveniently disguised among more innocuous accounts.)

Maryfield was the physical manifestation of the Anglo-Irish Agreement. But in other respects the Agreement was busy 'below the water'. The full institutional impact of the Anglo-Irish Agreement has never been highlighted or documented. With good reason. Seeing how mad the Unionists were at its symbolism, they would go crazy altogether if they knew its full practical detail.

In one sense, however, this is a pity for it would give the lie to those who said that the Agreement was ineffective. On the contrary, the Union could never be the same again. How could it be? The Agreement gave the Irish Government a consultative role in all aspects of Northern Irish life, economic, social, administrative and cultural and paved the way for the later Good Friday settlement, including Sinn Féin. No need to include the Political aspect here; in the absence of a settlement or assembly, the Agreement *was* the political system, assisted by a raft of quangos. There was not a hospital closure, fisheries initiative or cultural programme that the Irish Government didn't have a 'view' on.

On Public Appointments, the Division would nominate the names of local worthies, good constitutional nationalists, usually close to the SDLP. But not always. One of the more interesting aspects of the Agreement was the State's almost subliminal desire to create its own 'allies' up North, separate from the SDLP or the dreaded Sinn Féin. Even when Dublin had no names to offer, existing appointments were often sent to Dublin for perusal. An arch Unionist I knew was disgusted to discover that the latest senior promotions at the Public Record Office in Belfast had to await clearance from Dublin.

Of course, Dublin was not always heeded and many parts of the Agreement went unimplemented. But the very fact that the facility existed was almost as important as its effectiveness. Also, in cynical diplo-think, the lack of implementation, and foot-dragging, provided more sticks with which to beat the British and keep the momentum of discontent going. The good old British. They never let you down by not letting you down. Everything they gave was done so begrudgingly and slowly that by the time it trickled down it was accepted in the same spirit, and replaced by some new demand.

So recalcitrant were the British that they would not yield on even the most innocuous issues. For example, RTÉ reception in the North. For years, we had been trying to get more coverage for Irish television in the six counties, only to be continually thwarted by the British excuses about transmitter problems, frequencies already filled and general buck-passing. The files make extraordinary reading. Who could it possibly hurt to allow RTÉ to be received in Belfast? But their attitude was that nothing is given away without a fight and anyone who worked on this issue came away boiling at such stubbornness. I remember one female DFA colleague, a hitherto benign sort not given to atavistic nationalism, returning furious from meetings over broadcasting with the British. Almost more so than after a UDR harassment case, or a shoot-to-kill.

The security area was the major aspect of the Agreement where there was a lack of progress and where harassment of nationalists still continued. The issue of police accompaniment for patrols by the Ulster Defence Regiment (UDR), the ill-disciplined and mostly sectarian back-up force, was hotly pursued by the Irish Government and then lost. Even where agreement had apparently been pinned down with the British on foot patrols and army behaviour, such guarantees would be made meaningless within days by some macho stand-off in a small garrison town.

But at least the facility to raise such matters existed mainly through the 'log system' in the Agreement Secretariat. Northern politicians, or community workers, would contact Dublin, or directly contact Maryfield, who would then raise such cases with 'The Other Side' (the actual nomenclature on our notepaper). The British, or Northern Irish, officials didn't actually live in the Secretariat, but they were always in close proximity. They would contact the appropriate military people and an explanation/assurance would come back; details of an arrest, reasons given. Some areas were obviously more active than others, as were some politicians — notoriously so. Having opposed the Agreement, Sinn Féin cottoned on to its nuisance potential and soon we were receiving ready-made Harassment Forms hastily filled in with amazingly similar details.

The log system was a day-to-day affair and the banks of filing cabinets testified to the long years of such activity, just as did the files on Fair Employment and District Councils. Through these, and other material, a huge volume of information was being built up on Northern Ireland. Tacked to the walls were large laminated maps of the North's urban districts, coloured according to religious breakdown, as well as charts of

British army and police cap badges and insignia for easy recognition.

To 'monitor progress', our senior officials attended Liaison Group meetings with the British. These prepared for the Intergovernmental Conferences (IGCs), the high profile meetings of the Tánaiste and the Secretary of State for Northern Ireland (Dick Spring and Sir Patrick Mayhew respectively), after which a bland press release was issued, probably no different from that for the previous IGC.

If I was a journalist, I'd go crazy at these things. After each IGC, there was the same hubbub of activity, with the media scrambling into the room, cameras and microphones aloft, to hear Patrick Mayhew and Dick Spring reiterate exactly what was in the Communiqué and speak, through gritted teeth, about their 'constructive dialogue' and 'determination to proceed'. 'Now see here,' Mayhew would tell one journalist, while Spring followed up with, 'Quite frankly, the situation is ...' Eventually Spring had to be taken aside by Press section and told to stop saying 'Quite frankly'.

There was nothing frank about it. But of course it suited the two Governments to say as little as possible. Mayhew could hardly say 'We are very happy with the gradual dismemberment of decision-making in Northern Ireland and its hiving off to Free State-inspired quangos.' The other reason was more fundamental and sinister. Even the smallest of remarks on the North can bring people onto the streets and have Paisley on his soap box. Sometimes, the less said the better, as I'd discover myself. Keep it bland. Indeed, in one way, the whole Peace Process has been about the annihilation of language and the search for a form of words which will accommodate everybody.

The atmosphere of Anglo-Irish reflected this ambitious involvement in Northern Ireland. Along the floors in different rooms, people stayed late into the night dreaming up schemes for a United Ireland by stealth.

There was no knocking off at five or six. You were expected to stay late, even if you had nothing to do, which many people hadn't, thus adding to the gossipy, intrigue-laden atmosphere. The place was absurdly competitive, as Northern politicians realised when they discovered that their complaints about harassment were more effectively passed on when they went to the right 'contacts'.

Among the rest of the Department, the Division was half-despised. And with good reason. In the early days, after the Agreement, its people would go around puffed up like roosters, saying things 'Like, sorry can't talk to you' and belittling the work of other Divisions. They would arrive into Hourican's an hour or two after everyone else. It was even claimed that they circled the Green just to burn up time. But once things settled down and it was clear that the Agreement was not going to lead to a larger, more-inclusive settlement, such self-importance declined somewhat.

At one stage, the work was considered so sensitive, that no rookie Third Sec could come into Anglo-Irish, without having been blooded elsewhere first. It was also very masculine, and referred to as 'The Locker Room', such was the air of frustrated testosterone around the corridors. 'Oh, look they're washing their jockstraps!' said a girl, loudly, one day, when she saw a group of men, standing around the Secure fax, with their sleeves rolled up and their ties loosened. It was like something from Wall Street. But the women too got into the spirit, chewing gum and snapping their fingers for the 'stiff list' — the latest list of fatalities. It was whiff of sulphur stuff. You were so close to real violence and intrigue that its atmosphere rubbed off.

The atmosphere did change gradually. By the late Nineties, the Division was much more gender-balanced and new Third Secs came straight in, having just joined the Department. Northern Ireland had become mundane and workaday and, horror of horrors, the politicians were starting to try and take some of the decisions for themselves.

In 1993, my own job seemed almost comically mundane. I was given a small room on my own and put working on a quiet part of Economic Co-operation. The desk was known as 'the Canal Job', for much of it involved the Ballyconnell-Ballinamore Canal, an old canal which crossed the Border and had recently been restored with EU money and the support of the two Governments.

Along with Southern and Northern officials, I had to oversee the allocation of jobs and monies. With most of the physical work done, the job was now reduced to taking calls from lockmasters and discussing toilet facilities in Fermanagh campsites. But more sensitive political aspects also arose; the real motive for DFA involvement. As ever with these projects, the reluctant Northerners wanted to keep it low-key, whereas we wanted a big, flag-waving launch with an 'independent' body. Even the eventual expansive title, Shannon-Erne Waterway, had to be fought for.

There was other work on the desk but most of it was sucked up by First Secs and David Donoghue, a Counsellor famous for his bureaucratic energy. He used to leap the stairs, three steps at a time, and personally re-edited even the most mundane of documents. In the meantime, we were supposed to come up with new schemes for North-South Co-operation. With political movement stalled, other avenues of advance were sought, like economics or even environmental projects like the Canal. 'A Thousand Bridges Across the Border' was how a reconciliation pamphlet put it, but from a unionist perspective, it was more like 'A Thousand Gangplanks for the Invaders'.

'After all, there's more chance of progress in the economic arena right now than in the political,' warned Seán Ó'hUiginn, when I went to see him in his office, overlooking the back garden. Ó'hUiginn was head of Anglo-Irish Division and, when you joined it, you were called down for these little encounters, where Ó'hUiginn stared at you and asked about your interests and hobbies, but also, more fundamentally, what you thought about life. Or as he asked one gobsmacked officer, 'What moves your lights?' It was 'on the spot' stuff.

Ó'hUiginn was an impressive figure. Perhaps the most impressive figure in the Department. Feared and loathed by the Unionists and British, for whom he was regarded as the tactical and intellectual rock they had to work around, he had earned the title, 'Prince of Darkness' in the press profiles now breaking his anonymity. (His subsequent departure to Washington as Ambassador was sarcastically welcomed by John Taylor MP at the Forum in Belfast. 'God Speed to this enemy of Ulster' he told the room, while Ó'hUiginn quietly smiled into his hands.) He later became a lynchpin in the Peace Process, holding out for Sinn Féin when all others had despaired. For this reason, he had a poor relationship with Bruton and got involved in a spectacular row in the Taoiseach's house in Meath, about which there was great speculation afterwards. One account has Ó'hUiginn barking like a dog, in imitation of the Taoiseach's expectation that he be a lap dog. The story sounds fantastic but not impossible, such was Ó'hUiginn's mild eccentricity but also the unflappable quality that would have him face down the Taoiseach.

When I told Ó'hUiginn that one of my interests was painting, he asked what sort. 'Expressionists,' I answered. 'Which ones?' he came back. It was that kind of exchange. Another hobby was travel — Texas, South America. He sunk back in his leather chair and said dryly, 'You'll get plenty of chances for travel here. To exciting places like Leitrim and Cavan.'

Bored with fighting Mayhew and the Unionists (and Bruton), Ó'hUiginn engaged in this sort of small-scale intellectual interrogation as a distraction. He would come up to quivering Third Secs in the pub and ask them what God they believed in. But it was a interrogation they were flattered to receive, such was the awe with which the man was held. It reminded me of Pádraig Murphy as Political Director; the same droll humour, the same analytical powers and ferocious appetite for work. Not to mention the same sense of everybody hanging on their every word and ready to be led into battle.

His other quality was that, like Pádraig Murphy, and many of the mandarins, he often gave the impression that, despite all the drama and excitement — and there would plenty over the coming years — he'd really prefer to be in his garden reading the Greek classics, flicking through Virgil's Odes of which he was so fond. A dark-featured man, almost Spanish-looking, he wore broad pinstripe suits and cut a dapper figure around the town. Unlike some of the officials who clung to their files and desk, Ó'hUiginn looked like someone who had other things to get on with. He was married to an Irish speaker from Donegal, now a sculptress, who in 1971 had presented the Eurovision Song Contest on television. At the Consulate in 1970s' New York, they were the ideal diplomatic couple.

I might as well have been reading the classics myself, for all the contact I had with the outside world in my tiny cubby-hole office at the back of the building. Behind me was Iveagh Gardens and one of the few distractions was watching the kids trying to climb in and reach the chestnuts. 'Mister, can we get the conkers?' they cried when they saw my shadowy figure. I nodded an OK, impressed that for all the security — fences, cameras, lurking Gardaí — they were still able to come in after chestnuts.

Other Third Secs had warned me about the boredom that came with this job. One girl used to actually fall asleep. Another chap, a former writer for satirical radio shows, used to drift off on reveries in the overheated room; 'Ah yes, long walks on the beach with my girlfriend. The moment of my birth and the light shining on my face ... And then suddenly the door would open and in would come Devoy prattling on about some Peace Group file. 'Stop talking so fast!' I felt like telling him. "You're taking up all the oxygen in the room."' (Later, the same chap got Moscow as a posting: 'Eamon, think of waking up with a hangover. Then, think of the hangover clearing and realising you're still in Moscow.' The interesting city of intrigue under Communism had given way to a mob-infested 'second world' capital.)

But think about waking up and realising you're still in Ireland. A month ago, I was the Vice Consul of Ireland in New York, living the high life and hopping into limousines. Now I was in a back room, looking out at the rain and working on a rainy canal in Leitrim. Relocation shock is something everyone goes through and because of that, it's regarded as bad form to bang on about it. You just get on with it. Having settled in a foreign clime, people have to uproot their families again and pull their children out of international schools. At least I was spared that. For older people in DFA, it was more difficult, in this and in other things.

You tried to keep up with your old postings. In people's in-trays, you'd see *Pravda, African World*, the Italian papers but, after a while, they went into the out-trays unread. It was the same with the *Irish Echo* and the *Voice*. They had already begun to look ethnic and provincial, reflecting an old-fashioned world of Long Island and Irish-American dances. It was as if I hadn't been there at all. If things had begun to seem two-dimensional as I left the US, they now looked entirely one-dimensional.

And there was Ireland to get used to again, with its big coins, smoky pubs and cut-throat conversation. It was also a rapidly changing place, and nobody wanted to know about New York and the thousands of emigrants who had left. Even the returned emigrants themselves colluded in this; we were here now, this is where it happens. But it wasn't much consolation for me, especially since from my window, I could see the OPW guys loading Diplomatic Bags into army vans, destined for warmer and more exotic places.

In my isolation, I felt like the character in Kurt Vonnegut's novel, *Jailbird*, who is banished to a basement room in Nixon's White House and given a job monitoring youth culture, writing up reports which are later handed in and shredded unread. Above him is the Oval Office, where he can hear Nixon's aides, Haldeman and Ehrlichman, jumping up and down and arguing with the President. Until one day he coughs heavily, and the advisers upstairs suddenly go quiet, realising that there is someone beneath them. Before long, people are coming in to visit him and board up the windows.

Next to me, for example, was a dead office used by the Secretariat people when they came down from Belfast. There was nothing in it, except a desk and a phone; through the partition, a sealed-up door, I could hear them making long telephone calls and greeting other officials dropping in for a chat. One day they were talking about Hume and Mallon having a fight — another fight — but also something more intriguing about Mallon's car being followed and how he needed more security. But then I coughed and the conversation stopped. I could imagine their mute signals — 'there's someone in there' — and, sure enough, a head suddenly popped round my door. 'Who are you?'

'I'm back from New York.'

He stared at me for a moment. 'Oh, right.' And then he went back inside to resume his conversation in grunts and signals. They were probably now writing it out on paper.

19

Border Travels

At this time, in Anglo-Irish Division, things were relatively quiet on the political front. The 'Peace Process' had yet to begin and the violence was going on unabated. The Taoiseach, Albert Reynolds, had yet to get fully involved and political progress on the North hinged on the direct relationship between the Northern Secretary, Sir Patrick Mayhew, and our Minister, Dick Spring, who was also Tánaiste, in the Coalition Government with Fianna Fáil (FF).

In Spring, a seasoned Labour Party leader, with a large, and reform-hungry, parliamentary party behind him (Labour had achieved unprecedented results in the sea-change election of 1992) we had a more powerful Minister than we'd had for many years. Other Foreign Ministers had been Tánaiste before, but Spring brought a new authority to the post, reflecting his uneasiness of coalition with FF. He'd seen how fractious the previous coalition had been between the PDs and FF. We even had the new departure of a special, enlarged Tánaiste's office being opened, over in Leinster House — just to keep an eye on them over there.

The North was expected to be a breakthrough area for Spring, but for him too it was frustratingly slow. As well as his ongoing, and relatively poor relationship, with the uninspiring Sir Patrick Mayhew, there was the ongoing talks process between the Northern political parties, which seemed to be stuck in an impasse. As Seán

Ó'hUiginn said, there was at this time more chance of progress on the economic front, than on the political.

O'hUiginn was right about other things, too. I did go to interesting and exotic places. But not so much Cavan and Leitrim, as Enniskillen, Derry, Downpatrick and Belfast. In the absence of political progress, the increasing level of North-South economic co-operation meant lots of travel, especially on behalf of the cash-rich International Fund for Ireland, which I was also pulled in on.

Travel brought home the realities of Northern Ireland, far away from the phoniness of Irish-American opinion. At meetings, you saw the raw sectarianism which is at the heart of the conflict, the unashamed tribalism of one community pulling one way, and another community pulling the other. Even as an Irish citizen it is salutary to see these contrasts; on the one hand, the small towns with war memorials and Gospel Halls which look (and as far as their inhabitants are concerned *are*) just like England. And then you get to Newry with its Irish-language street signs and its floating crisp packets and you feel you're in Ballinasloe.

'The Border starts here now,' SDLP councillors told me quietly in Newry, meaning that south of here had been nationalised, cleansed. The tug of war had a physical manifestation; the Nationalists pulling westwards, the Unionists pulling east. 'Back towards the sea, where they came from,' said one Councillor, in the sort of remark that chills Unionists.

Little wonder the Loyalist paramilitaries wanted to shoot us as we travelled around as representatives of the Irish Government, assisting the process. Not blatantly, of course, but through concepts like 'parity of esteem' and 'cultural agenda'. The very dynamic of increasing Irishness was, by its nature, stripping the place of its Britishness.

On my first trip to Stormont, I travelled up with Michael Lyons, a sceptical Cork chap more interested in his sideline theatrical career than his day job (despite the tough entrance exam, many Third Secs gave the impression they'd sooner be doing something else). We thought it was hilarious going into this huge empty building, once home to the now abolished Northern Irish parliament. Later, of course, it would house the new Assembly, but in 1993, it was still eerily empty and yet dutifully cleaned each day, with the brass fittings rubbed down by headscarved Belfast Sadies, in the forlorn hope that the good times might return. Stepping into the deserted hall, our shoes echoed around the statue of grim-faced James Craig, ready with his sword. 'You're all very welcome,' said the Stormont official, but it was a limp handshake. You could see the look in his eyes; 'Paisley's right, they're coming to take us over.'

Upstairs, we went out on to the famous balcony where Brian Faulkner told the huge crowd, 'You will never be pushed into a United Ireland.' Little did he reckon with the creeping hand of constitutional Nationalism. Or the presence of cheeky Third Secs in Hugo Boss suits mocking the archaic atmosphere and the stuffy restaurant, with its heavy sauces and trifle deserts. By contrast with the go-ahead South, the North was living in the past. Ian Smith, the former Rhodesian premier, said he loved Northern Ireland because it reminded him of England in the 1950s.

Ironically, the building now housed the Belfast office of the International Fund for Ireland, dispensing monies under the hated Agreement. At a meeting with Northern Civil Servants, we discussed the various applications, pushing hard, for example, to give money to Derry's Protestant Fountain Estate. This surprised our Northern colleagues, but it was consistent with our new confidence. The Protestants were, in their own words, being 'driven off' the West Bank of the Foyle, as Derry became more Catholic, and the Southern Government was here to help. Such projects enhanced the Fund's legitimacy.

'Protestant' projects also benefited from the winding up of the Sailors and Soldiers Trust, a fund for British army veterans living in the South, which, through judicious re-investment had, over the years, become quite lucrative. With the veterans dying off, the money was directed by DFA and the Taoiseach's Department towards reconciliation work and projects in Northern Protestant areas, which, given the Trust's origins, was perhaps appropriate.

After the meeting, we went, not to the building's restaurant, but across the road to the Stormont Hotel, with the Union Jack flying over. The Hotel, with its 1970s' decor and slightly camp waiters, was to Stormont as Buswell's Hotel was to the Dáil, except that this Buswell's was half-empty, since there was no parliament. 'Now, gentlemen, can I take your orders?' said our waiter, with pen at the ready. 'You most certainly can,' said Michael, laughing.

Much of my travel was to monthly meetings of the East Border Region Committee (EBRC), a cross-border grouping, comprising the Councils of Louth and Monaghan from the South, and Newry-Mourne and South Down from the North. Interestingly, its existence pre-dated the Troubles and was tolerated by Unionists, mainly because its economic and social brief might drum up investment for the area — although the definition of 'social' was a broad and often controversial one, as I discovered when I was asked to take their views back to Dublin.

The Committee was also seen a useful regional rival to a similar grouping in the North West, which was much more successful, with Derry as the pivot and the active support of two MEPS, John Hume and Neil Blaney. The EBRC were obsessed about the North West. It was interesting how politicians could postpone their political differences, for the sake of geographical rivalry.

The EBRC members were constantly whining for more resources, often with no particular projects in mind, and one could see the detrimental effect of the EU funding bonanza which had killed off any idea of sourcing funding elsewhere or locally. It was all 'Brussels, Brussels'. One time, Eddie McGrady, a local MP, told them all to 'stop whining and get their house in order'. They were stunned. But they respected McGrady, a former EBRC Chairmen, who was a lot like they were. The EBRC crowd had a solid quality compared to the more glib and ambitious word-*meisters* that you met in Belfast or saw on TV. Stuttering, in old suits, they were mostly farmers, publicans, or teachers, for whom the conflict was both far away — Dublin, London — and very near — shot neighbours, cratered roads. Talking to them, it was clear they were caught up in a struggle they found both bewildering, and yet strangely normal.

Almost all of the Northern Councillors were SDLP and, their participation in this North-South committee was tolerated by Unionists the SDLP kept Sinn Féin off it (This was before the Ceasefire). Not that they needed encouragement. The SDLP people despised Sinn Féin and resented their ability to liberally fund electoral campaigns and constituency offices, as they put it, from 'rackets and robberies'. Such an ingrained attitude, after years, will be interesting as Sinn Féin engage fully in the political system. Certainly, John Hume's persistence in talking to Adams to explore a broad nationalist consensus, *before* an IRA Ceasefire — the so-called Hume-Adams discussions — caused great tension and puzzlement among the SDLP rank and file, as did Hume's leadership generally.

After each EBRC meeting, the real chat would get under way out by the coffee bar and there would be new and more outrageous revelations about Sinn Féin. Silly stuff sometimes; a certain fellow 'just out of jail and already driving a flash car'. A particular woman, constantly on RTÉ radio talking about British Army harassment, was not only dismissed as 'Sinn Féin' but incidents from her personal life were also outlined. 'Was there nothing I could do to get her off the airwaves?' Clearly their memories of the old Stormont regime had led to them to exaggerate the powers of Government.

Despite their antipathy for Sinn Féin, the Councillors were just as Nationalistic. In fact, perhaps more so. While the 'Shinners' made austere references to 'a thirty-two County Republic' and 'military struggle' — all the time refusing to even acknowledge Unionism — the SDLP were fully engaged with actually achieving self determination, working away on an economic and social level, particularly at the middle-class Catholic coalface where the real power struggle in Northern Ireland takes place.

It was clear that this was a community on the rise, far removed from the downtrodden minority of 1969. They would speak gleefully about the economic buoyancy among Catholics, about how more of them were taking out bank loans than Protestants (I don't know where they got these figures). Or of how Protestant kids were studying in England and not coming back, whereas Southern kids were coming North to study. Everything mattered in this tug-of-war. When Allied Irish Banks (AIB) went into the North, buying Trustee Savings Bank, they called themselves First Trust, not AIB for fear of offending Unionists. And this disappointed the Councillors. They loved it when Southern companies moved into the North.

Such buoyancy had made them less sectarian but more Nationalist. This was the Unionist fear — that the more the Catholics got, the more they wanted, and that ultimately they wanted to get rid of the State altogether. Thus the quandary of Northern Ireland. Where is the balance? Or is there one?

It was quandary too for the South. Since 1969 (and before), the Irish Government had only done as much for the North as was needed to keep the Nationalists satisfied. And no more than that. Containment. But each time they try to pacify them, the Nationalists demanded more. Why wouldn't they. 'It's like a monster,' said one DFA official. 'The more we keep feeding it, the bigger it gets.'

Of course, such ideas played back to bedrock Nationalist beliefs; that Partition was morally and economically wrong and that it would of necessity melt away. 'Irish Nationalism is an irresistible force,' Seán Ó'hUiginn used to say, with satisfaction. His other great phrase was that it 'was like a shark. It must keep moving or it dies.' When Ó'hUiginn first came out with this, at a luncheon table in Dublin Castle during the Forum (for Peace and Reconciliation!), the people at his table nearly dropped their spoons. Even the SDLP were taken aback. He meant that Irish nationalism had to keep adapting its agenda and methods to be effective, now military, now cultural, but the image of the roaming shark was what remained.

Ó'hUiginn was only articulating what was about to happen, which was that even Sinn Féin were going to wake up to the fact that violence was achieving nothing and that the terms on which the struggle would now be engaged were economic, cultural and social. With the focus shifting completely to the constitutional arena, the shark would have to think up new angles to advance the situation. 'The conflict is over,' declared Ó'hUiginn grandly, before the ceasefire. 'It's only a matter of working out the terms on which it is settled.' A typical diplomat's comment.

Ó'hUiginn was much given to these bold statements although his predictions weren't always borne out. 'What can we do to prevent the SDLP from going the way of the Irish Parliamentary Party in 1918?' (i.e. immediate obliteration) he once asked. In fact, once Sinn Féin was eased into the process, Catholic voters went back to the SDLP, suggesting that not only was the conflict finished, but so too were the parties of conflict. (By 2001, Sinn Fein *were* making inroads but only by shedding their radicalism.) The process had become as bourgeois as the impulses which first brought about peace; prosperity, education, bank loans and cross-border funding. The shark had gone shopping.

However, in 1993, such peace was a long way off and there was a terrible atmosphere of menace in the North. More people were killed in my first month back, October 1993, than in any since 1976. The violence had also taken on new and more sinister directions. Figures like Johnny 'Mad Dog' Adair and 'King Rat' Billy Wright were rampant and Loyalists were outkilling the IRA by almost two to one. Personally, I believe this was another, perhaps key reason, for the IRA ceasefire; the realisation that a re-blooded UDA and UVF were prepared to escalate the situation into all-out sectarian conflict. Loyalist paramilitaries were even targeting SDLP Councillors, something that hadn't happened since the early Seventies and as I arrived for one EBRC meeting, I could hear them muttering 'Are you taking one?'

'No. Are you?' The RUC had offered the Councillors firearms for their personal protection. But many of them declined not wishing to give the threats undue credit. And yet afterwards, one of the SDLP members brought me for a coffee on Newry's main street and outlined the sense of fear in exposed nationalist areas; the cars revving at night, dark figures crossing fields. Apparently, at night, the electricity had recently dipped, dimming the lights and bringing back memories of just before the 1974 Ulster Workers Strike, when Loyalists were (literally) testing the current.

Listening to his talk about electricity dips and dummy runs, I looked out the café window and saw British soldiers, bored with patrol duty, accepting crisps from schoolgirls, also bored — bored with adolescence. But there was a weird sense of vigilance, with the soldiers shouting to each other in Lancashire accents while army helicopters hovered overhead. Northern Ireland was more normal than we think and yet, in its acceptance of this 'normality', it was abnormal. You could come here every week, but how much of it would an outsider understand?

I took down the fellow's suspicions and wrote a report which was put in the Box. 'The Box' was a weekly compendium of mostly confidential documents, and there was absurd competition to get into it. It was given to about a dozen key players, including the Taoiseach, Tánaiste and relevant Assistant Secretaries. It was from the Box that leaked reports were taken about Sinn Féin's relationship with Mary McAleese, reports which caused such controversy during the Presidential election of 1997.

At one stage, I had the job of sorting through three years of Boxes and putting them into appropriate files. Read like this, they offered a fascinating, chronological overview of events, with cogent analysis and vividly-rendered conversations. Unlike the Reports from Embassies abroad, there was no room here for tropical colour or poetic licence. But they did seem to be affected with a constant air of wish fulfilment; the Unionists are coming round, light at end of the tunnel. In private, many Unionist politicians had a mischievous habit of musing aloud about the 'inevitability of a united Ireland'. Was it a wind up? On some issues, the Box consensus was often wrong; Trimble will never become Unionist leader, Trimble will never agree a settlement. Such analysis was understandable, of course. Wined and dined by officials, the Northern contacts felt compelled to offer some class of news or speculation, and the officials, in turn, had to justify their position, and expenses, by passing it on.

Considering the status of the Box, there must have been an extra temptation for officers to exaggerate and dramatise, and I was conscious of this as I wrote my report about the 'dimming lights'. But on Northern Ireland, people's suspicions were enough to merit attention. The North was considered a deeply sinister place, especially at this time, and if a Councillor was genuinely concerned that was enough to win inclusion in the Box. Unfortunately, it was also a region awash in suspicion and conspiracy and very often it was hard to tell what was real, and what was not.

Consequently you had to be very careful about what you said, or promised. At one EBRC meeting, great anger was expressed about increased British army harassment in the South Armagh area. But also about the creation of a Unionist-controlled Select Committee on the North at the House of Commons. The fact that the two issues were linked showed how everything was reduced to a zero-sum game — 'them' or 'us'. And, at the moment, 'they' were getting everything. The Committee was perceived as a pay-off to the Ulster Unionists for their minority support of the Major's beleaguered Government — support which gave them key leverage on NI.

I listened to their denunciations and said I would report them to the Tánaiste. An Intergovernmental Conference was being held in Dublin and perhaps the issues could be raised. That's what I said. What I didn't say was that the Tánaiste 'would raise the matters at the IGC', which was what was being reported on local radio before I'd even left Northern Ireland. Clearly, the EBRC had fed the most optimistic line to the press. The next day, the unionist *Belfast Newsletter* gave a hostile account of the meeting, expressing concern that an 'Éire Civil Servant' should make such assurances.

The story had the area's Unionist Councillors 'jumping up and down', according to my Counsellor, and I had to go down and make an explanation to Seán Ó'hUiginn. You often had to go down and report to Ó'hUiginn, the great brooding mandarin, whose usual response was to raise his hands airily and say 'one must be careful'. Sound advice.

The experience made me much more careful in the future about any kind of promise, although I still had to provide instant and continuous emollient for their grievances — 'the Tánaiste is most concerned, the Government is doing everything it can' — including stonewalling on their oft-repeated demand that Tánaiste come and personally hear their tales of woe for himself. The publicity over my (mis)quote had another effect; the return to the meetings, after an absence of many months, of a Civil Servant from The Other Side, an Englishwoman who sighed humorously when she caught my eye — 'tsk, these local politicians' — but who was, in reality, there to keep an eye on me.

The incident also altered my attitude to security. The next time I went up North, to Omagh, it occurred to me that 'I am now a legitimate target' and I was sort of hoping that my SDLP friend had taken up that gun offer, so if a UDA hit squad burst through the door, he could fire back. What an irony; Free State diplomat defended by Northern Constitutionalist in pitched gun battle, the sort of 'act of violence', of which they are both supposed to strongly disapprove!

I mentally pursued this melodramatic scenario during the Committee's long and winding discussion about cross-border roads. My mind envisaged a State funeral, with Dick Spring, in his white mac, saying a few, sad words, while Mr Ó'hUiginn and Noel Dorr lay down the tricoloured wreaths (Or is it the State blue?). Funny. But not that funny. Later, my train stopped suddenly at Portadown and I sat stony-faced, while young Loyalist toughs got on and sat staring at me. When I got back to Dublin I signed up for the Life Insurance scheme.

20

'Our Friends in the North'

After about a year in the Economic side, I was gradually shifted over to the Political side of Anglo-Irish. "Gradually" because of both the amorphous nature of the Division — at one time, I was working to three different First Secs — but also the continuing cutbacks. Although the early Nineties saw recruitment begin again in earnest there remained a strong ethos of maximising resources. Unemployment rates reached their peak in 1993, although within two years, the economy would begin to change dramatically.

Related to these cutbacks, there was now considerable tension over the continuing lack of promotions in the Department, particularly at First Sec level where a lot of officers seem to be stuck. The huge intake of the mid-Seventies and early Eighties had bottlenecked in the system. I've mentioned this before — the gripings of Napoleon and others in New York — but the related tension was now manifest, especially in Anglo-Irish where many of the malcontents were located. Additional strain was caused by the fact that some hungry officers, 'fast trackers' who did oversized amounts of work, felt that the Department should now simply abandon its seniority roster (the old 'buggins' turn' system) and promote people out of line.

One group were so impatient that they even declared a 'fatwa' on the Department's management. Their dissent focussed on Administration Division, but more particularly on the Secretary, Noel Dorr. The openly expressed dissent was often puzzling to junior officers who didn't understand the complicated personal politics involved. But for two years running, the dissidents boycotted the Department's Christmas party, a policy which hurt only their colleagues; the party is organised by the staff, specifically the most senior unposted Third Sec (my privilege in 1989), not the Department. In many ways, the officers were using the political tactics they had so long monitored in Northern Ireland (cold-shoulders, boycotts, open dissent) against the Department itself!

However, the dissent became a serious issue and talk of it even reached the newspapers. The Secretary found it particularly perturbing, presumably feeling that his hands were tied by the Government's reluctance to open new Embassies. At an Introductory Coffee Morning for new Third Secs, held in his ornate ante-room, with its golden shag carpet (memories of Christmas past) he even referred to the tension in his speech, puzzling the new intake. But then perhaps he felt that he had to explain the diminished turn-out, since the dissidents had boycotted this as well! The whole impasse created a sour atmosphere with DFA and prompted me to begin considering my long-term future. Even if you gave your talented all, as the 'fast trackers' did, where could you ultimately go? I'd never planned to stay in the foreign service for life, but I now began to contemplate an earlier exit than I'd previously envisaged. In any case, by this stage, I was already quietly writing fiction in earnest so I had a parachute if I chose to leave. (Although another remark by Dorr, at the same depleted Coffee Morning, made me wonder if I shouldn't stay on. Recounting his own arrival in Iveagh House as a raw recruit, Dorr told the Third Secs of how he was taken to meet one luminary after another. 'That fellow's writing a novel,' he was informed afterwards. 'Oh, and she's completing a poetry collection.'

'It made me wonder; is everyone in here writing a book!?' the Secretary told the starry-eyed intake, to gentle laughter. Perhaps, I thought, this is the place to stay for such a noble pursuit, and *not* be a fast tracker.)

The most serious, but also amusing, effect of the dissent was the tension it created among the officers themselves, especially those whom the 'fatwa' group felt had got undeserved promotion. Some officers hadn't spoken to each other for years, a puzzling sight, no doubt, for Northern politicians to behold. Piquantly, the tension meant that when I shifted over to the Political side I got a full office to myself, on the Political/Security floor, an unusual privilege for a Third Sec. It had been intended for a newly promoted officer but it was felt unwise to have him working on the same floor as his detractors. I was now on the other side of the 'hospital block', overlooking the back of the Loreto residence on St Stephen's Green, where elderly nuns could be seen, reflected behind pimpled glass, making their beds and crouched in occasional prayer. Praying for peace, perhaps.

Beside me, was another 'dead' room, from which you could hear the whirrings of the centralised computer system. For security reasons, this was where everyone's hard drive was located. We also had to change our password every month and there were no floppy drives on our PCs. Even with such precaution, senior people were still reluctant to send documents by e-mail. Instead, it was used for gossip, chat groups and the conspiratorial mutterings of disaffected First Secs.

The other key effect of the discontent, of course, was its influence on the development of policy, with disgruntled officers quick to dismiss the ideas of those perceived to be Departmental favourites. Now, in addition to the divisions of Northern Ireland and the rivalry of the Taoiseach's Department and DFA, we had a new layer of intrigue, with embittered officers sniping at each other within the Division itself, often in league with disaffected elements in the SDLP. The historians of the future, looking for the causes of minor permutations in Northern policy, would have their work cut out for them!

These tensions sat atop the traditional rivalries you'd expect between the Political and Security sides, who often had different, and quite divergent aims, especially in the pre-Ceasefire period. One wants to coax the British and Unionists, the other wants to attack them for harassment and collusion. Many officers were also 'Travellers', particularly on the security side. This was a long running system the Department had which enabled people to travel very quietly in the North and meet all kinds of shady characters. The Travelling system was very useful but it also contributed to the rather self-important 'cloak and dagger' atmosphere which many in the Division found so satisfying. There was a squalid sort of glamour in the intrigue of consulting near 'men in hoods', an attitude shared by much of the media dealing with Northern Ireland. Such individuals who dealt with suffering on this level also made much of being inured to it. There was a macho toughness, a cool *realpolitik* about one's attitude to the violence which suggested that if you got excited or distressed about it, you were being weak and emotional. Not seeing the larger picture.

I remember one day we were all watching the aftermath of some IRA atrocity on TV, with bodies all over the street. 'What bastards,' someone said and there was this weird silence in the room, a fastidious thin-lipped surprise. The reaction was too human. Jaded cynicism was better; it was a war after all. Such silence was cowardly, of course — whatever you say, say nothing — and it was one of the reasons the IRA were able to keep going. For it overlapped neatly with the 'sneaking regarders', of whom there were many in the Division, despite all the denunciatory speeches we had to script.

Really, all that concerned the officials was the overall political situation, and the way it might be charted. Human beings were secondary. One day we got a letter to the Minister from a man whose father had been shot dead by the IRA. It was an angry letter, and reasonably so for it related to media references to early prison releases for paramilitaries. I drafted a response but it was never issued. People were too busy with speeches at the time to be bothered with letters. Also when I showed it to the security side, someone said 'Oh, that family has questionable connections', repeating an unsubstantiated allegation by SF about another part of the family. Even as it was, the reason for the man's death — his father's company was accused of collaboration — had to be 'seen in context'. But there was a more general reason for inaction; individual deaths just did not matter.

'If my father's killers go free,' the man wrote, 'I will personally hunt down them, wherever they go.' I wondered why he was so concerned. The killers had been sent down for life and there seemed no real prospect of their being released in the near future. But within months, once the Ceasefire was in place, prisoners were getting out. The letter-writer had correctly anticipated the atmosphere that was about to ensue. It reiterated an ugly truth; individual victims mean little in the context of politically motivated violence. Hardly are the bodies buried but the killers are being welcomed in. The British were secretly talking to the IRA right through their bombing campaign. Why should they have sensitivities? They were only white-shirted officials in Whitehall.

Curiously, however, one group to whom the dead did matter were the Irish Republicans; they showed a constant and solemn respect to their own dead. Indeed they were so reverential towards their previous fallen comrades, that it began to seem that what they were really fighting for was to keep their legacy alive. As if they were slaves to the dead, fearful of letting Bobby Sands down. 'From the prisons, comes pressure for a ceasefire,' said one Republican. 'From the cemeteries, comes pressure to keep going.' By 1994, Sinn Féin were about ready to break the cycle and start living for Ireland.

Letters on the North arrived in by the bag-load. Whatever about mail on Eastern Europe or the Middle East, the Northern part of our own country prompted an endless stream of correspondence, much of it angry, much of it poignant, and all of it full of ideas and suggestions. Many of the writers presumed the Minister actually read the letters, as might have happened in the 1950s. But others were aware that their correspondence was rarely seen by the Tánaiste. 'And I don't just want a reply from some Civil Servant,' people would warn. Thanks a lot. In fact, they'd be lucky if they even got that. During the Peace Process, we stopped replying to letters altogether, not just because of the changing situation but also because of time pressures. In other Divisions, you could have a draft cleared quickly and sent to the Tánaiste's office for issue, but such was the sensitivity of NI that any reply had to be cleared right up the line. It took so long, that they simply stopped doing it. I always thought this was a pity. Most of the letters were thoughtful and a reply from a Minister, one of the few direct contacts which a member of the public still had, could easily have been delegated to junior officers.

On their receipt in the Tánaiste's office, where a three-person team handled correspondence, all letters got at least an acknowledgement, a 'holding' reply, perhaps with a rubber stamp signature, saying that the letter will be brought to the Minister's attention. Meanwhile, the original was sent to the relevant section. On not getting a proper reply, some people wrote in again. Other letters, of course, couldn't be ignored; invitations, representations from TDs and County Councils. Oblivious to new developments in NI, one quixotic TD used to send us long, meandering solutions to 'the problem in hand', for which I had to draft Spring's equally thoughtful response. At such moments, you saw the merits of not answering letters.

However, the volume of post brought home the passion and sincerity with which the Northern problem was beheld. Crabbily hand-written letters, poorly spelt, came in from Irish immigrants in Huddersfield and Leeds, offering their suggestions for peace. Or from

British army veterans, who now saw the 'other side', or even people who had no connection to Northern Ireland at all. As with the Consulate, many letters came from retired people who now had the time and the life experience to reflect on these matters. Booklets were enclosed, and pamphlets and suggestions for a new Ulster flag and coinage; many people fantasised about a post-settlement era. One woman suggested different police forces for each of the six Counties. 'That was Garret's idea,' said a colleague, remembering some of the former Taoiseach's brainwaves. And, of course, there was the bitter hate-mail of old-style Nationalists — 'sell-outs', 'Quisling Spring, more like' — but much less of this than you'd get from Irish-America.

There was also hate mail from Unionists (on the North, you could please no one) and in October, my first month in the job, a UVF letter bomb addressed to Spring was intercepted at the Belfast sorting office. But generally the protests were from softer Unionists of a milder, more thoughtful variety. There were also letters on specific topics, or atrocities, like the 1974 Dublin car bombings about which the victims' families were convinced there was a 'cover–up'. On the Enniskillen bombing of 1987, there were entire cabinets, including the extensive foreign reaction. 'Bombing a Remembrance ceremony,' said a colleague; 'that was the day the Provos really threw it away.' And reading through the horrified European news coverage, I could see what he meant. It wasn't just the directly sectarian nature of the attack, but also that it was a World War commemoration, in remembrance of a conflict in which almost all Europeans — and crucially, Americans — were involved and for which they hold similar ceremonies. 'Jaysus, the IRA lost a lot of foreign friends after that.'

Our main partners in the North were the Social Democratic and Labour Party (SDLP), the moderate Nationalist, constitutional party, led by John Hume. In theory, we were absolutely cheek by jowl with them, but it was a strange relationship which had its ups and downs over the years. Haughey apparently distrusted them, and abolished their special seat in the Irish Senate. He felt that Fianna Fáil alone should speak for Irish Nationalists. It is also conveniently forgotten that Albert provoked Fianna Fáil heckles when he initially dismissed the Hume/Adams proposals. On the other hand, the government was so keen to hear what Seamus Mallon was saying in 1984 that, when he came to Dublin, the house he stayed in was bugged.

On a day-to-day basis, however, the relationship was an intimate one. Many officers would talk to their SDLP contacts almost daily, gossiping about politics and backbiting about their respective masters. SDLP people thus became quite *au fait* with the workings of the Department. And with the workings of their own party. Often it was only by talking to DFA that SDLP members found out what their party leaders were up to. On practical matters, Anglo-Irish Division was a virtual constituency office for the SDLP and every day, bags of rushed-through Irish passports would come over from Molesworth Street to be forwarded to their Derry or Belfast offices. Some of their requests were bizarre. On one occasion I had to try and acquire a rescue boat for the River Foyle. A lot of people in Derry were committing suicide and were doing so by jumping off Craigavon Bridge. 'Hume is upset,' I was told, 'especially since he built the thing. Also, the suicides are mostly middle class, so he could be losing voters.'

I dutifully made enquiries, but even the Departments of Marine and Defence were surprised by the request. 'Can they not get a fucking boat in Derry?' they asked, not unreasonably. Of course, usually when it's the North, other Departments jump for Anglo-Irish, but by now it was wearing a bit thin. Also, as more and more Departments dealt directly with their Northern counterparts, the mystique of dealing with Northern Ireland was gradually being diminished. I called the

SDLP and said I was 'still looking into it', but the boat had been overtaken by new and more immediate requests. Most critical amongst these was saving SDLP MP Eddie McGrady's Westminster seat.

In a general review of Northern constituencies, the Boundary Commission had recommended abolishing McGrady's South Down seat and replacing it with a smaller area. The SDLP were outraged, since the new seat would have a Unionist majority. My friends at the East Border Region Committee were particularly incensed, regarding South Down was part of their natural hinterland. 'First, we have to stomach the Select Committee, then harassment, now this!' Again all the issues were connected.

One of the big planks of the SDLP's appeal was that South Down was 'a historic constituency going back years' and its abolition would be 'a violation of tradition and geography, etc.' A submission to the Boundary Commission and thus some clandestine historical research was required, so off I went to the National Library in Kildare Street to look up old books and Hansards. Of course, this being Dublin I bumped into people I knew. One fellow, doing a thesis on the Church of Ireland, was even able to point me towards the appropriate records. I said I was working on a 'cross-border cultural project', but given my suit and wide-eyed demeanour, I could see he was suspicious. (Ironically, he has since himself gone into Government, working as an adviser in Health and Education.)

Conveniently ignoring what historical detail didn't suit the case, I drew up a passionate defence of the geographical and historical integrity of South Down, which, in fairness, had been a Westminster seat for a long time. Its long-standing balance of urban and rural was outlined, along with colourful Parnellite MPs. Once drafted, the submission now had to be 'de-jargonised' and cleaned of any DFA phrasing. A few local colloquialisms would make it look home-grown. Completed, it was passed onto the SDLP who presented it as their own. Asked about the controversy on TV, Spring would feign vagueness and say; 'I understand the SDLP are making an appeal.' The fiction of the SDLP's independence — mirroring, they would argue, the fiction of an independent Boundary Commission — was illustrated by the fact that having written the document on their behalf in the first place, we then had to draft Spring's response to this 'interesting submission'.

McGrady later won the seat with 25,000 votes, the biggest SDLP majority in Northern Ireland. 'He might at least have sent us a thank-you note' my First Sec grumbled.

By contrast with SDLP, the IRA were still killing people and their political wing, Sinn Féin, were well out in the cold. As with New York, and Noraid, it was policy not to meet Sinn Féin (SF) or have contact with them. Even in context of the 'Travellers', this was quite consistently adhered to. (Of course, once 'out of office', it was somewhat different and, later, during the Peace Process, it was revealed that former Minister, Brian Lenihan, and former diplomat, Michael Lillis had separately met SF representatives.)

For us, however, it was different and such was the quarantine on SF that every week a Third Sec would have to go down to the GPO in O'Connell Street to buy their newspaper, *An Phoblacht/Republican News*, rather than have the Department subscribe to it. Again, it was like New York, where the equivalent paper, *The Irish People*, was bought at a subway outlet. The vendor on O'Connell Street must have been more than surprised to see some posh-sounding young fellow — or, at one stage, a glamorous young blonde in designer outfits — come along to buy ten copies of the latest 'War News' from up North.

Later, I was sent to the Sinn Féin head office on Parnell Square to buy *Iris*, the Republican Movement's ideology journal. Seán Ó'hUiginn wanted to read a 1988 article by

Mitchell McLaughlin, regarded as a key text in SF's path to negotiation. In the article, McLaughlin talked about the 'rights of Unionists'. It took this long for SF to recognise the people they lived around.

I was buzzed in through security doors reminiscent of the submarine doors in Iveagh House, although rougher looking and made of painted steel. I was stared at as I lolled around the Parnell Square bookshop in my suit, pretending to check out the Republican memorabilia and hunger strike memoirs, before going up and asking for an *Iris* issue from 1988. It was fairly obvious I wasn't a casual customer. I muttered something about 'academic purposes' and asked them to wrap it. I felt like a sordid businessman in Soho.

So distant were SF kept, that if people called us looking for their address, we'd say 'It's in the phone book.' Even on the day of the Ceasefire itself, with people running around like headless chickens trying to get a definitive version of the declaration — three different versions were in circulation, all taken from the media — we still couldn't ring SF for an official text. 'No way,' shouted a Counsellor, not impressed with pleadings that they were now 'no longer engaged in violence'.

But as with New York and Noraid, there were grey areas where our worlds had to mix, long before any ceasefire. Not just with SF, but with the IRA itself. Abroad, there were extradition cases and prisoners. And 'about to be prisoners'. One colleague got a call from the famous Sister Sarah in London, a nun who tended to the spiritual needs of Republican suspects. 'The girl is with me now,' said Sister Sarah, as the British police closed in to arrest a woman. Such situations required delicate judgement and huge caution.

Sinn Féin, meanwhile, had City and County Councillors, with whom TDs and Senators had to engage, particularly those representing Border areas. Often such TDs would get onto us about constituents and problems and, through answering one such query from a Fianna

Fáil TD (let us call him Seamus) I subsequently became his personal contact inside the Division. 'Eh hello, Eamon,' and I'd hear the small voice down the end of the phone with another 'small query'.

One query was about two local lads who had been stopped entering Britain under the Prevention of Terrorism Act, because of something they'd done years ago. One fellow, the TD didn't know about, but the other one, was 'a good fellow' and a 'lovely lad'. 'Ah sure, he was only driving a truck or something'. Subsequent enquiries revealed that the truck was weighed down with about 400 pounds. of explosives.

The TD had that low-key, non-committal way of talking where you imagined he was speaking out of the side of his mouth. It was like the Cavan man asked his opinion of a neighbour; 'he's that class of a sort, you wouldn't know what type he is.' Not that the TD was particularly sympathetic to Sinn Féin. Far from it. Even after the ceasefire, he still wanted a steer on whether he and his colleagues should meet locally with a major Sinn Féin figure. 'It's up to you,' I said, 'the situation has now changed.'

'No, but what do you think?'

'What we think is that there is now a ceasefire, the Taoiseach has met Adams and it's up to you how you wish to deal with them.'

There was a pause.

'But what we want to know is what your recommendation would be?'

This went on for ages, like a ping-pong match. Seamus' voice had now dropped to the conspiratorial whisper that people assume when they talk about the North, even over the phone. The distinct impression was that having ostracised Sinn Féin for years, he and his (presumably Fianna Fáil) buddies would prefer to keep it that way. Except that Seamus wanted me to give them the official nod to do so, so we could be blamed if there was any fall-out. Likewise if there was a controversy about meeting them, Dublin could be blamed for having recommended it. Eventually, I passed him over to my First Sec. 'Here, I'll tell him,' she said, going up a notch in aggression.

Sometimes, you had to go up the line, if people got persistent, like the politician who demanded a meeting with President Clinton. We said we'd do what we could but later the politician phoned us from Washington – unbelievably he was sitting in a limo circling the White House. 'All I want is one minute. One minute with the President' – our First Sec was sweetness and light in telling him to please fuck off and stop being a stupid man. One overseas Ambassador got shorter shrift. In a telex marked by nuances and permutation, he wanted to know if he should attend a talk by a visiting Sinn Féin bigwig – it was around the time of the Ceasefire. 'His Excellency is paid £60,000 a year,' barked a derisive First Sec on the security side. 'Tell him to use his loaf!' For which answer, obviously, I had find a more tender form of words.

Despite the DFA's paranoid caution about meeting Sinn Féin, inadvertent contacts were still made which could land you in hot water. Well before the Ceasefire, the office of Tom Kitt, our then Minister of State, asked DFA to meet a delegation from Tyrone, led by one of Kitt's constituents, a Dublin woman and Fianna Fáil member. They wanted to talk about the situation in Coalisland, where the British army had been running amok and relations were very bad with the local people.

Our Security people were away, so I met the delegation and brought them into a downstairs room. The Dublin woman introduced another woman and three men, one of whom had facial bruising and was on crutches. They described, in detail, the behaviour of the British soldiers. The aggression of the RUC or, more particularly, the UDR/RIR is, though deplorable, at least understandable since there is a sectarian dimension and they come from the same community, with their friends and relatives getting picked off by the IRA. But there is something bizarre about the British army, the much vaunted NATO lynchpin, coming over to Ireland and behaving like drunken football hooligans. In the newspapers, amazing photographs had appeared, taken by locals, of English squaddies pulling off their guns and jackets and challenging local youths to fist-fights in the streets. All discipline had broken down. After IRA attacks on their regiment, frustrated off–duty soldiers would go into local pubs and start smashing them up.

I was struck by the quiet dignity of these people and what they had to put up with. The woman with her broad vivid face and bleached white hair had the face I'd see so many times in the North; tough, resilient, the people on the front line. They seemed glad to have their story listened to by an official. No wonder, for one of them let slip that he was a Sinn Féin representative. It was almost subliminal, a flash reference. Oh dear, I thought, but if they saw my reaction, they didn't let on. From here on I tried to bring the meeting to a close. But, obviously, not quickly enough. When I wrote my explanation, an officer helpfully changed it so that it looked like I had immediately truncated the meeting as soon as the Sinn Féin revelation was made. An important change, as it happened.

It all seems quaint now, but at the time it was a big deal. Our Counsellor went bananas, feeling I'd broken all ground rules and should have vetted the group. I was helped by the fact that Kitt's office had suggested the meeting, but what could they have done, the request having come through a Dublin constituent? What particularly caused consternation was that it had been in Iveagh House itself, not a parish hall in Coalisland. 'I believe you've been meeting the Provos?' said Ó'hUiginn, drolly, when I dropped in to explain. But Ó'hUiginn was probably the least excited about it all, accepting that it was a mistake. He even found in it a black irony that the group stayed longer in the House because the man on crutches had some difficulty getting out through the submarine doors. 'With all due haste' was how I described the meeting as having concluded. 'Or even undue haste,' said Ó'hUiginn, smiling darkly.

The Security side also went mad, but for different reasons. I had come onto their turf. Whereas they had to be circumspect about whom they met, I had actually brought Sinn Féin into the House, admittedly by accident. There was also a competitive annoyance that the Coalisland people hadn't come directly to the Irish Government, rather than bringing in Sinn Féin. And the sad thing is that the Sinn Féiner became 'the issue' rather than the legitimate concerns of the group. This so annoyed me — I mean, maybe the SF guy was beaten up too — that I made sure to follow up on the Coalisland representation long afterwards, and see that it went up the line. 'Ah, God bless you, for all your help,' the woman told me, weeks later.

Sometimes, you had to do this anyway, since if people didn't get onto Security directly, but went through other sections, their concerns might not get the same priority.

21

The Script Factory

One of the most useful things you could do for politicians was provide speeches. I say 'politicians' because we were not just writing for our own Minister. Other Ministers expected material, as did Ministers of State and Chairs of Committees. This was especially so on Northern Ireland, where the issue of 'sensitivity of subject' could be cited as a reason not to risk speeches of their own.

When I began in the Division we were doing two or three speeches a week but with the onset of the Peace Process, it rose dramatically, often to as many as two or three a day. Every politician wanted to talk about the North and we wanted them to talk about it — to put pressure on the dissidents and keep the momentum going. The Peace Process was about speeches, and language and text. If you spoke enough about peace and a new beginning, you might bore people into a settlement. As one Counsellor put it, it was 'death by a thousand speaking points'.

Language, the same language, was constantly regurgitated and turned around. This created a problematic paradox; each speech had to sound 'fresh' and 'different', while essentially saying exactly the same as previous speeches. The language on Northern Ireland was tightly controlled. It had to be. One false phrase or wrong note and, as I've said before, bells could go off. And worse than bells. After years of honing and fine-tuning, the lexicon was down to a familiar patter. Some called it 'gobbledegook', others called it 'boilerplate', although strictly speaking, this phrase only described the standard text which you began with.

The language went something like this; the situation was a tragedy, and needed a new beginning, an agreement in which all sides could be accommodated and in which one tradition does not dominate over the other. The two Governments must ensure that negotiations lead to a settlement which honours the rights and aspirations of both communities equally. Unionists must be assured that Northern Ireland will remain a part of the United Kingdom for the foreseeable future, while Nationalists must be assured that their cultural identity will be secure in Northern Ireland, as well as in an all-Ireland context. We need to open doors, not close them. The three sets of relationships. Et cetera, et cetera, et cetera.

I wrote so much of this stuff that I could have written it in my sleep. Where did it come from? Its careful phrasing had been worked upon for years, as the State sought to engage Unionism and row back from the angry anti-partition rhetoric of an earlier era. But, in recent times, much of the credit must go to John Hume, who introduced a sort of New Age pleading to the peace-speak. From Hume, the Irish Government took the language and spread it like the gospel, or high quality manure, until it had fertilised everywhere, from newspaper editorials to the speeches of Tony Blair, for whom, of course, such language was second nature. In time, even Gerry Adams — indeed *especially* Gerry Adams — was coming out with it.

One time, listening to the Sinn Féin TD, Caoimhghin O'Caolain on the radio, I nearly got sick. 'That's our language!' I protested as I listened to a regurgitation of our familiar speaking points, except that O'Caolain had such a superior, pompous tone, it sounded even more scripted than it did with our Ministers. It reminded me of the Soviet Union or Cuba — the revolutionary turned jargon-spouting *apparatchik*.

To prevent such blandness among our own politicians, one had to constantly come up with new ideas and new twists within the language. For example, I had to draft an article for the Tánaiste relating his recent Middle East visit to the Peace Process at home. The piece was for the *Kerryman*, an innocuous but politically important forum. It was Dick Spring's local newspaper and, in 1987, he had only held his Kerry seat by seven votes. (For the same reason, invites for Spring to attend St Patrick's Day events abroad were always turned down, with the simple explanation, that the Tánaiste will be attending celebrations in Tralee. This year, and every year.)

In *The Kerryman*, Spring described (or I wrote), how the recent bombings in Israel had not diminished the resolve of Yitzak Rabin and Arafat to pursue their peace process, but increased it. Each atrocity made them more determined. Because, once started, there is no going back, etc. Parallels were drawn, and historic connections invoked; Michael Collins as an inspiration for the Israeli Independence movement, but also as figure who'd made the transition from war to negotiation.

The strange thing was that writing this stuff, you started convincing yourself. You got into the swing of it, picking up rhetorical momentum and bearing down towards the final paragraphs, with your argument-clinchers in full view. You also got into it for noble reasons. Unless you were a hardline Provo or Unionist, you usually *did* believe that the idea of outright victory, or domination, for one side was outmoded, and unfeasible, and that the only option therefore was for some form of compromise or accommodation. Even if, at heart, it was just as a postponement of your ultimate ambition.

In the finished texts, the hands of different writers were visible. For example, the robust concepts and American jargon of X, who had spent a lot of time in the US, or the reasonable 'let's all hold hands' pieties of Y, a former priest (one of many in DFA). By contrast, one official's speaking points could be so tough and argumentative that a rival (ridiculously) blamed them for the break-up up the 1992 Talks. To us, the politicians were only mouthpieces delivering our lines, pitching our ideas. And our rivalries. They were the Punch and Judy through which people could bash each other about and fight for career advancement.

Media impact was the key. Thus, X could point to one day's newspaper and say, with respect to the Taoiseach's speech the previous night in Philadelphia, 'Look, most of my speech survived.' A summary headline on the front page declared, 'Reynolds Lists Priorities for Progress in North'. But the real comparison was inside, where a full synopsis went across the top of page four; 'Each side holds part of the solution, says Reynolds.' By contrast, at the bottom of the page was the Tánaiste's statement at Ashford Castle — 'Spring Calls for End to NI Violence'. The headline and space for this was much smaller and X was delighted, since the latter statement had been drafted by Y, his main rival and superior. Appearances in the *Irish Times* were the key barometer, since, as the self-styled 'paper of record', it recorded all these speeches and was apparently read closely by opinion-makers in the North.

Of course, in a hierarchy, people could tamper with each other's drafts. And then there were the inputs from outside the Division; the Secretary, Noel Dorr, or the Tánaiste's advisers, like Fergus Finlay, or people in the Department of the Taoiseach. In the case of Albert's Philadelphia speech, for example, a key paragraph was inserted by Martin Mansergh (the Taoiseach's adviser on the North), calling for British troops to be withdrawn to barracks. Some ambitious speechwriters often tried to skip a layer and go straight to an Assistant Secretary or Private Secretary. As with Dermot Gallagher, who had an almost Roman attitude to encouraging rivalry, Ó'hUiginn liked to play people off each other, although in his case, it had more to do with seeking ideas and expression. Sometimes, Ó'hUiginn reached right down to the lower levels, hoping to unearth new talent and perhaps jump-start an often jaded process.

Usually, of course, Ó'hUiginn himself would have the final say and, as befits the 'Prince of Darkness', his speeches were often masterful, a skilful blend of steely determination, conciliatory phrasing and yet another 'new' insight. His draft for a Dick Spring statement to the UN General Assembly (UNGA) exemplified this. In his draft, Ó'hUiginn broke away from the older language and spoke about a new architecture, likening Northern Ireland, in a complex but comprehensible fashion, to a house with separate foundations. People spoke about the text for weeks, including the way Ó'hUiginn had stepped around – but also clearly invoked – the joint sovereignty aspect, which usually drove the British and Unionists mad.

In the UNGA statement of 1995, Ó'hUiginn's hand is again evident in trying to get over the by now ludicrous impasse over decommissioning, arguing that to make it a precondition for entry into negotiation as opposed a goal in the process 'is to ignore the psychology and motivation of those ... who have resorted to violence and,' (mindful of Spring's audience), 'the lessons of conflict resolution elsewhere'.

An indication of Ó'hUiginn's tight control over language was when he put his head into my room and asked to see the Irish language text of the Downing Street Declaration, before it was sent for official printing. The Irish version was important, not just for cultural reasons but also because, as the first official language, it might well have been the one which would be challenged in the Courts. Within hours, the draft came back, littered with changes and amendments. My Irish, unfortunately, wasn't good enough to understand all the corrections, but they looked more than technical. It was amazing. Here was a major bilateral agreement but Ó'hUiginn appeared to have cleared his fine-tunings with the Minister, and the Taoiseach, in no time. Fast phone calls, they must have been. I was most impressed. I got the thing retyped and sent it off to the printers, thinking how nice it would be if Seán had slipped in a phrase somewhere about 'the long term reality of a United Ireland'.

When he spoke himself, Ó'hUiginn had a fine delivery, modulated with a dry wit. At a dinner to celebrate the completion of the Shannon-Erne Waterway, held in the ESB's rooftop restaurant on Fitzwilliam Street (ESB International had done much of the Canal's engineering) he offered up such heartfelt tribute that the guests were nearly crying into their soups. Curlew cries from bog swamps were evoked, along with jumping perch and otters. But sometimes he was too clever and the tortuous logic of his constitutional concepts could make de Valera look straightforward. Nor did he take kindly to others questioning his scripture. One time, he agonised over the phrase, 'the peoples of Ireland', a key nuance since the plural suggested recognition of the Unionists as a separate people, as against the Hume orthodoxy, to 'heal our divided people'. ('Heal your divided party!' a Press Officer shouted one day at the TV screen) Ó'hUiginn toyed with the phrase 'all the peoples of Ireland' and asked a junior officer what he thought. 'It sounds like something from Lilliput,' said the baffled officer and Ó'hUiginn looked at him menacingly.

For speech material, history was ransacked with abandon and ever more outrageous analogies were made, especially later as Fianna Fáil began to abandon the core rhetorical aims of Nationalism and wanted to cover its ass. Parnell was constantly quoted, appropriately, given that, at this time, the Government was at Parnell's sneaky game of threatening a 'worse scenario' if constitutional nationalism didn't get its way. Even Isaac Butt, Parnell's predecessor, was being hauled out of his dusty crypt to support the Peace Process. I suggested John Redmond, the subject of a novel I was then writing, but this was dismissed; 'Always remember, at the end of the day, we are writing for a North Kerry Republican.' As in, not

Spring himself, but his seat, which he inherited from his father who resigned from Fianna Fáil because of de Valera's treatment of Republicans (thus, perhaps, the seven vote majority). 'And besides, he's a loser.'

'Spring's no loser!' said someone defensively, before it was explained that the reference had been to Redmond.

Since they were for a greater good — peace — these distortions could be forgiven but some of them were rich indeed. If anything they became even more distorted with the later arrival into office of the Rainbow Coalition, replacing Fianna Fáil, and comprising Fine Gael, Labour and Democratic Left. For example, I had to draft a speech for Avril Doyle, a Fine Gael Minister of State, attending the Byrne-Perry Summer School in her Wexford constituency. Byrne and Perry were pikemen who had been out in 1798, causing revolutionary mayhem and killing people. But I had to write a speech full of pacifistic sentiment and condemnations of violence. It was enough to have Byrne and Perry spinning in their pitch caps. A colleague had to produce similar prose for a Liam Lynch Commemoration at Knockmealdown, in County Limerick. Lynch was a Republican fanatic, who wouldn't accept the ending of the Civil War in 1923, and with whom even de Valera despaired. Now he was being used to preach non-violence and reasonableness as the State, as ever, tried to cut the ground from under modern-day Republicans.

Nor had the direct attacks on Republicans ceased. As late as October 1994, IRA violence was described as 'evil and perverted', a phrase written by Q, a skilful drafter from a Southern Protestant background. Not that this would have affected his prose. As with liberal lefty types who batted even harder for the State when they were in positions of responsibility, Q was most robust against the British on issues like Fair Employment and their army's collusion with Loyalist paramilitaries, and even more so against the Unionists. It was simply that the phrase was required and not only did Ó'hUiginn, usually more

Nationalist, leave it in, but he even changed it to 'sick and perverted' (on the North, 'evil' sounds banal).

Poets were also employed. Yeats was constantly invoked — 'Too long a sacrifice' etc. — but so too modern poets, like John Hewitt and Seamus Heaney. One officer suggested we should be giving Heaney royalties such was the man's constant usage. He even began turning up in Clinton's speeches. A lot of people didn't realise that Clinton's speeches on the North usually came, in their first drafts, from the Irish Embassy, drafts which often stayed quite intact until delivery. So impressed was President Clinton with Heaney's poetry that he used the line, 'when hope and history rhyme' as the title of a book.

The demand for speeches grew so much that eventually we just had to turn them around quickly — literally, a scissors and paste job. Bits from speeches were slapped into other speeches, with a few phrases changed. One trick one was to take a fourth para from an old text and put it second, or make a third para the fifth, and then give the whole thing a new 'top and tail' — the introductory references which open and close a speech. 'Rinse it, head, rinse it!', an Irish newspaper editor used to tell his staff, when they'd 'lifted' an English or US feature, meaning to drop all the local references and replace them with new (Irish) ones. With a similar turnaround, you could take an already delivered text and present it to another Minister's office as a brand new version. Little wonder a commentator of the time praised us for the 'consistency' of the Government's statements!

However, you did have to tailor your speech according to the speaker, and audience. Thus a draft for Meryvn Taylor's address to the UCD Law Society had to be slightly simplified when rehashed for Jimmy Deenihan's delivery to the Rotary Club in San Francisco. As Minister for Equality and Law Reform, Taylor would be expected to go into complicated concepts of rights and law. But for Minister of State Deenihan, a former Kerry footballer, it was straight down the middle, 'ye boy ye', with the Americans. And so the text was made more direct, with shorter sentences; peace and understanding *good*, violence *very bad*. And it was also made more muscular. The language on Northern Ireland might have been tightly circumscribed but that didn't mean we couldn't indulge in a bit of old-flag waving now and then, especially in the US, where phrases like 'discrimination' and 'human rights violations' went down a treat. Even a subtle phrase-change like 'the British Government' to the more sweeping 'British' gave it a little *frisson* of aggression.

As well as supplying material for President Clinton, we also gave language to American politicians and anyone else who wanted it. At one stage, the British Labour spokesperson on the North, Kevin McNamara, was in danger of losing his job and we were asked to quickly produce previous speeches which praised McNamara's role. He clearly hoped such references would save him. But I wasn't that energised, mainly because I didn't really like McNamara who I thought was a bit pompous but also because his position was already doomed, as our Counsellor admitted. For Blair and New Labour, McNamara was old hat, and too Nationalist to begin with.

More alacrity was shown for Senator Kennedy. In the 1994 mid-term Senatorial elections, Kennedy was under real threat and we had to get the finger out to help him. Kennedy is very important on the North, and to Irish politics, which is one reason why the British are so hostile to him. In 1994, Reynolds and Spring visited Massachusetts to show their support, including attending a special ceremony honouring the Senator in Boston. For the Taoiseach's speech, G, a First Sec and star speechwriter, excelled himself to produce an emotional tribute to Ted and the whole Kennedy legacy, with references to water-logged Famine ships and ragged emigrants coming up the shoreline. For such speeches, G would do multiple drafts and then take it home to be mulled over with a glass of whiskey. 'They'll be crying in the aisles when they hear this,' said G proudly as he put the finishing touches to his final draft.

He wasn't far wrong. Some months later in Hourican's, we met Trina Vargo from Kennedy's office. 'That was an amazing speech you guys gave in Boston,' she said. 'People were so moved! Like, our Republican challenger for example and his friends in the *Boston Herald*, who wanted to know what the Irish Government was doing making such "electoral speeches". Who wrote that speech?' I grabbed the Duty Officer's mobile and called G, still at his desk at 8 p.m.; 'Come down immediately and receive the plaudits.'

G also had a gift for instant messages of sympathy 'from' the Tánaiste or Taoiseach. (Although not as quick as one Government Press Secretary, who on being called at home for an official reaction to a statesman's death, used to pause, clear his throat and say 'The Taoiseach is greatly saddened ...') Again, the Kennedys featured, including messages on the death of Rose, the mother, and Jacqueline, JFK's widow. But on the latter, there was a row with Protocol who were often ultimately responsible for the delivery of such messages. A nerdy character in Protocol objected to our description of Jacqueline as having 'bravely faced her husband's death'. This, he said, implied that somehow she foresaw and had prepared for her husband's death, which in the realm of Dallas conspiracy theories would be an amazing new angle. We accused them of being overly pedantic and an unseemly row developed which delayed the Tánaiste's message. Did Spring even read such messages? I wondered. On Nixon's death, G wrote a paean so fulsome and positive about the former crook that I felt sure it would not go through unchanged. But it did.

Worse, perhaps, than a bereavement was the loss of an elected position. Not only was Kennedy in trouble in 1994, but so was the fifth Horseman, Congressman Tom Foley, who was falling behind in Oregon. Separate faxes had been cleared and readied for issue, one of congratulation and one of sympathy, but such was the confusion, as the election results emerged, that faxed messages of congratulations were sent to both Kennedy and Foley. In fact, Foley had lost. Luckily, the over-optimistic fax was retrieved at the other end, before it could fall into the hands of a mischief-making journalist.

Finally, there was the issue of the use of jargon in speeches, the peace-speak of consensus and non-confrontation. In the long journey from 'Six Counties', 'anti-partition' and 'Orange Mobs', Dublin appeared to have retreated from its traditional nationalist goals. But it could also be argued that we simply found a more innocuous language in which to cloak our deepest desires. 'Peace-speak' sucked all the contentiousness out of language and developed a blander lexicon which permitted further progress in the political debate and went down better abroad. Ah, those fair-minded Irish, said the Europeans. Meanwhile, the Provos were stuck outside with their fighting talk. In this regard peace-speak fulfilled a secondary goal of outflanking the Republicans and cutting them from underfoot.

But what of the Unionists? Let us do a breakdown of how the peace-speak, the gobbledegook, might sound to someone more suspicious. 'What we want is a final and comprehensive settlement, bringing lasting peace.' Decoded; 'the settlement of 1921 is wrong, did not, and *will not* bring lasting peace and the basis for partition needs to be re-examined, if not eroded.' Crucial to this were 'the three sets of relationships; that between the two communities within Northern Ireland, that between the two parts of Ireland and that between Britain and Ireland'. This was an ingenious formula which allowed the South to broaden the terms of debate so that the political relationship between the two communities in the North would not work unless bolstered by new relations between North and South. In widening concentric circles, the South was broadening a problem which the British had always tried to internalise. Or to use their own language, 'securitise'.

The European context was also mentioned but this was baloney, and another smoke-screen; as if we cared how the North sat in an integrated European context. Essentially, with the three sets reflected in the three-stranded talks process, the South wanted to unravel the whole situation and start again. The beauty of it was that the sets were interlocked and could only work in full. Not bad for a political framework which preceded the Ceasefire and for which even Paisley's party had signed up. Did the entry of Sinn Féin make the settlement any more ambitious from the Irish point of view? It seems not.

Other phrases can also be usefully deconstructed. For 'Agreed Ireland' read 'United Ireland'. For the 'island as a whole', also read 'United Ireland'. For 'bringing together our divided peoples' (Hume's favourite) the implication was that the Unionists were 'our own people', who had to be 'undivided back into the Irish family'. By an extraordinary process of language, the Unionists have gone from being a majority in NI to a sympathised-with minority on the island as a whole. On all sides they were being co-opted by language, soothed and seduced by reasonableness of the Irish. And if they refuse? They are being belligerent and unforthcoming. They are saying no. How could they object to President Robinson, nice Mrs Robinson, travelling North again to 'understand them' and 'bring them in'?

In reality, how could they not? Mary Robinson had more impact than a hundred car bombs. Bombs they could deal with. They strengthened resolve and bolstered partition. But love-bombing, the Unionists couldn't handle. The long arm of 'friendship' is much more insidious. Irish nationalism takes many forms and peace-speak is just one of them. Again the shark must keep moving. But a better analogy is a creature which takes many forms; now a shark, now a worm, now a cuddly bear. It's like the horror movie, *The Thing*. The Thing is everywhere!

So ingrained is Irish nationalism, that Irish people don't realise how nationalist they are even when they think they're being non-nationalist. Deep down, almost all Irish politicians and certainly all Ministers are regarded by Unionists as a threat to the North. Not necessarily because of their views but because their script is the State's tightly calibrated script. Thus, Republicans and the like are surprised that Liz O'Donnell, for example, of the un-nationalist PD's, should bat hard in the Talks, or that Proinsias De Rossa, usually so anti-Republican having been one himself, should then, as a Minister, deliver forthright statements. But why the surprise? The Ministers are locked into the State's mode. Again, Ó'hUiginn; 'Irish nationalism is an irresistible force'. Recovery of the North is a constitutional imperative which, even when amended, is still an imperative. 'Why are you afraid of peace?' the Nationalists mockingly ask the Unionists. But how can they not be?

As well as writing material, we also did oral briefings within the House; to Danish MPs, German church groups or gum-chewing American students, who yawned their way through presentations. It was a useful chance to rhetorically rehearse the issues, speaking for twenty minutes about the conflict, tracing its origins, development and the Government's hopes for the future. And then you took questions. Sometimes, however, as you heard yourself trundle through the well-run 'peace-speak' or gobbledegook, you could see their eyes glaze over, especially if they were young Americans, whose education system seemed to assume the attention span of a gnat. One day, a colleague was airily offering the 'three sets' of relationships to an Indian journalist over a three-course lunch. But the Indian was bewildered by the torturous interlocking 'strands' and suddenly exclaimed, 'I'm sorry, but I don't know what you're talking about!' 'Right, then scratch all that,' replied my colleague and he went into a more simple and direct explanation, comparing it to India and Pakistan.

On another occasion, briefing some London stockbrokers, we started talking about an incremental 'window', feasibility and the 'likelihood' of a ceasefire. 'Yes, but when exactly will the ceasefire occur and for how long?' they asked. They were financiers and they wanted hard facts. For a moment, we were quite flummoxed, being more used to the euphemisms of mirage and speculation.

These briefings also produced the one bad row I had with a First Secretary. We were briefing a group of Americans, accompanied by some Derry people. One of them asked about integrated education — the mixing of Catholic and Protestant schoolkids — a touchy-feely issue for Americans, but in Northern Ireland, just touchy. Very touchy, in fact, with even the most progressive of politicians often being lukewarm about it. This was understandable, since either side saw non-denominational education as a threat to their culture. For the Catholic side, in particular, non-denominational schools would most likely be British-style comprehensives eating away at their children's Irishness.

However, I spoke about the Irish Government's 'desire' for more integrated education in the North which wasn't a strictly accurate reflection of government policy. I should have said something like 'the Government supports an improvement in the atmosphere in Northern Ireland which would allow integrated education to properly develop etc.' These qualifications would have been fine. But on the specific issue of education, the Irish Government has no official view. It supports the general freedom of choice but otherwise bites its tongue on this issue. Which is what I didn't do here. With impatience creeping into my voice, I witheringly described the Catholic Church's stubborn control of education in Northern Ireland and why this had to change.

After I finished, there was a pause and one of the Derry people (a brother of the novelist, Seamus Deane, I discovered later) exhaled softly and said, 'Well, now that's certainly putting it clearly.' I immediately knew I'd gone too far. Afterwards, the group had hardly gone out the front doors, when the First Sec turned on me and said 'you do not quote the Government like that!'

'Yes, but that's what we want — integrated education.'

'Maybe, but it's not the Government's view. For fuck's sake, Eamon! It's the Government we are speaking for. What you and I think doesn't matter.' I said nothing. He was furious and went mute while some Protocol people passed us in amusement. It was the last time I gave 'my' views on integrated education. Or anyone else's views, for that matter.

22

The Peace Process

The main search for a political settlement in the North was based on trying to revive the Talks process which had lapsed in 1992 (see below) and which attempted to work out a deal between the two Governments and the main political parties in Northern Ireland. The paramilitaries, engaged in violence, were not involved. However, from 1993 on, a new strategy was developed to try and draw in Sinn Féin, and the IRA, on the basis that if the Republicans called a ceasefire, a settlement could be built around that. This strategy became known as 'the Peace Process'.

So how did it begin? Those most honoured in recent accounts are often those most anxious to be honoured, with a lesser mention for those whose position requires them to be more modest, such as senior civil servants, clergymen, and former gunmen. At a political level, there has also been an absurd reaching out to credit all sorts of politicians, including Charlie Haughey, which some regard as more like an absurd attempt to make the settlement palatable to Fianna Fáil backbenchers. (This was before Haughey's Tribunal come-uppance.) It is quite similar to the credit handed out for Ireland's economic boom, which, by some generous accounts, seems to involve just about every investor and allegedly far-sighted politician.

The Peace Process starts with Albert. Or rather with Albert running with the ideas coming out of the Hume-Adams discussions. Albert's can-do, 'Let's sort this out' attitude to the economy and the liberal agenda was now applied to the North. Albert came relatively baggage-free. The fact that he wasn't even a rhetorical nationalist, like most Fianna Fáilers, was a big help. Nor was John Major a British nationalist. It was two grey men getting together to sort it out. (Although the British would also have been mentally prepared by their own, yet to be revealed, secret dialogue with the IRA.)

Albert was lucky in that key officials were already in place. In his own Department, his advisor on the North, Martin Mansergh had been keeping the lines open to Sinn Féin, as had people in DFA. Mansergh was an important figure and, for DFA, the fact that he was ex-Foreign Affairs had both positive and negative aspects. Like Charles Powell in Britain, who 'defected' from the Foreign Office to work directly for Thatcher, there was always a bit of suspicion with DFA about working to someone who had jumped the fence (as we shall see later when Bruton made Seán Donlon his adviser on the North). In the Division's Control room, you could gauge someone's importance to the Process by looking at the speed dials on the fax. Mansergh's personal button was there, well smudged from use, as was the Embassy Washington, the Embassy London, the US Embassy Dublin, the SDLP and the Tánaiste's office in Leinster House. Faxes to Maryfield were sent in code. In effect, these fax numbers represented all the key bases for the Northern Peace Process.

There was a fortuitous continuity in the fact that Seán Ó'hUiginn was head of the Anglo-Irish Division, and that Dermot Gallagher (Dag), as Ó'hUiginn's predecessor at Anglo-Irish, was now Ambassador in Washington. Dag had strong nationalist views, as had Ó'hUiginn, and both were equally dogged. While Ó'hUiginn was a thinker, Dag was a 'fixer' and operator. Dag's position in Washington was very important, since — and this cannot be stressed enough — there would have been no ceasefire, or settlement, without the Americans. The equation was relatively simple; Adams talked to Hume, who spoke to Ted Kennedy, who spoke to Bill Clinton. In Dublin as US Ambassador, Kennedy's sister, Jean Kennedy Smith was a crucial conduit, gloriously antagonising her London counterpart by getting directly involved in Northern Ireland.

Likewise, in Washington, the National Security Council had bypassed the State Department in bending the ear of the President towards a settlement which included Sinn Féin. The State and Justice Departments were much more cautious about such an approach having adopted an explicitly pro-British approach since the days of the Thatcher-Reagan Special Relationship. Thus the importance of this bypassing cannot be underestimated. The key officials here were Tony Lake, the NSC adviser and his deputy, Nancy Soderburg. Again, there was a useful overlap; Soderberg had formerly worked in Ted Kennedy's office, and was predecessor to Trina Vargo to whom we supplied Irish material. Dag was in weekly, sometimes daily, contact with Lake and Soderburg — in future years, an airing of these notes and telexes will complete the picture of the US contribution to the overall process.

So it wasn't just perceived arrogance which caused Hume to jump on a jet to the US the day after claiming to have lodged with the Irish Government, the 'synopsis' of his discussions with Adams. In retrospect, America was the place to go. With Dublin cautiously on board, it was thereafter a matter of carrot and stick with Sinn Féin (SF), who were themselves applying carrot and stick to the IRA. Through 1993-95, there was a lot of carrot and stick, and a lot of false dawns and missed deadlines. But, for the Irish side, the US were always there as guarantors, driving the process on. When in November 1995, Major invited Bruton to London to announce the 'twin track' plan on 'political talks and decommissioning', it was because Clinton was flying in the next day. The US had to continuously force Britain to take the process seriously.

In the early period of the Process, it was amazing how inaccurate and begrudging some media stories were about US involvement. For example, after a lengthy and crucial meeting between Spring and President Clinton at Martha's Vineyard, in spring 1994, one Irish Sunday newspaper belittled the encounter in a front page lead, describing the meeting as having only lasted for a few minutes. In fact, even a glance at the meeting transcript, along with Dag's long and detailed report on the discussion, reflected Clinton's total engagement with the process and his commitment to push the British to do more. Most immediately, and specifically, he promised to get them to respond properly to Sinn Féin's famous list of questions demanding 'clarification' of what would happen in a post-Ceasefire situation.

At the Official Opening of the Canal, I mentioned the newspaper story to Dag, as a bit of a wind-up. 'The quality of the British replies [to the IRA request for clarification],' he said sharply, 'was a *direct* consequence of that meeting.' He was annoyed, and rightly so, at the begrudging coverage of some of the Irish media. It was as if some people didn't want the process to work.

American involvement internationalised the situation, which is why the British Government, and British press hated them for it. It is part of the reason they so disliked the Kennedys and, later, Clinton. (Such mistrust is not entirely unjustified. For all their official neutrality, the US is emotionally and instinctively on the Irish side. I saw this when I was there, and not just in Irish-America. The British constantly dismiss US involvement as a pandering to the Irish-American vote, but it goes much deeper than that. The US are themselves a former British colony and see the wider picture on an issue like Northern Ireland. Would, indeed, that there was a disciplined Irish-American vote for us to avail of.)

Like Albert, the Americans saw something that needed sorting, that needed some risk-taking, and recognised that only their power could shift the British to do likewise.

They drove the Irish peace process and this incensed the British. It was a dream come true for Irish nationalism. The shame was that it didn't happen years ago, but then we had to wait for the end of the Cold War, and the end of the Special Relationship, before it could. To paraphrase Bruce Morrisson's remark, we had to change two Governments — the Tories and the US Republicans.

The pursuit of Sinn Féin was a high-risk strategy but in 1993 it seemed to be the only gig in town. However, in retrospect it appears that as early as in 1992 the three-stranded (or Brooke) talks offered a real prospect of a settlement between the SDLP, the Ulster Unionist Party (UUP) and the two Governments, a settlement which might have worked from the centre outwards and eventually sucked in the paramilitaries.

I spent a week reading the main files on the 1992 Talks. You'd need that time just to absorb all the different reports and corridor discussions; the 'talks' were really a shuttle between different rooms. It is clear, however, that an agreement was tantalisingly close. What went wrong? Accounts differ. The most plausible is that the SDLP were about to settle until Hume overruled them, feeling they should go away and work for a larger settlement (perhaps he already had a feeling that SF wanted to come in). There was talk of shouting in the SDLP 'dressing rooms'. But SDLP sources say that it was the Irish Government who torpedoed the chances. That it was they who felt that a larger settlement was possible. On a drive up to the Border to check on the Canal — and do a 'wet run' for the official opening, a barge ride by Mayhew and Spring — Z, a senior official at the 1992 talks, took us through them at length, confirming that half-way through the Irish Government realised that, as he put it, the Provos would have to be 'stitched into a settlement'.

This might confirm the Unionist accusation that the Government was negotiating in bad faith, and wasting their time. But the Irish Government weren't in a great position overall. Their negotiating team was unwieldy;

the lugubrious John Wilson, the laconic David Andrews and, because it was a Coalition Government, the moderate Des O'Malley. At other stages, the team was joined by Padraig Flynn, who became Justice Minister.

The failure of the 1992 talks made it more difficult to start again. Technically, the main responsibility for doing so fell to Dick Spring as Tánaiste and Minister for Foreign Affairs in the FF/Labour coalition. As leader of the Labour Party, with ostensibly no historical baggage, he came into office promising he would engage constructively with Unionism. However, from 1992 on, renewed allegations about security forces collusion with Loyalist paramilitaries and an increase in the British army harassment of nationalists, meant that Spring soon found himself reverting to bog-standard Brit-bashing and criticising the Northern security forces. Useful for a North Kerry Republican, perhaps, but not getting us anywhere on the political front.

As things proceeded, Spring advised caution to Reynolds regarding the latter's pursuit of Sinn Féin (SF). In fairness, someone had to be cautious. Carrot and stick again. Soft cop, hard cop. This was more or less the pattern over the next two years. Reynolds coaxes SF, Spring speaks tough. Also, the whole exercise looked much more risky at the outset, than it appeared in retrospect. From WT Cosgrave to CJ Haughey the State had spent fifty years protecting itself against militant Republicans. Spring was also busy as Foreign Minister, and had to travel the world. True, Reynolds was Taoiseach and had a Government to run but most of its programme was Labour's, which also kept Spring busy. In that context, there was another factor; Spring and Reynolds distrusted each other. Albert had already fallen out with the PDs as Coalition partners. Would the same not happen with Labour? As with the PDs, there was the legacy of the Beef Tribunal and its potential for political fallout. Those old beef exports to Iraq; they hadn't gone away, you know.

Meanwhile, Spring dealt with the British through the existing Anglo-Irish Agreement and the Inter Governmental Conference. As co-chairman of the IGC, it was his Department which serviced the Agreement. The hope had been that he might continue to develop its machinery in tandem with Reynold's pursuit of SF, and a larger settlement. The Agreement, after all, was a creative blueprint, with open-ended potential, and there was disappointment that aspects of it had been allowed to lapse.

Of course, not building up the Agreement suited the British who were always trying to slow it down and even have it temporarily stalled. The by-now retired Thatcher had said that she regretted ever signing it and backbench Tories had come to resent its impact. Thus, during the 1992 talks, the British had demanded that the Maryfield Secretariat stop working and become a mere 'post box'. This was always presented as aimed at Unionist sensitivities, but it was soon revealed to be a core British ambition. Spring was prepared to give such a pause a chance, although Irish officials were against this, feeling that any suspension in the working of Maryfield would cause the Agreement to die. Either way, it created a furious row.

Within DFA, Sir Patrick Mayhew was regarded as a poor successor to the amiable Peter Brooke; as Secretary of State for Northern Ireland, and seemed to have a poor relationship with Spring. By contrast, Brooke was regarded as the person who laid the foundations for the entire Process when he stated in 1990 that Britain no longer had a 'selfish, strategic or economic interest in Northern Ireland'. This phrase would grow into the Hume-Adams discussions and subsequently feature in all successive guiding documents.

The phrase really came to the fore in the Joint Declaration (Downing Street Declaration) of December 1993 and more especially fourteen months later in the Joint Frameworks Documents of February 1995. In both documents, Brooke's original language was interpreted in such a fashion that it essentially suggested that the British would henceforth adopt a neutral position on the matter of the Irish peoples working out their political future. However, original Irish hopes that the British might go further and 'join the ranks of the persuaders for Irish unity' did not come to pass, nor indeed did the explicit endorsement of something close to joint sovereignty, as was once ambitiously hoped — although we were, by now, further down that road. However, the Irish side were happy with the fudge, feeling that in the smorgasbord of language from which everyone can take their pick, there was enough to unstitch the existing settlement.

The language of Downing Street and the Joint Frameworks Documents was essentially a distillation of what we'd been churning out in speeches for our Minister and other government officials over the previous twelve months; the three sets of relationships, parity of esteem, and the principle of consent, to reassure the Unionists. Both sides had given voice to their ultimate ambitions, but had agreed to postpone their realisation. It was ingenious. However, at times I thought our willingness to accept a share of the blame for the situation went too far, in a 'there are faults on all our side' kind of line. But what fault was it of ours? We didn't create or administer Northern Ireland. Granted the development of an avowedly sectarian state in the South didn't help things (still evident as late as the X case) but this seemed minor, compared to the security blunders in the North, and the decades-long discrimination. But such language was the price to pay. It was almost as if we were pretending to take on this blame, as a way of taking on more responsibility and getting more involved.

In dealing with the North and other issues, Spring was aided by his omnipresent advisor Fergus Finlay. By now, the role of Special Adviser had become much more developed than it was when I first arrived in the

347

Department. In the 1980s, the Adviser was a somewhat remote figure usually attached to the Minister's constituency office and generally keeping watch over party theology. Brian Lenihan and Gerry Collins used to have Virgil Bric, an affable history lecturer on leave, who used to dwell up in the attic of Iveagh House in a skylight office. He didn't travel much, unlike one of his successors, a flamboyant character (whom we shall call Magnus) who the Minister used to bring around the world. Mockingly, the girls would mimic his phone calls from the super phone on the Government jet, sitting on the runway in Bangkok or somewhere. 'That's right, I'm calling up from the airport in Thailand.' But perhaps his real offence was that he wasn't DFA and had come in at a time when the role of such advisers was still undefined.

At the UN, he would join the gaggle of officials behind the nameplate and try to get involved but it was awkward for him. The Political Director and others, busily redrafting, would consult with him in an almost desultory way — 'Oh Magnus, you're here as well, you might as well look at this.' Perhaps feeling he had his position and world travels to justify, the Adviser would then over-scrutinise the document, leaning back ostentatiously with a pencil in his mouth, then come back with the most pedantic of reservations: 'I really don't know if you can say this.' The officials would stare at him blankly; 'Eh, why Magnus ?' And so having asked for his views, they would ignore them, or absorb them in such a way that they would obviously look bad and have to be removed again.

However, with the arrival of Labour in 1992, this all changed. Labour were reform-driven, in office with a restive Fianna Fáil, and they had an agenda to fulfil. The Political Adviser system became much more developed, even institutionalised, and overlapped with a new position of Programme Manager. Cleverly, the Labour Advisers would meet half-an-hour before the weekly meeting with their FF counterparts, so that when the meeting commenced they would just push through their policies, which is probably appropriate since they had effectively written the Programme for that Government. Understandably, the Civil Servants were initially distrustful of the system but it definitely improved things, building up trust between a new Minister and wary mandarins and sending regular shockwaves through the system to bring up work from below. FF and others criticised the system but they soon emulated it and, indeed, expanded it, so that today we have such a proliferation of managers, advisers, and personal press attachés that one wonders if daily spin control rather than evolved policy is the guiding principle.

During Spring's time, Fergus Finlay worked very effectively with the senior officials, especially on the North. It also put the Department at the centre of things since Finlay was not just the adviser for Foreign Affairs but for all of Government, in tandem with Spring's role as an enhanced Tánaiste. He would become a controversial figure, however, as was probably inevitable, given the tensions between FF and Labour and the continuing fall out of the Beef Tribunal. Later, in Reynolds' libel trial against the *Sunday Times* in London, his lawyer would refer to Finlay as a 'snake in the grass'. With his balding head and Parnell-style beard, Finlay was an unmistakable figure around the House, but it was as well to keep your distance. One Third Sec used to meet him coming in on the morning train where he'd gently mock the Department's pomposity and try to draw him into comment. But the Third Sec would say nothing; 'I just kept smiling and nodding my head.' Even though Finlay sat on the key Liaison Group dealing with the British, there was feeling of 'Don't tell him too much; he's an adviser'.

Likewise, you weren't supposed to say anything to the Press. Throughout the Department, there was a strict policy of routing all press queries to the Press section. But, in practice, there were a lot of unattributed remarks and 'off the record' comment, especially on Northern Ireland where the press was virtually part of the process, the medium through which positions were adopted and dialogue broadcast. As with speeches, we could tell who the sources were from give-away phrases — 'bedrock views' or 'crossing the Rubicon'. Someone even told a reporter about Ó'hUiginn's famous shark of Irish nationalism, 'which must keep moving or it dies', and thereafter the shark began breaking the surface of newspaper articles, its dorsal fin visible below the cloudy peace-talk waters. The shark became so well known that, later, when the Department tried to exploit the discontent of Northern (and mainly Unionist) fishermen, a press officer commented 'Before, it was a shark, now its fucking herrings!'

DFA made useful trade-offs with the media; in return for tip-offs and leaks, journalists would give information to officers, which often ended up in the Box. The information journalists wouldn't, or couldn't, publish, was often more interesting than what they did. But again there was usually a reason why they didn't publish such stuff. Some of it was outlandish speculation which only fed the extraordinary rumour mill of Northern Ireland, but it was useful nevertheless.

For example, from one source in New York, close to hardline Sinn Féin elements, I got a tip-off on the impending Ceasefire. The same prospect was unwittingly confirmed by someone in Dublin who was then going out with an assistant to the US Ambassador, Jean Kennedy Smith. The Division was particularly appreciative of these insights, since the US Embassy was, by then, a key conduit for SF intentions. Possibly my best source was an old friend from student days, once active as a hardline Unionist, who over the course of time, would correctly predict the election of Trimble and the corresponding rise, and stance, of Unionist dissenter Jeffrey Donaldson.

Advance copies (not technically leaks) of key documents were often sent to sensitive background figures, such as Cardinal Cahal Daly in Armagh. This reflected the close relationship Dublin had with the Catholic church in NI, a relationship the Unionists might criticise but it was for a reason they would appreciate; to stem the flow of support to the IRA. Daly was very anti-Provo, but he was a tricky figure for officialdom, as were many of the Northern Irish clergy. Slightly more amenable were the SDLP to whom advance copies were also selectively sent. Why not, since they'd probably worked on them with Dublin officials. But even if they hadn't, they were given a sneak preview on the clear expectation that the British showed practically everything to the UUP.

On the day of the Joint Frameworks Document (JFD), a crowd of us watched UTV get the first reactions of politicians. 'Well, I'm not exactly sure,' replied the SDLP's Mark Durkan in the Derry studio, 'because I've only just got the thing.' For a moment, Durkan looked sternly at the camera and we all started laughing. 'There you go, Simon,' someone shouted, 'rebuked over the airwaves!' Basically, Durkan was saying, 'What the hell was the delay?' Officers would have been expected to firm up their personal contacts.

In November 1993, however, a serious leak occurred when the journalist, Emily O'Reilly, published an early version of the JFD in the *Irish Press*, under the headline 'Blueprint for a New Ireland'. Much speculation ensued about who leaked it. There were only about ten copies and DFA people believed (partly confirmed by Finlay) that it was probably a Cabinet Minister or spin doctor who gave it to O'Reilly as background, not expecting that she would publish it. Or, a more conspiratorial scenario; that she would publish it and this would be good, because it would draw out Unionist anger early and so blunt their protest for when the real thing came along. A balloon going up.

Either way, the leak had major implications for DFA, with much discussion in the media about the security system in Anglo-Irish, discussion which was rehashed later with the leak of memos concerning Mary McAleese. The Gardaí came in to do long interviews with officers in their rooms, requesting that they be shown safes, shredders and files. Many of them, apparently, went away more confused about the procedure than when they arrived. In a way, it was all quite humiliating. For the investigation was across the board, from the photocopying people to Seán Ó'hUiginn, who was with them for an amazing two hours. 'Perhaps he's asking them if *they* think there'll be a ceasefire?' said someone afterwards.

But this being Anglo-Irish, some people were upset at not being interviewed, feeling it implied they weren't important enough. 'Not in the loop,' as the phrase went. Others, however, were very happy. Given the time lag between the document's composition and the inquiry, many people were well embarked on Postings and had to be flown home from New York and Brussels to recoup their memories. This was even more so with the McAleese leaks where, again, the Gardaí had an inquiry. Interestingly, while the first investigation seemed almost Inspector Clouseau-ish — bureaucratic intrigue not being a strong point of the Gardaí — the second was much more thorough.

But the conclusions on both occasions were the same. Lock up all files every night, shred constantly and keep changing combinations. But after a few weeks, people drifted back to their old ways. Counsellors used old 'Boxes' to prop up PC's and, with the Control Room churning out briefs, no one had time to put everything away, especially when it's Friday and someone shouts 'Let's all go to the pub!' It's human nature and it happens everywhere; from the Pentagon to the smallest bank. 'Lets face it,' admitted a Counsellor, 'one Provo cleaning lady comes through here, and we're all doomed.'

But if we were bad, the British were much worse. The concept of confidentiality seemed alien to them and they leaked right through the most sensitive negotiations. In the run up to the 1985 Anglo-Irish Agreement, they had babbled like over-excited debutantes. Leaking was always particularly bad under the Tories, given their proximity to the gossipy world of London clubs, and old boy networks of public schools, country estates and regimental ties. The closed world of upper-class Tories and military elites which Irish nationalists identified as the true centre of British power was very real. And not to be underestimated. After Liaison Group Meetings and IGCs, our people would open the London *Times* and read the details of so called 'confidential' meetings.

So fearful were we that the British would break the embargo on the Anglo-Irish Agreement (AIA) in 1985 and get to work early, spinning it to their own advantage, that elaborate precautions were made to have Embassies primed. The joint nature of these agreements was, in this sense, largely illusory; each side wanted to sell a particular take on the idea to their respective constituencies, home and foreign. All Missions abroad were given advance copies of the AIA, with background material, Q & A and Speaking Points. A colleague, posted in the Hague, described how his Ambassador, a nervous fellow, sat on the carpet like a child on Christmas morning, carefully following the instructions, as he opened the relevant parcels. 'Now dispose of pink paper and proceed to parcel B, putting envelope Y in the safe.'

The Irish also had memories of 1977 when the British broke the embargo on the judgement of the European Court of Human Rights that they hadn't used 'torture' on suspects in NI, but rather 'inhuman and degrading treatment'. A small difference, I suppose, when you've got a hood over your head and are threatened with being dropped from a helicopter at 800 feet. But the distinction was one the British could profitably leak to their tabloids. 'UK didn't use torture' was the servile headline; a pre-emptive strike which the Irish then found hard to reverse. Even the name of the Downing Street Declaration is itself the result of a pre-emptive strike. Rightly, it should be the 'Joint Declaration', but the British cleverly got the more resonant 'Downing Street' into the early spin.

In February 1995, a major leak occurred on the British side, when the London *Times* published excerpts from the upcoming Joint Frameworks Documents. In this case, the leak was clearly politically motivated, with the *Times* quoting selectively from the document to make it look more Nationalist than it was. The *Times* wanted to rouse the Unionists, and this they did. The story was even written by Matthew D'Ancona, not a staff member (he is now with the *Telegraph*) but a political freelancer with strong Unionist links.

It didn't take long for the Embassy in London to find out the alleged source. In the gossipy, politically divided world of the London media, journalists were only too happy to finger others. Details were collected on D'Ancona's friends and a link was made to the carnation-wearing Lord Cranborne, who had had access to the document and was said to be a huge influence on the Prime Minister, John Major. 'You'd better ask Robert,' was an expression MPs heard Major using on Ulster, and on Europe. Is it any wonder that the Peace Process stalled under the Tories? Cranborne, as Leader of the House of Lords, was trying to halt what he saw as appeasement on the North. Heir to the Marquis of Salisbury, Cranborne apparently feared that Sir Patrick Mayhew might be replaced as Northern Secretary by Michael Ancram who, as heir to the Marquis of Lothian, came from an older and even more noble peerage than he. My God, and these were the people we expected to show imagination on Northern Ireland! How the UK cried out for the fresh winds of meritocracy and open Government. (Although ironically, within a few years, Cranborne was later fired by William Hague for trying to do a 'deal' with New Labour over reform of the Lords.)

An e-mail pointing to Cranborne as the leak came in from the Embassy, but frustratingly (to me, anyway) the information was not passed on to the media. Perhaps they hoped to use it in private, but I thought the State should have been more forceful in identifying publicly the source of these destructive leaks. So I took the note, chopped off its top and tail, and quietly passed it to Maeve Sheehan, then of the *Sunday Tribune*, suggesting that she quote from it. Two days later, I nearly dropped when I saw the *Tribune*. The leak was the main story, including the alarmingly specific detail that, through its Press Office in London, the Irish Government — and, apparently, Patrick Mayhew — believed Lord Cranborne was the source of the document. Reached at his country estate, Cranborne denied leaking the document but expressed his strong displeasure at the direction of Major's Northern Irish policy. His denial was not very convincing.

I now had to worry about my own denial. I had loudly discussed the e-mail in the Press section the previous Friday and, given the way the story appeared, I now felt I'd be the obvious suspect for the 'leak about the leaks'. But in fact, leakers always feel they're more exposed than they actually are and by the following Monday, the controversy had moved on so fast, with accusations flying, that the *Tribune* story had been well overtaken. But discussion of it still came up. 'Yeah, I wonder how the *Tribune* got that,' a Press Officer said to her colleague and then she looked at me, pointedly. The moment passed.

I felt better about my patriotic gesture when I stood beside a senior colleague and listened while she dictated an entire scoop to the UK *Independent on Sunday*. The hack was an old friend from UN days but, despite repeating the details three times, the hack still got it wrong in the eventual story — 'Sir Christopher Mayhew', for example. Perhaps he was mixing up the Northern Secretary with the architect of St Paul's! And this on the front page. 'Jaysus,' my colleague grumbled, 'he'd never make a note taker in the Chinese Lounge.'

But the rest of the story was accurate. It was 22 August 1994 and an American team were in Ireland to try and pave the way for an IRA ceasefire. After the half acceptance by Sinn Fein of the Downing Street Declaration, further intense work was done in public, and behind the scenes, to try and bring the elements together. The British had offered clarification of the Declaration and the basis for a new and wide-ranging agreement was in place. The US delegation was acting as a go-between, but also a sort of guarantor, for the Republican movement to lay down arms and included Congressman Bruce Morrisson (he of the visas) and Niall O'Dowd, publisher of the *Irish Voice*. It was good to see familiar faces from my time in New York. I even met them one night trying to get into Pink Elephant nightclub. Morrisson might have got thousands of visas for Irish kids and possible peace for Ireland, but he still had to deal with a nightclub doorman. (Mind you, not to be recognised in Ireland, on this particular mission, probably suited them.) I interceded with the manager – 'Sound man, Robbie' – and in they went.

During a visit by same American group the previous March, the IRA had held a three-day ceasefire although the gesture caused more resentment than favour: 'Oh, so now you don't get killed till Wednesday,' was how someone put it. The SDLP's Seamus Mallon was especially impatient with such gestures and his criticism of the partial ceasefire caused him to have a major row with Hume. Spring supported him, consistently stressing, throughout the period from March to August 1994, the importance of achieving a 'permanent cessation'. Indeed at this stage, Spring might have been taking his cue from Seamus Mallon on the dithering of Sinn Féin, by contrast with Reynolds who seemed to be led by the 'just follow me' approach of Hume. With his wonderfully caustic tongue, Mallon said that he 'hadn't spent 30 years in politics to play wet nurse to the IRA'. He also memorably described SF's new found flexibility as 'Sunningdale for slow-learners'.

SF's procrastination about a ceasefire (which seemed so close since the IRA's partial acceptance of the Downing Street Declaration in March) caused great tension in the SDLP, but so too did Hume's lack of information about what was happening. 'Trust me,' was his refrain, 'I've got peace in my grasp, a settlement is only around the corner.' The perspective of SDLP rank-and-file, however, was that they had a party to protect and SF were, at the very least, the electoral enemy. It seemed that Hume was content to sacrifice his party to gain peace. A noble idea but what if he sacrificed both? As it was, his leadership was not bringing young people forward, and many heirs were waiting in the wings. There was a suspicion, for example, that Hume had not helped develop the party in South Derry for fear that a power base might emerge to rival his own. Strabane had a nationalist majority, so why was its Council in Unionist hands? One story had the Irish Government going to Hume, at one stage, and suggesting that he try and secure the area for the broader Nationalist cause. 'Fuck off, it's our party," he allegedly replied. In this he was at least consistent: he also refused to allow the SDLP to set up a lucrative Dublin branch.

As the Process continued, many Fianna Fáil people were also in the dark about what was happening. One day, I bumped into a FF backbencher in the street. 'What's happening?' the TD implored 'My constituents are all asking.' 'I'm sorry, it's confidential,' I felt like replying in a cocky, unelected way. But instead I just gave him a verbal version of the Overall Steering Note and said that he probably knew as much as I did.

The path to the ceasefire was long and painful, but in fairness to Hume he doggedly persevered. Apparently, he gave SF/IRA about five final deadlines to commit, all of which they bypassed, and he certainly also gave DFA the dates of a few D-days, which also passed. On 22 August, we were told it was 'coming'. On the 24th, it was coming 'in days'. On the 26th, a Friday, some people didn't go for lunch for fear they'd miss it. It was like waiting for the

Postings announcement. But nothing came. On the 29th, a Monday, it was 'coming again — definitely the next day'. Instead, it came on Wednesday, August 31st 1994, at around 11.00 am.

By now people were wound up so much, that they were running around like headless chickens; faxing statements, collecting comment, watching the TV. The competitive atmosphere of the Division became absurdly high-pitched and shameless. It was a once-in-a-lifetime opportunity and people were hiding radios and fighting over photocopiers. The Locker Room boys had loosened their ties, and were pacing the corridors with their sleeves rolled up, sucking on pencils. (It was thus with some pleasure that I went in a week later and said 'I've just spoken to Conor Lenihan' — then a journalist — 'and the Loyalist ceasefire is coming tomorrow'. The security people were disgusted. They had said it wasn't coming for another week).

Phones rang off the hook as Missions abroad begged for more material. In middle of it all, Garret FitzGerald, our former Premier, called up looking for some election statistics on Sinn Féin. It was a surreal intrusion. Old Garret, architect of the Anglo-Irish Agreement, and of the modern Department, and suddenly he was like a voice from the past. 'Here, Eamon, you talk to him,' someone said and I had to go off and dig up the statistics.

Meanwhile, people were watching the TVs, with clipboards propped on their knees. This was a regular activity, monitoring parliamentary debate, so that the Minister's replies could be drafted immediately. With the ceasefire, naturally, the coverage was constant and voluminous and one chap got so tired listening to the 'guarded welcomes' and 'new dawns', that he switched over to an old episode of *The Rockford Files* on another channel. The same fellow got into trouble later for watching the Rugby World Cup in South Africa, when he was supposed to be noting a debate in the Senate. Devoy, our manic Counsellor, burst in to find him struggling for the remote.

But, on the day, not everyone was so inured. Going home that evening, there was an eerie calm on the streets of Dublin. So, it's all over. People stared quietly at the *Evening Herald* headlines in shops. In time, the Ceasefire would break — perhaps we even knew it would break — but effectively the war was finished. Ó'hUiginn was right, the 'conflict was over'. But now came the hard part, 'working out the terms on which it was settled'. But this sentence could be turned on its head. After all, 'working out the terms on which it was settled' — wasn't this what 'the conflict' was all about? Since 1920, and before.

23

The Fall of Albert

On September 6, 1994, only a week after the Ceasefire, the Taoiseach met Gerry Adams. 'Indecent haste,' said Y, a joke on my controversial encounter with the people from Coalisland, but also expressing genuine concern at the rush to bring in Sinn Féin. Later I was over in Government Buildings when the famous Hume-Adams-Reynolds handshake took place on the steps of the building. There were about 200 journalists there, including James Higgins, from the *Irish Voice* in New York and the sheepish faces of SF activists. The tripartite handshake was Albert's idea, on the suggestion of a photographer, and you could see Adams's pleasant surprise.

But not everyone was so impressed. Afterwards, I met a Fianna Fáil Dublin TD who said that FF backbenchers had their 'stomachs turned' by the sight of Adams in Government Buildings. People forget that, as well as sneaking regarders, there would be strong antipathy towards SF in FF, the peaceful Republican party. 'But what is the alternative?' said the TD. 'We have delivered the IRA. Now can the British deliver the UDA and/or the Unionists? The Unionists need new leaders, but from where will they come?'

One reason for the meeting was to put pressure on the British. Already they were stalling and a rift had opened between London and Dublin on the 'permanency question' — the insistence that the IRA make a real commitment to a permanent ceasefire. The previous evening had seen a very tense meeting between Spring and Mayhew, with the British being very negative; no lifting of the broadcasting ban on SF, no opening of border roads and no give on the permanency issue. It was as if they felt annoyed, cheated by the Ceasefire. Throughout the meeting, Mayhew had thrown in abrasive *non sequiturs* like 'Of course, you know the Unionists regard the US interest as an unwelcome intrusion' (i.e. we British do). Or 'Tell the Taoiseach, to cool it − he's frightening the horses.' This was usually prefaced by 'excuse my temerity, but ...'. Without excusing his own, Spring rightly shot back that the Taoiseach had 'corralled certain horses that others weren't prepared to approach'. Spring was robustly defending Reynolds but, unfortunately, British stubbornness was only beginning.

Two days later, the Taoiseach met Al Gore and it was through the Americans that the Irish would try constantly to put pressure on the British to move the process along. But it was a difficult game and when the IRA broke their ceasefire, the doubters were able to say 'told you so'. The (as it turned out temporary) collapse of the ceasefire sent Ó'hUiginn into depression. At least, when he went to Washington as Ambassador in 1996, he had the satisfaction of knowing that the process was up and running again. But after the Canary Wharf bombing and the unwillingness of then Taoiseach, John Bruton, to continue trying to coax SF in, Ó'hUiginn walked the corridors in despair.

In fairness, first Reynolds and then Bruton were dealing with a British Prime Minister, John Major, whose government was beholden to the UUP MPs for parliamentary survival. Bruton however could probably have brought in more US pressure. After a lunch in Iveagh House in early 1995, George Mitchell, Clinton's adviser on Northern Ireland, told Spring that the US were anxious to move the process forward. He said that he had mentioned to Bruton that he was meeting the British next week; was there anything more he could do? 'No,' Bruton had apparently told him, 'Sure, what more can you do?' Mitchell was surprised. Spring, and his mandarins, were even more surprised. What a wasted opportunity.

Bruton's elevation to Taoiseach at this stage was due to the sudden, and infamous end, to Albert Reynolds' government. The same stubbornness which helped him achieve the Ceasefire would, in November 1994, directly contribute to the downfall of his own Government. His refusal to relent on appointing the Attorney General, Harry Whelehan, to the High Court infuriated his Labour partners who wanted someone other than Whelehan. Worse, the appointee concerned would not step aside as the controversy deepened. 'I am the President of the High Court,' he repeatedly insisted like a bearded robot.

Word of Albert's impending doom came through on a Friday evening. I was standing in the corridor, when someone put their head out. 'The Government could collapse! I've just been talking to Leinster House. There's ructions over there.' The fall of any government is an interesting process to observe. The Department is often quite removed and even a bit indifferent. One Government is much like another, after all, especially where foreign policy and Northern Ireland is concerned. Personalities may be different (new Minister, new Taoiseach) and there are new election promises to be fulfilled, but even these, as we know, are a variable commodity.

This dispute, however, was different, mainly because of the dramatic nature of events. Albert in the Dáil admitting he was wrong about the appointment and revelations that the Attorney General's office had accidentally delayed the extradition of a paedophile priest to Northern Ireland compounded Labour's reservations. Albert in the Dáil, a few days later, watching as Spring is unable (and unwilling) to form a replacement Coalition because Fianna Fáil Ministers had known more about the earlier confusion that they had been prepared to admit. Bruton stepping in and forming a new Government, a

Rainbow Coalition of Fine Gael, Labour and Democratic Left (in Government for the first time). Even the loss of Albert didn't concern us too much since Spring would remain as our Minister, and Tánaiste, in the new Cabinet.

Crowds gathered in the Control Room and Press Section to watch events unfold on TV. People wouldn't directly express their political opinions, although later when the new Attorney General, Eoghan Fitzsimons, started explaining everything to a special Dáil Committee, one officer, an old style Gaelgeoir called O'Braonain, let out a cry; 'This man isn't helping the situation at all!' In other words, this AG was being far too forthcoming. The main reaction, however, was cynical laughter and amazement at Albert's antics. And there was the spotting of fellow Civil Servants. For the dispute directly involved officials and missing paperwork. An extradition request had not been processed because the AG's office was allegedly understaffed and didn't have computers. Albert, meanwhile, didn't give the correct information to the Dáil because he'd been handed the wrong folders. 'Who's he landing in the shit?' we asked resignedly, expecting the worst for the Civil Servants.

Afterwards, we were encouraged to go back and look in our own trays, just in case any of us had similar papers lying around. We all had! I found a letter from Sir Ninian Stephens congratulating Spring on the Peace Process. Sir Ninian, an Australian Judge, had been Chairman of the 1992 Talks. The letter should have at least got a Thank You. Oops, too late for that now. So I spoke to the Tánaiste's office about getting some kind of retrospective acknowledgement from the Private Secretary but, before we could issue a reply, Sir Ninian suddenly died. Which sort of solved the problem.

I also found a letter from a prominent NI academic, inviting Spring to speak at a conference in Liverpool — a good opportunity to grandstand on British-Irish relations. Again it was well out of date. But because it wasn't really 'my side', I went down the corridor and stuffed it under the tray of the Lobster, an anecdote-telling character whose desk was always heaped with paper. There, that should do it.

Although Albert was gone, it took a while for him to go. In his book *One Spin On the Merry Go Round*, his Press Secretary, Seán Duignan, describes the surprise of world leaders when Albert kept popping up at international meetings. 'We thought we said goodbye to you.'

But the best drama was at a CSCE Summit in Budapest, as the crisis first unfolded. Thatcher had gone to one in Paris and came home without her job: now Albert was in a similar fix. Ironic, really; the CSCE process was supposed to embolden democracy and dispose of despots. Mindful of such parallels, Tommie Gorman of RTÉ News challenged Reynolds as he emerged from the meeting. Albert had spent much of the Summit avoiding the press, but Gorman was in the conference centre lobby as Albert came out. 'Taoiseach, you've just been in there talking about transparency and accountability in politics.' Albert nodded that he had. 'What about your own honesty, in not being straight with your Government partners?' Only with a terminally damaged Premier could you be this brazen. Albert, stunned and annoyed, turned away, and Gorman went after him, shouting 'Taoiseach, what about your own transparency?'

On that night's News, you could see the drama of confused suits and jostling cameras. But Albert moved quickly and, like a fop from a Restoration Comedy, he simply pushed open the nearest escape hatch and went in through a door in the wall, bringing with him various Press Officers. At one stage, they went through the hotel kitchens, as surprised to see the flambé-throwing chefs as they were to see a fleeing Prime Minister. Eventually, on the other side, they managed to lose the journalists but the wolves were waiting at home. In the infamous words of Finance Minister, Ruairi Quinn, 'We've come for a head, Albert, yours or Harry's.'

Upstairs at the summit, Albert sat in his room, making long and desperate calls to Dublin, including to Harry Whelehan, who was presumably keeping to his mantra of being 'the President of the High Court'. Downstairs, all thirty-five leaders were assembling for the 'family portrait'. But Albert wouldn't get off the phone. 'Will you go in and talk to him?' people asked each other, but no one dared. Eventually Tom Kitt, our genial Minister of State, went in and tried but he was bawled out of it by Albert. Kitt was thus going to have to take his Premier's place in the group portrait, an amazing fluke which caused great amusement since Kitt had recently become known as 'Mr Photo Op', such was his penchant for prominent publicity.

In fairness, it was hardly a situation he could have foreseen and so, to this day, if you look at the photo of the world leaders — Yeltsin, Clinton, Kohl — you will see, up in the corner, the smiling, boyish face of Tom Kitt, although, given the circumstances behind the photo and the crisis surrounding his Government, not smiling too much. When Albert finally came downstairs, he was in livid form. 'What about my meeting with Clinton?' The US is always the key meeting for an Irish Premier, especially Albert. 'I'm afraid Clinton's gone, Taoiseach,' said someone gently and Albert cursed again.

'I've missed something else, as well. What is it?'

'The family photo, Taoiseach. It's been taken.'

Another torrent of abuse as Albert realised he'd lost his chance to be photographed among his 'good friends', Jacques, Helmut and John. At this stage, everyone kept away from Albert, except for one brave official, who perhaps because of his tenure as Ambassador in the Middle East, must have been inured to such moments. The complicated car plan of thirty-five countries was about to swing into action and the official walked firmly up to Albert. 'Taoiseach,' he announced, 'the cars are going to be leaving now. Alphabetically — and in the French language.'

The Taoiseach stared at him. His reply, sadly, is not recorded. But it certainly wasn't French.

The length of and confusion over Albert's departure created problems on the Protocol front; who was going to be in Government next week ? In our case, this involved American visitors. Since our section also covered North America, we had a lot of US politicians to deal with, especially during this period; securing them meetings, setting up itineraries and providing briefings. We also had a lot of Irish visitors going the other way, and talking up the Peace Process with Americans. So many indeed, that, at one stage, when we tried to get yet another engagement at the White House, we were told, in a memorable phrase, 'Sorry, guys, but we're kind of Irished-out at the moment.' Understandable; the Middle East and Bosnia were also crying out for attention.

The Unionists were also going back and forth and, one occasion, when a UUP delegation were in Washington, the Americans called and said that, if we wished, there was a chance the UUP could meet the President. 'What do you think?' an official asked 'It'd do them the world of good. It'd be like the spinach for Popeye.' But Ó'hUiginn said no, not yet; 'that privilege was to be kept for the SDLP only.'

And what access the SDLP had, with Hume popping in and out of the White House, with regularity. Would that one could publish the letters from Dag in Washington, and follow the clearly detailed choreography of Irish politicians, Northern and Southern, along with key players and Irish officials, including Dag himself. One letter described the look of shock on Douglas Hurd's face as he saw Hume emerge from the President's office ahead of him. The British had been trying for weeks to secure such a meeting. With Clinton and Major, the Special Relationship had definitely broken down.

However, at home, the crisis over the Reynolds crisis created a few problems. For example, a banquet was to be held in Dublin Castle, in honour of Ron Brown, Clinton's

Trade Secretary, who had been tasked with encouraging investment in Northern Ireland. (Brown was later tragically killed in a plane crash in Croatia.) The Taoiseach was to host the banquet, except that technically there might be no Taoiseach by this particular time. The Taoiseach's Department proposed that their Secretary, Paddy Teahon, would chair it — a laudable elevation for a Civil Servant — but the US Embassy rejected this, saying that a Prime Minister was required.

Then, in the week leading up to the formation of the Rainbow Coalition we had a visit from the Republican Governor of Massachusetts, William Weld, who was leading a trade delegation and accompanied by the Speaker and Majority Leader of the Massachusetts Senate, both old-style Democrats and red-faced Irish-Americans. It was good to see that bitter disputes were not exclusive to Irish politics, as the Americans brought with them some interesting tensions, which the travelling press pack gleefully seized upon. Weld was then embroiled in a major legislative battle with the Democrats in Massachusetts.

William Weld was a strange fish, whose demeanour seemed to personify the silver-spoon quality of New England Republicans. In the magazine profiles we were sent, much was made of his family lineage, taste in literature and languid air of confidence — he was very tall — and, certainly all the time he was with us, he walked around with a sort of superior quizzicality which was really irritating. But much was made also of his great political skills and he was being spoken of as a possible future Presidential candidate. Except that this was unlikely, since the US Republicans, like the UK Tories, were much more conservative than their electoral base, and they weren't going to warm to someone like Weld who, though a fiscal conservative, was also a social liberal. 'Tight money, loose morals,' the Americans call it. (Weld was later controversially rejected by the Senate as Ambassador to Mexico.)

Some of the entourage he brought were hilariously self-important. The Trade Office people were fine, but there were these clear-eyed Young Republican types who just would not relax. They were like young interns, with hair gelled back and firmly gripped mobiles. One chap called Rick was particularly wired, rushing up to me every so often, and asking, *sotto voce*, if we could 'advance this situation'. I could see our Counsellors laughing. After leaving Weld and party to the IBEC office on Baggot Street one morning, Rick and I walked, or goose-stepped, the short distance to Government Buildings. Until we met, as you do in Dublin, a woman I knew out walking her dog. Stopping to talk for a moment — her son was working for the EU in Sarajevo — Rick suddenly burst in, 'Sorry, but is this in the programme?' He looked like a panic button had gone off in his head.

Later, just before we closed the door on the Secretary's Ante Room in Iveagh House where dinner was about to be held, Rick put his finger up and insisted on walking around the table to check again on all the place settings. 'Yes, they always have salmon,' he said disdainfully to a fellow robot, casually insulting our Protocol people. Such rudeness was quite at odds with his political masters who, led by Speaker Bolger, had an after-dinner sing song, which went on into the early hours. Even the WASPy Weld joined in. You'd think Rick and the robots would learn from such old-style US conviviality.

Then something happened to Rick. Our dislike of him and his mates had clearly got to the Trade Office people, who didn't like him much either, and Rick was told to 'cool it' for the rest of the trip. Stripped of his phone, he sat slumped in a seat and stared at us, loosening his stripy tie, like a beaten stockbroker. He reminded me of a friend's story about meeting these Young Republicans in New York. Utter control-freaks by day, they just went bananas on their night off, phoning in the cocaine and the Chinese hookers. From the way Rick's lip was curling, he looked like he was in the mood to get ugly.

But, for all his studied languidness, Weld himself also had an element of this control neurosis. We were told that he got deeply upset if he was late for anything, but also if he was too early. Rather than go in and sit waiting for someone for two minutes, he would prefer to 'sit in a car, reading a book'. How much of a book do you read in two minutes?

As it happened he would be made wait but thankfully the cause of it was an inter-American row for which we couldn't be blamed. At a reception in Heritage House, St Stephen's Green, the US Ambassador, Jean Kennedy Smith was to come and meet him beforehand in an upstairs room, and then they'd go in together to greet the roomful of guests. Kennedy Smith was the quintessential Boston Democrat, Weld was a Massachusetts Republican. Was this why she was over half an hour late? Or was it just carelessness with timekeeping?

Weld was furious and went on into the reception, mingling with the guests. I started panicking, wondering how Ambassador Kennedy Smith would react. Even though it was a US affair, it was still our Protocol, and our visit. I asked an Embassy official, a foppish chap with a tasselled white silk scarf, but he raised his hands and said 'Who knows?' Some odd sorts were working in the US Embassy. When the Ambassador finally arrived, she emerged from the car with an obviously high-spirited man who quietly crept away. She then wanted Weld to leave the reception and come back upstairs to greet her. But Weld, busy mingling, refused. And that was that. It wasn't until a party later, in the Ambassador's residence, that they sort of mended fences.

In Derry, Hume gave Weld a tour of his empire. It was also a coup to get meetings with Bruton, Spring and others in the very week a Government was being formed. A useful distraction from the political drama, perhaps, but also a sign of how forthcoming our politicians can be for American visitors. Bruton was ebullient as he waddled out to see us. Pink-faced and power expectant, he would be Taoiseach within days. 'I just hope these Americans appreciate it,' said a hassled Private Secretary. As a reward, Weld's delegation gave us paperweights embossed with the Governor's crest, and little key-rings in which his favourite fishing flies were preserved in plastic. More for my collection. But I was sort of hoping I might get Rick's red braces and his now disconnected mobile phone.

As part of the post-ceasefire process, it was decided to have a Forum for Peace and Reconciliation which would meet in Dublin Castle, a gathering of all the parties North and South. The idea came from the Taoiseach's Department and there was scepticism about it in DFA. To work it, they 'wanted bodies', an unfortunate phrase in the context, and DFA people were not enthusiastic. 'It's a train that's going nowhere,' said Ó'hUiginn, in one of his cryptic utterances. 'And we don't know who is driving the train.'

In fact, the Forum, which opened in October 1994, was quite a success. Mainly because there was so little happening elsewhere, with the process stalled over the 'permanence' issue. It was also a useful 'cleansing' operation for SF, which was one of the reasons behind it in the first place, allowing them to come in and mingle with elected democrats, including those of a softer Unionist variety. The main Unionist parties stayed away however, which was a pity. And yet the Forum's consequent mainly Nationalist image didn't make the organisers any more amenable about who'd they invite to attend.

An electoral-threshold was set and, pretending to be a 'student doing a thesis', I had to call Workers Party HQ to find out the number of WP Councillors in the South. (I couldn't say I was calling in relation to the Forum.) 'Five, at the moment,' the woman said, hopefully. When I told the officer organising the Forum, he said 'Ah, good. That means they have eight overall, one more than the Conservatives.' Although the WP were disliked, the UK

Conservatives were even more so. 'But the Conservatives are just in the North,' I said. 'Exactly,' he said, which I thought was a bit unfair. 'And besides, there is also the fact that they are a British party.' Stranger still, what did that make the DUP? 'Surely we want as many parties in as possible, so as to lessen its pan-Nationalist image.'

'Well, yes,' he said, 'and in fact we are looking at giving the UDP and PUP some form of observer status. But we are waiting for the Loyalist ceasefire.'

When such a ceasefire came, the Loyalist fringe parties were practically love-bombed by the Division. It was typical of the crudity with which the Department (and the South, in general), sought out amenable elements of Unionism, done in a way which would make any Unionist immediately suspect. Billy Hutchinson was taken to The Commons restaurant by three First Secretaries. For Rack of Ulster Lamb, perhaps, and constitutional treacle. Over postprandial brandies in Iveagh House, it had got down to 'Sure you don't really like Trimble anyway, do you?'

The South saw the fringe parties as more reasonable than mainstream Unionism, but we had been down this road before; Reg Empey and the McGimpsey brothers were the South's 'reasonable' contacts in the UUP, but in the 1992 talks the Government crudely tried to 'secure' Empey during negotiations only to see him, understandably, back off. However, there was one difference with the smaller Loyalist parties: they as yet had little electoral support. In a bizarre subtext, confidential soundings were made with moderate Nationalists (i.e. SDLP) to see what could be done to bolster the base of well-disposed Loyalists.

In the end, neither the PUP or UDP attended the Forum. I had to send the invites, triple checking the addresses — this was one post you didn't want someone saying hadn't arrived. (I also did the Tánaiste's Christmas card list, changing some of the addresses, like those for Ian Paisley and Peter Robinson, from their Party HQs to their homes. I wanted to give them a rise in their dressing gowns. Ruin their eggs for them.)

This cultivation of the Loyalist fringe, and Sinn Féin, with their links to paramilitaries, was interesting given our apparent utter disdain for the Workers Party, which seemed to have increased now that the more reformist elements had split to form Democratic Left. In 1993, DFA advised against the Taoiseach meeting a WP delegation, on the grounds of their marginal support and 'dubious activity'. The First Sec's strong recommendation was backed by the Counsellor and even more strongly by the Head of Division. It seemed odd given that the WP appeared to be working for 'a peaceful, non sectarian alternative'. Nor were they nearly as 'marginal' as some of the tiny reconciliation groups which the Taoiseach regularly met, and funded.

The antipathy was stronger than that usually heard from elected politicians. Perhaps because of the belief that elements of the Official IRA (linked to the WP) still existed. But perhaps also because, despite all their murder and mayhem, Sinn Féin/IRA were actually more palatable to bureaucratic nationalists and sneaking regarders than the WP, with their alien Marxism and neo-Unionism. 'Partly,' an older hand told me, 'but it's also because, in here, they feel they can tame SF. Take away the violence, and the old style Republicanism, and what are SF? But the WP are much more independent and intellectually challenging. Look at the Dáil, for God's sake. They're the most effective opposition.'

He was speaking of DL and WP in the same breath, a still common confusion. By now, of course, DL had become partners in the Rainbow Coalition and we had the ridiculous situation of one Counsellor, the afore-mentioned O'Braonain, questioning whether to give a Brief (or a copy of the Box) to one of the DL Ministers! 'You know, that fellow … he's not sound at all,' he said ruefully, and he painted a subversive picture of left-wing anti-nationalists. O'Braonain was a funny character, much imitated by the younger officers. One girl even managed to get into his PC and send a circular e-mail, announcing the formation of an informal research group on 'the National Issue' — 'needed now more than ever' (a reference to the new Rainbow Government) and looking for the services of a 'few sound men, and women'. So plausible was it, that quite a few people came knocking on O'Braonain's door!

I was surprised that the NI Conservative Party weren't invited to the Forum, but they might have driven people mad. They were certainly good value when they showed up at the Tory Party Conference. Because they were actually from NI — the only 'British' party represented there — they had to be given quality podium time, usually on Northern Ireland, and you could see that this pissed off the more representative delegates from the UK proper. With good reason — the NI delegates were usually a succession of batty, well-heeled incoherents from North Down who came out with the kind of stuff which gave even the Tories a bad name. Which is why our Press Officer chuckled delightedly, behind his desk, when we all watched them on TV. 'Look at that wanker!' he shouted, pointing. 'Keep going Missus!'

British Party Conferences were closely watched, and officers would spot old friends trotting up to the podium. Tory MPs, once hostile on Ireland, were now 'on side'. 'You see. We worked on him well. He's sweet now,' someone would say, listening to some Right Hon's fulsome support for the 'solid work' of the two Governments and, like a scene from *Goodfellas*, the other officers would nod their heads sourly. Sweetening the ruling Tories had been one of key successes of Irish diplomacy. And the incoming Blairites. One of the revelations of working on the Interparliamentary Body was discovering how tough on Northern Ireland some of the Labour MPs were, especially the ones from Lancashire and Yorkshire, where so many of the British soldiers came from.

The Forum, then, was mainly a Nationalist body, and a sounding board for grievances. One day, Bill Flynn, the Irish-American financier, gave a long speech attacking Ian Paisley. Flynn is a honourable man who played a helpful role in getting the ceasefire. But his speech was sentimental and ponderous, with much about his parents and origins. (How impatient I'd become with this culture now that I was back in Ireland — *real* Ireland.) His speech was warmly applauded, including his attack on Paisley — Flynn repeated some of Paisley's more outrageous remarks — but as a colleague whispered, 'That's tomorrow's papers in Belfast; "Paisley attacked at Dublin Forum".' It was a pointless exercise and sent completely the wrong message.

It was the same, in a more subtle way, with Gordon Wilson, who was given his own seat at the Forum. Wilson was a truly heroic figure. His daughter had died in the Enniskillen bombing, and he had become a tremendous, tireless figure for reconciliation. But the Irish Government could not get enough of him. They brought him out on every occasion. They quoted him in speeches — otherwise nationalistic speeches. They even made him a Senator. Within time, predictably, he expressed his quiet wish for a United Ireland; he was a Leitrim Protestant, after all. Equally predictably, given the poisonous atmosphere of the North, an anonymous Unionist wrote to Wilson saying it was no wonder his wife had died recently (of natural causes), given the way he was down there with 'those people in Dublin'.

It was a horrible thing to write and when Wilson relayed it to the Forum, there were shocked mutters around the table. I could see Mary O'Rourke TD going, 'Oh, my goodness. Such people.' But, if anyone was curious, they might have asked how a situation could come about where someone could write such a thing. Especially, someone who felt bitter, betrayed and constantly bombed. Could it be because they felt that Wilson was being used by the Irish Government? Could it be that in the comfort of Dublin Castle, we just didn't understand the depth of suspicion and hatred in Northern Ireland, and of how our arrogance towards the place came across. Wilson, the poor soul, seemed to have no idea of his totemic value. Beware the South-speak of 'reconciliation' and 'healing', for behind its velvet glove can lurk much greater ambitions.

The Forum was interesting socially and drew an unusual set of visitors; F W De Klerk, the former South African Premier, delegates from the Orange Order and EU representatives. The EU does not get the credit it feels it should on NI. They give as much money, and more, as the US does and have greatly helped economic regeneration, a long-term goal of the Irish Government, which — in a classic reversal of liberal unionism — sees in a buoyant NI, an area more amenable to peace, Southern influence and the control of the Catholic middle-class. And less prone to the influence of deprivation-fed paramilitaries.

The party leaders came and went. Initially Albert gave the Forum a lot of his personal time. And then all his time, since it was to the Forum that he retreated when he lost his job. It was also to the Forum that Bruton came the day after he was elected Albert's successor, waddling into the room like a man who'd just sucked on a helium balloon and couldn't stop laughing. By contrast, Albert sat, lantern-jawed, like a man who'd put all his money on a horse called *Attorney General* which didn't even make it home.

There was a good social atmosphere around the Forum, which brought back memories of the EU Summit. Foreign journalists came for photo–ops and a long line of former politicians and experts came up to offer their wisdom. Before Christmas, the Forum broke up temporarily and politicians and hacks drifted towards the Oak bar, underneath the Castle. It had been a good year and people were in a festive mood. In one corner, we nursed our brandies and listened while Neil Blaney, the

Donegal TD and Father of the House, filled his pipe and told scandalous tales about Jack Lynch and Charlie Haughey. I wished I could have remembered more of it (Blaney died shortly afterwards) but the drinks were flowing. Something to do with someone's wife standing on the steps and shouting to Lemass 'Don't give him the job' — Haughey or Lynch, I wasn't sure.

By the counter, I saw Seán Ó'hUiginn chatting to Michael O'Kennedy of FF, John Hume of the SDLP and Pat Doherty of Sinn Féin. It was an interesting sight, the four of them standing together, deep in the vaults of Dublin Castle, the former headquarters of British rule. I mean, if this wasn't a pan-nationalist front, I don't know what was. One big, happy family. It was still tribalism at the end of the day. But it also gave new meaning to the comments of Unionist, John Taylor, who described the Forum as the political equivalent of Alcoholics Anonymous for Sinn Féin/IRA, its purpose being to wean Republicans off violence for good!

Afterwards, we walked over towards St Stephens Green, where the DFA party season had started. Another Christmas. I felt older now, but it was still great crack. If anything the social life in the Department had increased over the years especially in Anglo-Irish which had a culture of people working late, and then drifting over to Hourican's or the Conrad Hotel to meet others returning from London or Brussels. Or from 'travelling' up North. With Labour in power, there were seemed to be many more Iveagh House functions, as new Ministers sought to build profile. The ballroom could be used for all Government functions, not just Foreign-related ones, and for these Protocol always need extra 'bodies'.

Social life was also boosted by a new intake of Third Secs in the mid-Nineties which helped to overcome the existing social divisions created by the promotions impasse. Reflecting the jobs' hiatus, however, many of the new intake were older and over-qualified, and often projected an unearned cockiness which would soon be brought up short when they had to deal with consular cases abroad. Or even by Ó'hUiginn in the pub, idling over to interrogate them about their 'existential values'. 'So you're at the Vatican,' he asked a nonplussed Third Sec beside me. 'Tell me, who were the Saints canonised last month?' To which he got a long and beatific silence. Others reminded me of myself when I first joined; impressed, idealistic and eager to know more. One night I told a gang of them, fibbing, that I'd had an advance look at the Frameworks Documents. 'Go on, tell us, what's in it!' they chorused. But I waved my finger — it's a secret — and, for a moment, became the patronising toad that I'd once despised.

We even had a party for the Frameworks Documents, held in Roly's Restaurant in Ballsbridge. Actually, it was a Thank You party for all the staff of the Division and the work they'd put it over the past year or so, but the menu billed it as a 'Celebration Party', which was a bit insensitive, given that the Frameworks were supposed to be non-contentious and conciliatory. Just as well the papers didn't hear about it. Or about our antics, which were a great laugh, with Spring and the mandarins cracking jokes and slagging each other, and Fergus Finlay telling me about a novel he'd written, a political thriller in which the Taoiseach gets killed. 'Not Albert?' I exclaimed.

A singsong developed but, in the climate of reasonableness, some wag insisted on non-violent rebel ballads, such as 'The Rising of the Constructive Dialogue', or 'The Wearing of the Speaking Point'. 'Oh, how wearing,' sighed someone else wearily. It all became somewhat debauched, and at one stage a couple who had gone outside to 'get some air', were now sitting up on the restaurant's copper windowsill and visibly getting oxygen from each other. 'Cross-Border bodies!' someone shouted to laughter while the couple carried on regardless, blithely ignored by the Minister's driver and the Gardaí outside the US Embassy, across the road.

The Gardaí, incidentally, were ever present on these social occasions, and on Protocol generally, and, after a while, you struck up a discreet, nodding acquaintance. Later, I went to a publishing party in the River Club, overlooking the Liffey, at which a surprise guest appeared; Salman Rushdie, then under death threat and understandably not advertised. But I should have expected something from the door, where a group of well-built men were scanning us, one of whom gave me a nod. He was Special Branch man I knew. My fiends looked at me; what was that all about? Another time, coming out of Lansdowne Road Dart station, we saw a large crew of riot police, awaiting the end of a soccer match. 'You're not inside anymore,' said a familiar voice from under one of the helmets — he made it sound like prison — and, by this time, I wasn't.

Sometimes, the slightly sloppy nature of the Gardaí annoyed me, especially when they were on Protocol duty where a slouching gait or foot up on the car might let the whole image down. But colleagues told me to relax; that's what the foreigners like about Dublin, the relaxed informality, especially the British. In my prickly defensiveness, I didn't know if I found this endearing or patronising, but apparently it was true. Tom King loved playing golf here, and had one or two Gardaí who were regular partners. The British politicians were grateful for any relief from the intense security they were subjected to. One colleague described how Douglas Hurd, now out of office and at a function on the city's northside, was almost in tears of joy to be on a real Irish street with school children and shoppers, in a way you wouldn't see in Whitehall. It showed the absurd state of abnormality between two close and interconnected neighbours, which is now hopefully changing. But no chances could be taken with security and after each IGC, the British cavalcade would literally scream away at high speed.

One time, I had to jump into the back of a car, as a 'body', but such was the speed and confusion of our arrival at the airport, that I found myself swept inside, and suddenly, when the cops peeled away, in a room with Veronica Sutherland, the British Ambassador, who turned around to her officials and said, angrily, 'Look, sort out what *that's* about, OK?' It had been a difficult IGC and for a moment I thought I was going to be privy to some British insight, but someone nodded in my direction — he's not one of us — and everyone shut up. Another time, we found a filofax that a British official had left behind after a Liaison Group meeting. I jokingly suggested opening it up to find out their 'real' positions but this earned a frown which I felt was unfair, given the British Government's fixation with surveillance and intrusion, tapping our phones and recruiting informers.

From elsewhere in the Department, there was sad news on the social scene, including a sudden end for my old friend, Napoleon. I hadn't seen much of him since his return from the UN. Apparently, most of his time was spent in Harcourt Street, and around the bars there, cursing the Department; he'd been passed over again for Ambassador. One day, at an EU lunch in a city restaurant, he just keeled over and died. His funeral was a large affair, attended by old sparring partners from Doheny and Nesbitt's, that nest of lawyers, spin doctors and academics. At the graveside, the appointed orator was too overcome and someone else was sought. 'They must have been looking for Tom Kitt,' said a mandarin dryly, referring to our Minister of State's legendary ability to seek out an audience and a camera. Poor old Napoleon; even to the end — even *beyond* the end — he was the butt of his own black humour.

24

Buenos Aires or Bust

It was to Doheny and Nesbitts that another departure made his way. Robin Fogarty, the Deputy Secretary when I joined the Department, and the instigator of that Grey Door protest against the incoming Taoiseach, had finally retired. Apparently he now spent most of his weekdays, red-faced and brooding, inside the front snug of Nesbitts. Or in the nearby United Arts Club off Fitzwilliam Square, on the steps of which he had allegedly tussled with Haughey over the gossip columnist, Terry Keane. 'How are you, Robin?' someone asked. 'Well, the directorships have not exactly come flooding in,' he said grimly. He was not a happy man.

Not long afterwards, he died, and glowing tributes appeared in the newspapers — tributes whose anodyne quality were an injustice to the colour and volatility of the man. Still at least the accompanying picture was the same 1970s' file photograph they always used, with Robin staring at the camera like a handsome Christopher Lee who'd just risen from the crypt, his face decorated with bushy sideburns and a big knotted tie. It captured the man in all his lupine prime.

Retiring in better health was my former Deputy Consul General from New York, who generously held a big farewell party in the Ballroom to which, I think, the entire Department was invited. The CG himself, meanwhile, had gone on to bigger and better things as Ambassador in Finland. He never made it to Iraq, where the continuous EU boycott and sanctions seem to go on forever. But his ambition in Helsinki showed no sign of abating and he managed to get almost the entire Finnish Cabinet to come and hear a speech by the visiting Dick Spring, who, of course, was most impressed.

However, by this time, I didn't see such a fast track for myself and, in many respects, I had begun to withdraw from the Department. Partly because I was engaged in the writing of novels, but also because the novelty and discovery of being Third Sec was beginning to wane; increasingly, it was about paperwork, planning and areas which I had already encountered. Along with this, I was less comfortable with the decorum and bureaucratic procedures of the Department. Even if I was a fast tracker, I would still have to demonstrate the commitment and patience necessary for advance. In reality, the rank above me, First Secretary level, was 'get serious' time, often described as the true coal face of the Department. In 1995, the embittered raft of senior First Secs finally got their promotion, but incredible tension awaited the announcement. The fear was that one part of the fatwa group might be promoted and others not. Thankfully, however, they all got the nod, but the whole exercise, with its backbiting and endless intrigue, made me realise how much I didn't want to stay forever in DFA.

It also made one wonder about the utilisation of such talents. Some of the First Secs were very talented people, who you felt could make a fortune in the private sector, or as journalists or political consultants. Ultimately, there was a frustration that the foreign service could only satisfy, or reward, a portion of this energy.

Increasingly, my own priority was to get home and do more writing. The valuable hours that I spent scripting Dick Spring and John Bruton, I now wanted to give to more plausible characters. Like that other Civil Servant and writer, Flann O'Brien, the increasingly straight-laced nature of my daytime writing and duties was causing my night-time jottings to become wilder and more surreal, not to mention satirical. This was especially the case, by

May 1995, when I published my first novel, *The Casting of Mr O'Shaughnessy*, a blackly humorous look at Irish political history, and at the sort of Republican and revisionist issues which we had explored in our speeches.

Initially, there was some concern that a serving officer in Anglo-Irish Division was publishing such a provocative work at this sensitive time. At one stage, I was told they might have to be transfer me out of the Division. But in the end, it was fine. 'Just don't mention what part of the Department you work in,' I was warned. So I didn't. Not the least provocative part was that the eponymous Mr O'Shaughnessy was partly, but quite obviously, based on the career of the colourful Seán McBride, a former Foreign Minister in 1948. McBride, once an IRA Chief of Staff, went on to win the Nobel Peace Prize and then, at the height of the Cold War, the Lenin Peace Prize. Given these myriad and contradictory achievements, the potential for comedy was rich indeed, and one that I made savage use of. Later, McBride's name was given to a set of hardline guidelines on American investment in Northern Ireland, opposed by John Hume and the Irish Government, and called the McBride Principles. 'The ultimate oxymoron!' cried Napoleon, in one of his favourite parlour games. (The others were 'Mason Diplomacy' referring to the initiative of a bull-headed British Secretary for NI in the 1980s and 'Republican Movement', depending on your perspective on the decommissioning issue.)

Although I was free to do publicity for the book, the Department were less happy about me writing articles or expressing specific views, and with that kind of stricture I saw problems for the future. I considered taking a career break, a generous Civil Service facility by which you could take a year's leave, renewable for up to five years. If the writing didn't work out, I could return to DFA, long haired and contaminated by the outside world. But there was also the temptation to stay in the job and write on the side, as others had done. By now, we had quite a few writers in the Department; Patricia Cullen, a poet, Bobby McDonagh, who published a book on the Amsterdam Treaty and Paul Walsh who found himself fêted throughout Tokyo as an authority on Lafcadio Hearn, a famous Irish scholar of Japanese studies.

The temptation to stay was increased by a new round of Postings. Already I was being circulated again, after only two years home. Some of them were attractive — Copenhagen, Chicago — but I was warned that I would not get another North American post so soon and would probably be sent to Europe, as a matter of policy. In the style of the typist who urged me not to put Tehran too high the last time, my concerned First Sec examined my ballot and, in an appalled amendment, quickly redrew my second choice to last. 'You don't want Beijing, right now, I'm telling you.' What I did want was Argentina. Buenos Aires. Perhaps that was the place to ignite my diplomatic career and, more importantly, my writing. Gabriel Garcia Márquez, Mario Vargas Llosa, Pablo Neruda. As with India the previous time, I now had visions of sitting out each sunset evening on creeper-strewn balconies, tapping away at the Great South American Novel, and hanging out in nightclubs later with Maradona and his friends. (Well, perhaps not *all* of his friends.) Our Embassy there was, by any account, not the most taxing, and one officer described with joy how their fax machine was almost permanently broken. 'HQ was far away!' she said, twiddling her fingers. I immediately enrolled on a Spanish course in the Civil Service Training Centre on Lansdowne Road — in a class of eight, there were five cops (don't ask why) — while, back in Iveagh House, I sent off my Postings ballot paper, with Buenos Aires marked number one. Another spin on the roulette wheel.

At the upper end of the Department, however, it was less roulette than inter-party arm wrestling and, in 1995, we had our second 'Donlon Affair'. The first had occurred in 1980, when Haughey indulged in a bit of powerplay and tried to move Ambassador Seán Donlon, whom

Haughey considered insufficiently nationalist, from his post in Washington. Assisted by Irish-American politicians, such as the Four Horsemen, Donlon had successfully faced him down, one of the few people ever to do so and, in the process, becoming a folk hero in DFA. Now, after ten years in the private sector, Donlon was returning to Government but DFA were resisting him. Bruton wanted to bring Donlon into the Taoiseach's Department, as his Special Adviser on Northern Ireland.

Ó'hUiginn said it would be unfair that he would have to work with, or even to, a former Secretary of the Department. But he also felt that the arrival of Donlon, with his anti-Republican pedigree, would completely send the wrong message to SF at this highly sensitive time in the Peace Process. But, of course, much of it was pure powerplay. Spring didn't want his adviser on the North to be in a subsidiary role to Bruton's, especially to an ambitious hand like Donlon. The dispute thus became party political, with Labour supporting DFA against a Fine Gael Taoiseach, a neat turn around from ten years ago when a Department emerging from an FG government sought protection against FF. But Bruton, by now, appeared to have little time for Foreign Affairs.

And so Labour demanded that Donlon not be appointed or at the very least, if he was, that Ó'hUiginn be elevated to a position, and salary, equal to Donlon's. Spring didn't need convincing. Ó'hUiginn was threatening to walk away from the post if this wasn't conceded, bringing with him many of the slender hopes for the Peace Process and a renewed ceasefire.

Media coverage began appearing about the controversy and reference was made to Donlon's public stand against Noraid in the US in the 1980s. Sinn Féin voiced their concerns but such was the blurring now in operation that Donlon's anti-Provo line soon became non-Republican and even sort of non-Nationalist. Someone was spinning skilfully. But also disingenuously. Donlon had simply been delivering a Government line, which

many others were delivering and senior politicians even
more forcefully so (such as Jack Lynch and CJ Haughey,
when it suited him). Donlon, after all, had also been a
Unionist hate-figure during the time of the Anglo-Irish
Agreement.

One of the charges against Donlon was that he wasn't
sufficiently supportive of campaigns by Irish-Americans
to raise the issue of the wrongly imprisoned Birmingham
Six, and that he even tried to thwart their efforts. This was
a loaded charge, for all Irish Governments were wary of
these campaigns at the outset, mainly because they were
led by IRA sympathisers and activists — an odd
contradiction given that the men were trying to prove
their innocence. It was also loaded in that officials are
probably more sympathetic to such cases than senior
politicians, and certainly more than one FF Taoiseach who
privately dismissed the Birmingham Six case as 'closed',
regardless of how dodgy their conviction had been,
mainly because it had taken 'the heat off' the Irish
community in Britain. (This was before the Government
realised what a wonderful stick the Birmingham Six was
for beating the British.)

But the charge persisted against Donlon and mention
was made about a letter he had apparently written to
Congressman Hamilton Fish of New York telling him not
to get involved with the Six and even perhaps questioning
whether the men were innocent at all. I was now given a
curious mission. I was told to get the files out of storage
and look through them for the Hamilton Fish letter and
any other document penned by Donlon which seemed to
question the innocence of the Six. The people who asked
me to do this suggested that, given the nosy atmosphere
of DFA, I might lock my door for fear that someone could
stroll in and ask what I was up to.

The files came up from Registry, green belted and
dusty, and they made interesting reading. It is always
strange, speed-flicking through the papers, and seeing the
names of previous colleagues, and long-gone politicians

and events; a sort of de-ageing process like the newspapers flying away in an old black-and-white movie. Much of it was the same old issues, and the same old language. I couldn't find anything on the Six, but other oddities turned up, trenchant telexes from Jack Lynch about 'undesirable elements' in Boston and readers' letters on NI cut out of US newspapers, with the notation 'constructive person — could be of use for future publicity.'

Eventually, I found the Hamilton Fish letter, or the correspondence surrounding it. Firstly, a letter from Ambassador Donlon in 1981, robustly and clearly defending himself against the charges contained in a letter sent by the Embassy in London, which related a conversation they'd had with Fr Denis Faul. Fr Faul was 'not happy with the co-operation he was receiving' from the Embassy in Washington and had had a 'disagreement' with the Ambassador the previous year, when Donlon had allegedly dissuaded Fish from involving himself in the campaign 'to assert the innocence of the Birmingham pub bombers' (sic). Fr Faul had 'high hopes that the new Republican Senator from New York would play a prominent part in raising Irish issues'.

'These are serious allegations' wrote Donlon 'and you are aware that Fr Faul has made similar allegations about me to TDs, to the Minister and … in a letter to the Taoiseach. The fact is that I have received no correspondence, no telephone call, no personal approach, directly or indirectly from Fr Faul since my arrival in the US in October 1978. Nor can we trace any correspondence or telephone calls with any other officer stationed here in the same period … I am completely puzzled by Fr Faul's behaviour. I enjoyed a most constructive and personally friendly relationship with him from 1971-1978 … This then was 'the Hamilton Fish letter' — the letter was not to Fish, but about him. Donlon was therefore off the hook. He had merely warned Fish about the bone fides of some of the people taking up the Birmingham Six case and the dangers of being used by them, something which any Irish diplomat, or peacefully-inclined Irish politician, would have done.

I was not surprised then that when I gave the papers to the people who had asked me to find them, they seemed somewhat disappointed and said they probably wouldn't be 'used'. They clearly wanted something more juicy on Donlon. And so none of the correspondence appeared in the media. But I've no doubt that if it had been more damaging for Donlon, it would have and the whole experience made me think again of what someone said at the time of the Emily O'Reilly leak, 'Why are you looking around the edges for the source? – look at the very centre.'

In the end, Donlon was appointed Special Adviser to Bruton and Ó'hUiginn given a new post of Second Secretary within DFA, above Assistant Secretary and shadowing Noel Dorr, the Secretary; not unlike the old Deputy Sec position. The whole thing died down as quickly as it started. Donlon's name got its own speed dial on the Control Room fax – Mansergh had temporarily left the Taoiseach's Department – but in the coming months, it was hard to detect Donlon's influence on NI policy, despite his large salary. Bruton followed his own instincts which, as ever with a politician, can be a very dangerous thing.

Nor did Bruton take kindly to Foreign Affairs advice, either on a high-ranking level such as with Seán O'hUiginn, with whom he allegedly had a major row, or on the level of other officials. Apparently he didn't appreciate the idea of the Box, for example, and copies would return to us with incredulous hand-written notes along the sides of reports. 'Who permitted this line to be taken?' queried Burton about some hardline encounter between Counsellor David Donoghue and some Unionists. It was clear that Bruton didn't appreciate the creative role that officials had on Northern Ireland. Not the least disappointing aspect of the McAleese leaks row, for example, was Bruton's slow defence of the Department.

Nor were we helped by the revelation of Bruton's Fine Gael colleague, and former Minister of State Gay Mitchell (probably our least popular Minister of State in recent years). During the McAleese controversy, Mitchell nonchalantly told the media that when he was in Foreign Affairs, he used to see 'documents lying around, behind potted plants, and the like'. But then, curiously, he added that he himself had removed many boxes of papers from the Department, mainly to do with the EU Amsterdam Treaty which he was interested in.

Either way, after ten years of Fianna Fáil and Labour Ministers, DFA had very firmly its shed any image it had of being close to Fine Gael.

The new Second Secretary position didn't necessarily alter the power structure in DFA, but it would have an interesting effect later on, when Fianna Fáil returned to office. Ó'hUiginn's successor was the wily Dermot Gallagher (Dag) who, as Second Sec, found himself having a better relationship with new Minister, David Andrews, than the actual Secretary, Pádraic Mac Kernan, whose relationship with Andrews had completely broken down. In this situation, Andrews seemed to defer to Dag, in so far as he deferred to anyone, and Dag accumulated influence. Thus, the man who had disdainfully told me in 1987, 'Jaysus, Delaney, you're real Foreign Affairs' had become the ultimate power in the same department although, in temperament and perspective, he probably still saw himself as outside its culture. 'You know, of course,' a diplomat had told me despairingly as we stood by the Mediterranean at an EU summit, 'that he is not one of us. *At all.*'

But who was 'us', after all? Throughout DFA, Gallagher had cultivated an elaborate parallel world of dedicated followers and favourites. When such officers turned up in Embassies abroad, people would ask, drolly, 'Ah, do you come to us from Dagestan?' Meaning, the

Independent Republic of Dag. Nor was this a negative badge, since some of these followers were among the most hardworking and effective in DFA, good in the field and with a handy ability to cut through bureaucratic twittering. Nor was Dag's influence confined to DFA. He had a very good working relationship with Paddy Teahon, Secretary of the Taoiseach's Department and with Frank Murray, Secretary to the Government, and a fellow Leitrim man. The three of them were a powerful triangle at the heart of Government. Dag had close access to Bertie Ahern, his 4th Taoiseach in six years and, in 1999, he left DFA altogether to succeed Paddy Teahon, as Secretary of the Taoiseach's Department. But only temporarily and two years later he returned in triumph to Iveagh House, to run Foreign Affairs as Secretary.

All this, however, was after I'd left. Instead, my own time coincided, almost exactly, with the Secretarial reign of Noel Dorr, whose period now begins to seem benign compared to the somewhat public and divisive confrontations that followed. Dorr's legacy was the modern Department. A true DFA mandarin, he had consolidated its structures and resisted the intrusions of other Departments, especially during the long years of recession in the 1980s and 1990s. He could hardly have prevented the promotions blockage and, in general, he was a conscientious, selfless Public Servant, whose influence can still be felt in the background on matters like EU treaty negotiation.

Noel Dorr was what I wasn't, basically, and that became even more apparent on the day of the Postings. It was the usual excitement and drama, but the rapidity of the e-mail system meant that news unfolded more quickly, and gloomily. Buenos Aires went early, to a girl who, in fairness, already spoke Spanish, but so did Brussels and other liveable options. Each time a Posting disappeared, the others hung there like a threat, and it was with one of the least palatable of these that I ended up: Luxembourg. I got the short straw.

'Eamon, we expected you to write the great South American novel,' they chuckled later in Hourican's, 'but the Great Luxembourg ... novel?' Just to rub it in, a colleague sent me an article which had just appeared in the London *Independent*, a Letter from Luxembourg, entitled 'Journey to the Heart of Dullness'. Rich and nasty was the general consensus, with delusions of Eurocrat grandeur. One description was of a line of empty bars, their doors open in the rain, playing Pink Floyd covers at 2 a.m., an image I found particularly depressing. Broadway and the East Village it wasn't. Nor was it particularly endorsed by ex-Luxembourg hands. 'Limerick on a wet Wednesday,' was one assessment (Again, rain). 'True, you have three countries on your doorstep but the problem is that you're in none of them!'

Of course, once you get a Posting you must, in theory, go on it and I dutifully sent off my 'happy' letter of acceptance to the Ambassador, Aldyne Skinner. But, in reality, I immediately tried to find a way out and thought again of my original idea; a career break. I spoke to colleagues who pointed to the large number of people now on such leave, in academia or Public Relations or, in one case, restoring currachs in the Kerry Gaeltacht. In tandem with novel writing, I felt I could make a living doing freelance journalism. I went down to see the Master Mandarin himself, Seán Ó'hUiginn, and he was very sympathetic. He had read my novel, and its irreverence seemed to appeal to his own sense of adventure, as did my desire to take time out. Indeed, in such a spirit, he wondered why I wouldn't take the ultimate step. 'Are you not tempted to bite the umbilical cord altogether?' he offered airily in a typical utterance and I said that no, I'd hedge my bets. I didn't want to upset my mother too much, throwing away the good, safe job.

Ó'hUiginn immediately supported a career break, and put the case to Personnel. The Luxembourg Post was eventually re-circulated and, to their shock, those who had most ribbed me over it were themselves now in line.

Thus, the whims of the Posting system, although, in fairness, the chap who did eventually go enjoyed it very much. It's what you make of it, after all.

For me, however, getting it was a 'sign', along with some other curious 'signs'. For example, only weeks after launching my novel, a bust of its inspiration, Seán McBride, was unveiled in the Minister's Ante Room. 'Oh look, Spring probably feels the way we all do about McBride,' I was told wearily. 'But McBride was the only other Foreign Minister who wasn't Fianna Fáil or Fine Gael (McBride was leader of Clann na Poblachta, an independent party) and, as such, Spring wants his head up in the House.' But Iveagh House? I felt like protesting. It was as if the blood-spattered ghost of the Nobel laureate was coming after me and, like Oscar Wilde's wallpaper, one of us would just have to go. By a grim irony, I was almost asked to write the speech for the unveiling. And I was warned to definitely stay away from the ceremony. 'The family will bloody lynch you!' I was told firmly. Apparently, some of McBride's family and friends were not pleased by my scandalous 'portrait' of the man, complete with McBride's ludicrous faux-French accent and the strong insinuation, often voiced privately, that McBride was centrally involved in the 1927 murder of Kevin O'Higgins, ironically a former Minister for Foreign (then 'External') Affairs.

Understandably then, I didn't attend the unveiling. But I was unable to resist having a look and so, with an empty folder under my arm, I popped over to the Minister's chambers to peep in through the great oak doors. Inside, in front of a group of people holding wine glasses, I saw Dick Spring's nose grow like Pinocchio's, as he praised the 'integrity' and 'moral consistency' of the great Seán McBride. Later, in the throes of the Christmas Party, an excited Seán Ó'hUiginn broke from the dancing and announced, 'Come on, let's go upstairs now and throw that head out the window. Come on, what's wrong with you!' Ah, the spirit of the Christmas party.

Another 'sign', or curious coincidence, came with the National Commemoration Ceremony at the War Memorial Park in Islandbridge, a gesture of reconciliation by the Government to those who fought with the British, and Allies, in two World Wars. My novel had specifically explored these commemorations and featured the actual events of 1986 when a similar ceremony in the Garden of Remembrance provoked widespread protest. At that time, the then Taoiseach, Garret FitzGerald, had had coins thrown at him – thirty pieces of silver – while Haughey, playing the green card, stayed away. But now, with the new atmosphere, things were completely different. We even had Tom Hartley of Sinn Féin and Ken Maginnis of the UUP attending – the first time the two parties had officially attended an event together.

To soften the symbolism, the ceremony also commemorated the Holocaust, with Jewish representatives prominent among the VIPs. This made for a confusing speech, however, and when the draft text arrived over from the Taoiseach's department it was so bad that people read bits of it aloud for the laugh. It was binned and replaced by a fresh text written by Mary Whelan, with amendments from Anglo-Irish. When Bruton delivered it, in the open air, with the Wellington Monument dramatically in the background, someone said that he really knew how to 'choose his words' for such occasions. I had to smile.

After the Ceremony, the be-medalled elderly veterans were taken up Military Road to the Royal Hospital Kilmainham, which appropriately used to be a old soldiers' retirement home. In a reception in the stone-flagged vault, surrounded by suits of armour, they sipped whiskies and glasses of beer and seemed bemused that their commemoration had once been the source of such controversy to nationalists and revisionists alike. All they knew was that they had well-worn stories to tell. It was a great day. Some of the soldiers had fought in Malaysia, the Philippines and Korea.

Finally, word came through. I would leave the Department on July 14th, my birthday. The precision was because the next day I would be photographed for the newspapers, eating snails at a Bastille Festival in Portarlington, an old Huguenot town, and even for something as innocuous as this, the Department wanted no overlap. That's how strict they were about publicity, unless it was sanctioned. On Friday, I was DFA but the next day I would be a *citoyen* once more. I went down to Personnel to get my release papers and, by the staircase, passed Tommy Hillick, the messenger, busily bundling up all the provincial papers from Northern Ireland. 'They're clearing out,' he explained as musty old books and booklets were pulled out of wardrobes, and space made for a 'new dispensation'. In tea boxes, I could see the old material which the State used to explain its case on the North, 'outsiders' accounts, like reports from the Seventies by the *Sunday Times* 'Insight' Team, or Liam de Paor's *Divided Ulster* or, even *The Irish Landscape* by geologist, Frank Mitchell, an endearing attempt to link the geographic integrity of the island to its political unity.

Meanwhile, fish boxes of old files were on their way down to the National Archivist who was now working fulltime in the basement, trawling through the decades, and the thoughts and ideas of long-dead diplomats. Out the back, the Army were putting diplomatic bags onto the jeep, destined for the airport and foreign climes. No more of that for me. Behind them, by the Secret Garden, I could see the OPW gardeners clipping at the cherry blossoms, while Mrs Landy, the housekeeper, stood by the back entrance organising supplies for another function in the ballroom. On my way back, I looked into the deserted ballroom for the last time, with its polished floor and Versailles-type mirrors, and thought of the *Moll Flanders* filming. Since I first stepped into it, I had truly danced, dined, spoke, issued and lied for Ireland.

Upstairs, they got out the wine and cake. Q, our star speechwriter, and one of the First Secs recently promoted to Counsellor, gave a witty speech and wished me well, in the midst of which, Eithne, one of our oldest Clerical Assistants broke down into tears. 'Don't be too flattered,' whispered a colleague, 'she cries when anybody leaves.' And, indeed, on her own departure a few months later, she was inconsolable. It was people like Eithne who made DFA. Not the diplomats but the typists, clerical staff, drivers, accountants and Ambassadors' Secretaries, aptly likened to old style Priests' Housekeepers, such was their unswerving dedication. Many of these were also posted, not as much as diplomats, but more so than before, and almost always to 'sensitive' places like Beijing or Moscow, where local recruitment might be a security risk. 'Free at last!' a senior official wrote on my card, but again my colleagues – cynical to the last – urged me not to get too excited. 'He's referring to himself.'

And the Department got the last out of me. Days before my departure, I had to go down to Shannon airport to greet the incoming Mayor of Boston, Mayor Menino. Not an Irish-American, but coming here anyway – that Boston vote – and so he had to be looked after. He'd also heard about the visit of Governor Weld, the Massachussetts Republican. 'Hey, at least you're not jogging with Ray Flynn,' said a colleague, referring to the previous Boston Mayor, whose appetite for exercise meant that Consul Generals had to run alongside him, briefing him on our economy.

Menino was flying into Shannon at 6.30 a.m. and I went down the night before, so that I could meet him coming off his flight. For Public Service cost reasons, I didn't fly myself, but got the train. I'd only see him for about twenty minutes, but such gestures were valuable. Rolling in, alone and sleepy-eyed, the Mayor would be met by a friendly face – 'Irish Government, Welcome to Ireland' – who would take him to the VIP lounge for coffee and biscuits. Down in the airport, his own officials, who'd been in Ireland for a few days, were waiting. A young aide took his bags, excitedly. 'Hey Mayor, they're really looking after us. We arrived at the hotel and they had this bag piper playing for us!' It made me smile. It was like Irish-America, except it was in Ireland.

Shannon, with its hinterland of Bunratty and tourist attractions, was another echo of Irish-America and it brought me back. In the hotel bar the previous night I'd listened to a 'come-all-ye' band that could have come straight from the Astoria Manor. Afterwards, I went for a midnight walk around the old airport, built in the Fifties, and looked up at the stars and at the statue of Our Lady, there to protect travellers and emigrants. It was a strange feeling. I thought of all the other airports that my colleagues had been at, around the world, waiting for visitors. I thought of Napoleon and Fogarty, and of all the men and women who'd done foreign service. Of Freddy Boland at the UN telling Khrushchev to be quiet and, before him, Seán Lester at the League of Nations, trying to keep check on the Nazis. I thought of Vanessa and the Bluefish Dane, and of Forbes and myself signing in late for Dracula's Butler at the Plaza 50, much as a new generation of eager, young delegates must be signing in now. I even thought of my old friends, the Iraqis, sitting in the General Assembly, and I had no doubt that, seasoned diplomats that they were, they would go on twirling their worry beads, waiting for the world to come round.

Glossary

AG	Attorney General.
AIA	Anglo-Irish Agreement.
AOH	Ancient Order of Hibernians.
ASEAN	Association of South-East Asian Nations.
B'nai Brith	A New York based Jewish educational, humanitarian and cultural organisation.
CG	Consul General.
CIA	Central Intelligence Agency.
CJH	Charles J Haughey.
Comcen	Shorthand for "Communications Centre" at Iveagh House.
Copol	Key EU Political Committee staffed by senior Foreign Affairs officials from EU States. Their recommendations would then be considered at EPC (see below) Ministerials.
Coreu	Telex system between EU members – the main mechanism for European Union drafting of political statements and initiatives.
CSCE	Conference on Security and Co-operation in Europe. Established by the Helsinki Agreement of 1975, and involving 35 countries (all of the European States and the US). Since replaced by the OSCE, the Organisation for Security and Cooperation in Europe.
DCG	Deputy Consul General.

Deputy Perm Rep

    Deputy Permanent Representative (to the UN).

DFA	Department of Foreign Affairs.
DL	Democratic Left.
DO	Duty Officer.
DR	Draft Resolution.
DUP	Democratic Unionist Party.
EBRC	East Border Region Committee.
ECOSOC	(UN) Economic and Social Council.
EPC	European Political Co-operation – former system for co-ordinating foreign policies of EU States.
ETD	Emergency Travel Document.
EU	European Union. Formerly EC (European Community).
FACs	Foreign Affairs Councils.
FBI	Federal Bureau of Investigation.
FF	Fianna Fail.
FG	Fine Gael.
GA	General Assembly (at the United Nations).
GATT	General Agreement on Tariffs and Trade.
GCHQ	Government Communications Headquarters — main surveillance base for British Government.
GDR	German Democratic Republic.
IGC	Inter-Governmental Conference.
ILGO	Irish Lesbian and Gay Organisation.
ILC	International Law Commission.
INLA	Irish National Liberation Army.
INS	Immigration and Naturalisation Service.

Interpol	International Criminal Police Organisation, Vienna-based body coordinating cooperation between national police forces.
Intifada	Movement of Palestinian uprising in the West Bank and Gaza Strip beginning in 1987 and recommencing in 2000.
Irangate	1987 US political scandal revolving around covert US supplying or arms to Iran to facilitate the release of US hostages in the Middle East.
Iveagh House	Headquarters of the Department of Foreign Affairs.
JFD	Joint Frameworks Documents.
Les Douze	Literally "the Twelve", a reference to the then number of EU member states.
Maastricht	1991 EU treaty preparing the way for Economic and Monetary Union (EMU).
MAC	Management Affairs Committee within DFA comprising the Secretary and Assistant Secs.
Maryfield	Location of the DFA's former base in Northern Ireland.
NATO	North Atlantic Treaty Organisation.
NI	Northern Ireland.
Noraid	Irish Northern Aid Committee (US).
NSC	National Security Council (US).
NYPD	New York Police Department.
OPW	Office of Public Works.
P&Bs	Patriotic and Benevolent Organisations.
PD's	Progressive Democrats.
Perm Rep	Permanent Representative (at the UN).
PMUN	Permanent Mission at the United Nations.
PQ	Parliamentary Question.

PR	Proportional Representation.
PSM	Private Secretary to the Minister
PUP	Progressive Unionist Party.
RIR	Royal Irish Rangers.
SDLP	Social Democratic and Labour Party.
SEA	Single European Act.
SF	Sinn Féin.
SR	Special Rapporteur.
UDA	Ulster Defence Association.
UDP	Ulster Democratic Party.
UDR	Ulster Defence Regiment.
UN	United Nations.
UNESCO	UN Educational, Scientific and Cultural Organisation.
UNGA	UN General Assembly.
UNHCR	UN High Commission for Refugees .
UNRWA	UN Relief and Works Agency for Palestine Refugees in the Near East.
UUP	Ulster Unionist Party.
UVF	Ulster Volunteer Force.
VFW	Veterans of Foreign Wars.
WAC	Women's Action Coalition.
Warsaw Pact	
	Mutual defence/military aid treaty signed in 1955 by Eastern Bloc states. Counterpart to NATO.
WEOG	West European Organisation of Governments.
WP	Workers Party.